# SHORTCAKE CAKE

STORY AND ART BY

## suu Morishita

Characters

# SHORTCAKE CAKE

NEKOCHIYA HIGH SCHOOL

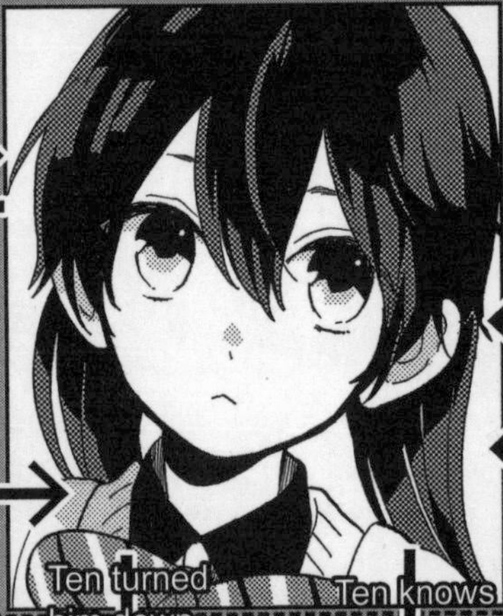

## TEN

First-year. She moved into the boardinghouse about a month after the new school year started. She has pluck.

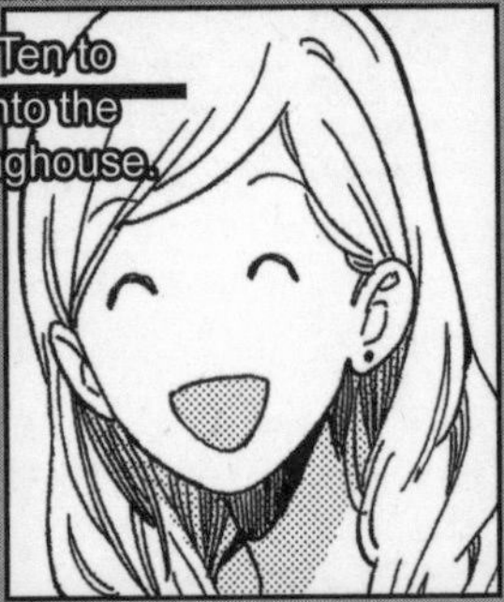

Invites Ten to move into the boardinghouse.

## AGEHA

First-year. She attended the same junior high school as Ten.

Ten turned him down once, but she likes him now.

Ten knows now that Chiaki has feelings for her.

Chiaki likes Ten even though he knows she likes Riku.

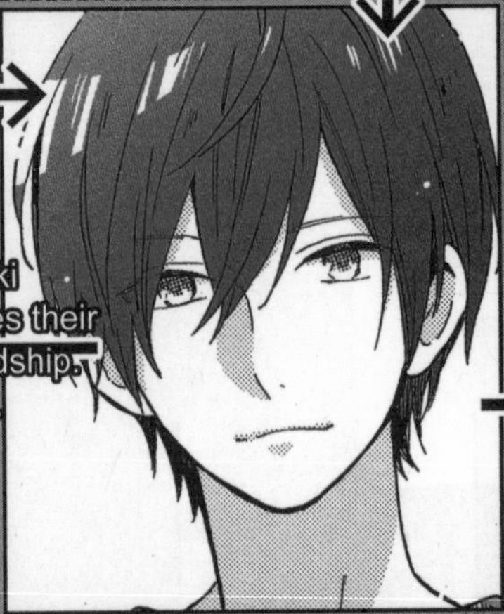

Chiaki values their friendship. But...

## CHIAKI

First-year. A gorgeous guy who loves reading books.

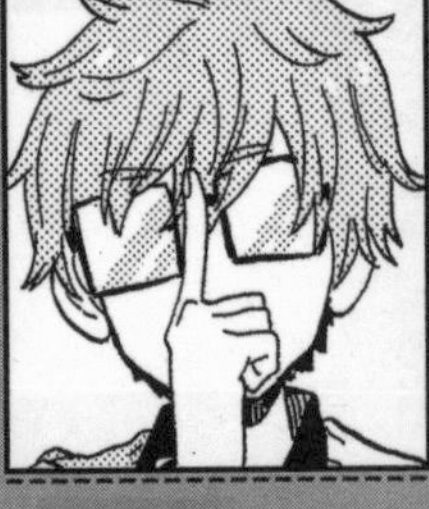

## YUTO

Second-year. He tutors Ten and the other first-years.

## REI

Second-year. The son of the owner of Hoshino Boardinghouse.

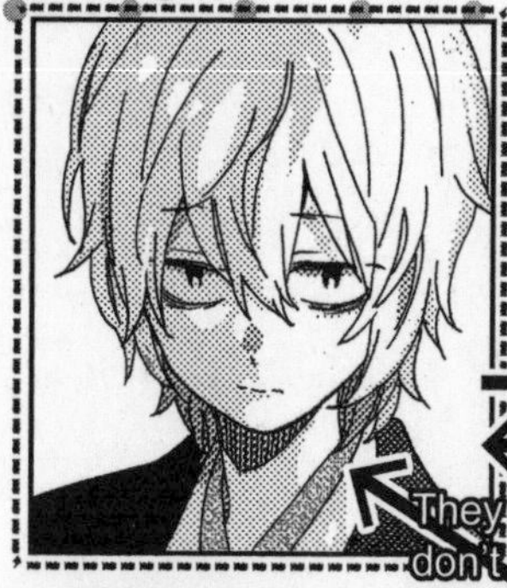

## SHIRAOKA

Rei's driver. What's his connection to Ran?

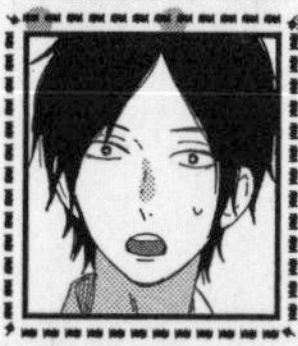

Hoshino Boardinghouse

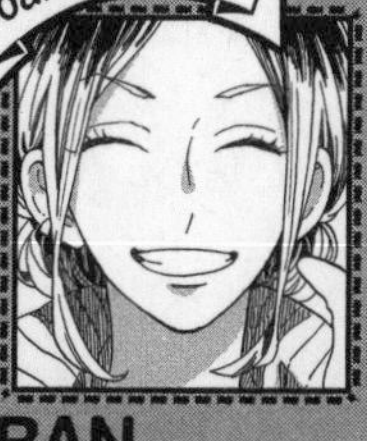

## RAN

House mom. She likes cooking and cars.

"Be my girlfriend."

She thinks he's weird.

They don't get along.

NEKOCHIYA SHOGYO HIGH SCHOOL

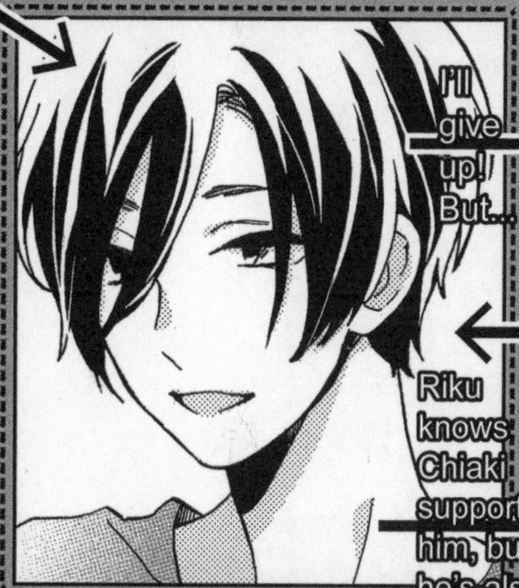

I'll give up! But...

Riku knows Chiaki supports him, but he's also a rival...

## RIKU

First-year. Lives in the boardinghouse though he grew up nearby. He's very friendly with girls.

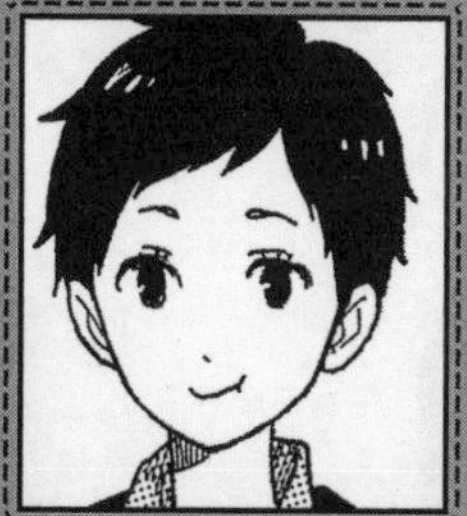

## AOI

Third-year. She's the oldest in the boardinghouse. She likes talking about relationships.

### Story Thus Far

Ten is a first-year in high school who lives in a boardinghouse with boys.

Over summer vacation, Ten realizes that she likes Riku, but she hasn't said anything to him yet. When the new semester starts, Ten and Chiaki's class visits the zoo. While there, Chiaki holds Ten close, leaving her in a state of confusion. But Ten's feelings toward Riku have grown. She leaves the zoo with only a souvenir for Riku.

Ten and Chiaki sneak into the sports festival at Riku's school. Ten is focused on the side of Riku that she doesn't typically get to see. Chiaki reacts by saying, "Look at me." Ten thinks he sounds jealous, and Chiaki admits that he is. Then he kisses her!

# SHORTCAKE CAKE

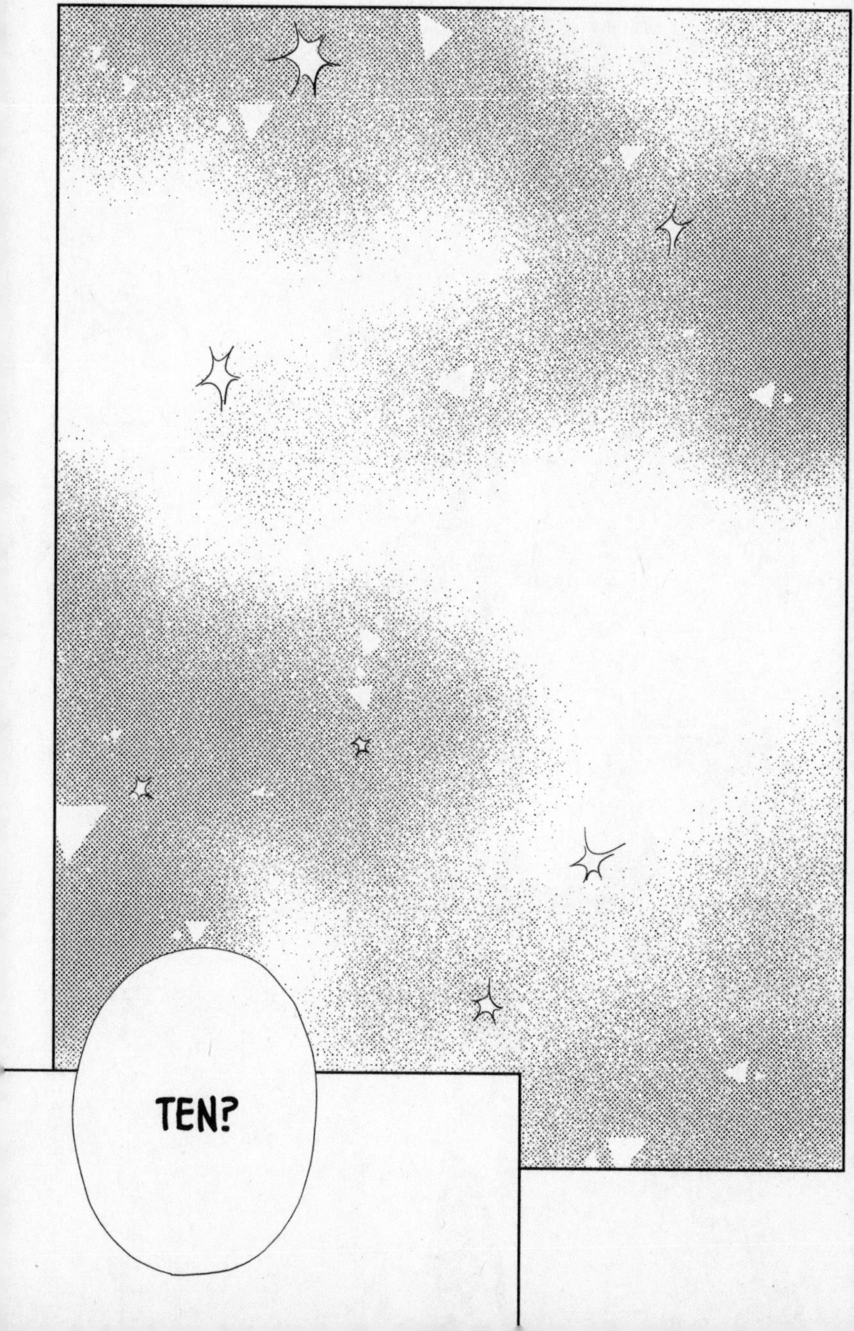
TEN?

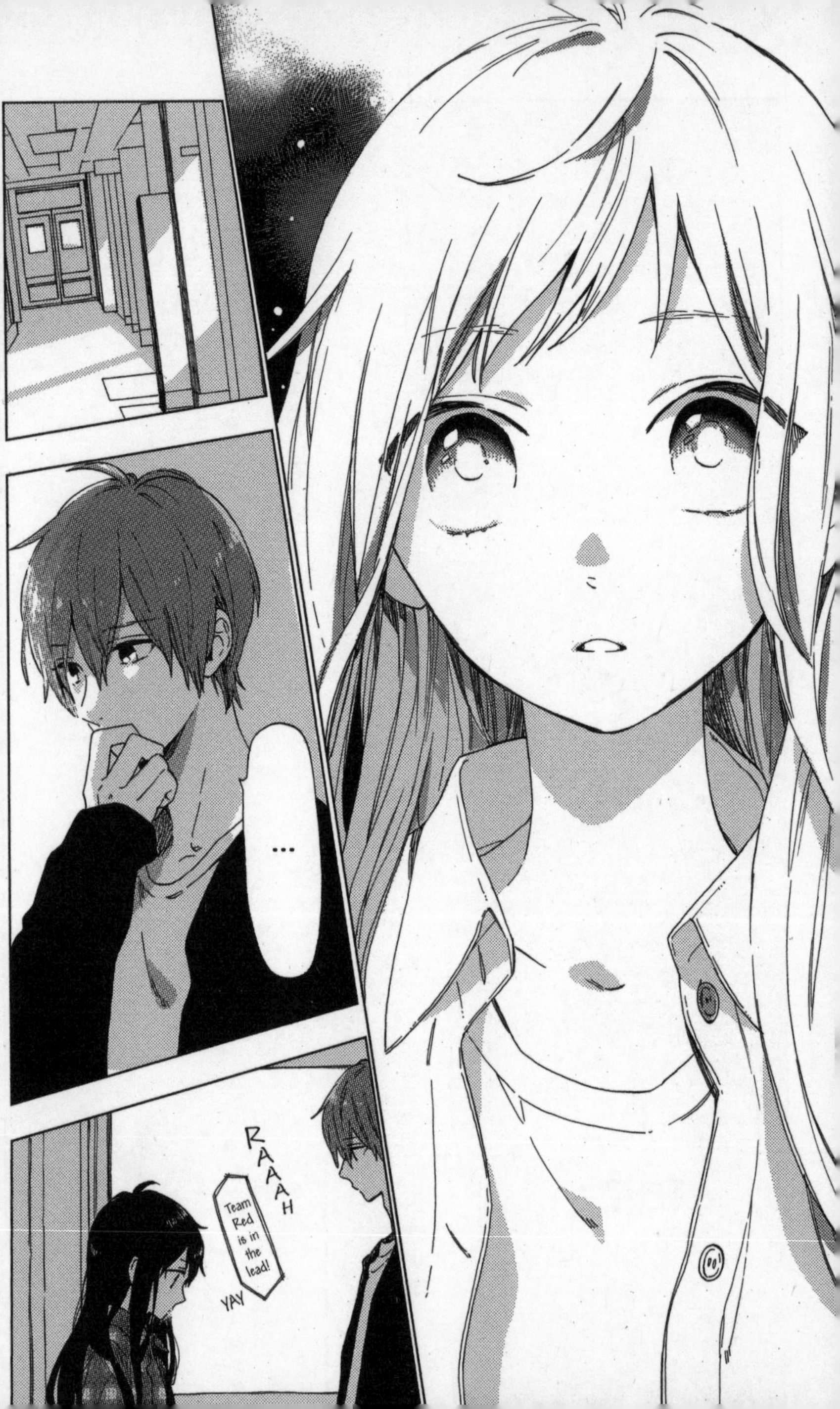
...
RAAAH
Team Red is in the lead!
YAY

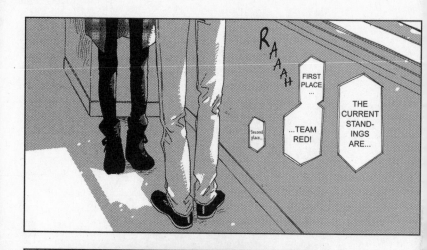

RAAAH

THE CURRENT STANDINGS ARE...

FIRST PLACE...

...TEAM RED!

Second place...

...

ARE YOU SURPRISED?

OF COURSE YOU'D BE.

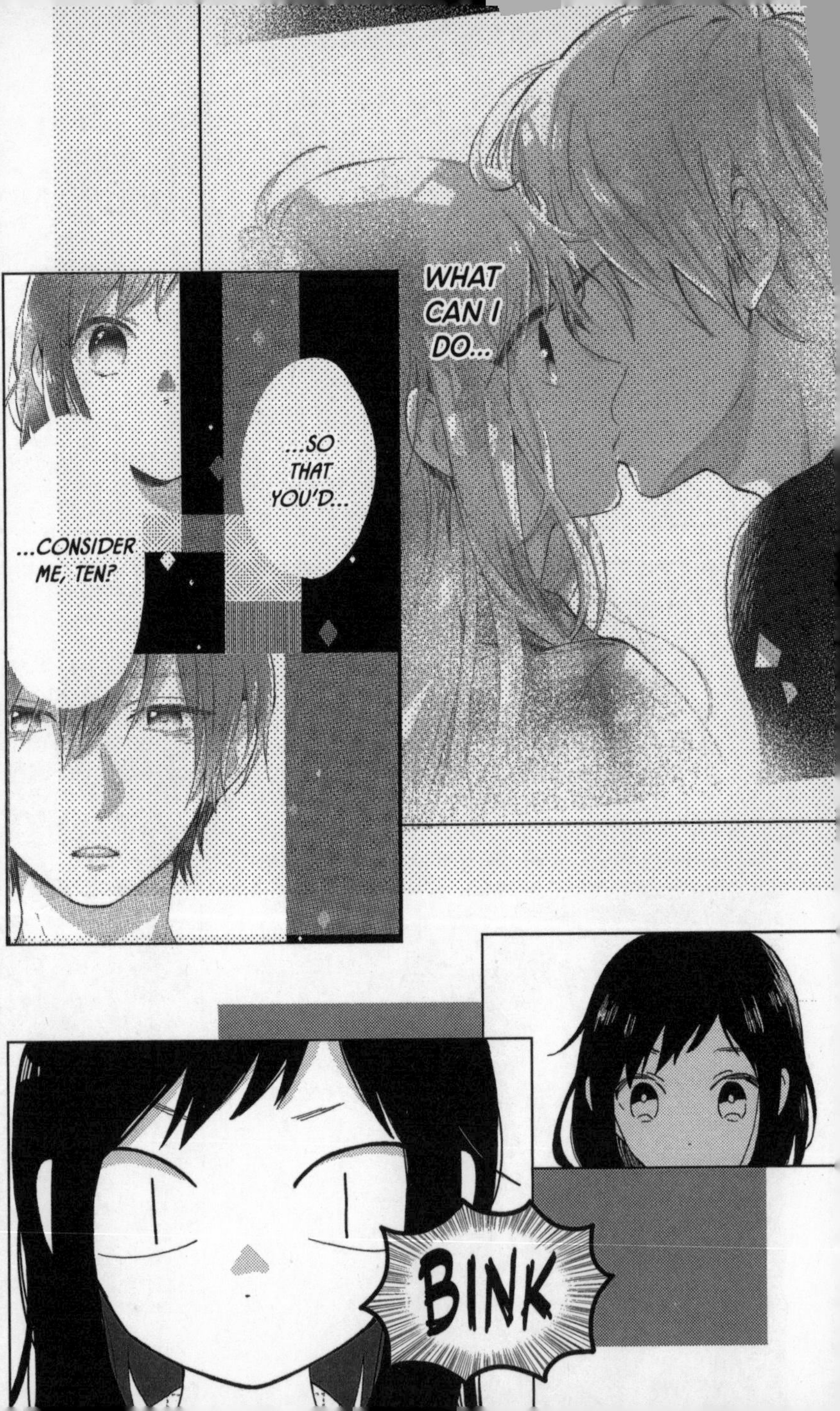
WHAT CAN I DO...
...SO THAT YOU'D...
...CONSIDER ME, TEN?
BINK

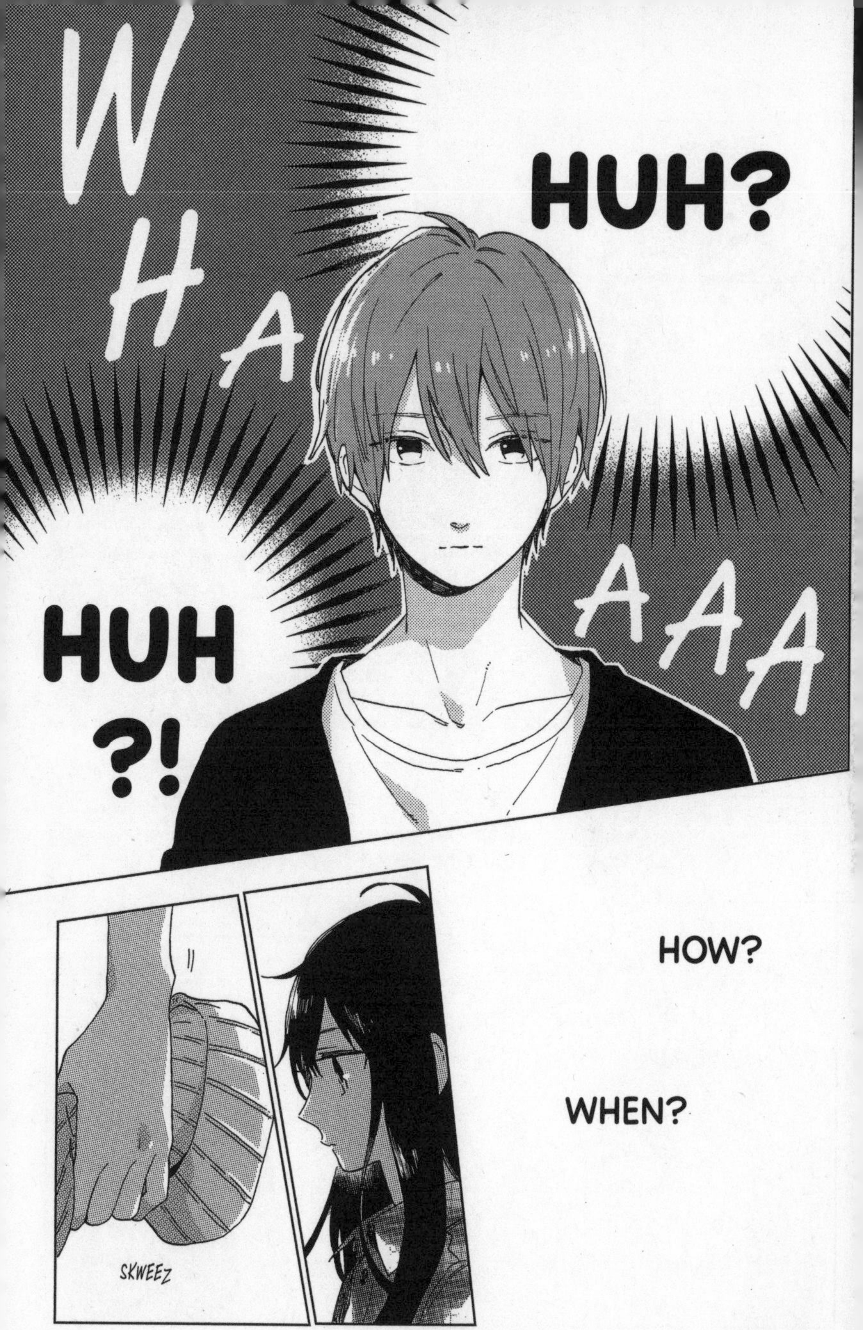
HUH?
WHAAAA
HUH HUH?!
HOW?
WHEN?
SKWEEZ

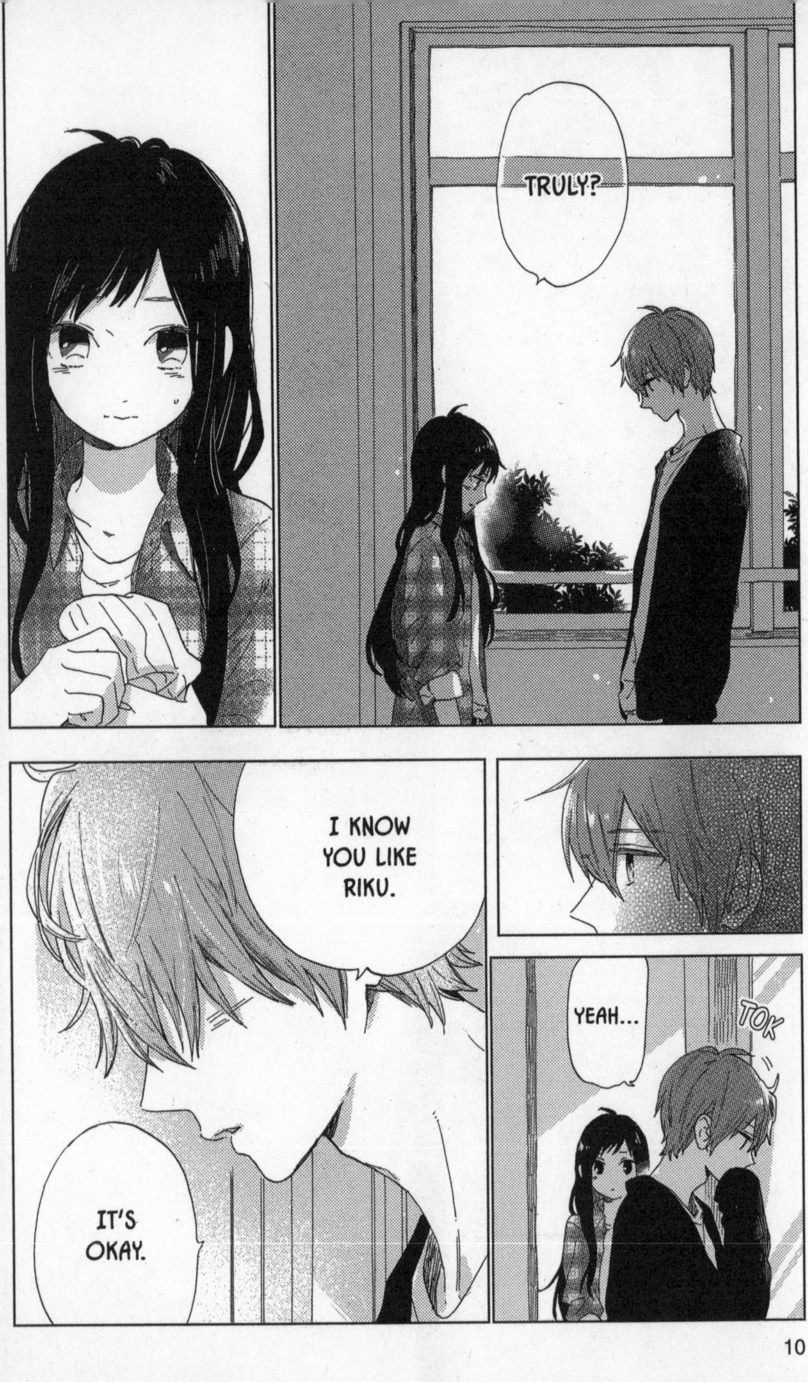
TRULY?
YEAH...
TOK
I KNOW YOU LIKE RIKU.
IT'S OKAY.

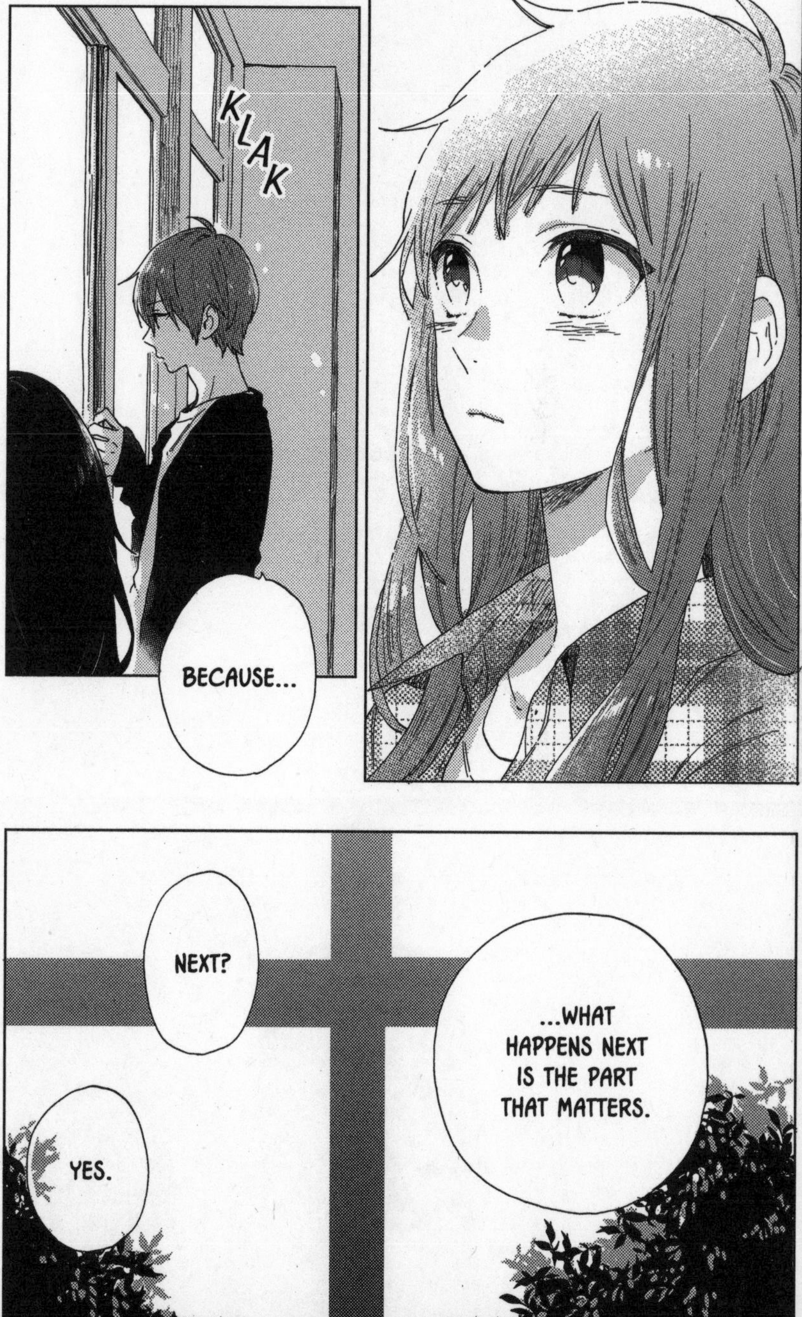
KLAK
BECAUSE...
...WHAT HAPPENS NEXT IS THE PART THAT MATTERS.
NEXT?
YES.

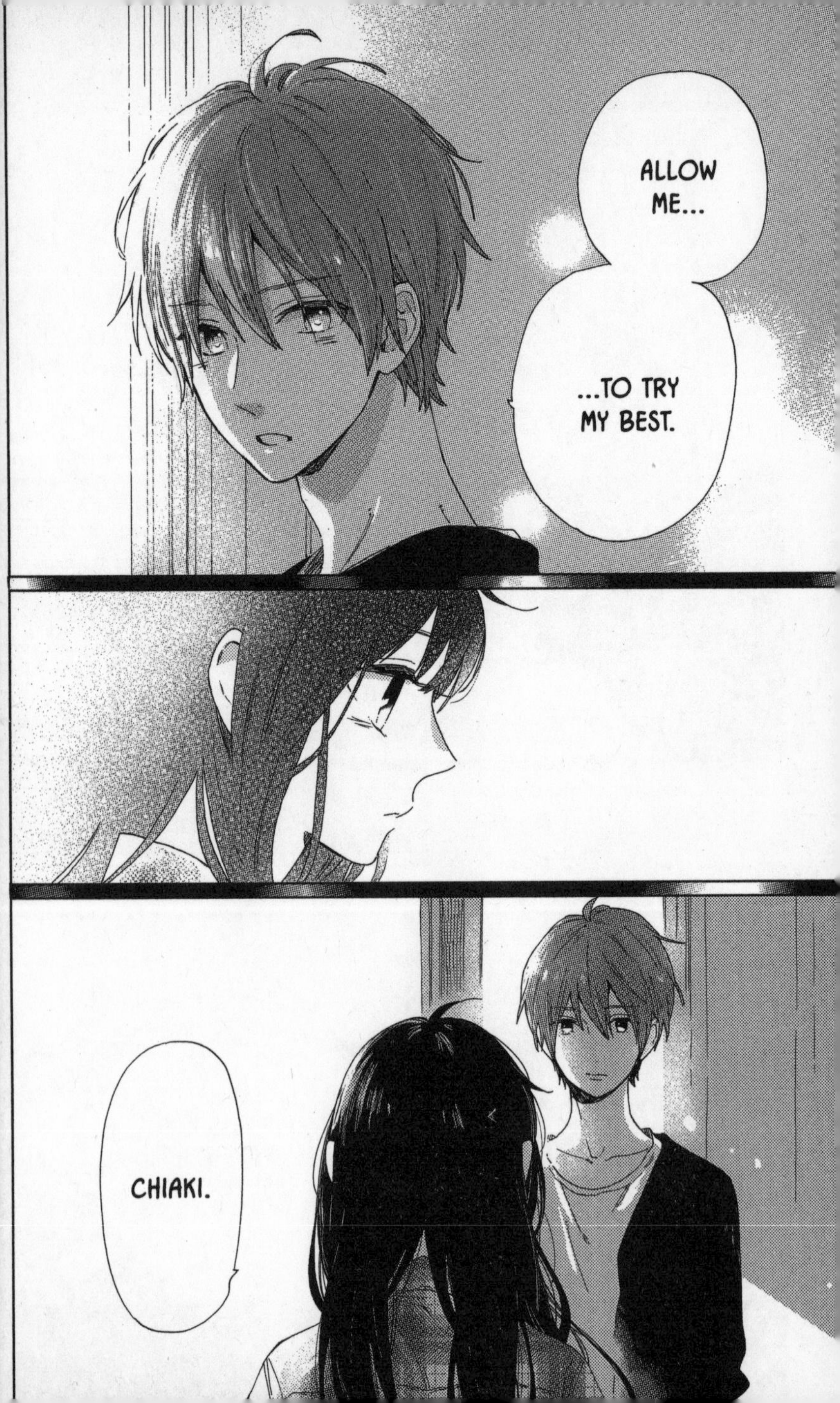
ALLOW ME...
...TO TRY MY BEST.
CHIAKI.

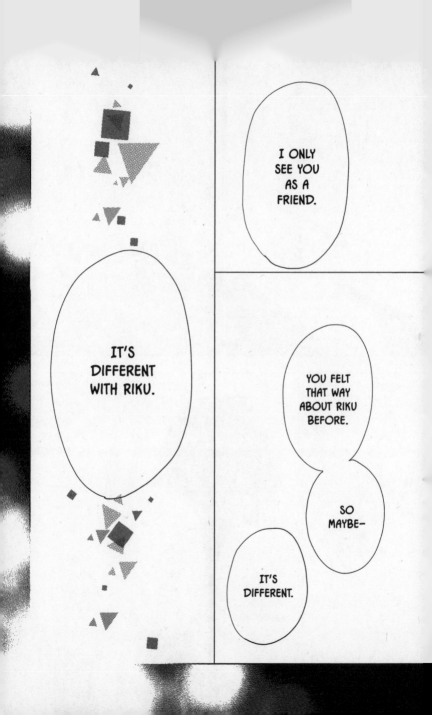

I ONLY SEE YOU AS A FRIEND.

IT'S DIFFERENT WITH RIKU.

YOU FELT THAT WAY ABOUT RIKU BEFORE.

SO MAYBE—

IT'S DIFFERENT.

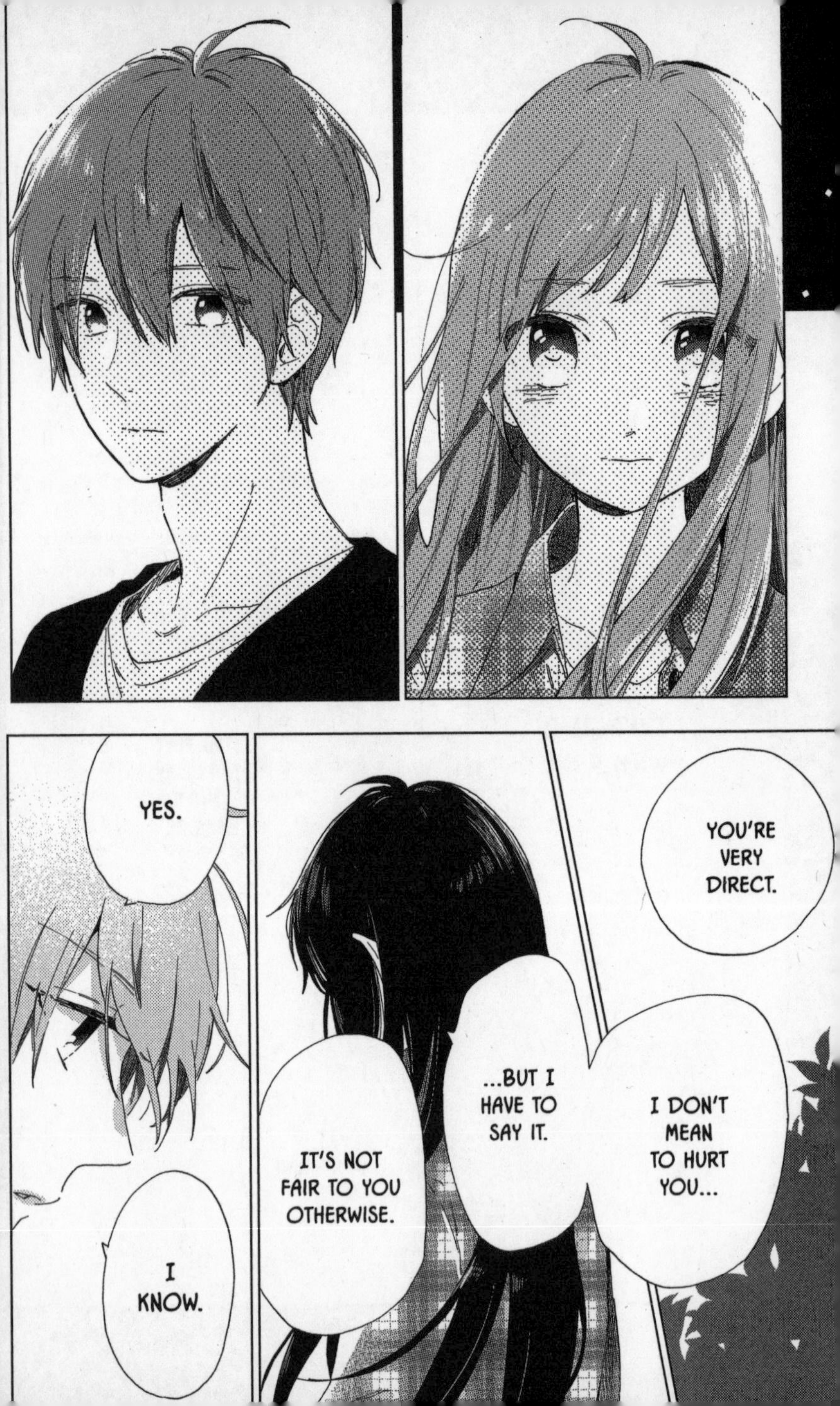
YOU'RE VERY DIRECT.
I DON'T MEAN TO HURT YOU...
...BUT I HAVE TO SAY IT.
IT'S NOT FAIR TO YOU OTHERWISE.
YES.
I KNOW.

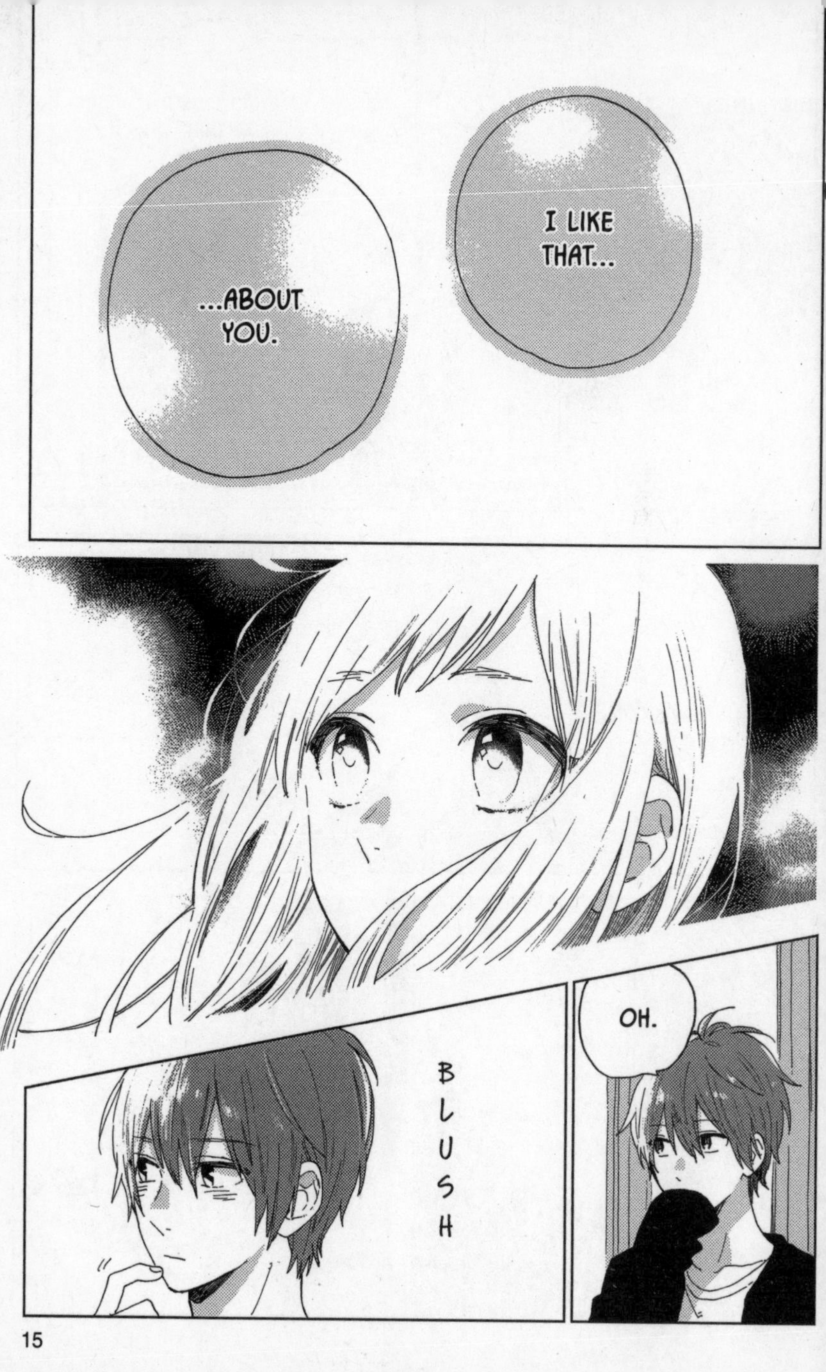
I LIKE THAT...
...ABOUT YOU.
OH.
BLUSH

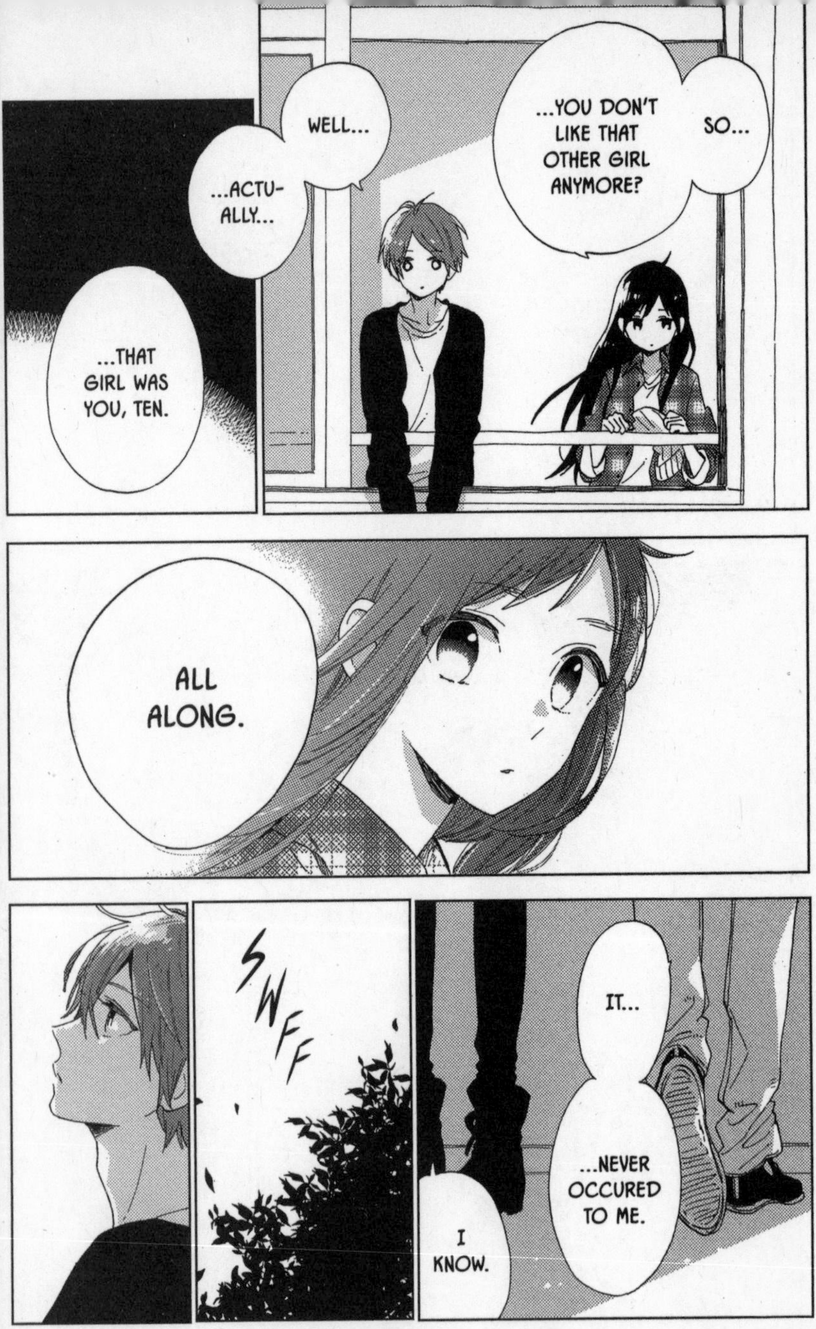
SO...
...YOU DON'T LIKE THAT OTHER GIRL ANYMORE?
WELL...
...ACTU-ALLY...
...THAT GIRL WAS YOU, TEN.
ALL ALONG.
IT...
...NEVER OCCURED TO ME.
I KNOW.
SWFF

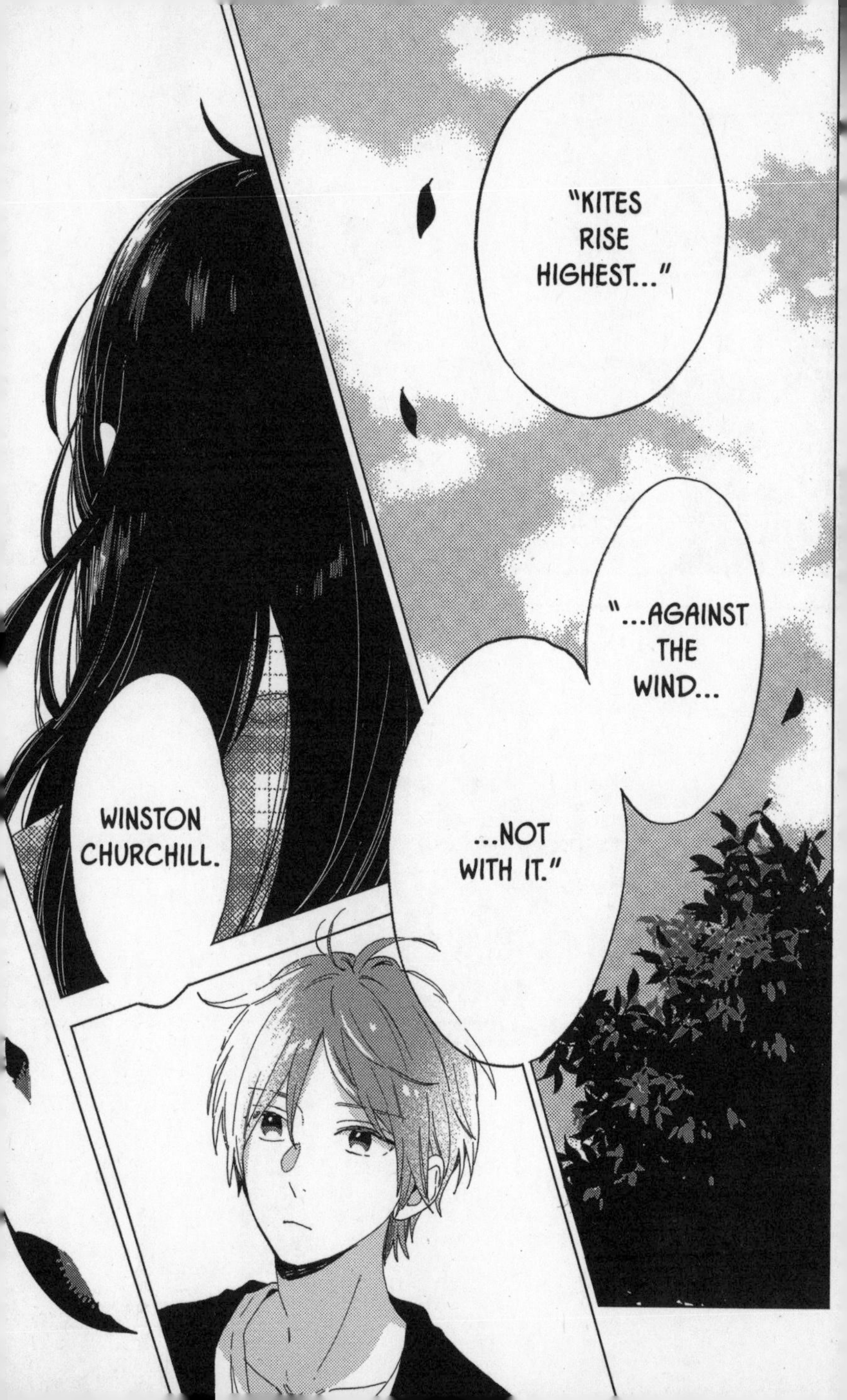
"KITES RISE HIGHEST..."
"...AGAINST THE WIND...
...NOT WITH IT."
WINSTON CHURCHILL.

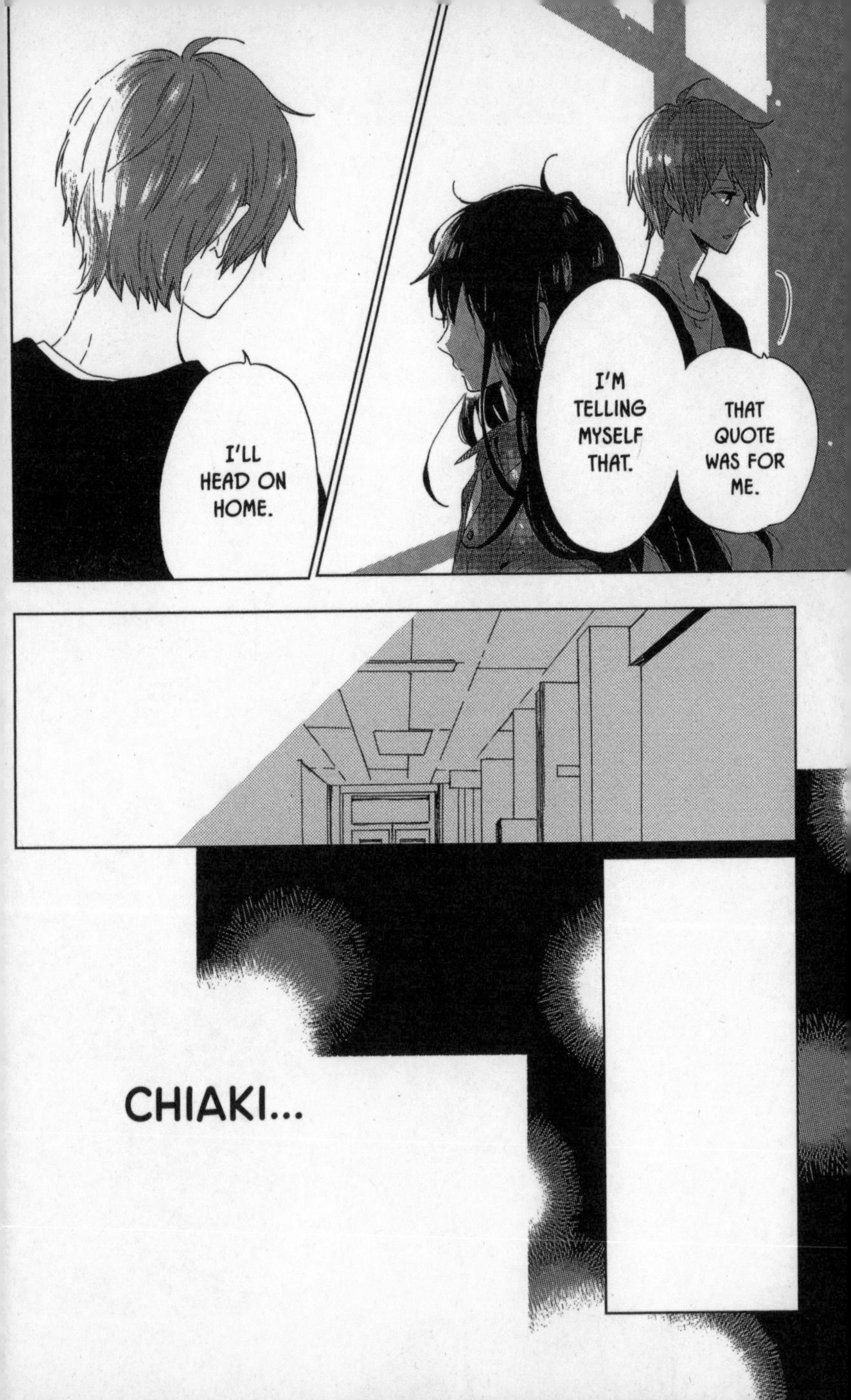
THAT QUOTE WAS FOR ME.
I'M TELLING MYSELF THAT.
I'LL HEAD ON HOME.
CHIAKI...

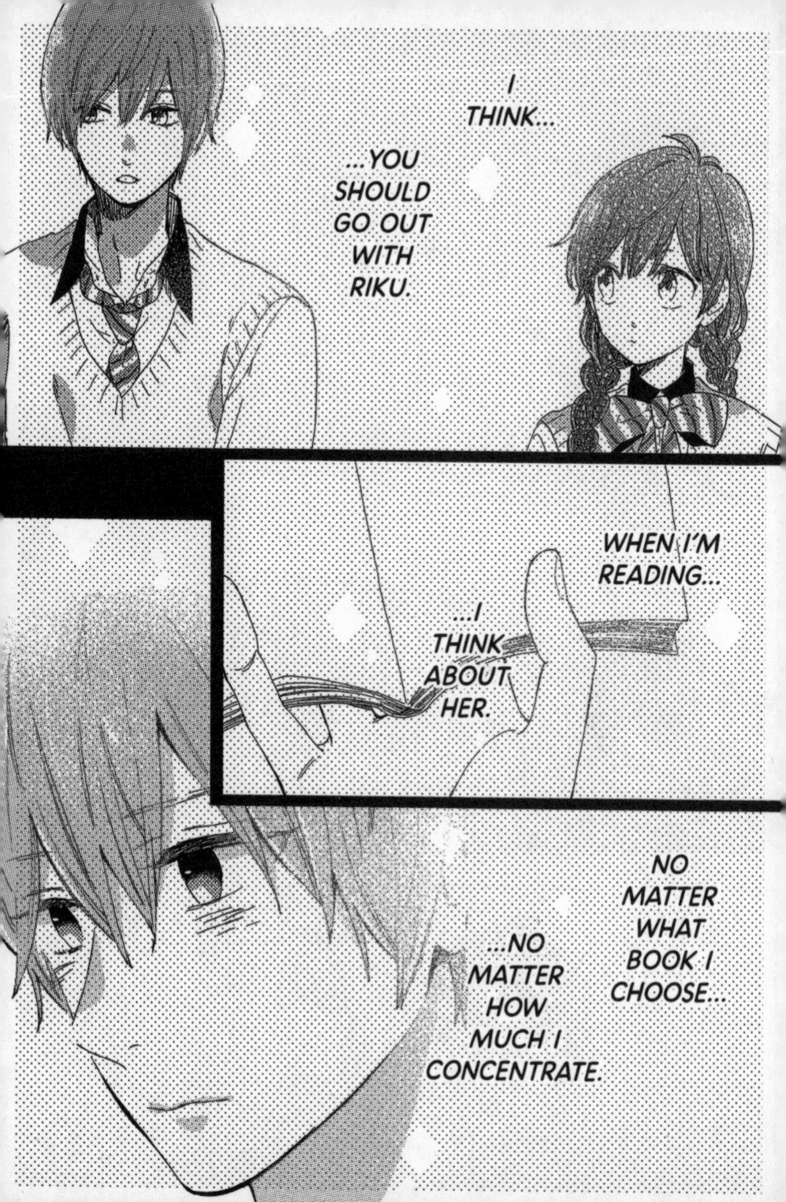
I THINK...
...YOU SHOULD GO OUT WITH RIKU.
WHEN I'M READING...
...I THINK ABOUT HER.
NO MATTER WHAT BOOK I CHOOSE...
...NO MATTER HOW MUCH I CONCENTRATE.

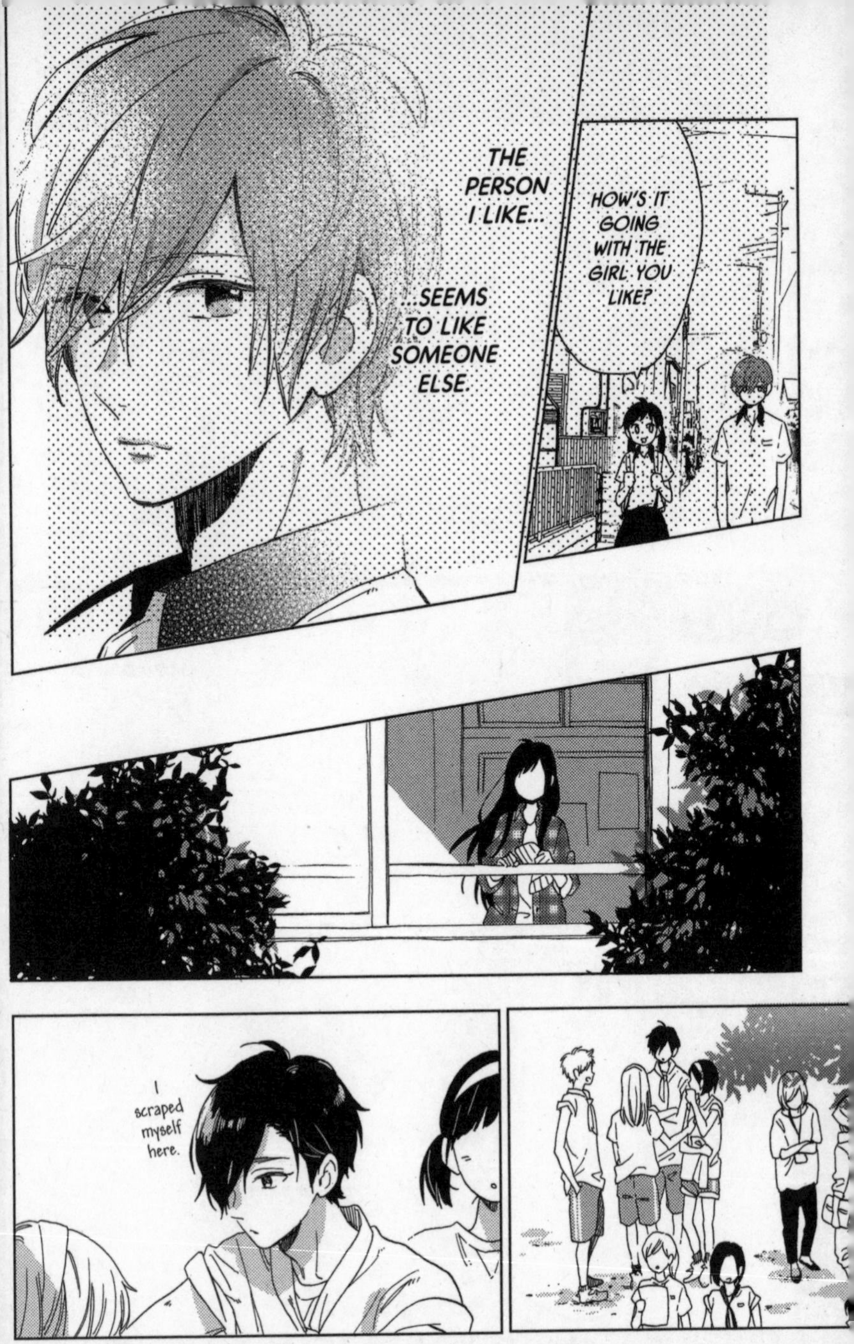
HOW'S IT GOING WITH THE GIRL YOU LIKE?
THE PERSON I LIKE...
...SEEMS TO LIKE SOMEONE ELSE.
I scraped myself here.

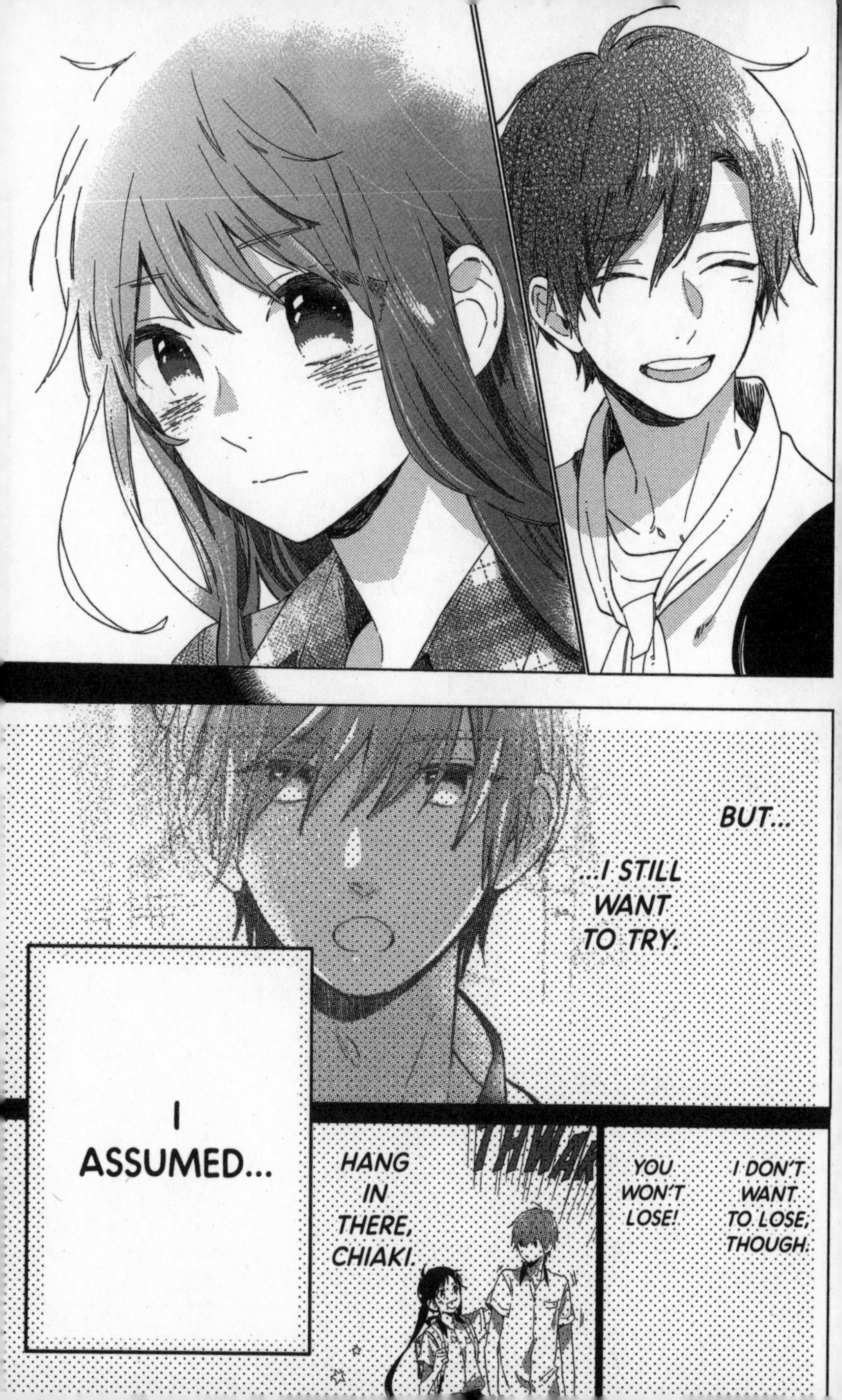
BUT...
...I STILL WANT TO TRY.
I DON'T WANT TO LOSE, THOUGH.
YOU WON'T LOSE!
THWAK
HANG IN THERE, CHIAKI.
I ASSUMED...

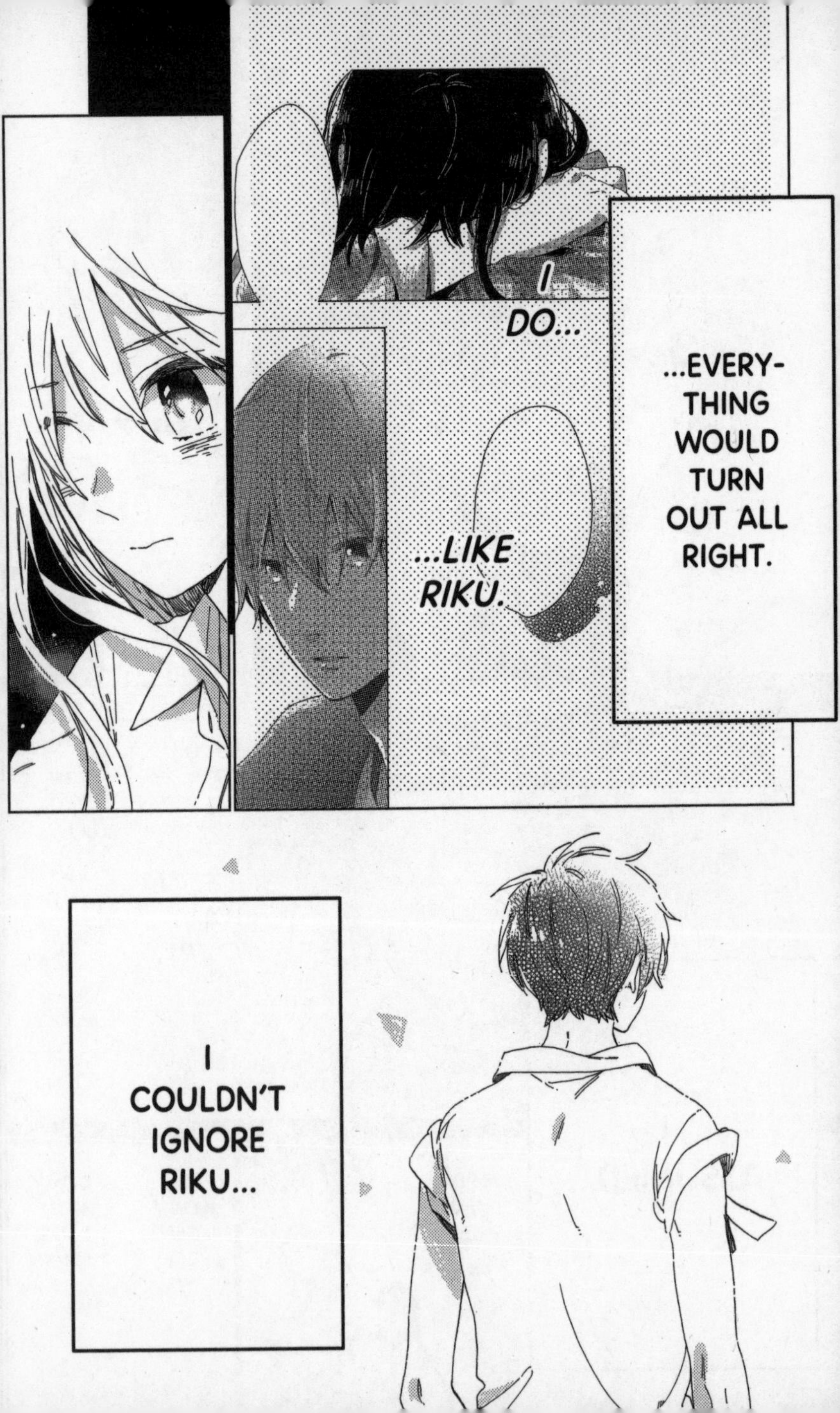
...EVERY-THING WOULD TURN OUT ALL RIGHT.
I DO...
...LIKE RIKU.
I COULDN'T IGNORE RIKU...

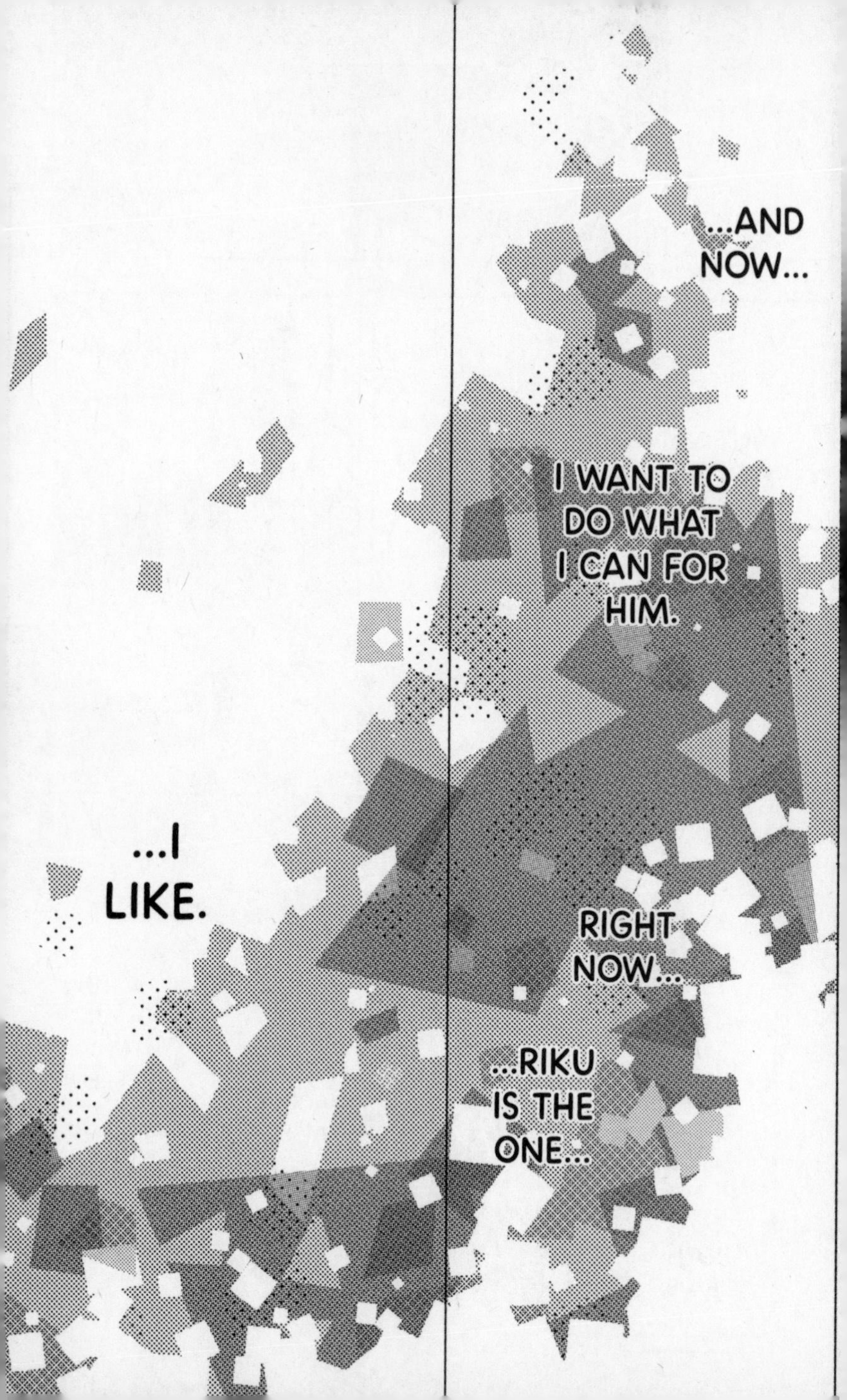
...AND NOW...
I WANT TO DO WHAT I CAN FOR HIM.
RIGHT NOW...
...RIKU IS THE ONE...
...I LIKE.

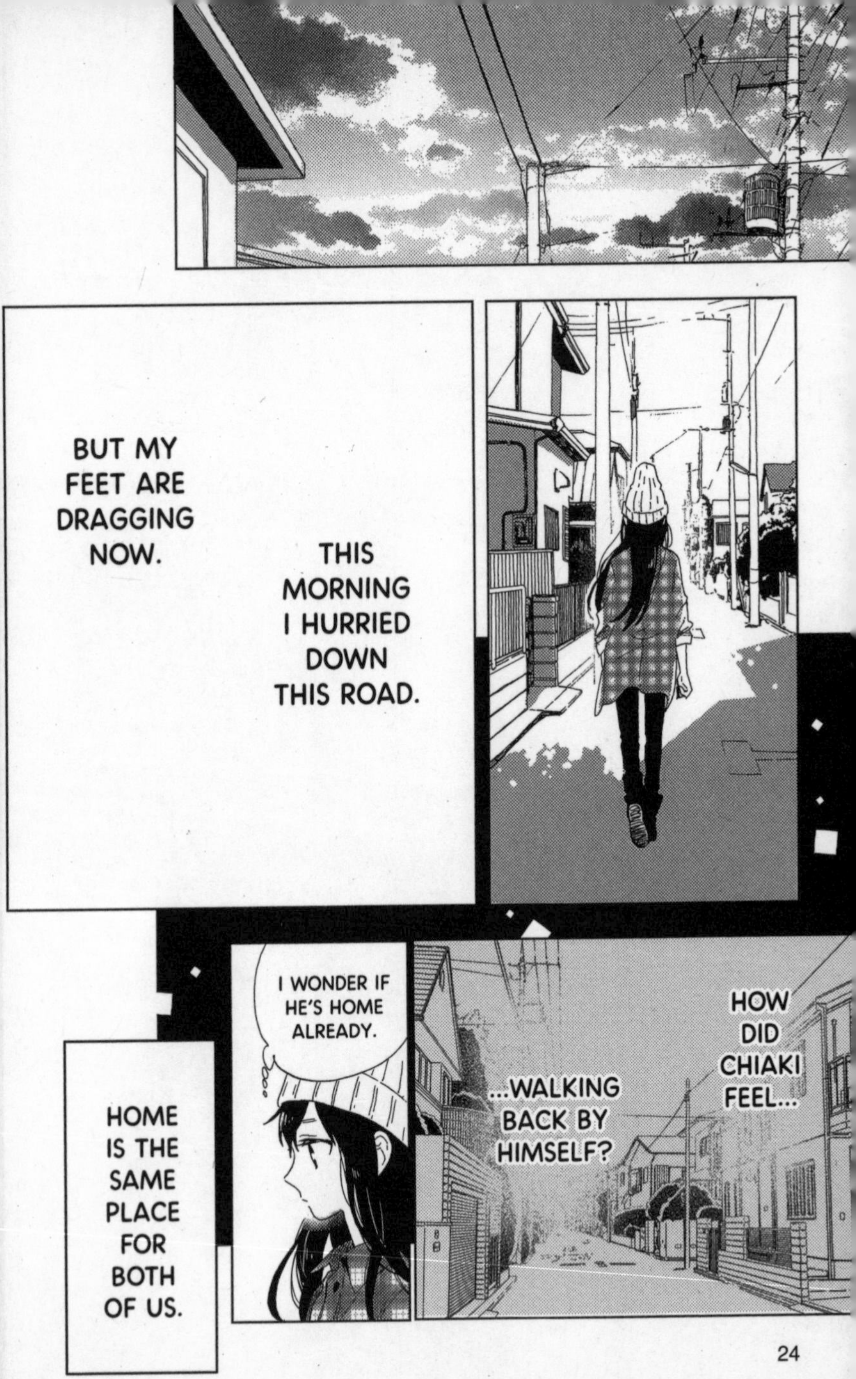
THIS MORNING I HURRIED DOWN THIS ROAD.
BUT MY FEET ARE DRAGGING NOW.
HOW DID CHIAKI FEEL...
...WALKING BACK BY HIMSELF?
I WONDER IF HE'S HOME ALREADY.
HOME IS THE SAME PLACE FOR BOTH OF US.

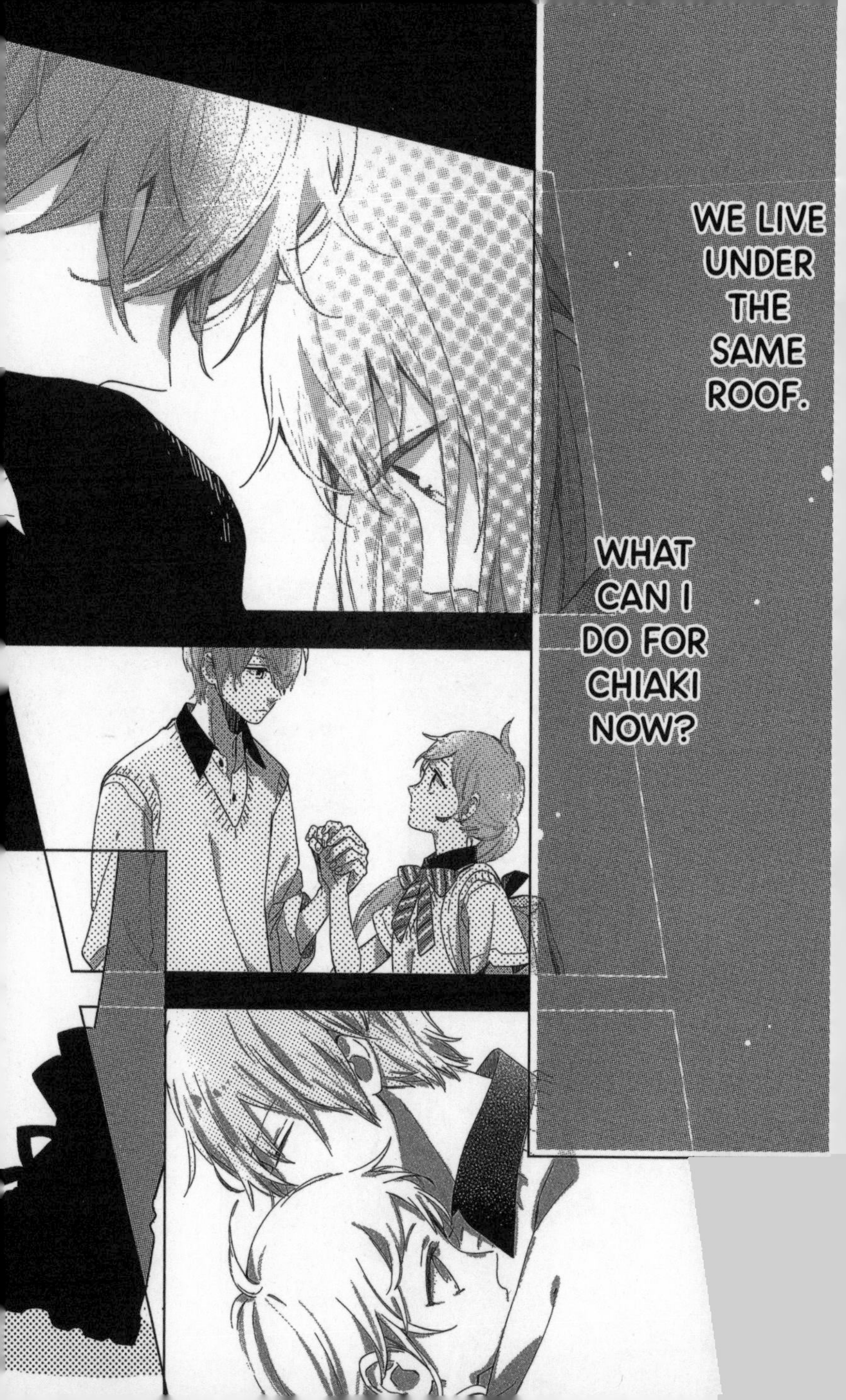
WE LIVE UNDER THE SAME ROOF.
WHAT CAN I DO FOR CHIAKI NOW?

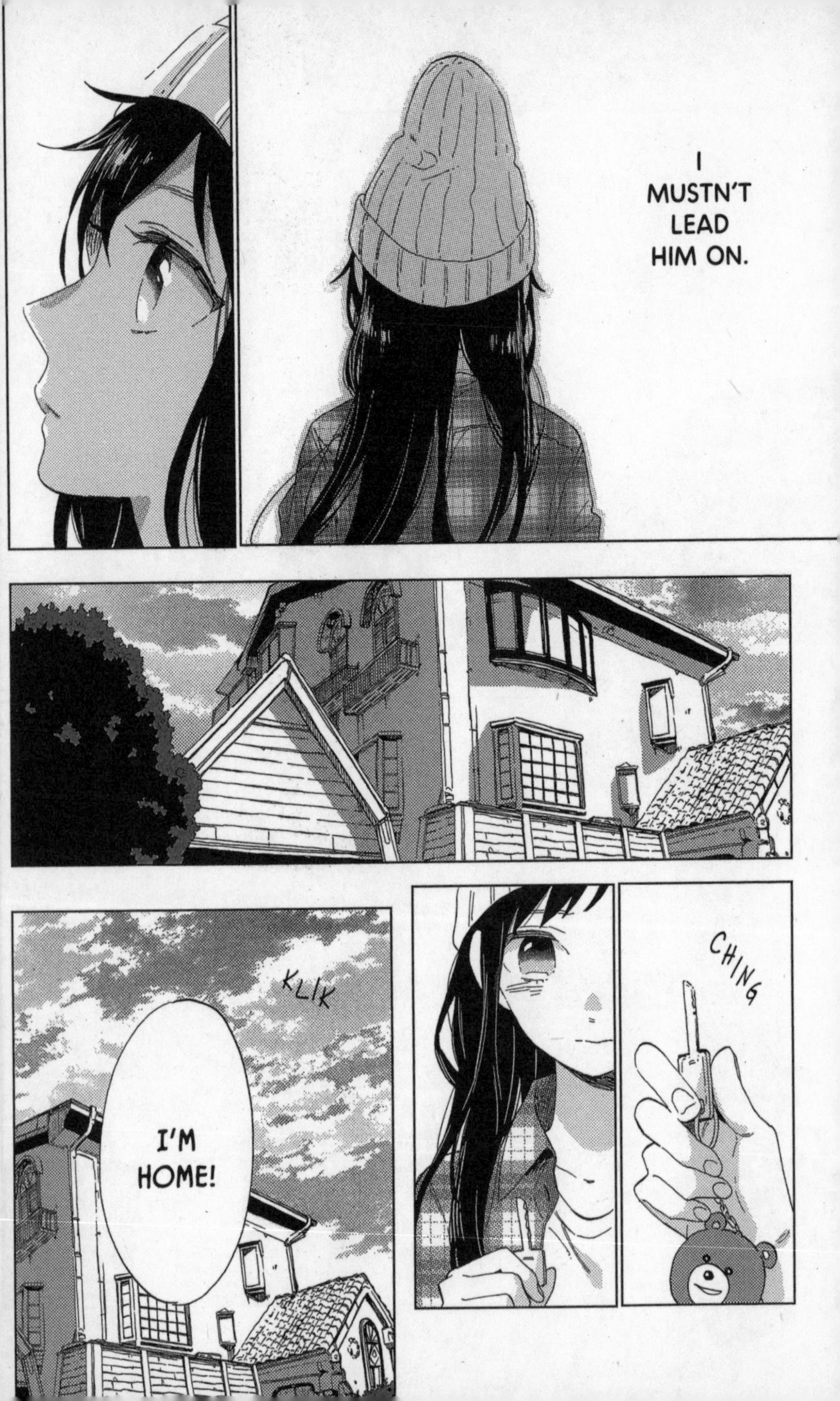

I MUSTN'T LEAD HIM ON.
CHING
KLIK
I'M HOME!

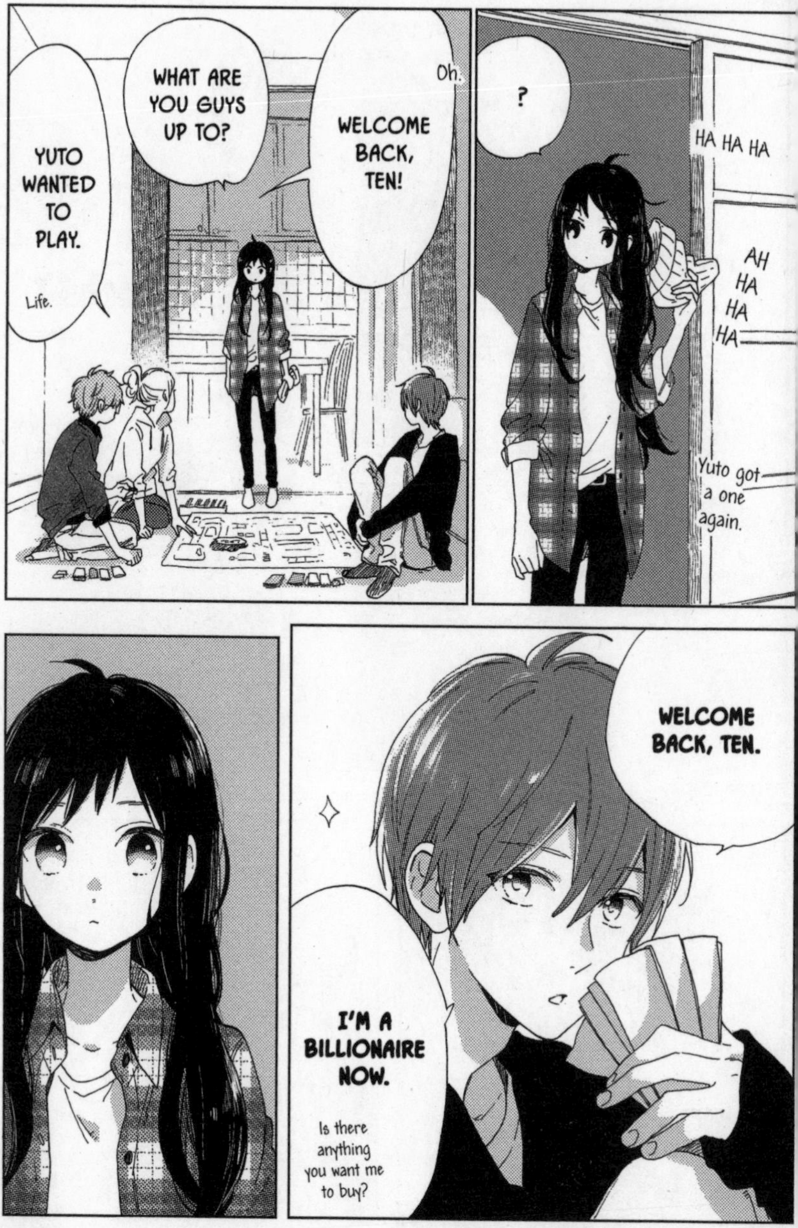
?
HA HA HA
AH HA HA HA
Yuto got a one again.
Oh.
WELCOME BACK, TEN!
WHAT ARE YOU GUYS UP TO?
YUTO WANTED TO PLAY.
Life.
WELCOME BACK, TEN.
I'M A BILLIONAIRE NOW.
Is there anything you want me to buy?

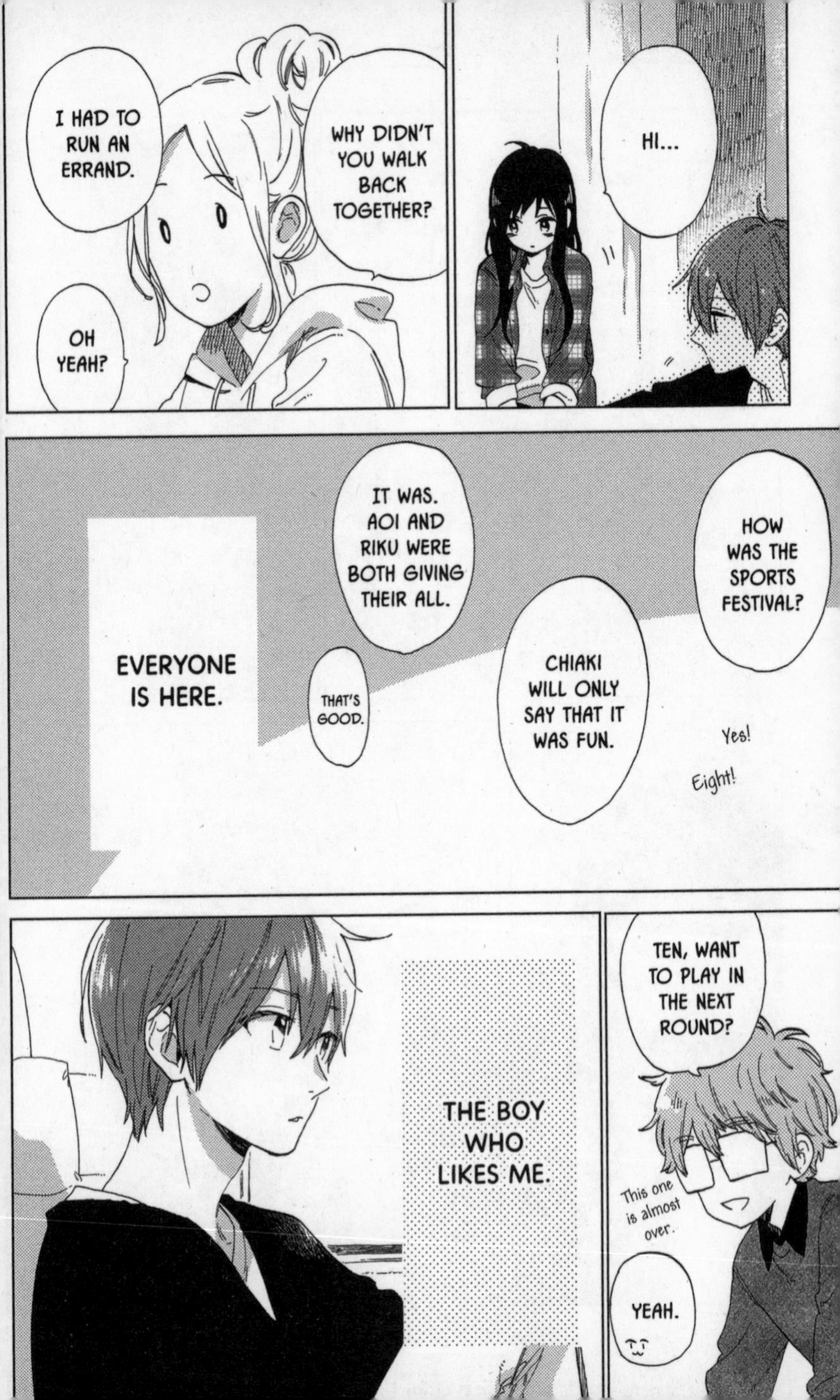
HI...
WHY DIDN'T YOU WALK BACK TOGETHER?
I HAD TO RUN AN ERRAND.
OH YEAH?
HOW WAS THE SPORTS FESTIVAL?
Yes!
Eight!
IT WAS. AOI AND RIKU WERE BOTH GIVING THEIR ALL.
CHIAKI WILL ONLY SAY THAT IT WAS FUN.
THAT'S GOOD.
EVERYONE IS HERE.
TEN, WANT TO PLAY IN THE NEXT ROUND?
This one is almost over.
YEAH.
THE BOY WHO LIKES ME.

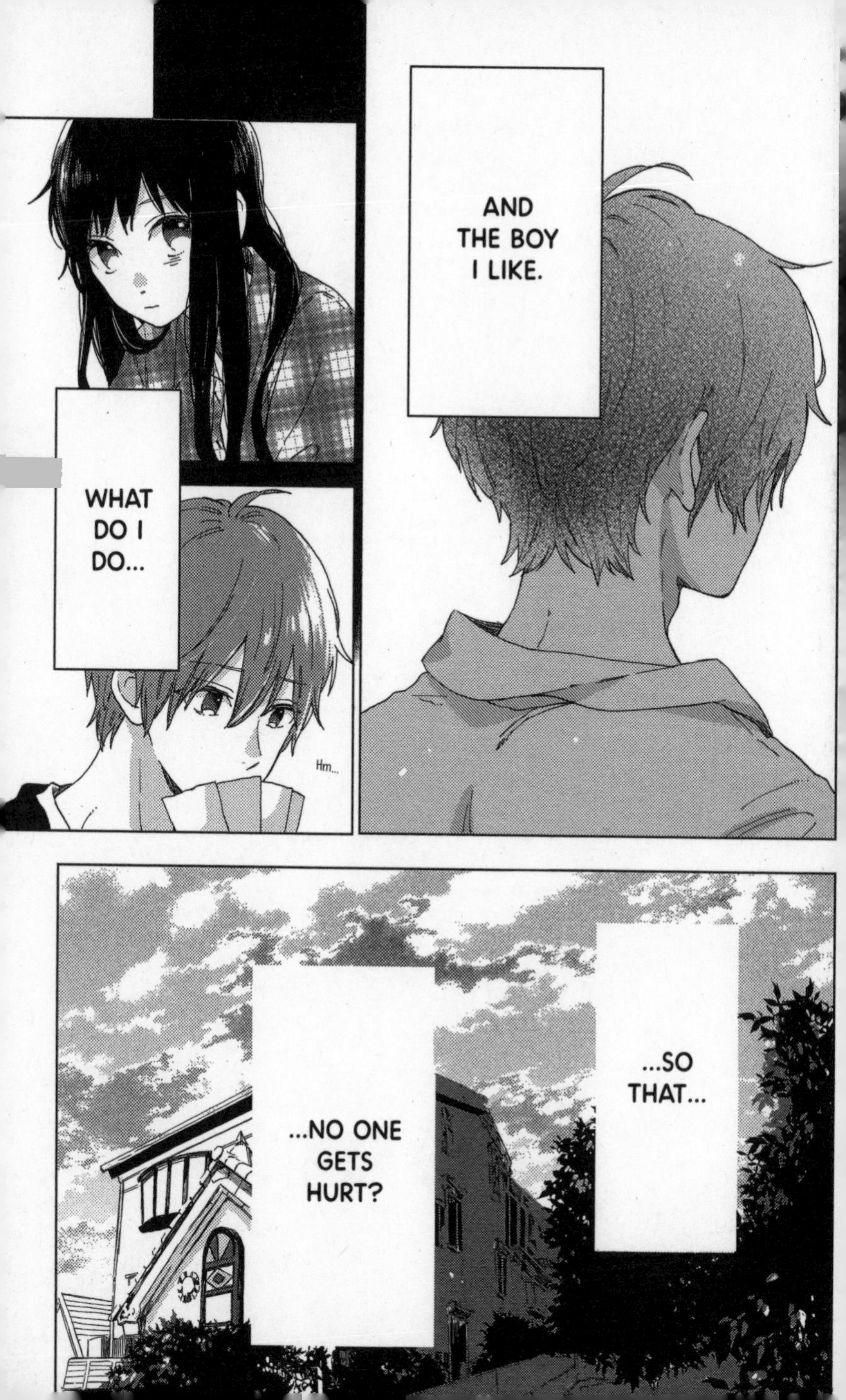
AND THE BOY I LIKE.
WHAT DO I DO...
Hm...
...SO THAT...
...NO ONE GETS HURT?

SHORTCAKE
CAKE

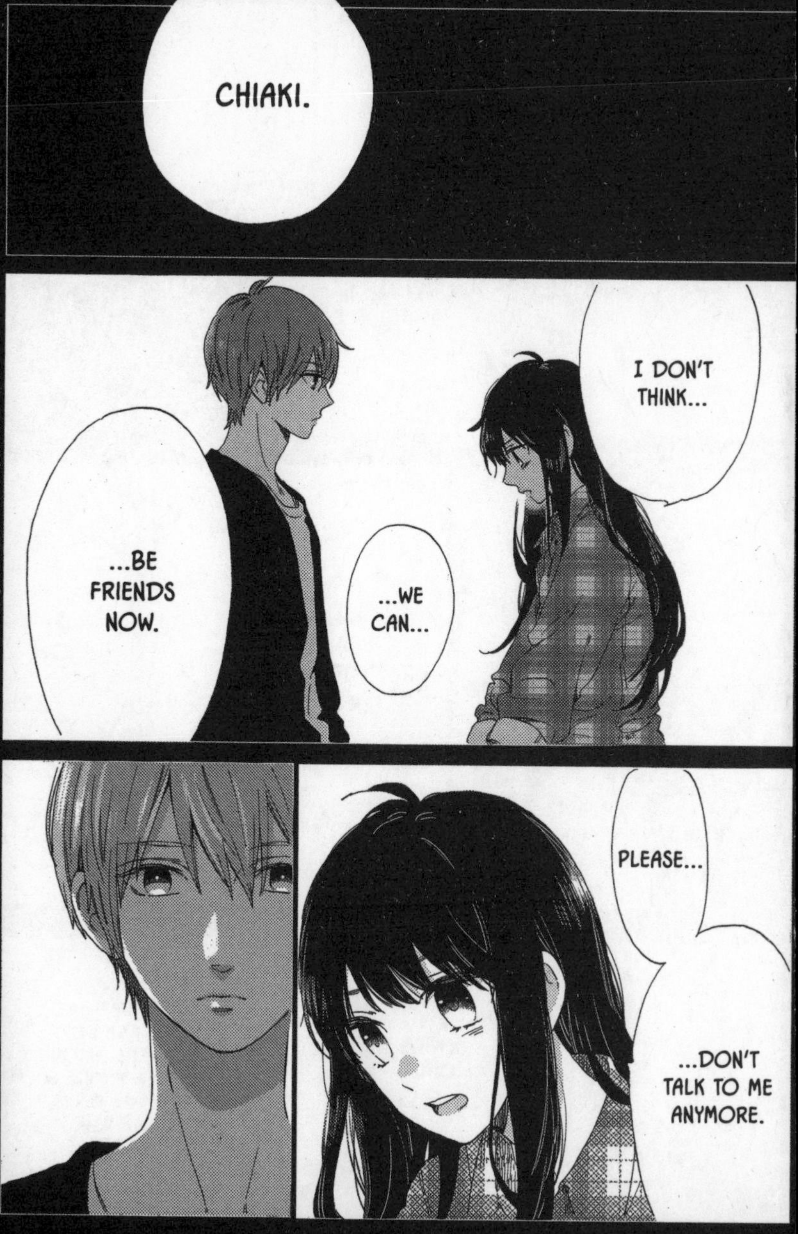
CHIAKI.
I DON'T THINK...
...WE CAN...
...BE FRIENDS NOW.
PLEASE...
...DON'T TALK TO ME ANYMORE.

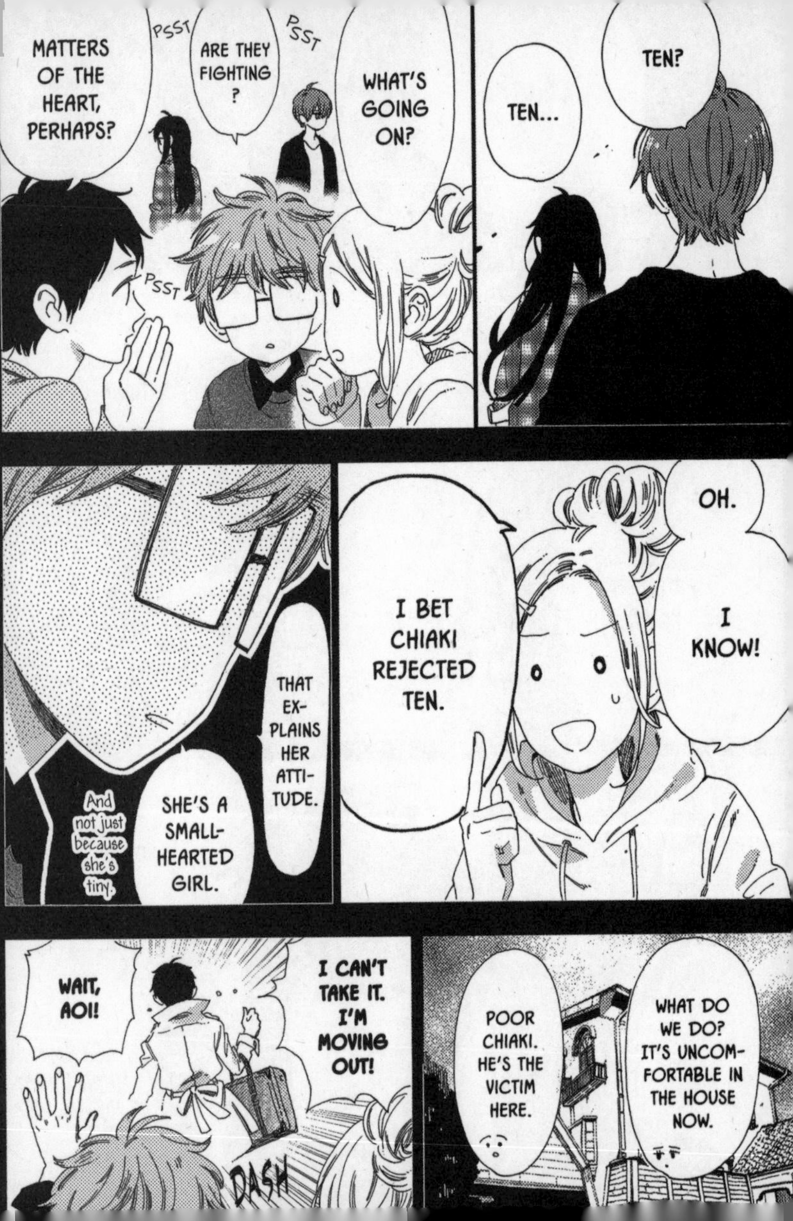
TEN?
TEN...
WHAT'S GOING ON?
PSST
ARE THEY FIGHTING?
PSST
MATTERS OF THE HEART, PERHAPS?
PSST
OH.
I KNOW!
I BET CHIAKI REJECTED TEN.
THAT EX-PLAINS HER ATTI-TUDE.
SHE'S A SMALL-HEARTED GIRL.
And not just because she's tiny.
WHAT DO WE DO? IT'S UNCOM-FORTABLE IN THE HOUSE NOW.
POOR CHIAKI. HE'S THE VICTIM HERE.
I CAN'T TAKE IT. I'M MOVING OUT!
WAIT, AOI!
DASH

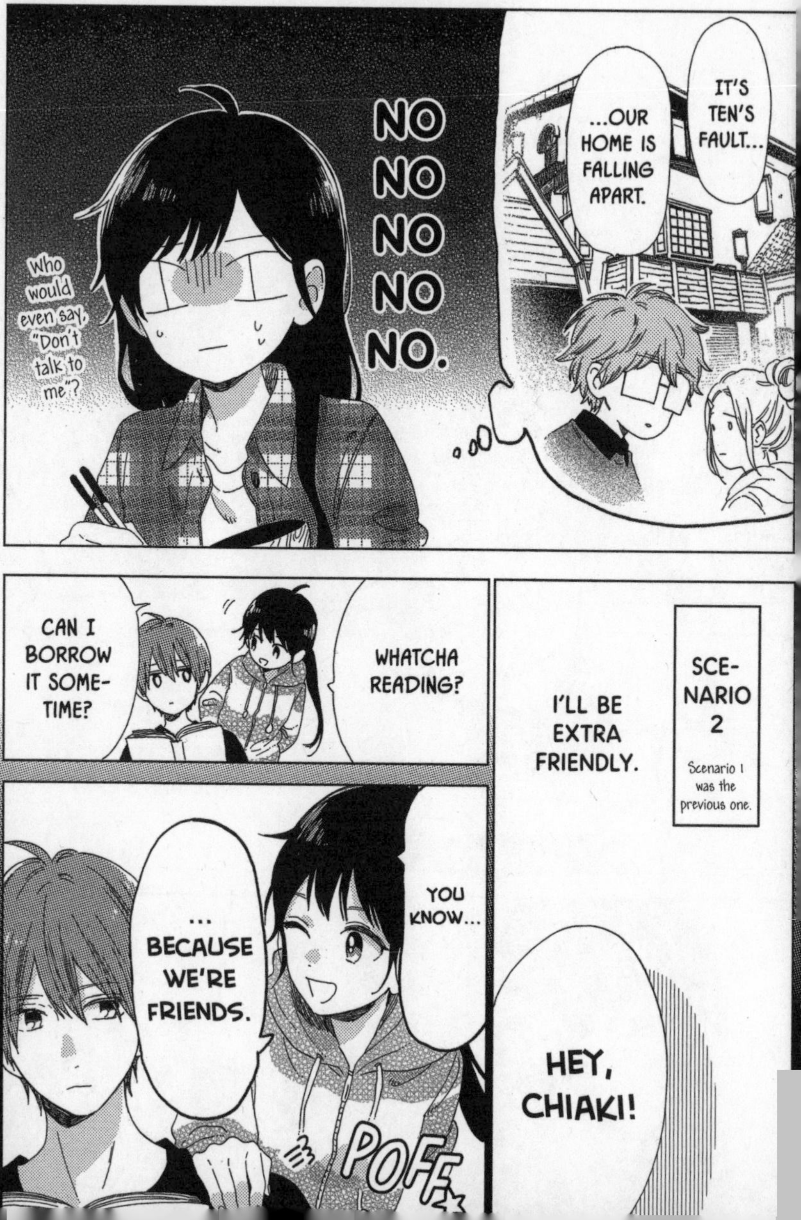
IT'S TEN'S FAULT...
...OUR HOME IS FALLING APART.
NO NO NO NO NO.
Who would even say, "Don't talk to me"?
SCENARIO 2
Scenario 1 was the previous one.
I'LL BE EXTRA FRIENDLY.
HEY, CHIAKI!
WHATCHA READING?
CAN I BORROW IT SOMETIME?
YOU KNOW...
...BECAUSE WE'RE FRIENDS.
POFF

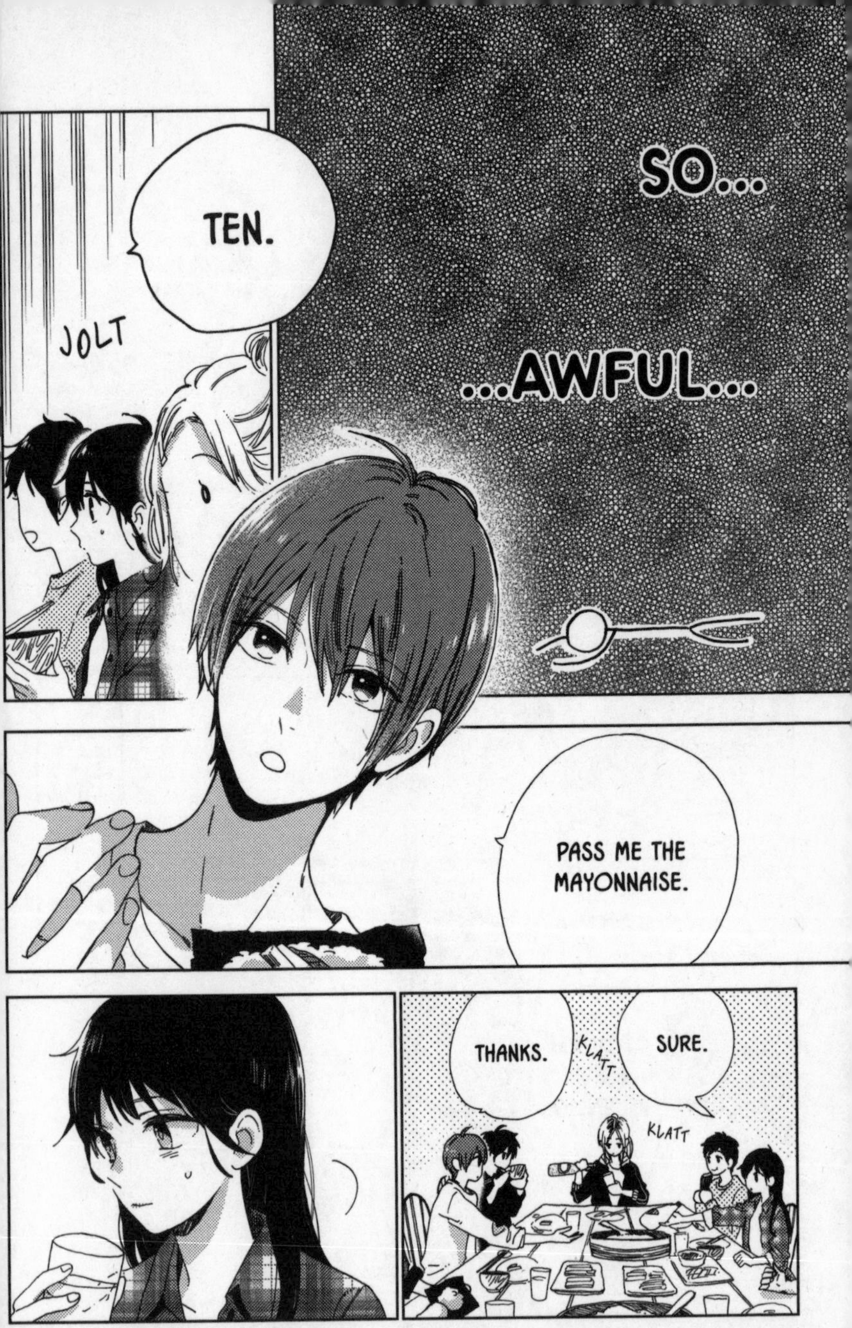
SO...
...AWFUL...
TEN.
JOLT
PASS ME THE MAYONNAISE.
SURE.
KLATT
THANKS.
KLATT

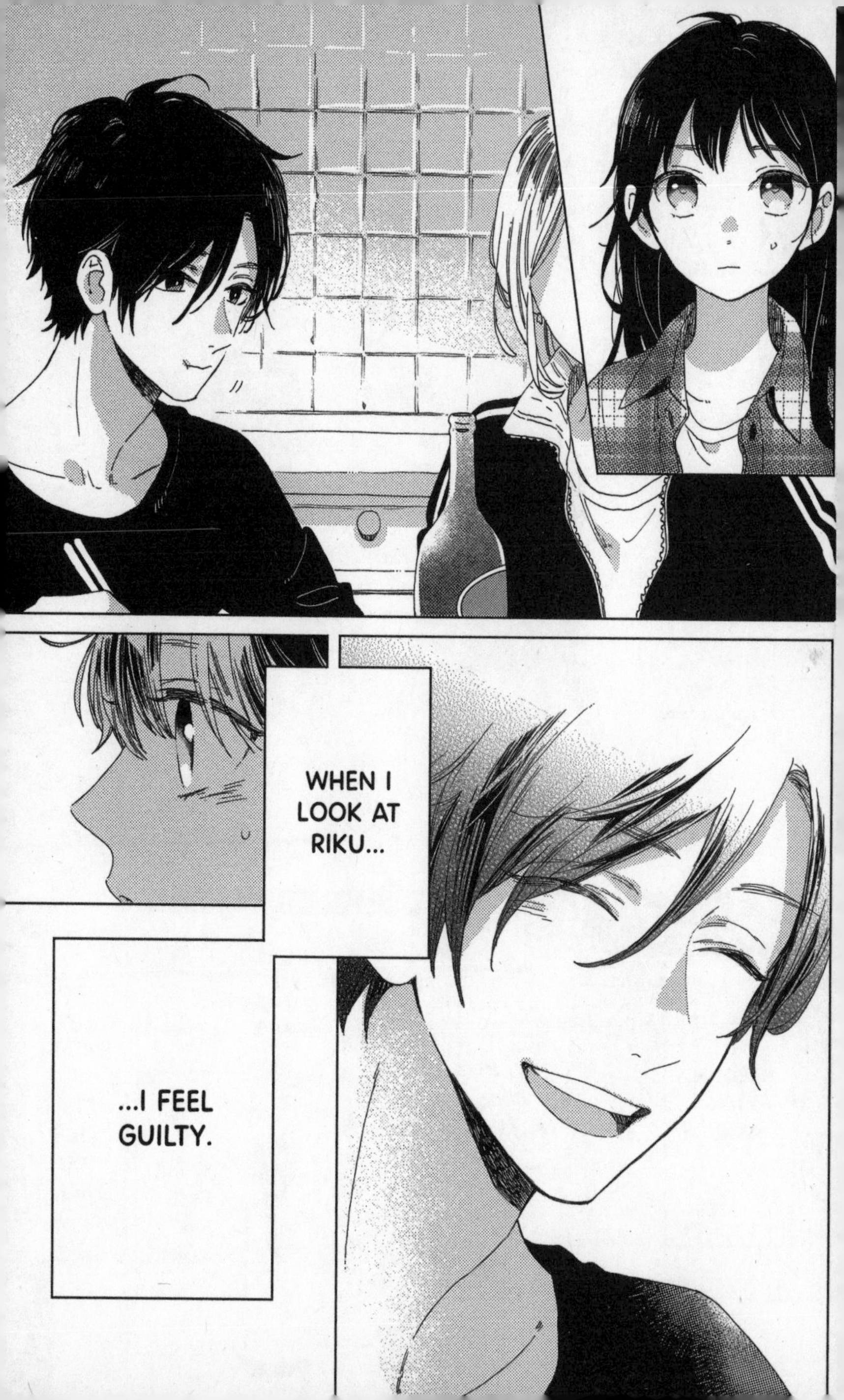
WHEN I LOOK AT RIKU...
...I FEEL GUILTY.

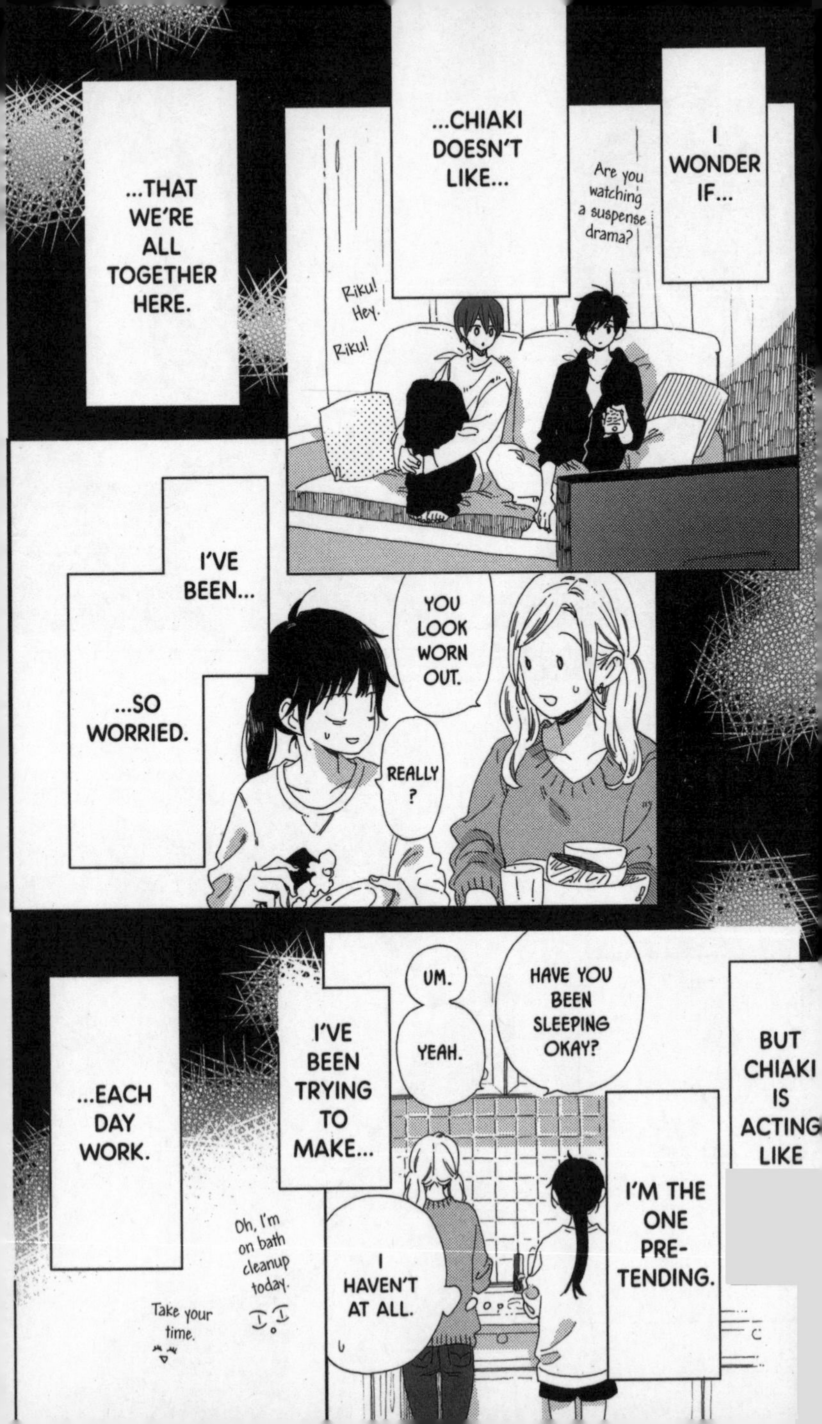
I WONDER IF...
Are you watching a suspense drama?
...CHIAKI DOESN'T LIKE...
Riku! Hey. Riku!
...THAT WE'RE ALL TOGETHER HERE.
YOU LOOK WORN OUT.
REALLY?
I'VE BEEN...
...SO WORRIED.
BUT CHIAKI IS ACTING LIKE
I'M THE ONE PRE-TENDING.
HAVE YOU BEEN SLEEPING OKAY?
UM.
YEAH.
I HAVEN'T AT ALL.
I'VE BEEN TRYING TO MAKE...
Oh, I'm on bath cleanup today.
Take your time.
...EACH DAY WORK.

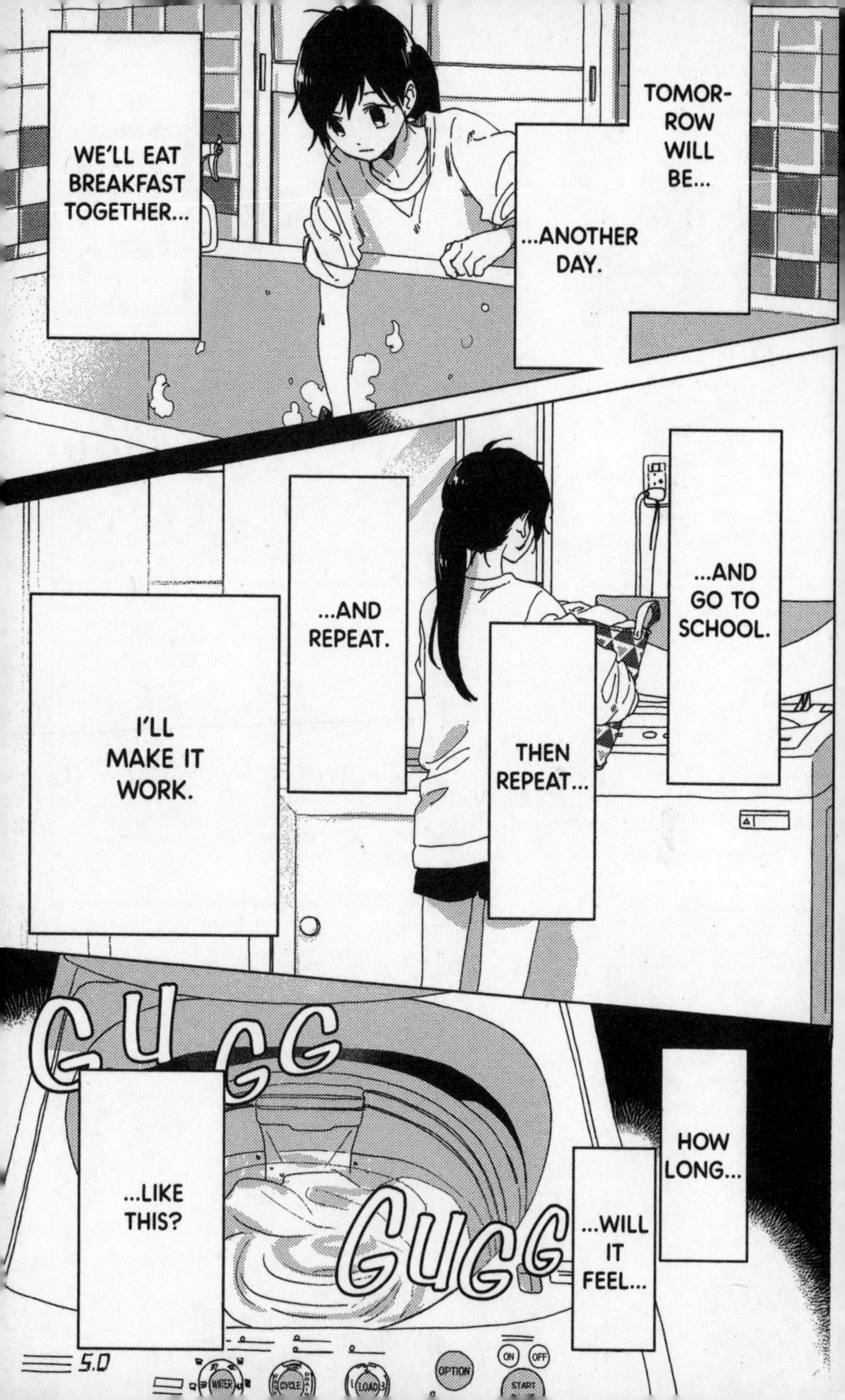
TOMOR-ROW WILL BE...
...ANOTHER DAY.
WE'LL EAT BREAKFAST TOGETHER...
...AND GO TO SCHOOL.
THEN REPEAT...
...AND REPEAT.
I'LL MAKE IT WORK.
HOW LONG...
...WILL IT FEEL...
GUGG
GUGG
...LIKE THIS?
5.0
WATER
CYCLE
LOAD
OPTION
ON
OFF
START

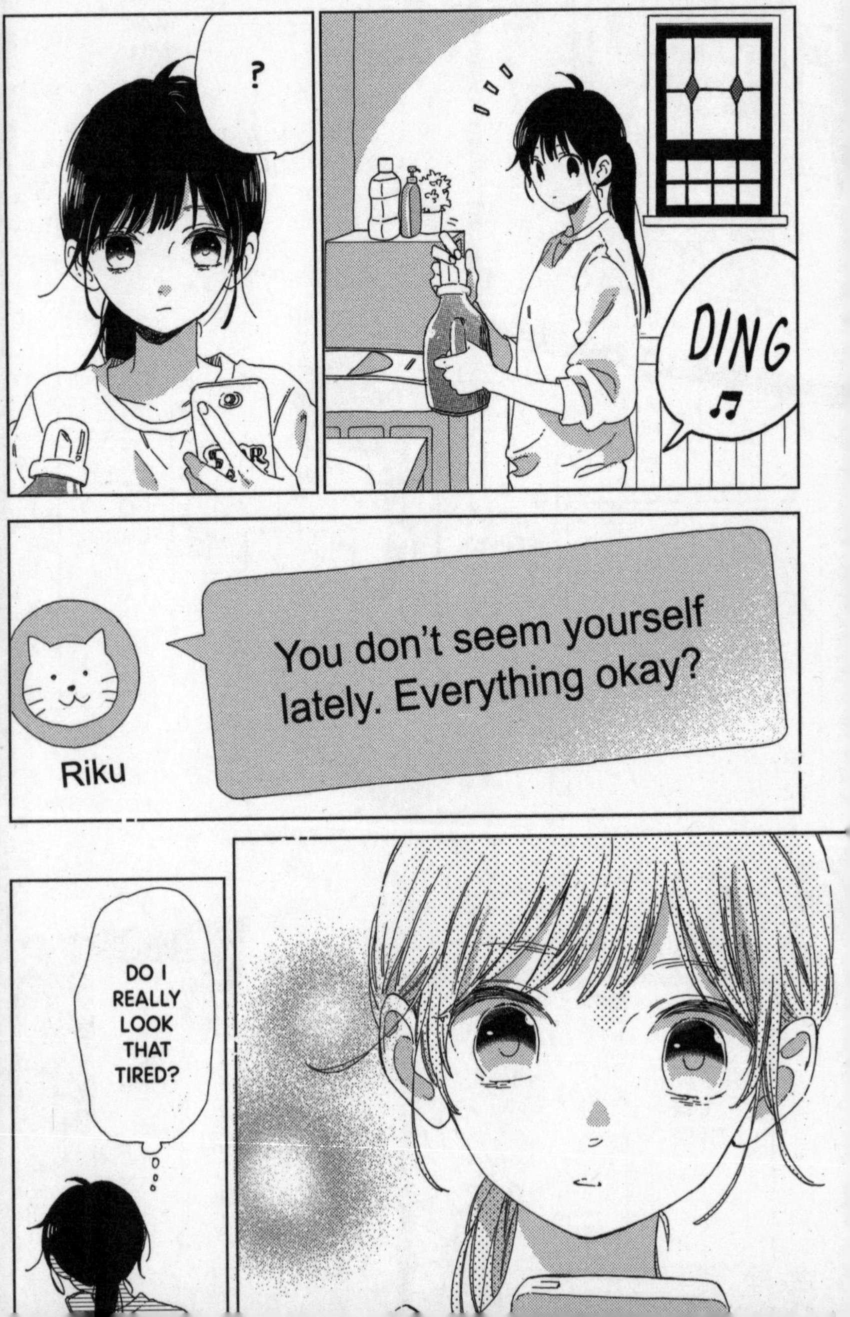
DING ♫
?
Riku
You don't seem yourself lately. Everything okay?
DO I REALLY LOOK THAT TIRED?

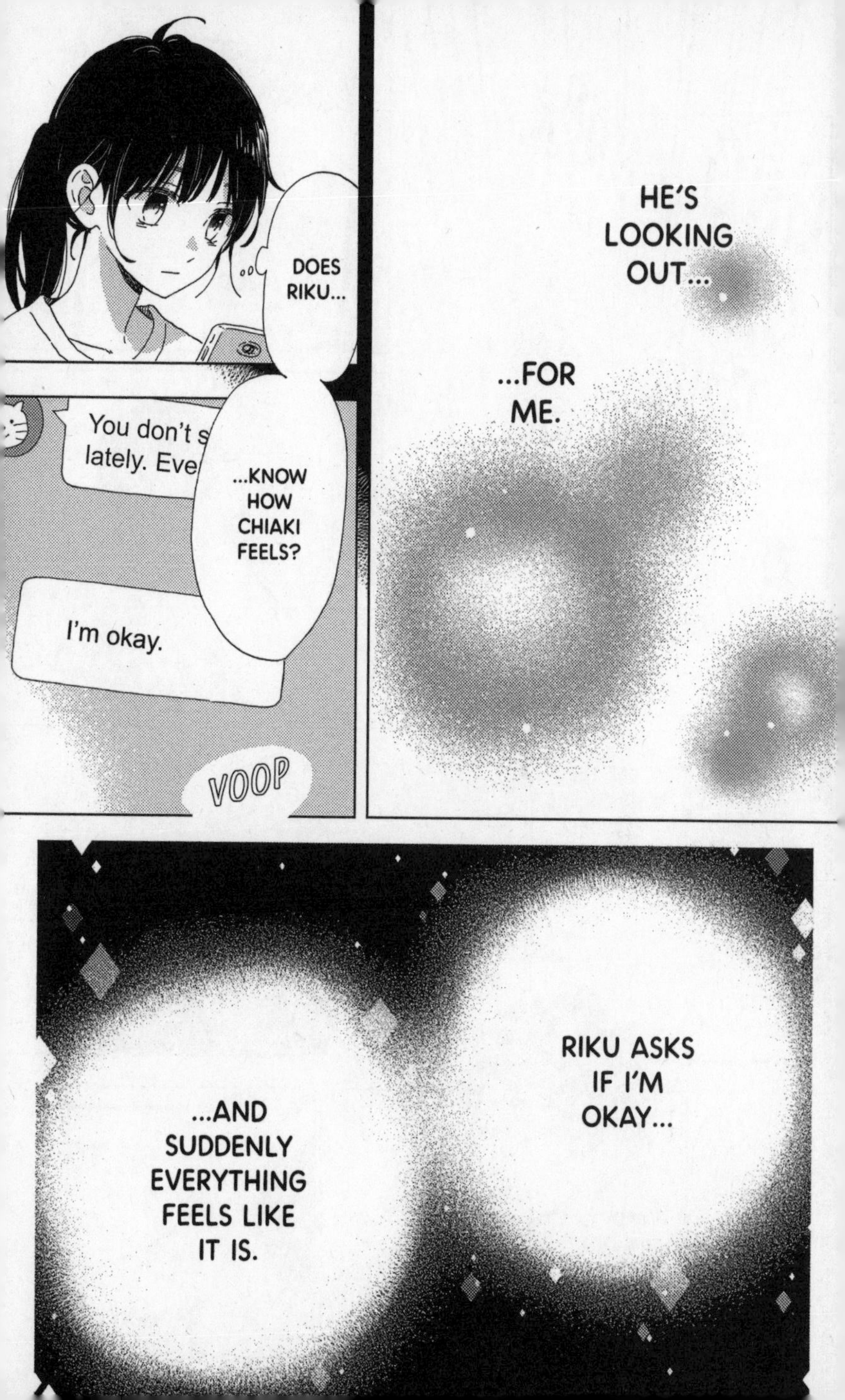
HE'S LOOKING OUT...
...FOR ME.
DOES RIKU...
...KNOW HOW CHIAKI FEELS?
You don't
lately.
I'm okay.
VOOP
RIKU ASKS IF I'M OKAY...
...AND SUDDENLY EVERYTHING FEELS LIKE IT IS.

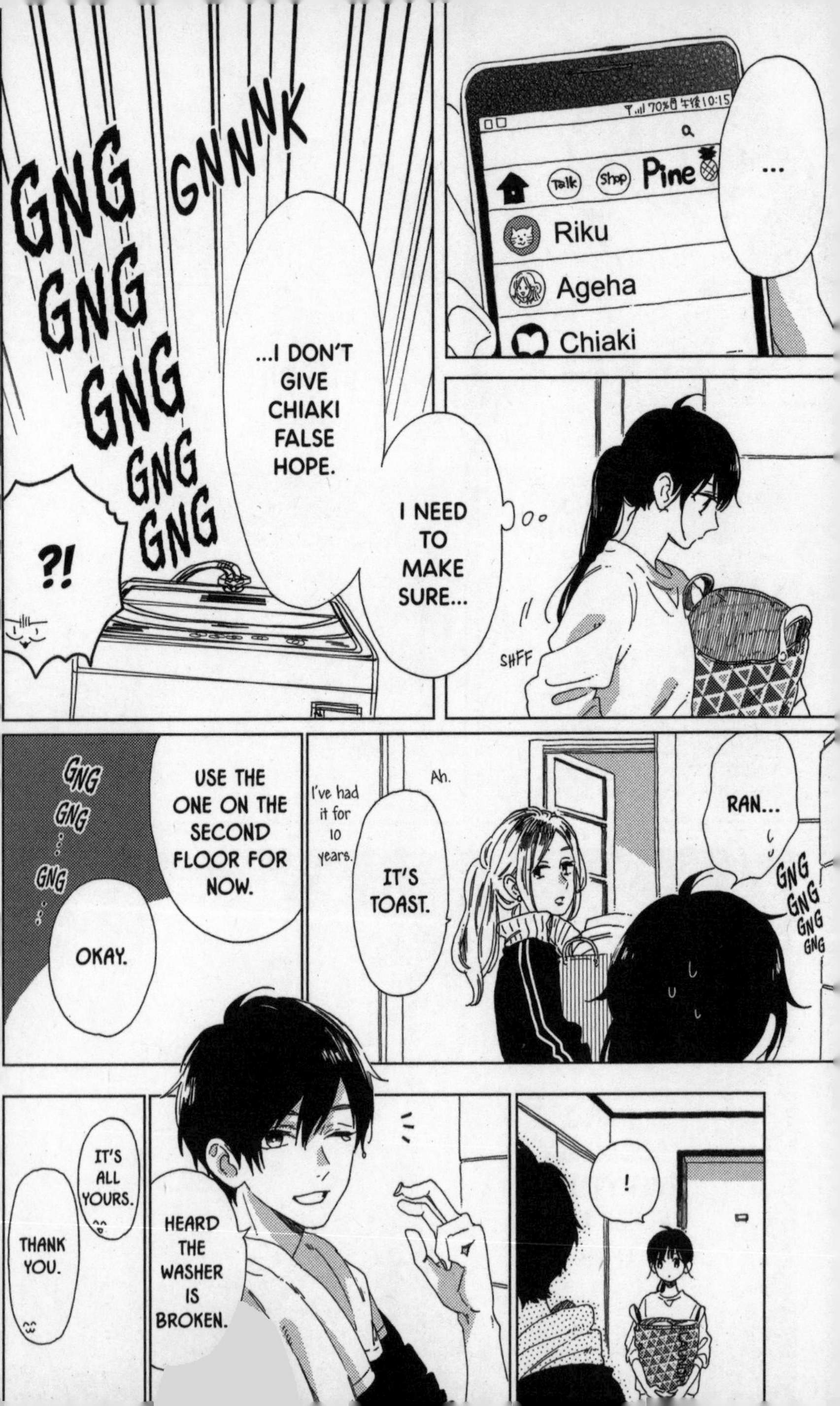
...
Pine
Talk
Shop
Riku
Ageha
Chiaki
I NEED TO MAKE SURE...
...I DON'T GIVE CHIAKI FALSE HOPE.
SHFF
GNG GNG GNG GNG GNG
GNNNK
?!
RAN...
GNG GNG GNG GNG
Ah.
IT'S TOAST.
I've had it for 10 years.
USE THE ONE ON THE SECOND FLOOR FOR NOW.
GNG GNG GNG
OKAY.
!
HEARD THE WASHER IS BROKEN.
IT'S ALL YOURS.
THANK YOU.

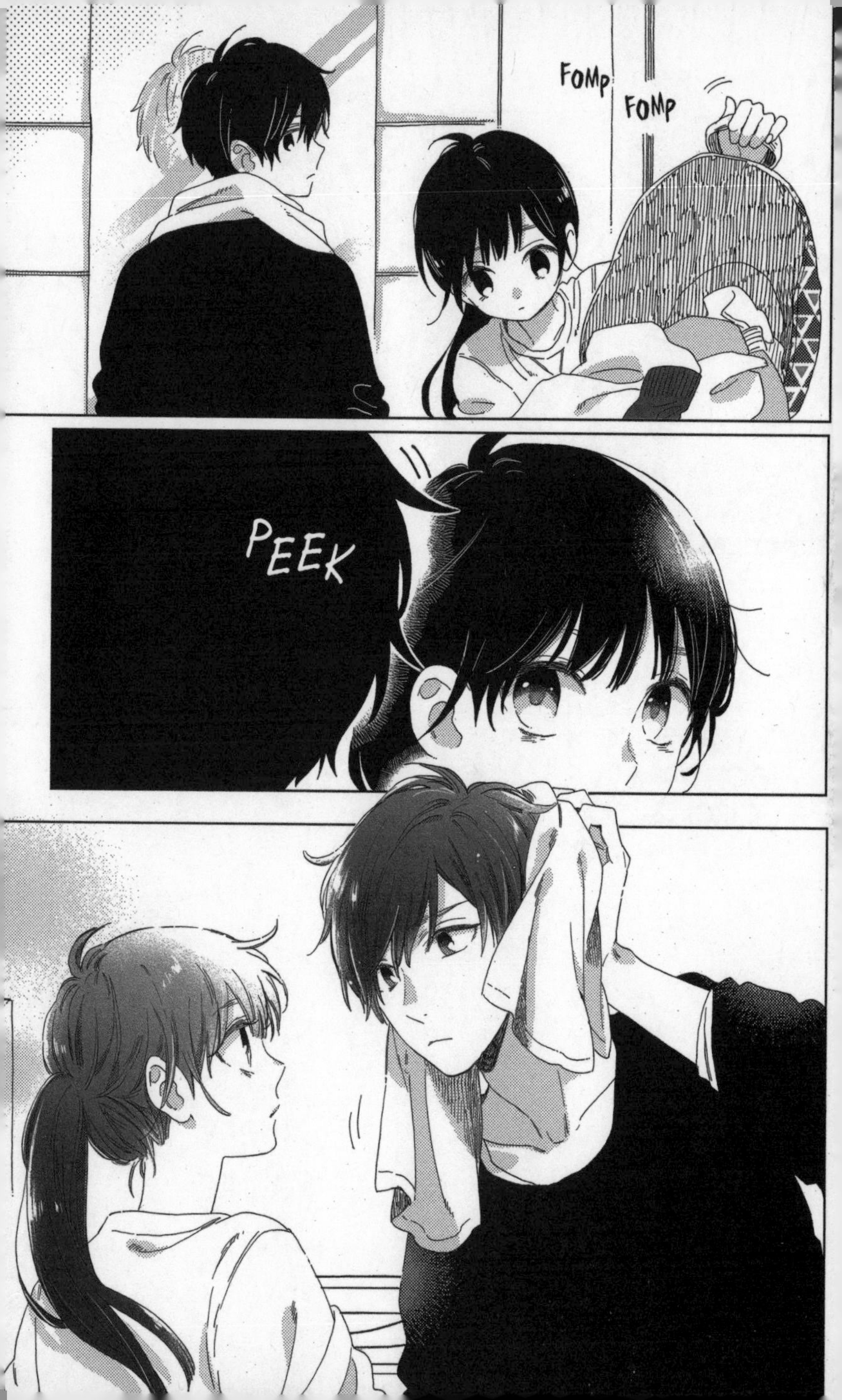
FOMP
FOMP
PEEK

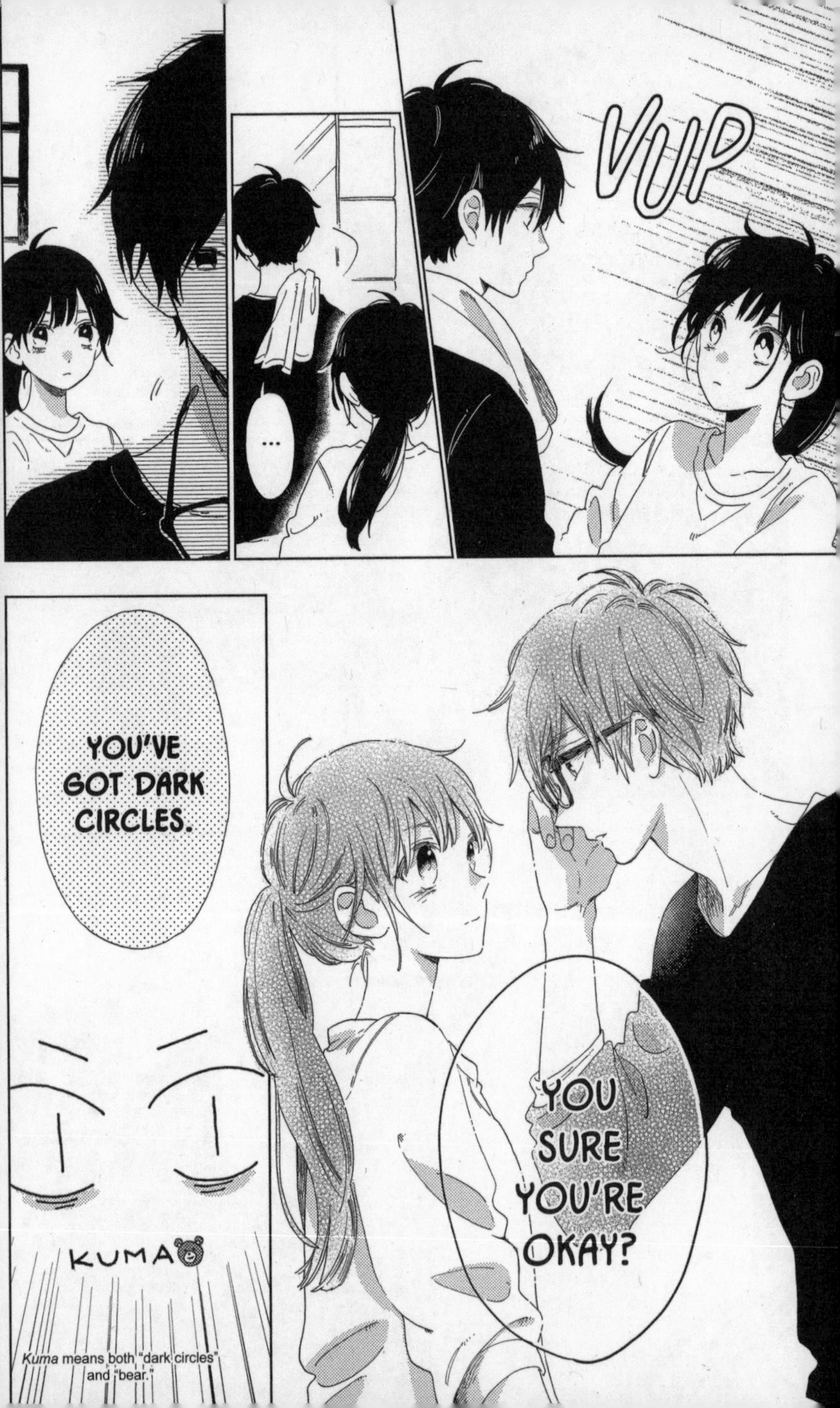
VUP
...
YOU SURE YOU'RE OKAY?
YOU'VE GOT DARK CIRCLES.
KUMA

*Kuma* means both "dark circles" and "bear."

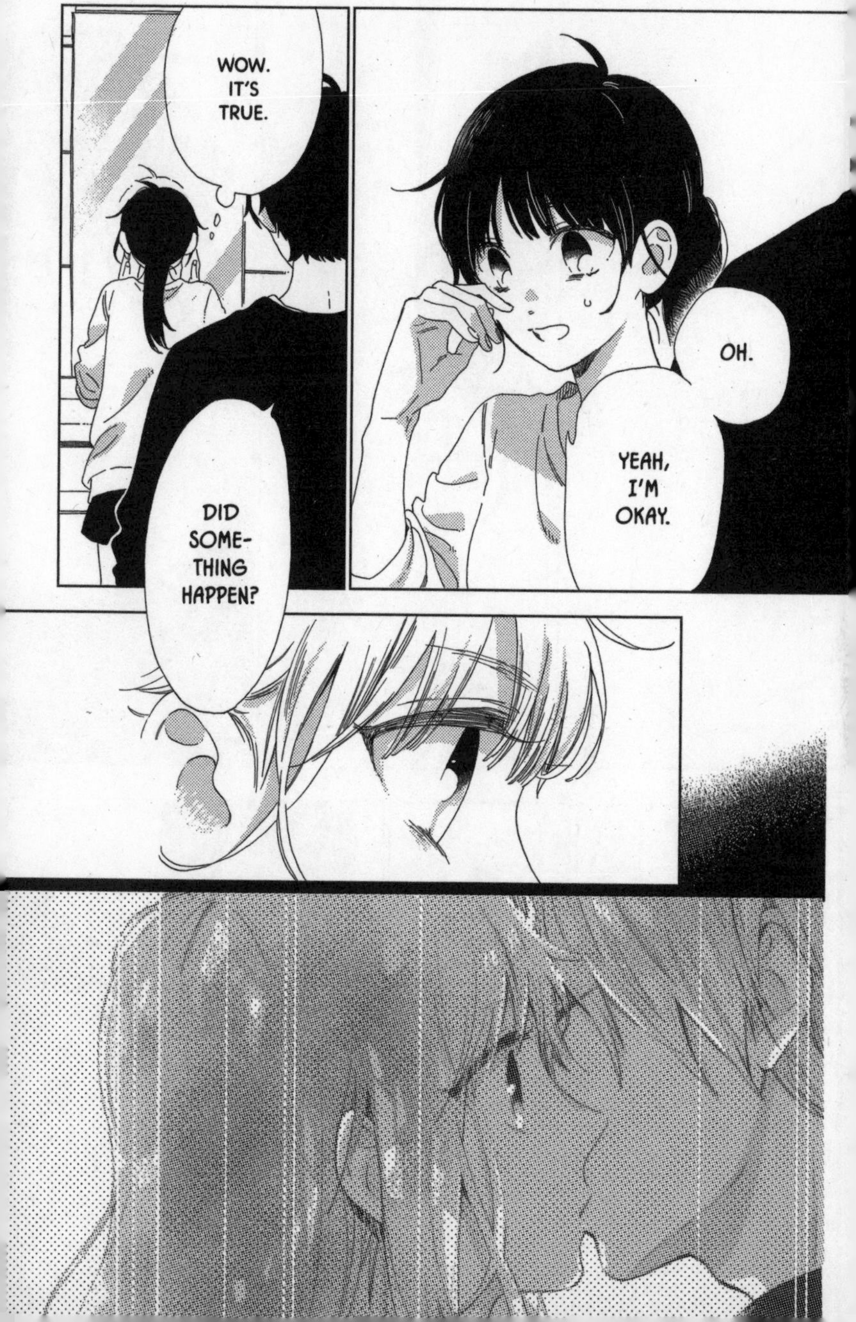
OH.
YEAH, I'M OKAY.
WOW. IT'S TRUE.
DID SOME-THING HAPPEN?

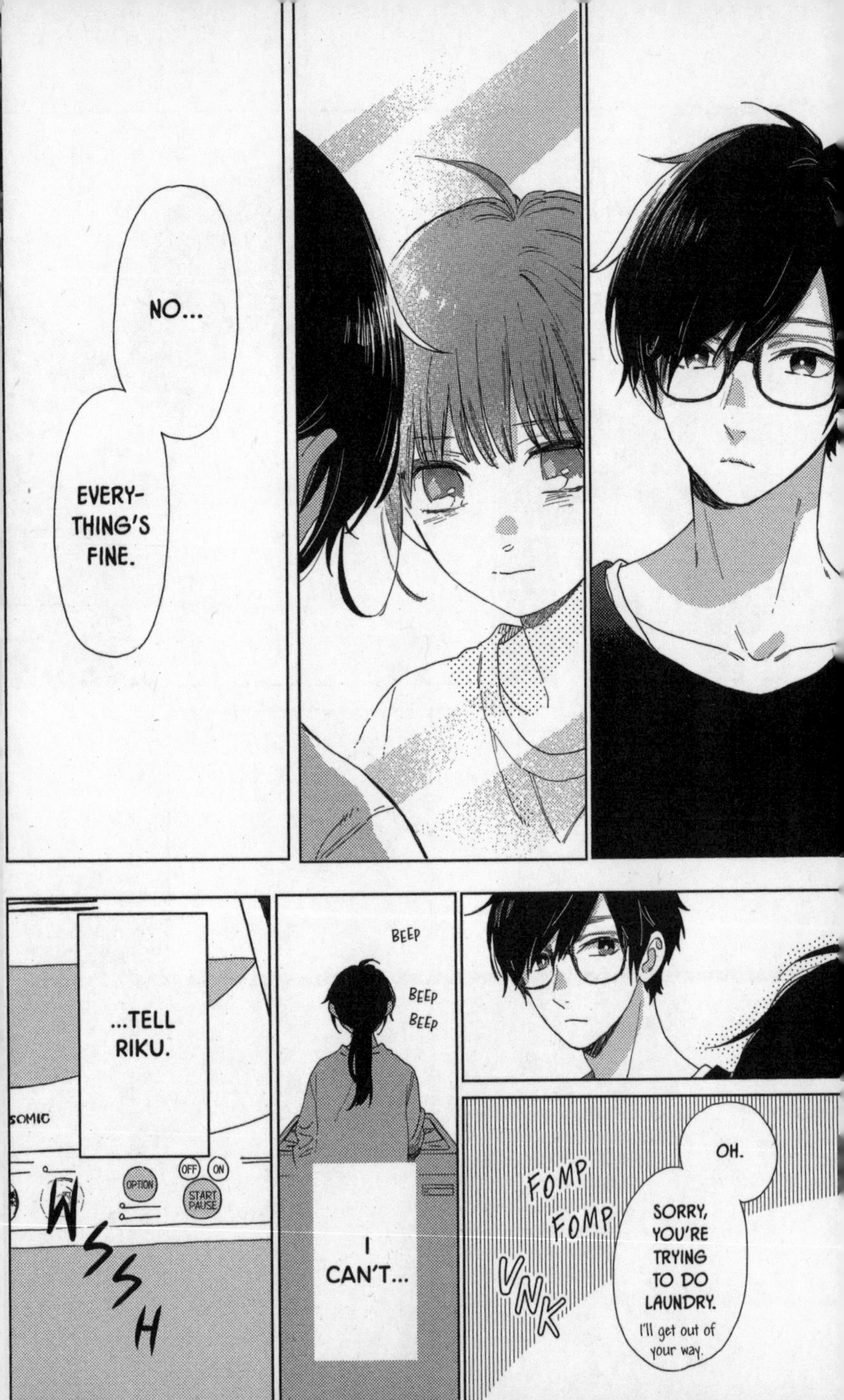

NO...
EVERYTHING'S FINE.
OH.
SORRY, YOU'RE TRYING TO DO LAUNDRY.
I'll get out of your way.
FOMP FOMP
VNK
BEEP
BEEP BEEP
I CAN'T...
...TELL RIKU.
SOMIC
OFF
ON
OPTION
START PAUSE
WSSH

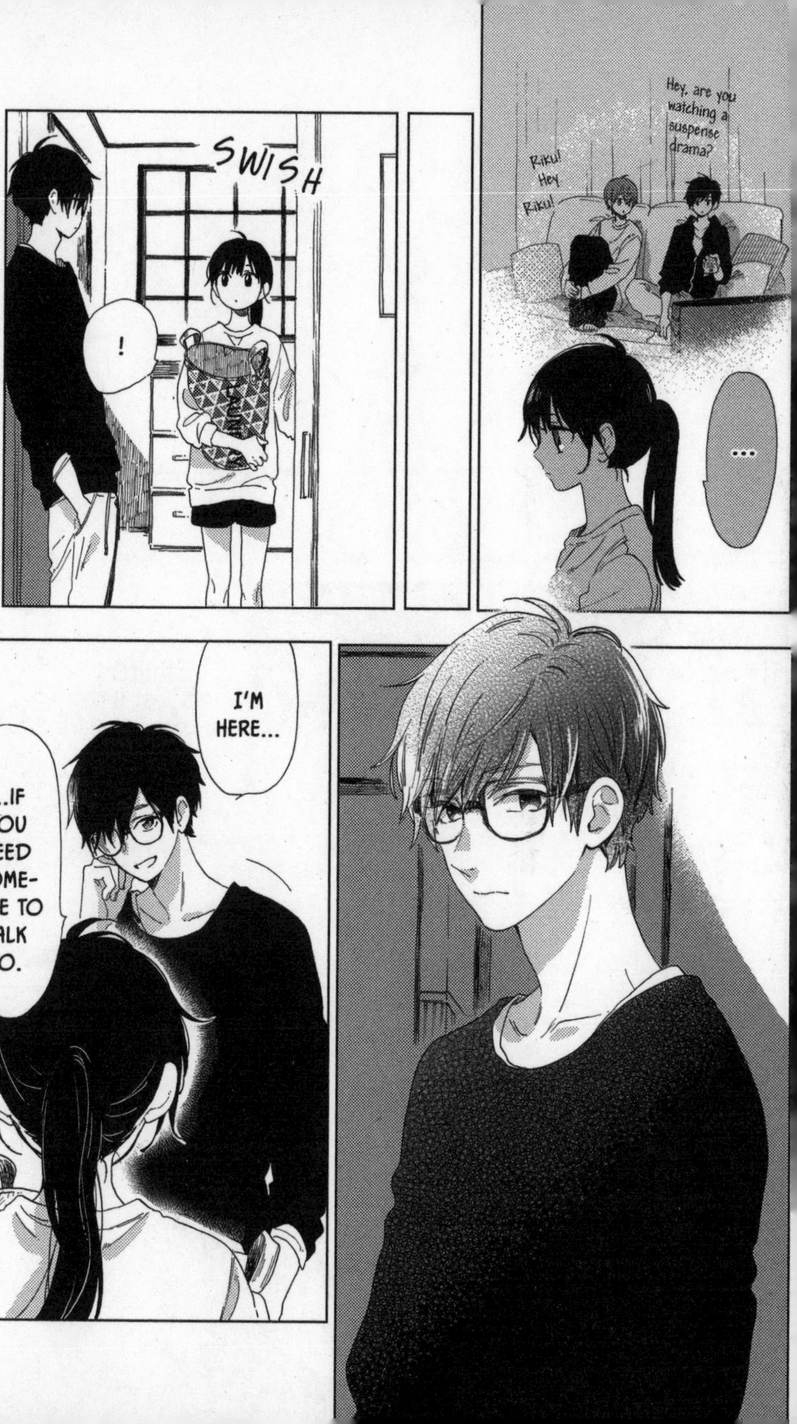
Hey, are you watching a suspense drama?
Riku! Hey Riku!
...
SWISH
!
I'M HERE...
...IF YOU NEED SOME-ONE TO TALK TO.

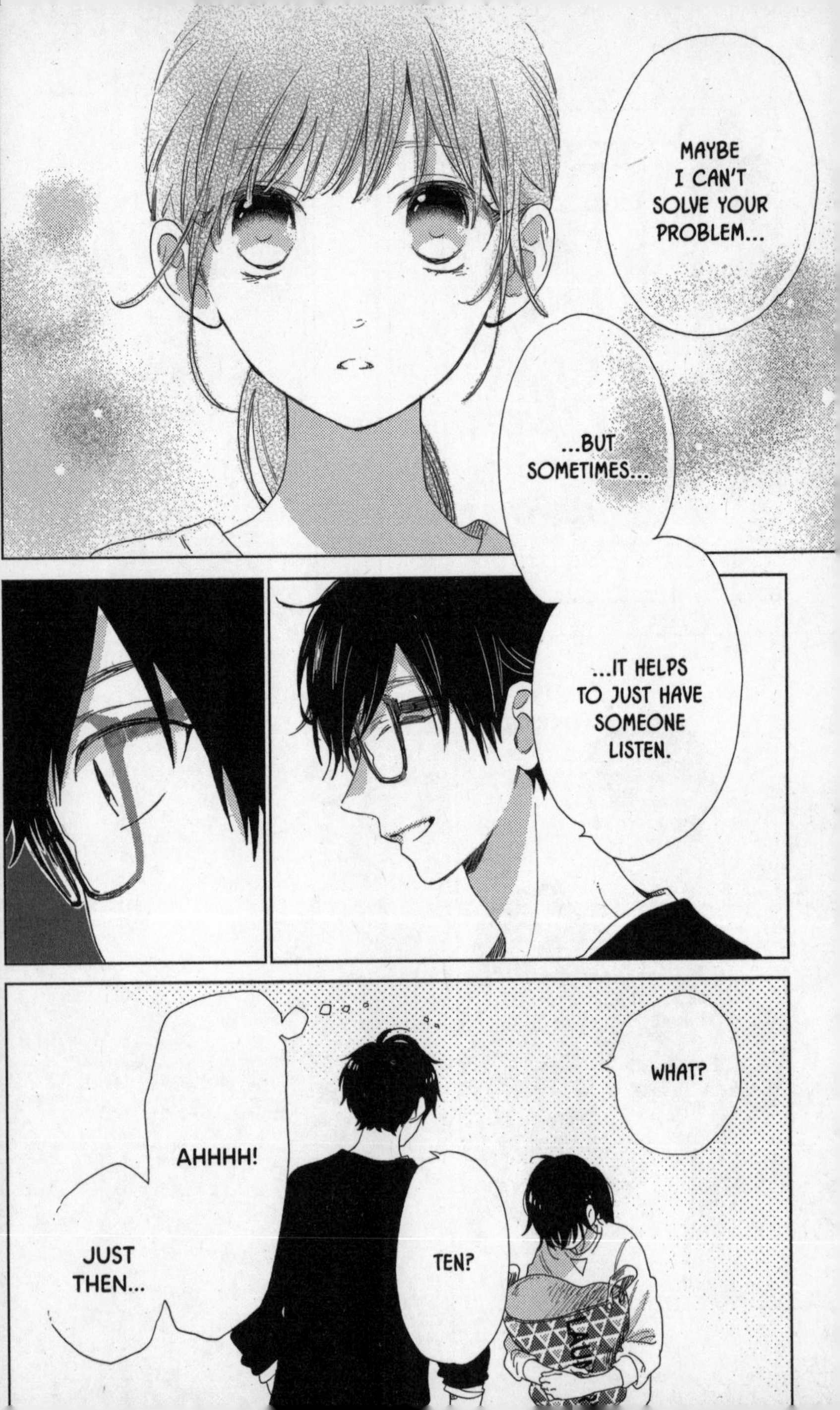
MAYBE I CAN'T SOLVE YOUR PROBLEM...
...BUT SOMETIMES...
...IT HELPS TO JUST HAVE SOMEONE LISTEN.
WHAT?
TEN?
AHHHH!
JUST THEN...

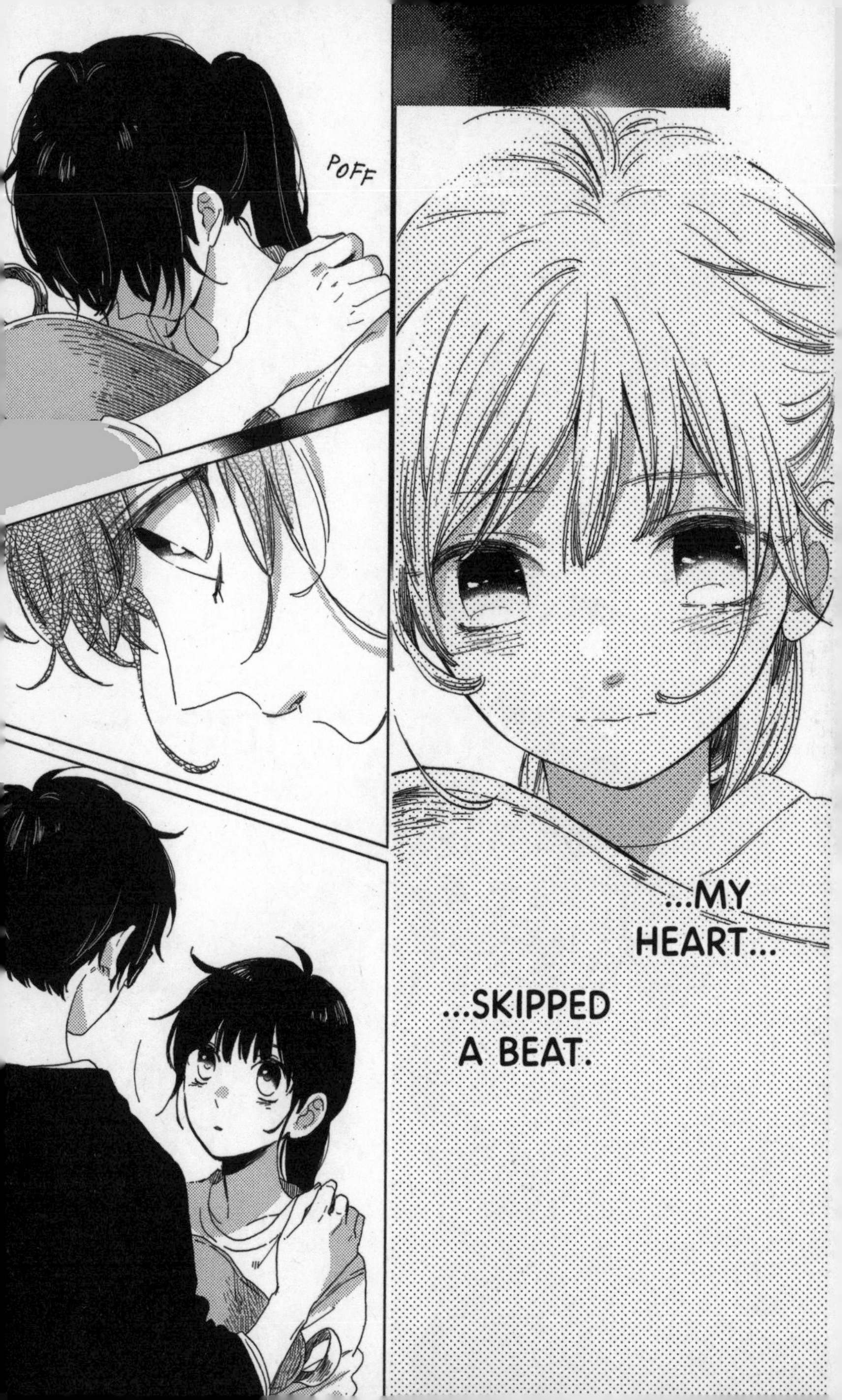
...MY HEART...
...SKIPPED A BEAT.
POFF

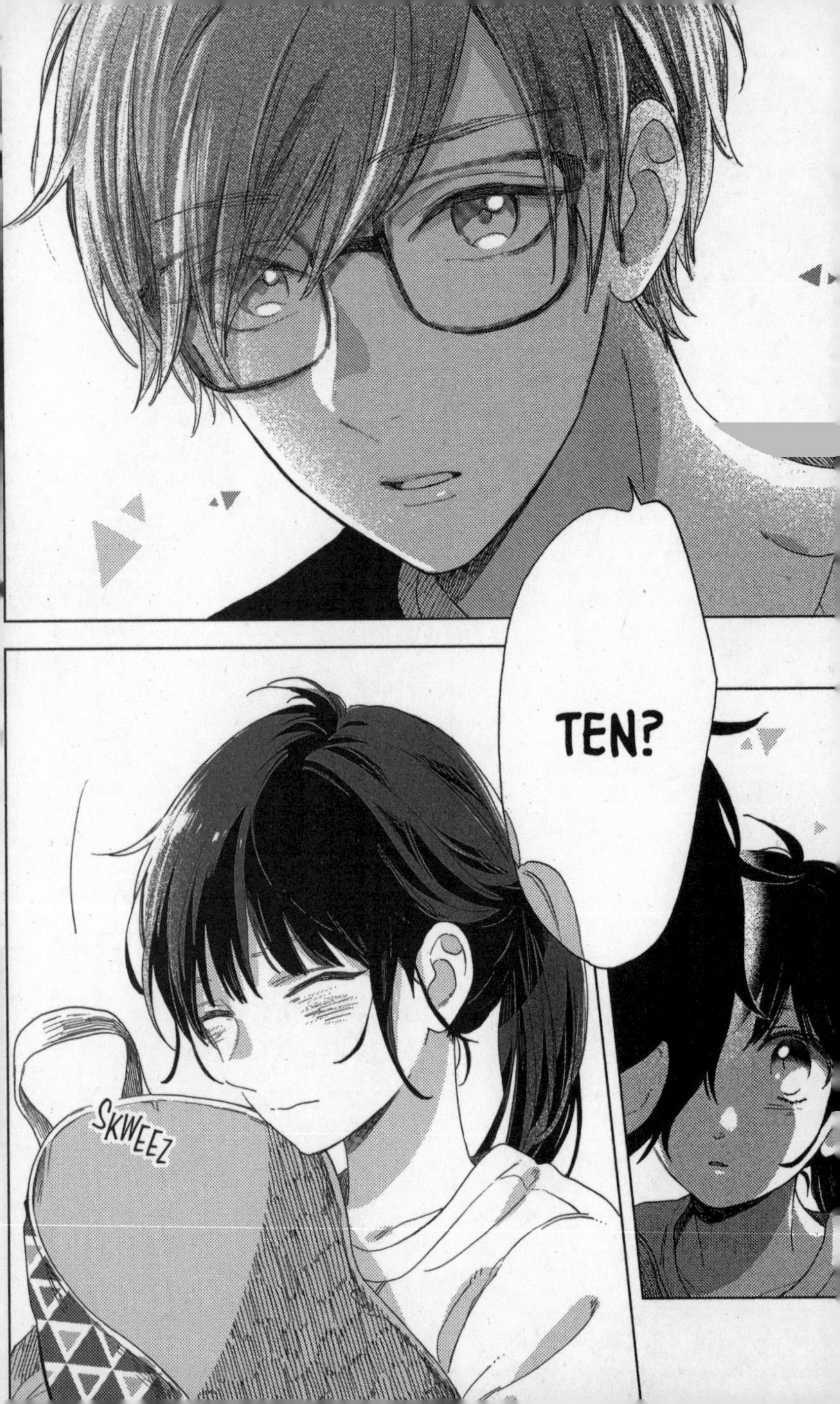
TEN?
SKWEEZ

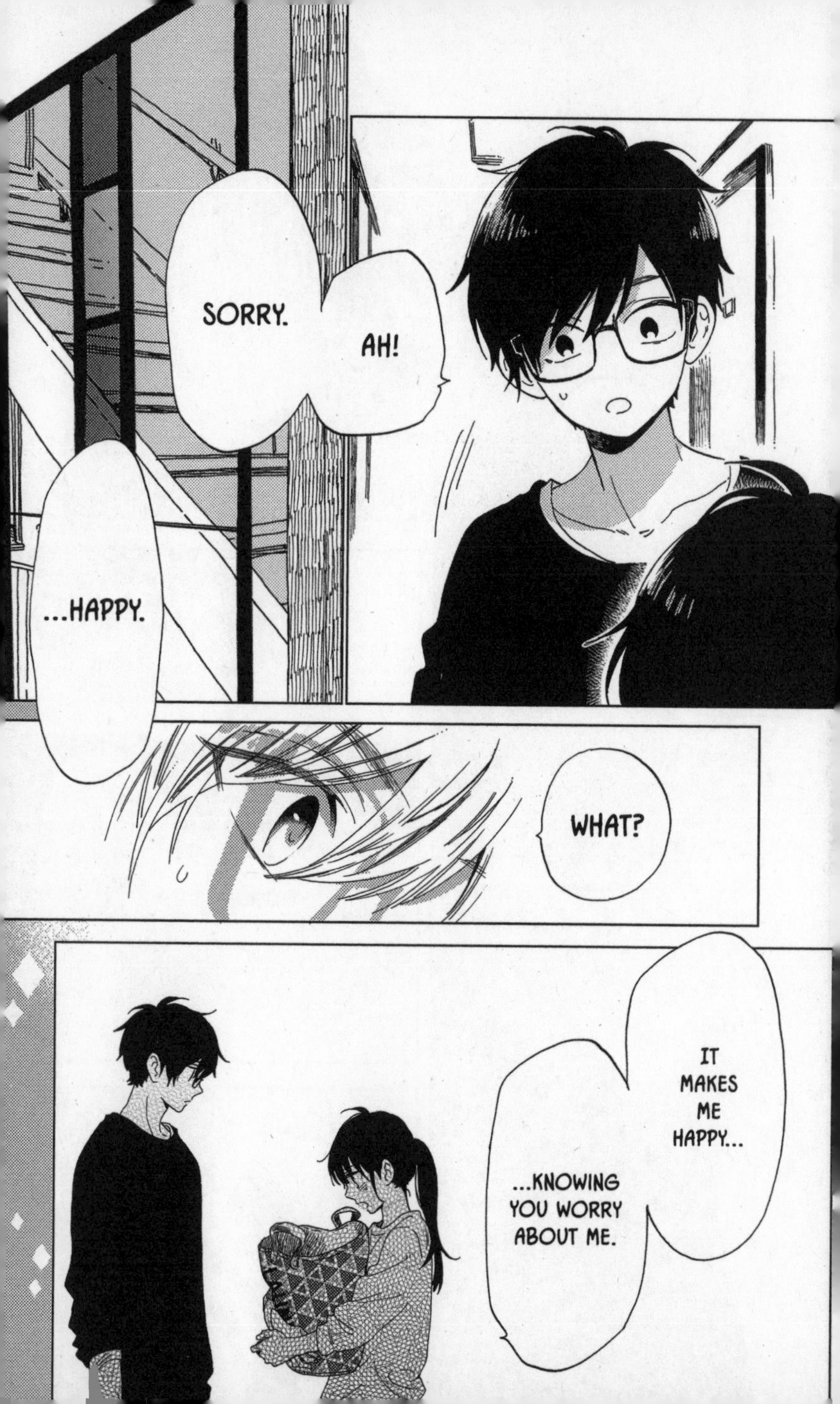
AH!
SORRY.
...HAPPY.
WHAT?
IT MAKES ME HAPPY...
...KNOWING YOU WORRY ABOUT ME.

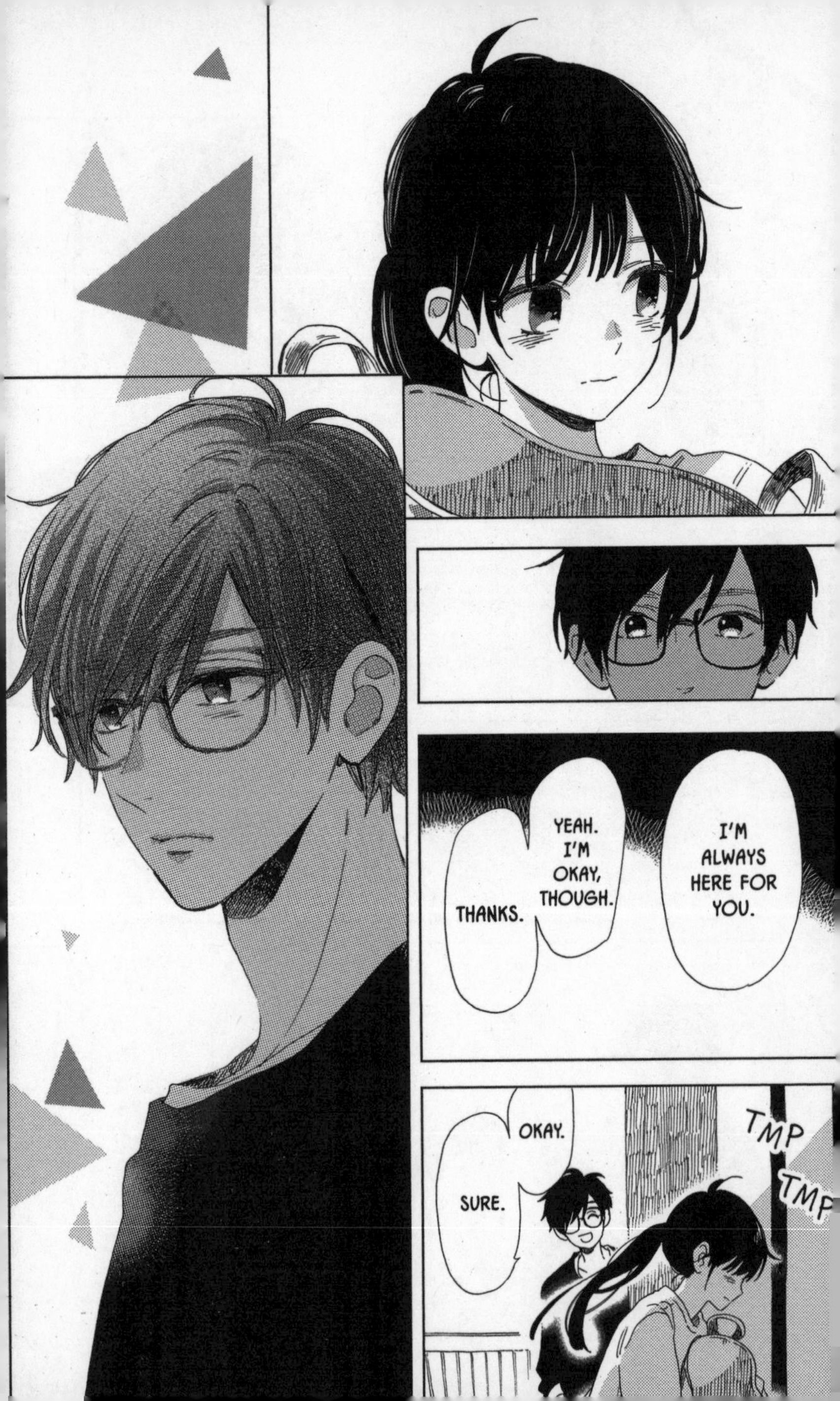
I'M ALWAYS HERE FOR YOU.
YEAH. I'M OKAY, THOUGH.
THANKS.
TMP
TMP
OKAY.
SURE.

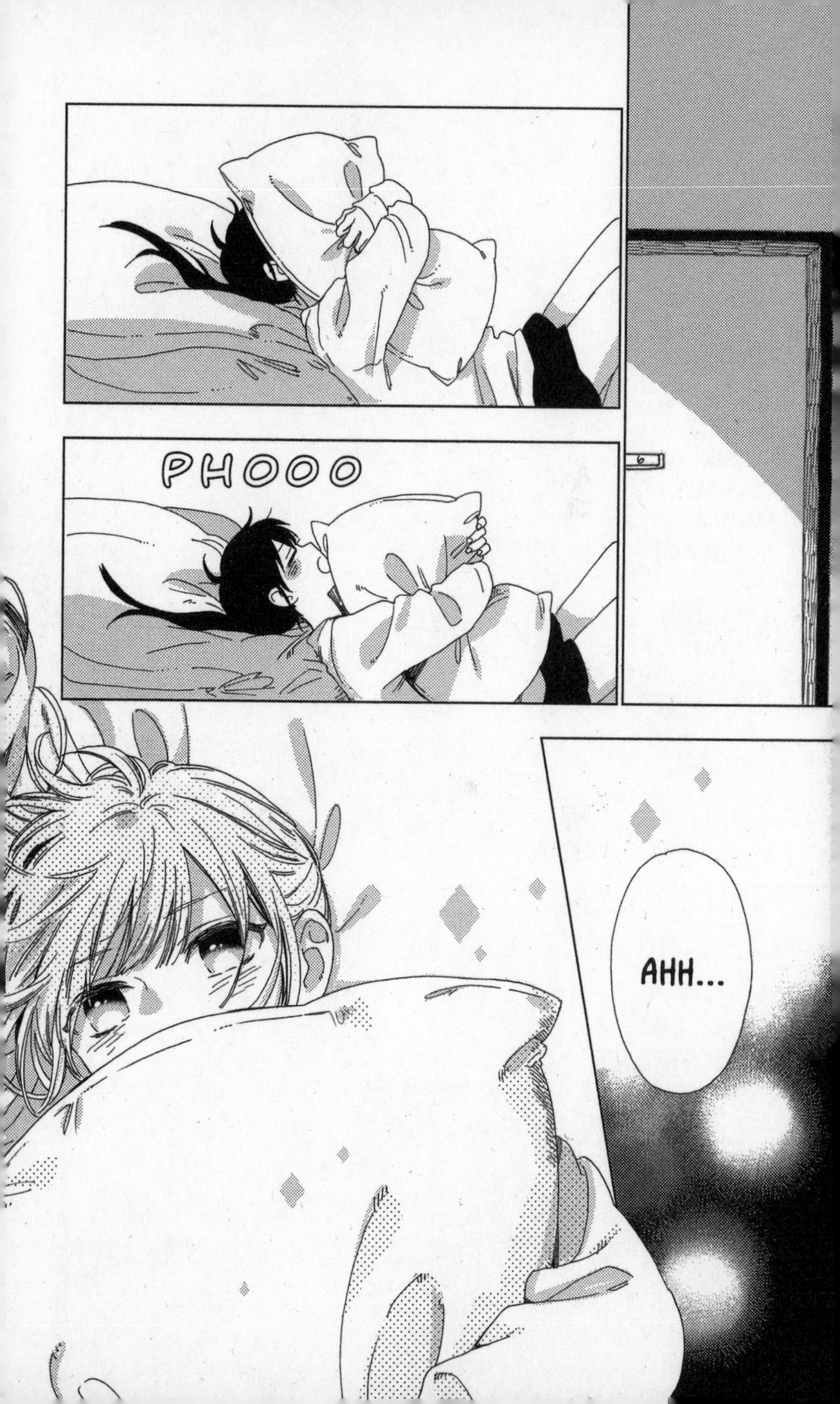
PHOOO
AHH...

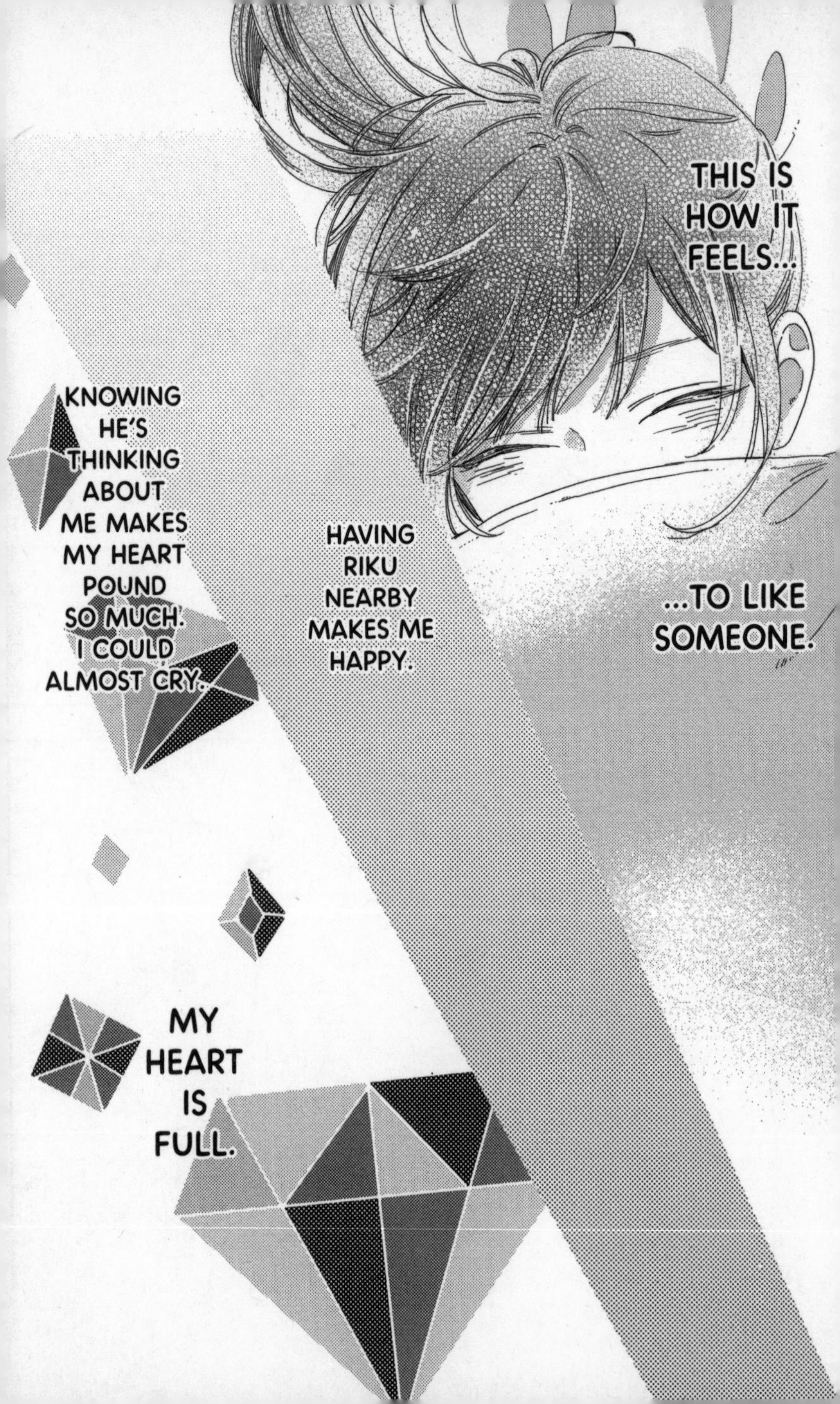
THIS IS HOW IT FEELS...
...TO LIKE SOMEONE.
HAVING RIKU NEARBY MAKES ME HAPPY.
KNOWING HE'S THINKING ABOUT ME MAKES MY HEART POUND SO MUCH. I COULD ALMOST CRY.
MY HEART IS FULL.

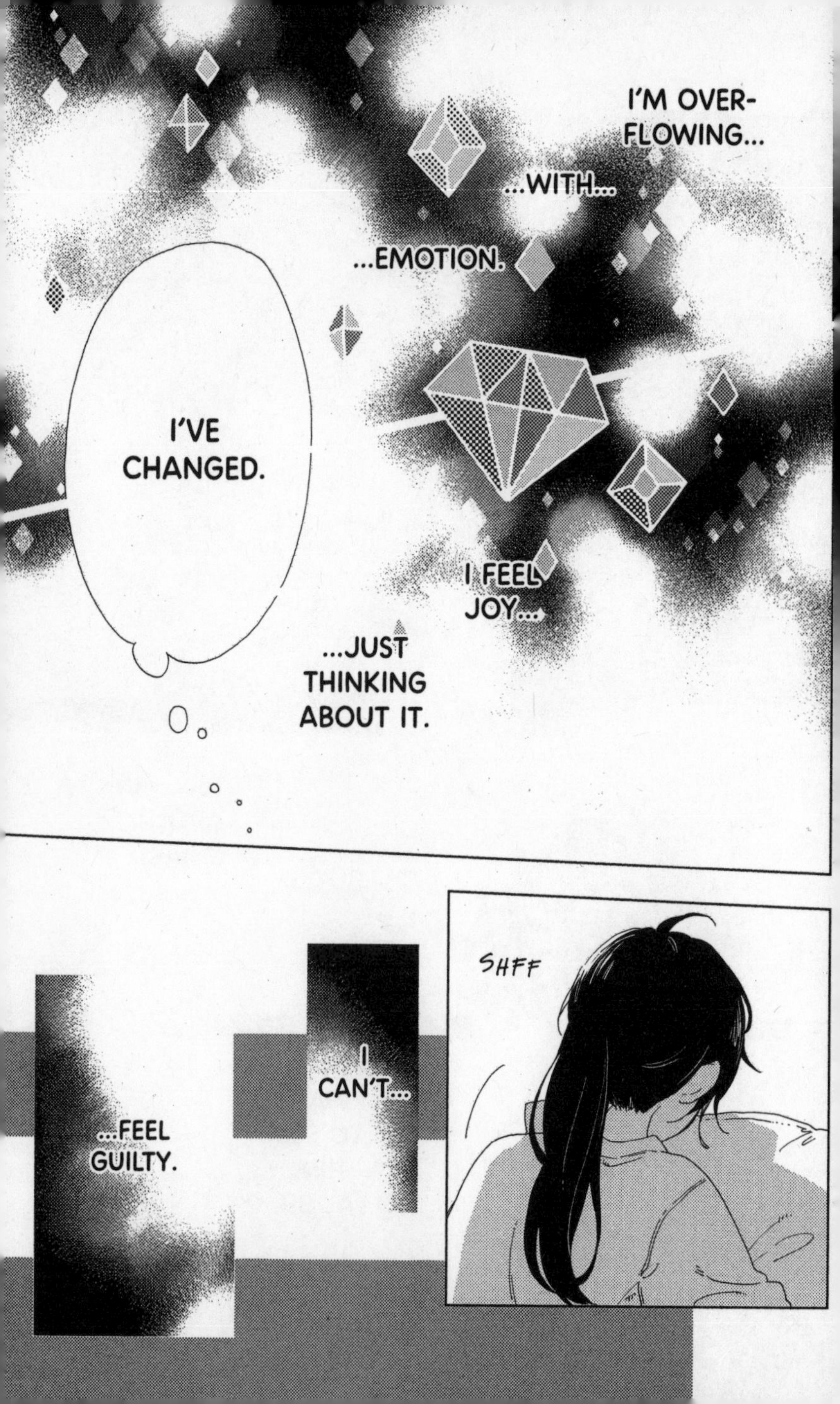
I'M OVER-FLOWING...
...WITH...
...EMOTION.
I'VE CHANGED.
I FEEL JOY...
...JUST THINKING ABOUT IT.
SHFF
I CAN'T...
...FEEL GUILTY.

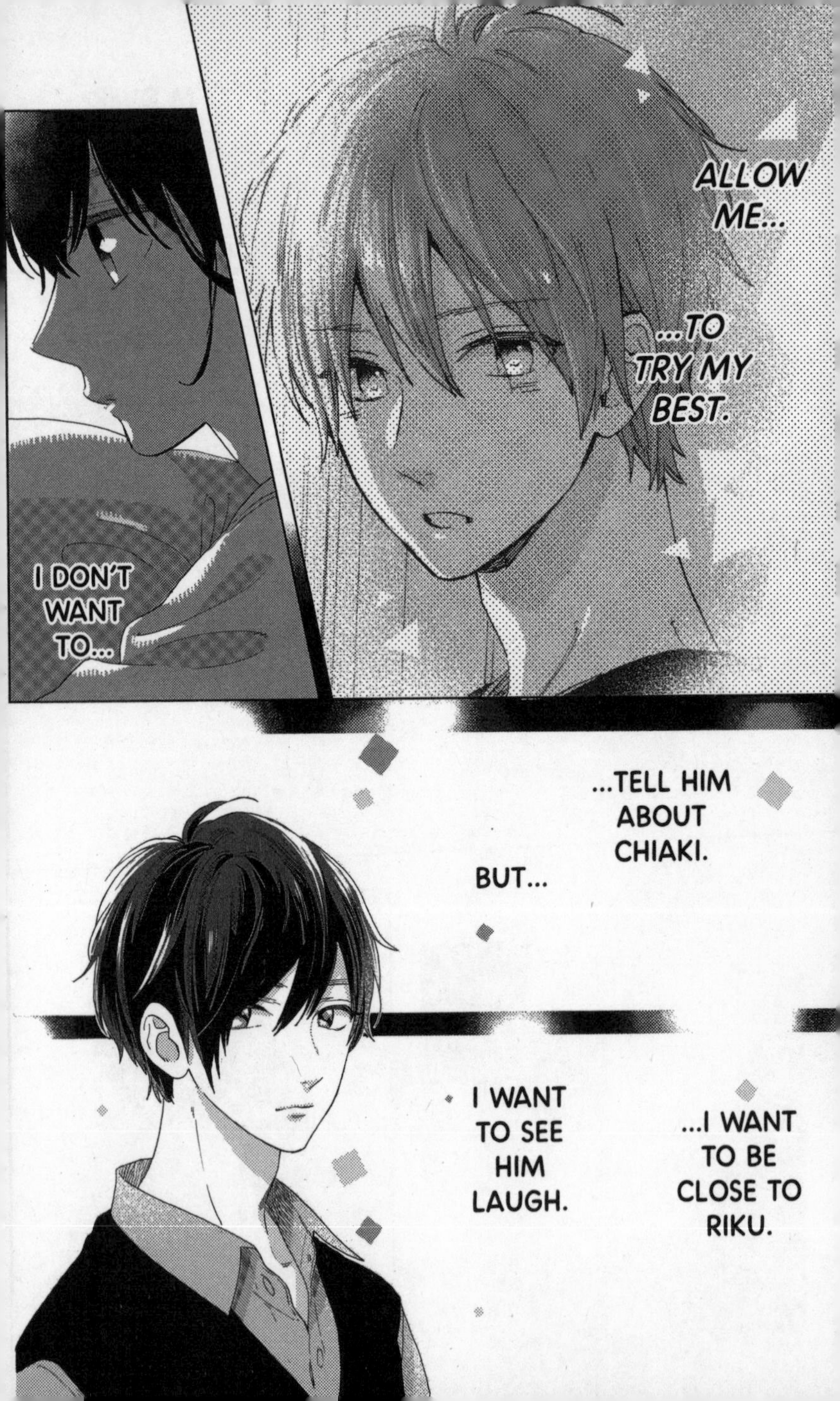
ALLOW ME...
...TO TRY MY BEST.
I DON'T WANT TO...
...TELL HIM ABOUT CHIAKI.
BUT...
...I WANT TO BE CLOSE TO RIKU.
I WANT TO SEE HIM LAUGH.

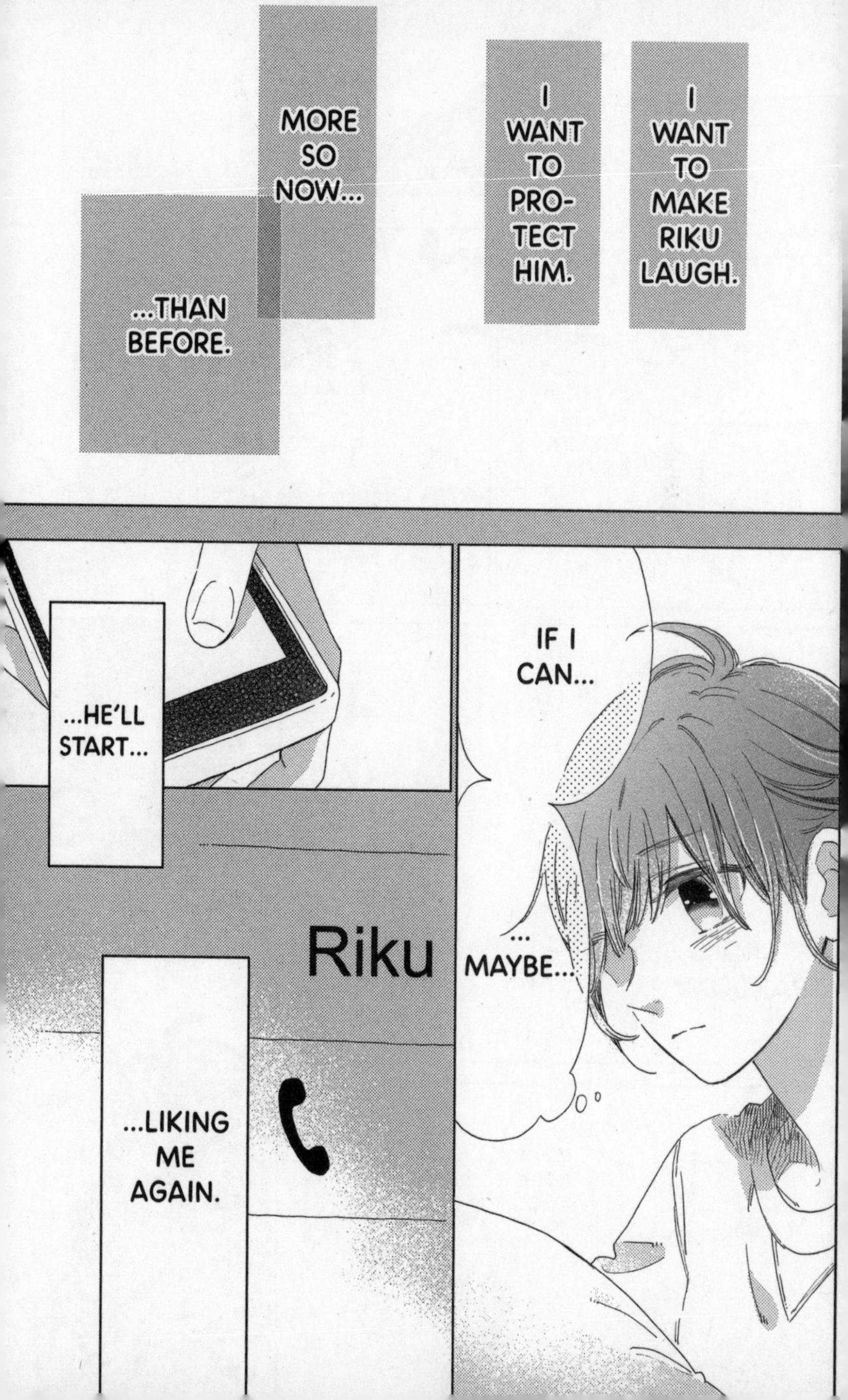
I WANT TO MAKE RIKU LAUGH.
I WANT TO PRO-TECT HIM.
MORE SO NOW...
...THAN BEFORE.
IF I CAN...
...MAYBE...
...HE'LL START...
Riku
...LIKING ME AGAIN.

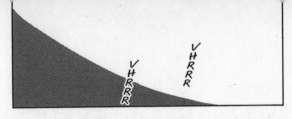

VHRRR VHRRR

THANKS FOR LETTING ME USE THE WASHER ON YOUR FLOOR.

OH.

UM...

HI!

NO PROB-LEM.

Ah!

WHEN IS YOUR BIRTHDAY AGAIN?

NOW WHAT...

...

...DO I SAY?

UM...

RIKU...

SO RANDOM!

WHAT?

OH YEAH?

AB.

So you're AB.

WHAT'S YOUR BLOOD TYPE?

!!

I MISSED IT.

APRIL 30.

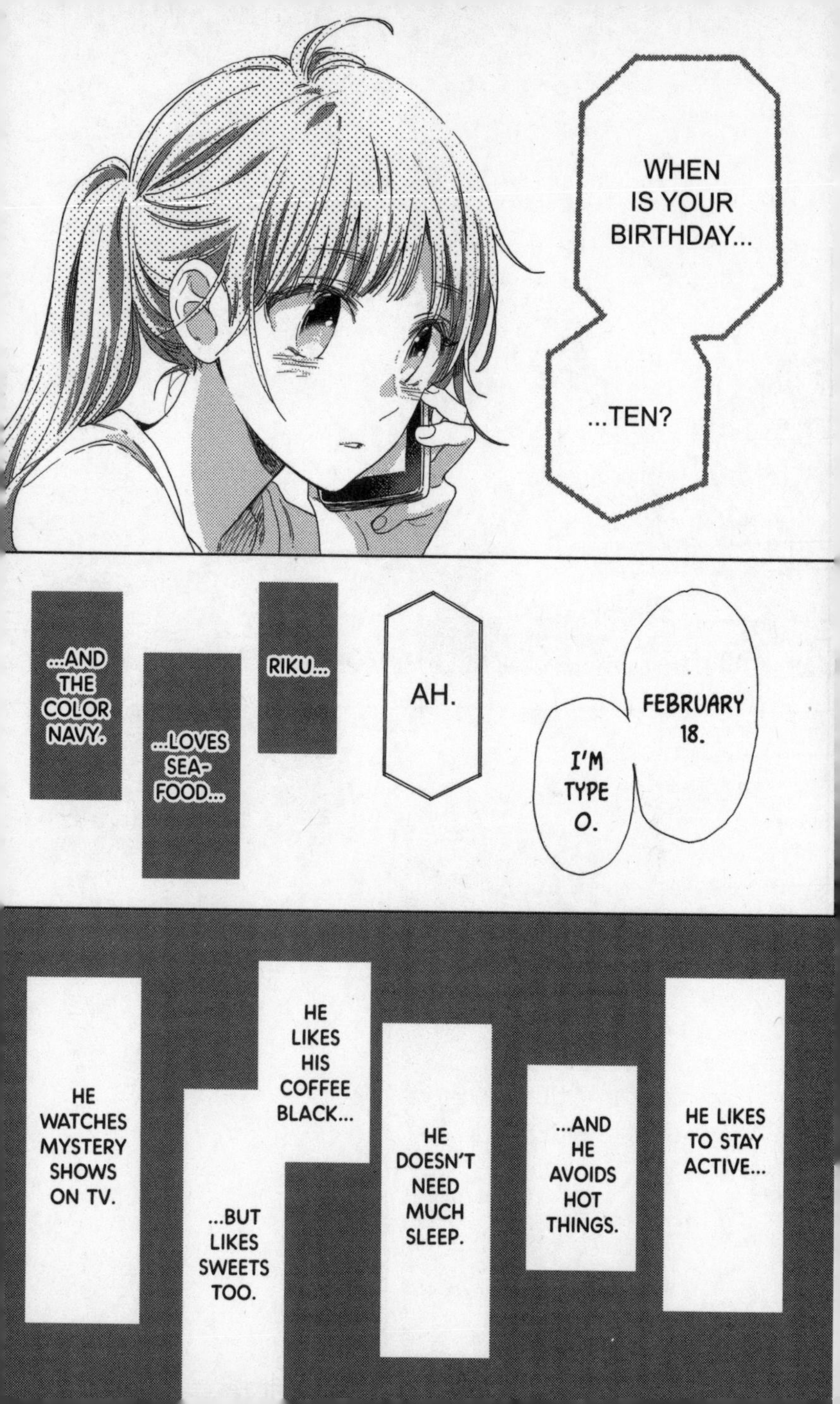
WHEN IS YOUR BIRTHDAY...
...TEN?
FEBRUARY 18.
I'M TYPE O.
AH.
RIKU...
...LOVES SEA-FOOD...
...AND THE COLOR NAVY.
HE LIKES TO STAY ACTIVE...
...AND HE AVOIDS HOT THINGS.
HE DOESN'T NEED MUCH SLEEP.
HE LIKES HIS COFFEE BLACK...
...BUT LIKES SWEETS TOO.
HE WATCHES MYSTERY SHOWS ON TV.

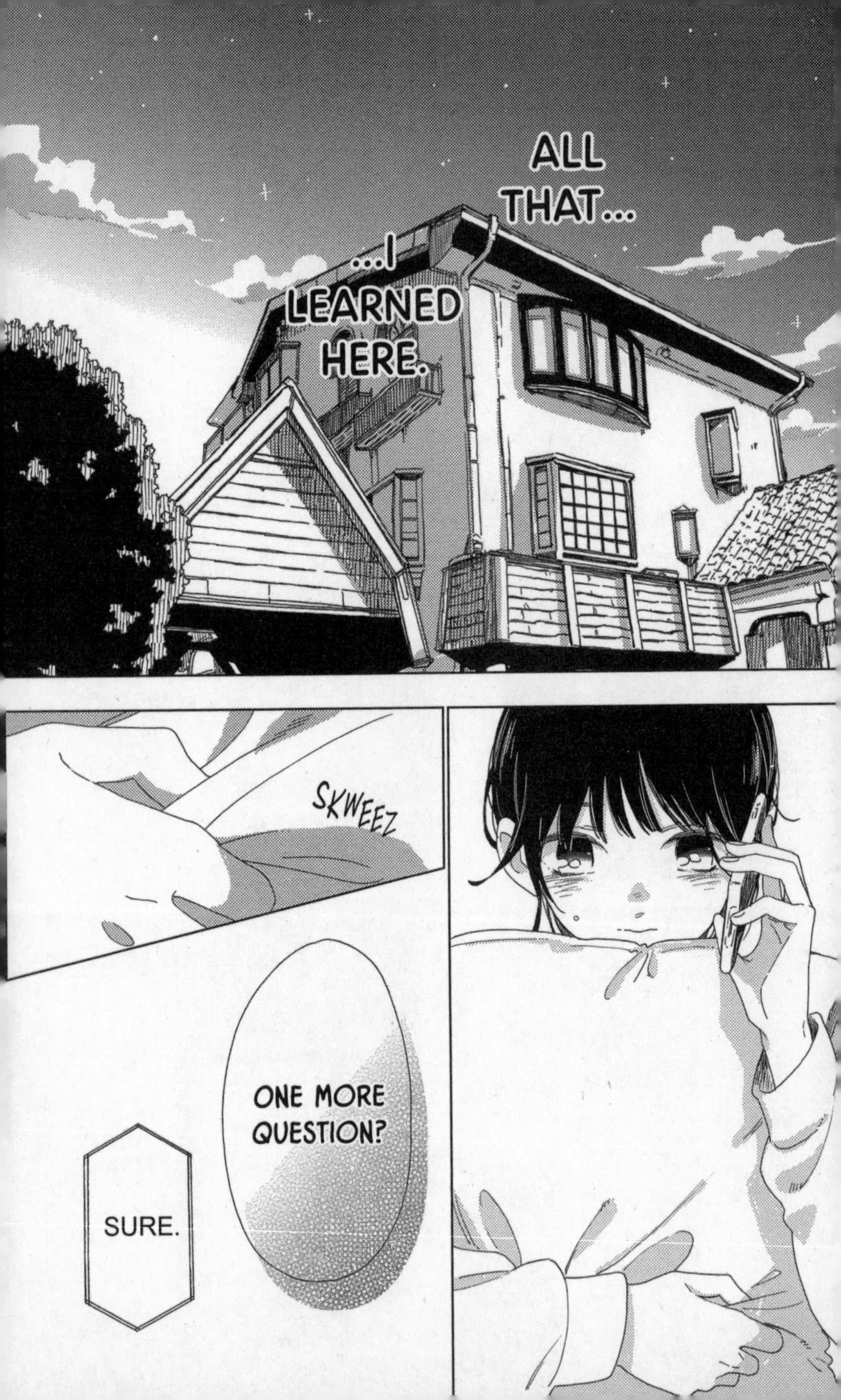
ALL THAT...
...I LEARNED HERE.
SKWEEZ
ONE MORE QUESTION?
SURE.

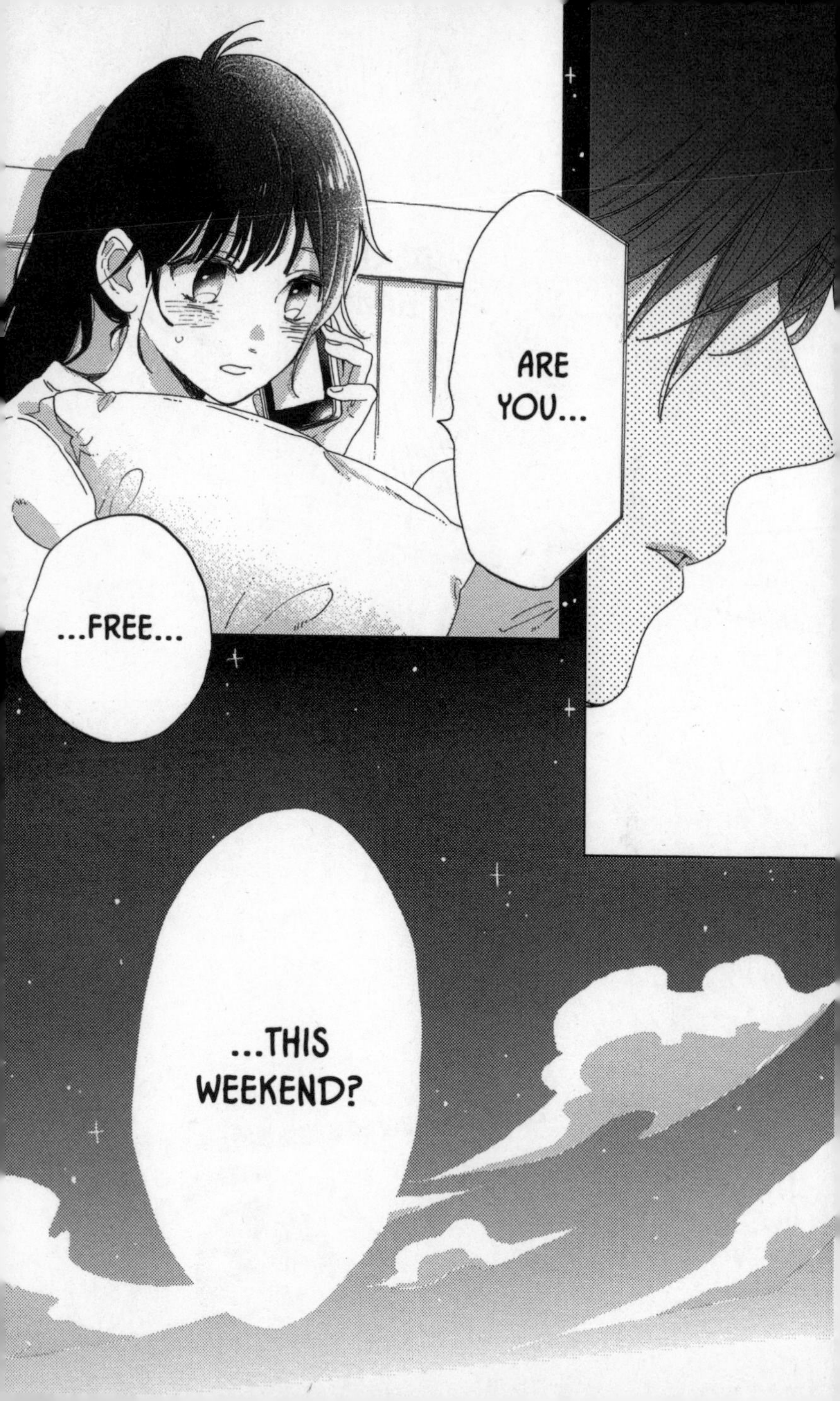
ARE YOU...
...FREE...
...THIS WEEKEND?

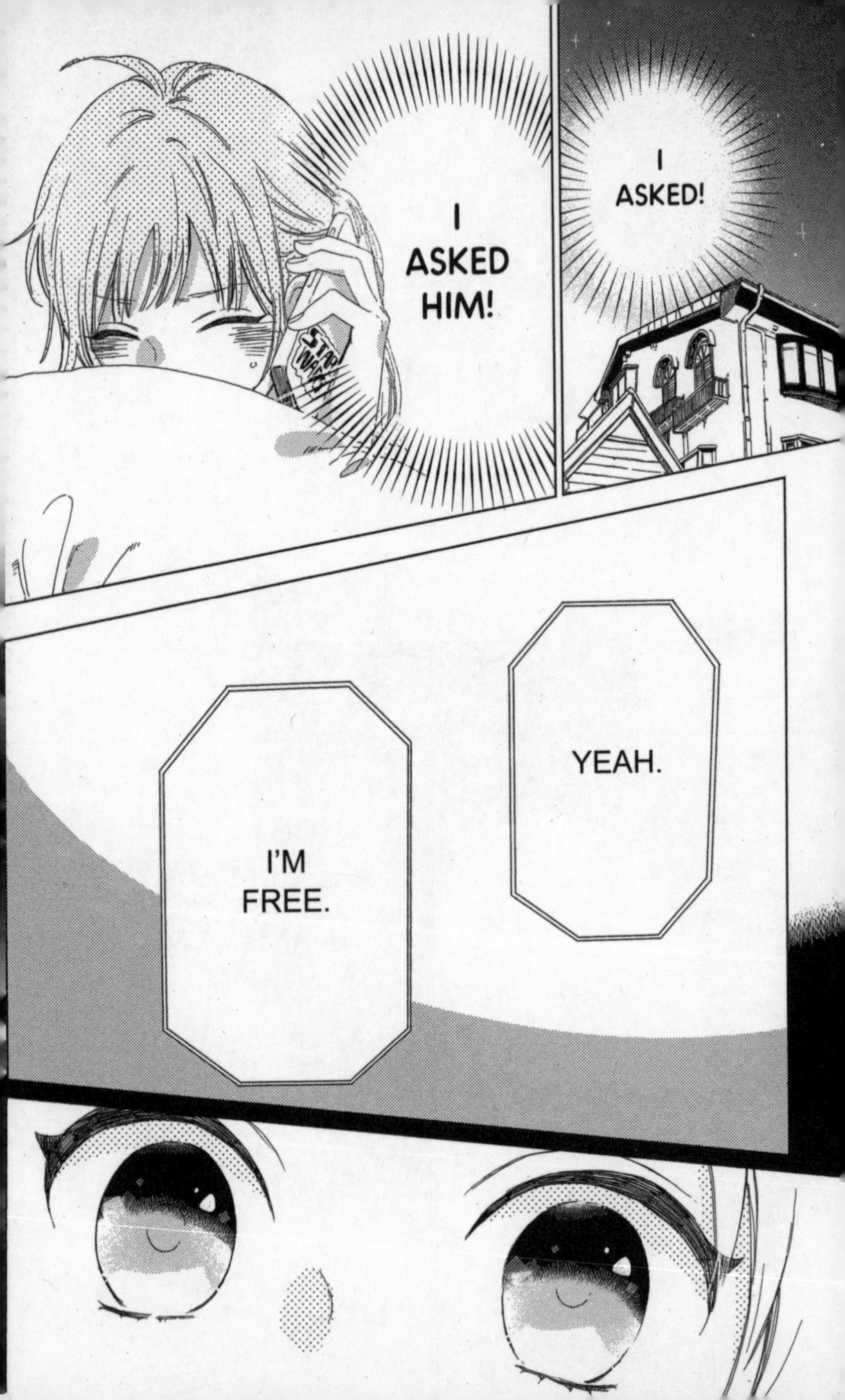
I ASKED!
I ASKED HIM!
YEAH.
I'M FREE.

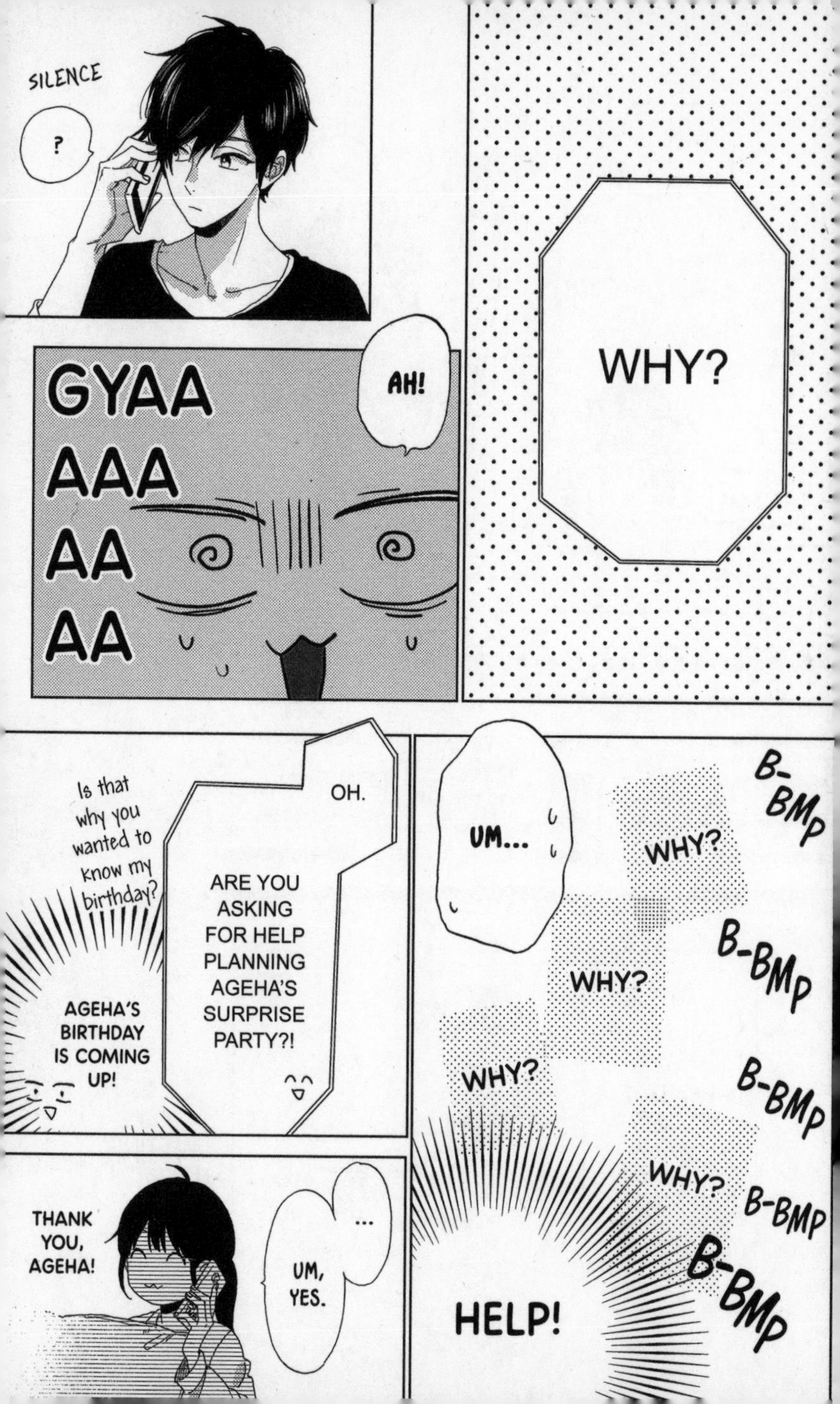
WHY?
SILENCE
?
AH!
GYAA AAA AA AA
B-BMP
UM...
WHY?
B-BMP
WHY?
B-BMP
WHY?
B-BMP
WHY?
B-BMP
B-BMP
HELP!
OH.
ARE YOU ASKING FOR HELP PLANNING AGEHA'S SURPRISE PARTY?!
Is that why you wanted to know my birthday?
AGEHA'S BIRTHDAY IS COMING UP!
...
UM, YES.
THANK YOU, AGEHA!

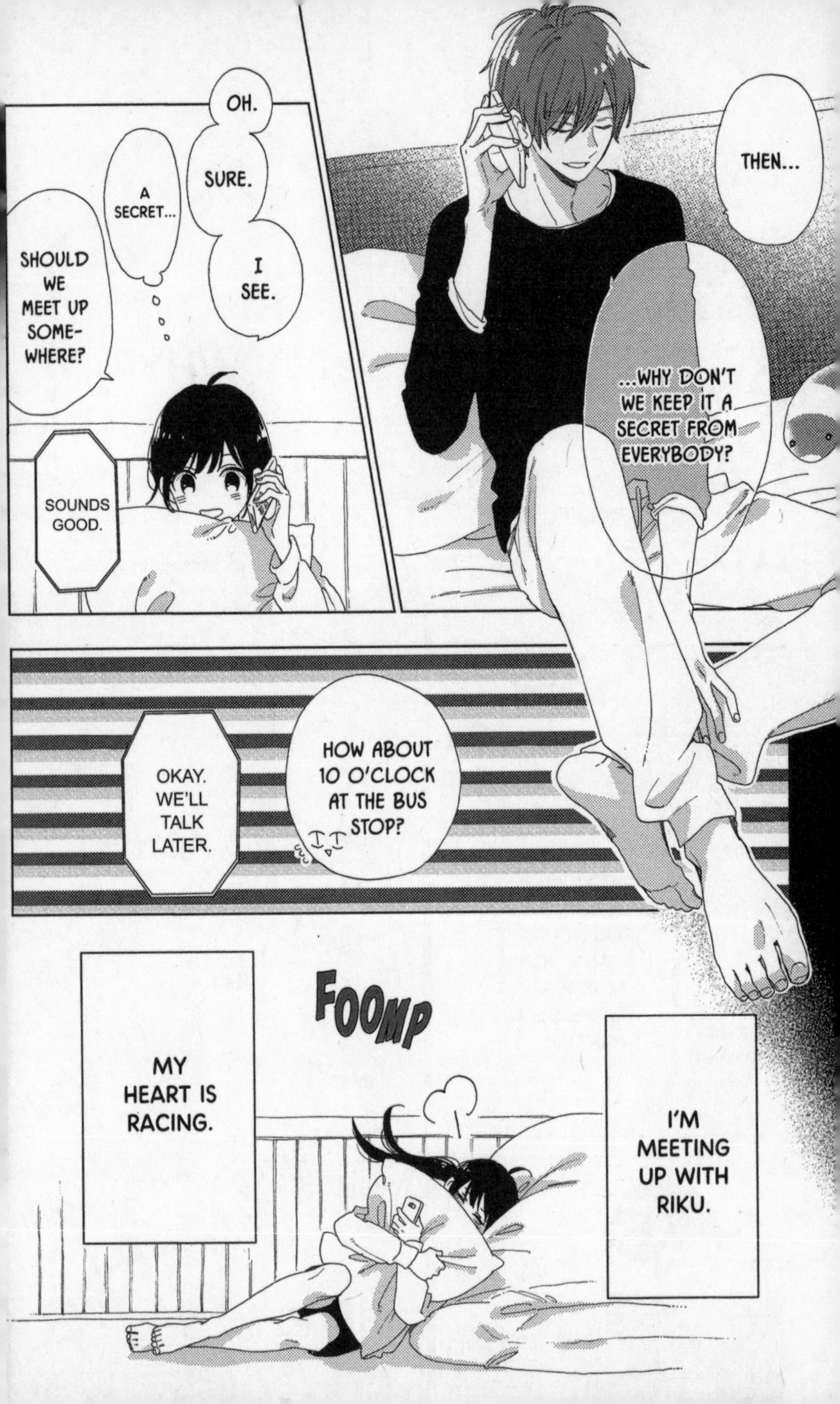
THEN...
...WHY DON'T WE KEEP IT A SECRET FROM EVERYBODY?
OH.
SURE.
I SEE.
A SECRET...
SHOULD WE MEET UP SOME-WHERE?
SOUNDS GOOD.
HOW ABOUT 10 O'CLOCK AT THE BUS STOP?
OKAY. WE'LL TALK LATER.
I'M MEETING UP WITH RIKU.
FOOMP
MY HEART IS RACING.

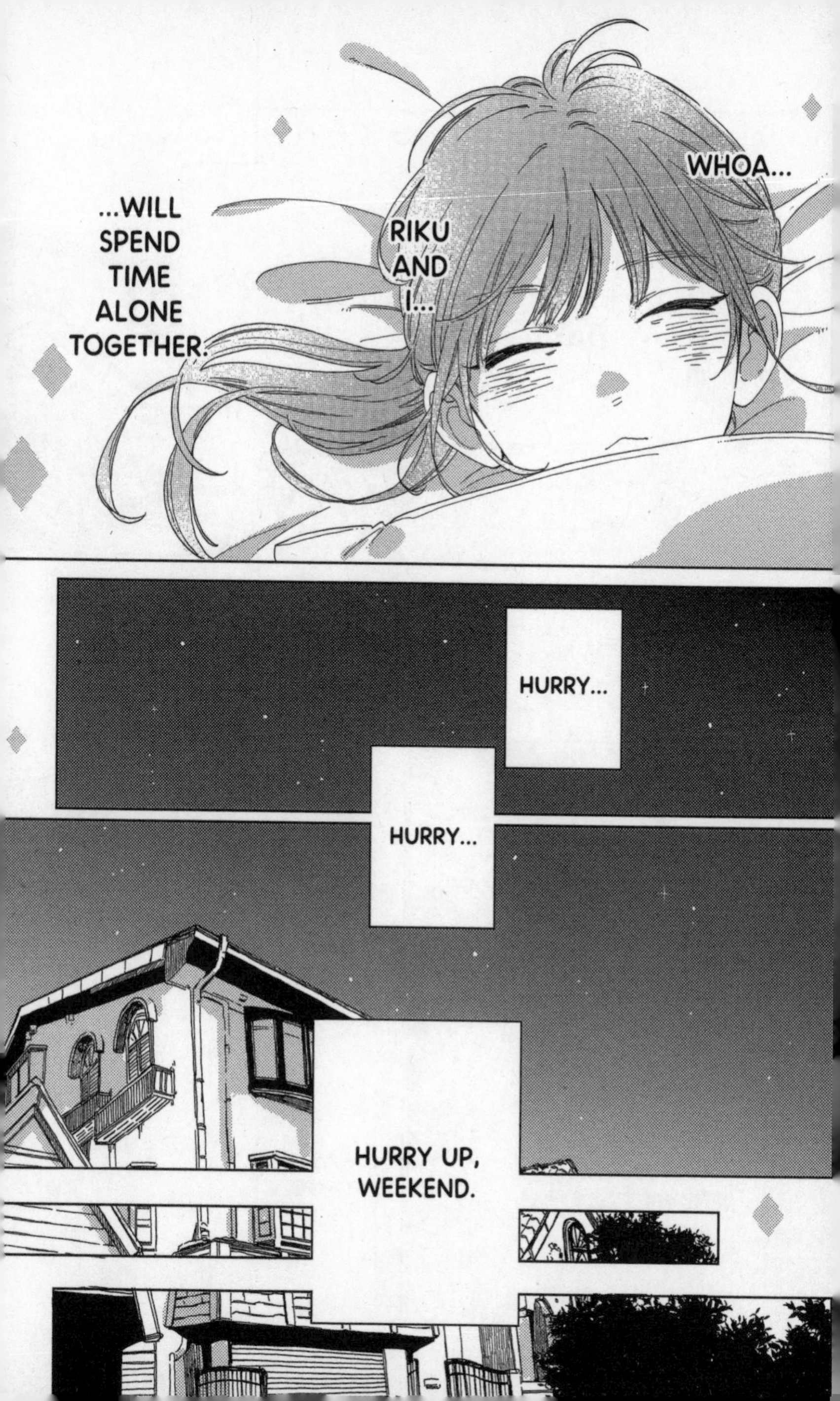
WHOA...
RIKU AND I...
...WILL SPEND TIME ALONE TOGETHER.
HURRY...
HURRY...
HURRY UP, WEEKEND.

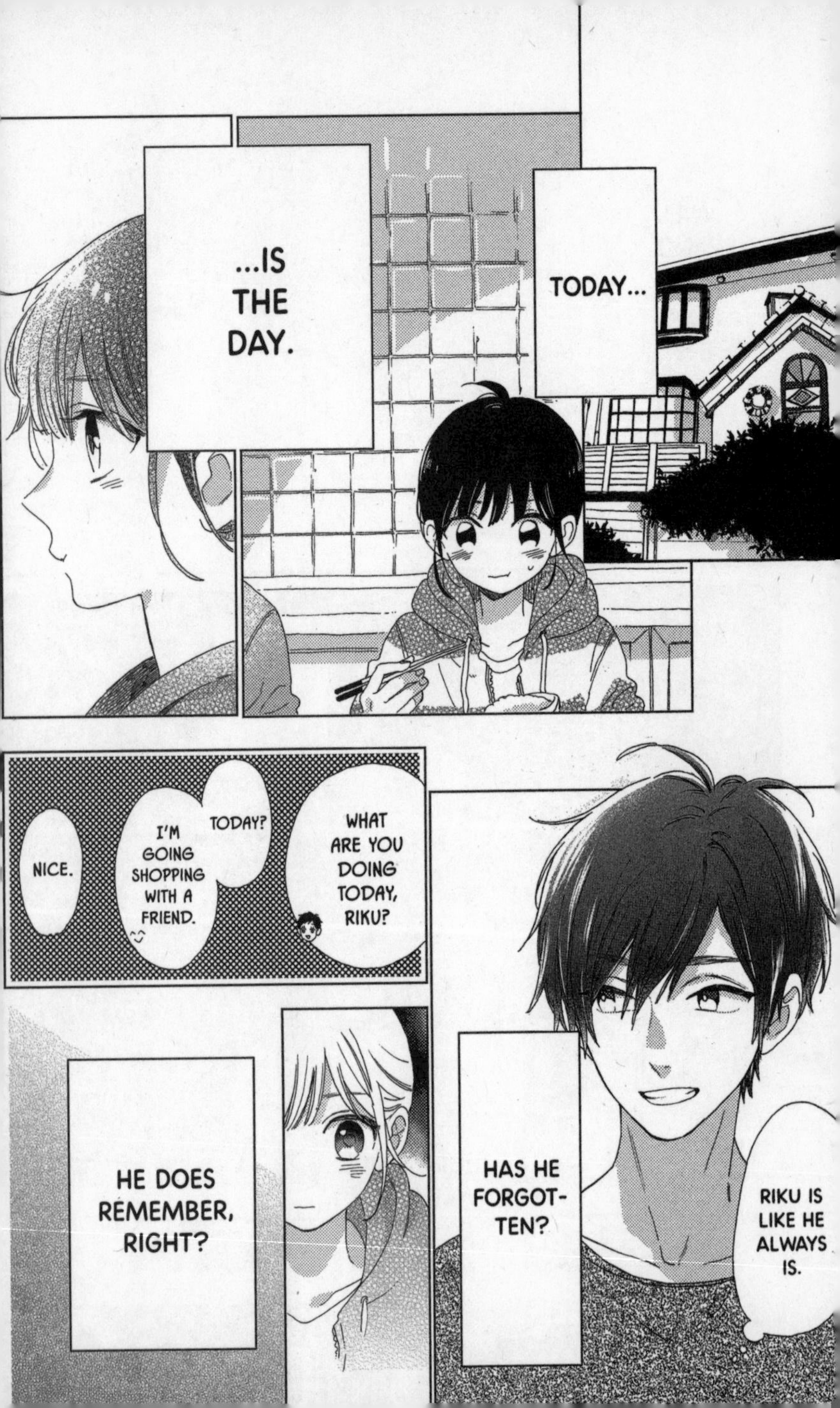
TODAY...
...IS THE DAY.
WHAT ARE YOU DOING TODAY, RIKU?
TODAY?
I'M GOING SHOPPING WITH A FRIEND.
NICE.
RIKU IS LIKE HE ALWAYS IS.
HAS HE FORGOT-TEN?
HE DOES REMEMBER, RIGHT?

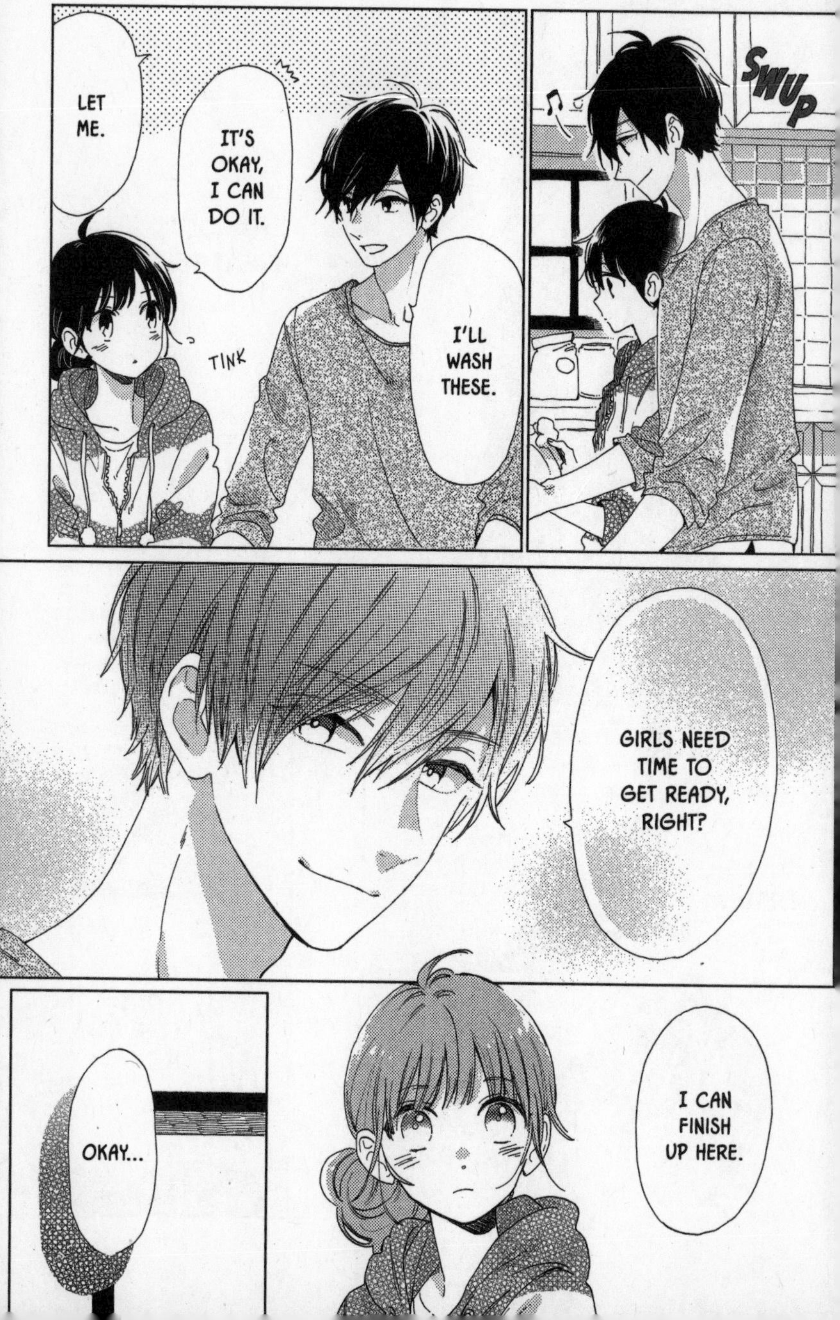
SWUP
I'LL WASH THESE.
IT'S OKAY, I CAN DO IT.
LET ME.
TINK
GIRLS NEED TIME TO GET READY, RIGHT?
I CAN FINISH UP HERE.
OKAY...

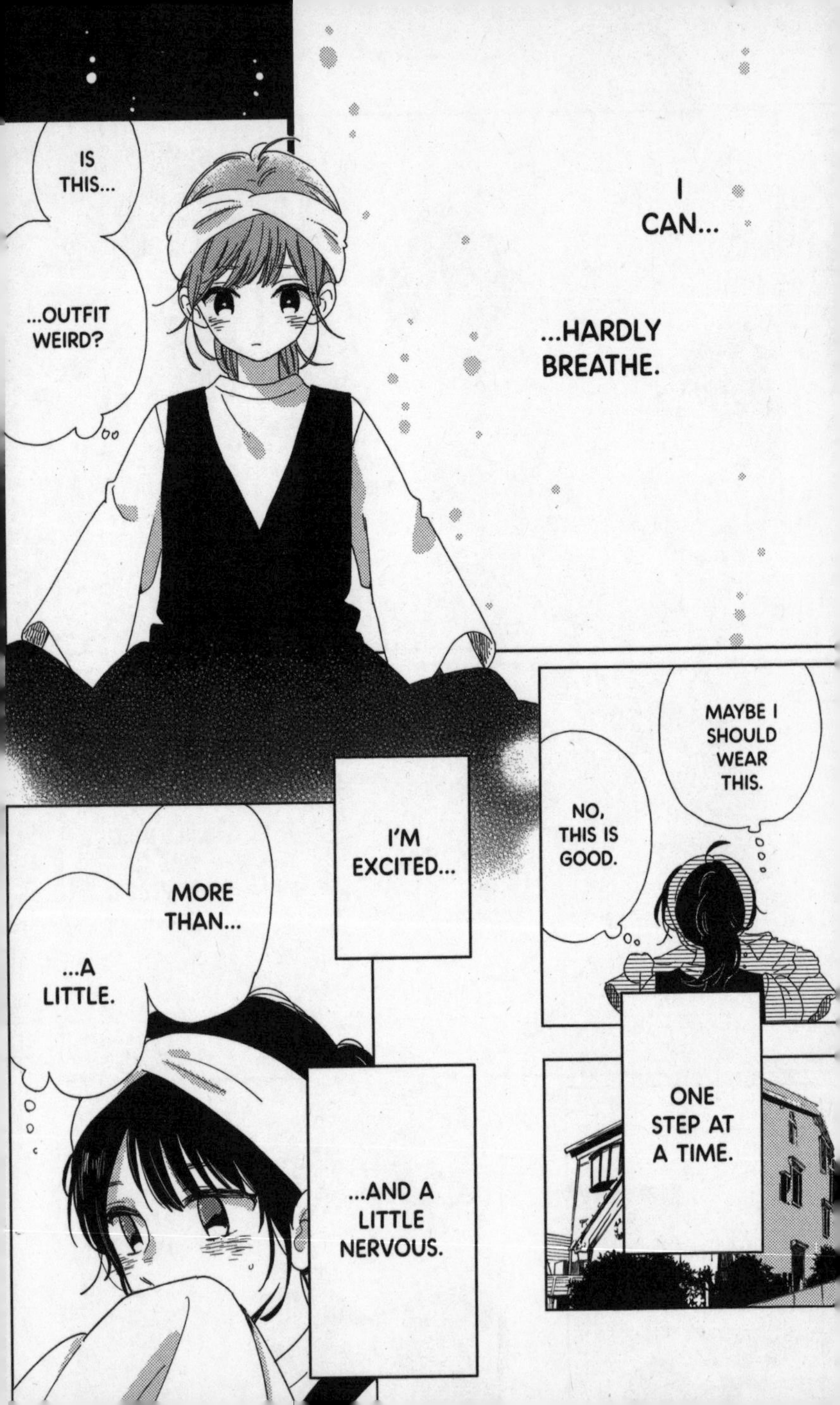
I CAN...
...HARDLY BREATHE.
IS THIS...
...OUTFIT WEIRD?
MAYBE I SHOULD WEAR THIS.
NO, THIS IS GOOD.
ONE STEP AT A TIME.
I'M EXCITED...
MORE THAN...
...A LITTLE.
...AND A LITTLE NERVOUS.

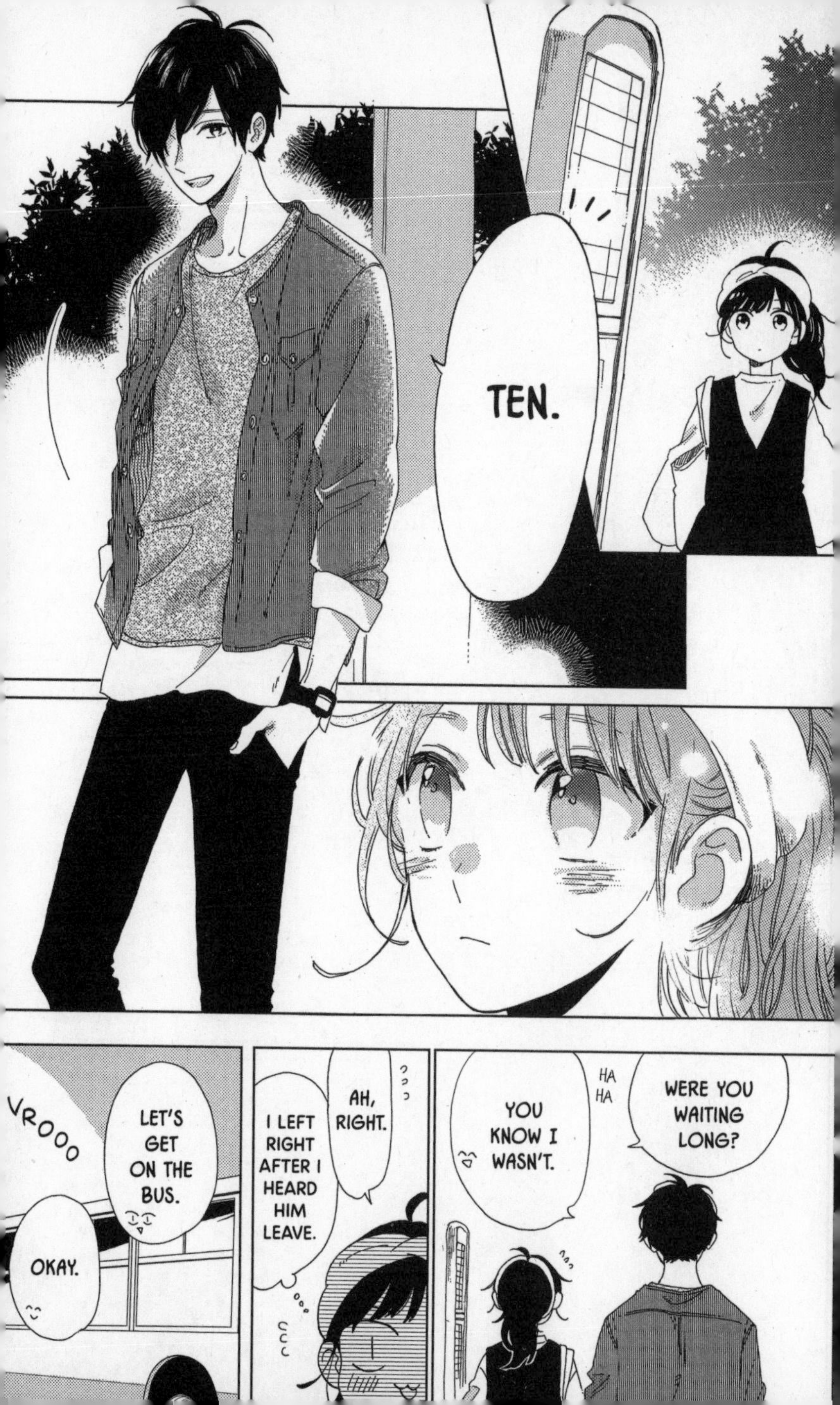
TEN.
WERE YOU WAITING LONG?
HA HA
YOU KNOW I WASN'T.
AH, RIGHT.
I LEFT RIGHT AFTER I HEARD HIM LEAVE.
VROOO
LET'S GET ON THE BUS.
OKAY.

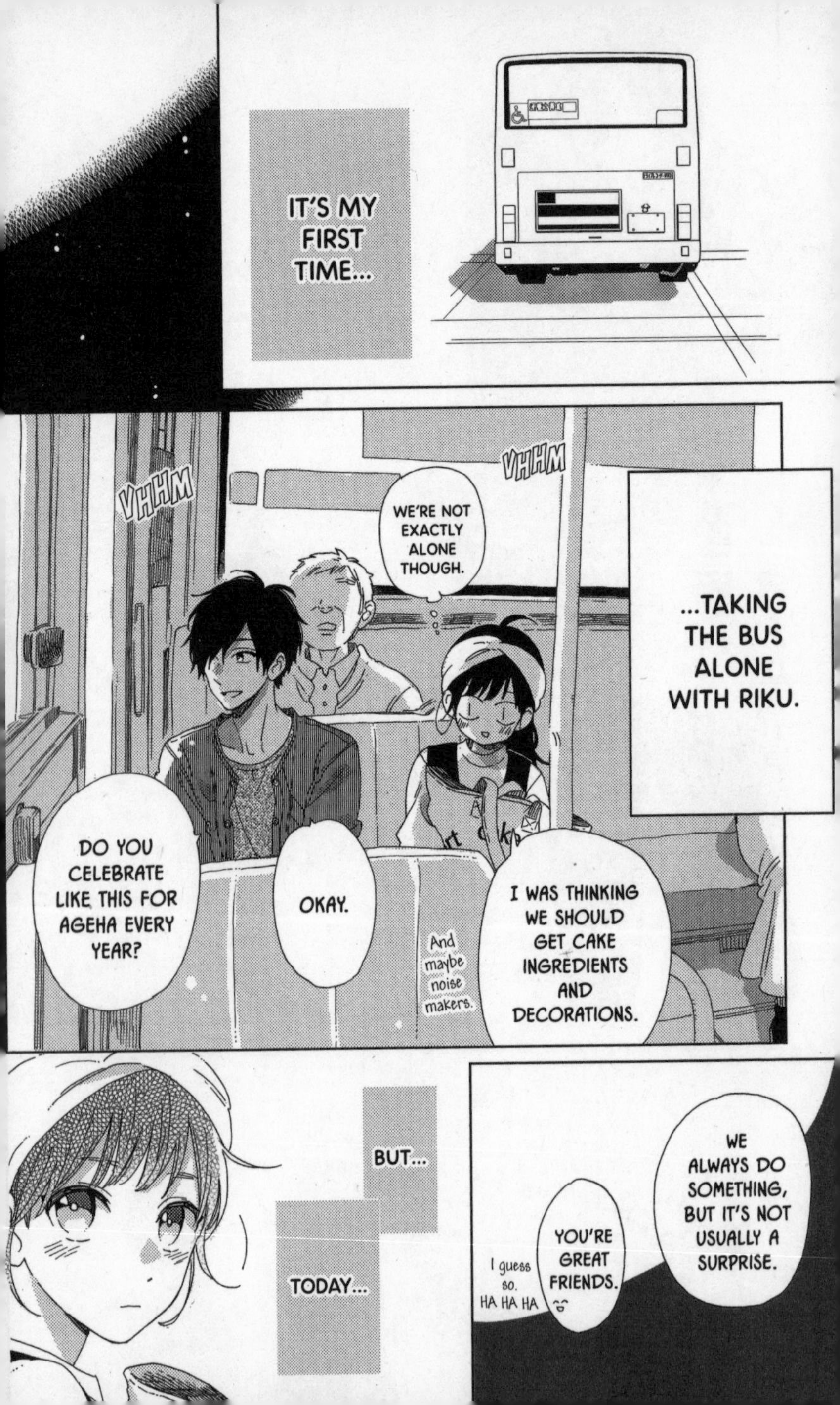
IT'S MY FIRST TIME...
...TAKING THE BUS ALONE WITH RIKU.
VHHM
WE'RE NOT EXACTLY ALONE THOUGH.
VHHM
I WAS THINKING WE SHOULD GET CAKE INGREDIENTS AND DECORATIONS.
And maybe noise makers.
OKAY.
DO YOU CELEBRATE LIKE THIS FOR AGEHA EVERY YEAR?
WE ALWAYS DO SOMETHING, BUT IT'S NOT USUALLY A SURPRISE.
YOU'RE GREAT FRIENDS.
I guess so. HA HA HA
BUT...
TODAY...

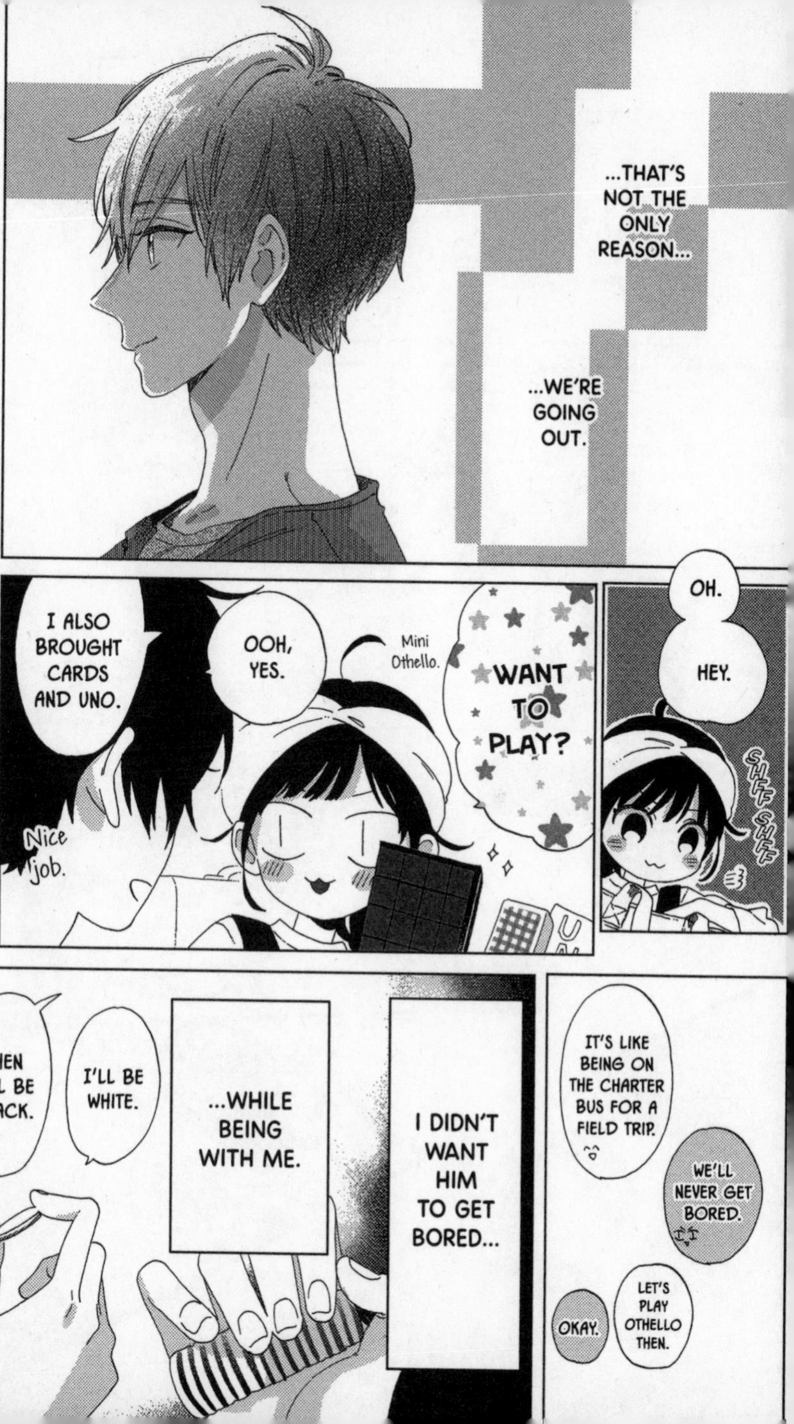
...THAT'S NOT THE ONLY REASON...
...WE'RE GOING OUT.
OH.
HEY.
SHFF SHFF
WANT TO PLAY?
Mini Othello.
OOH, YES.
I ALSO BROUGHT CARDS AND UNO.
Nice job.
IT'S LIKE BEING ON THE CHARTER BUS FOR A FIELD TRIP.
WE'LL NEVER GET BORED.
LET'S PLAY OTHELLO THEN.
OKAY.
I DIDN'T WANT HIM TO GET BORED...
...WHILE BEING WITH ME.
I'LL BE WHITE.
THEN I'LL BE BLACK.

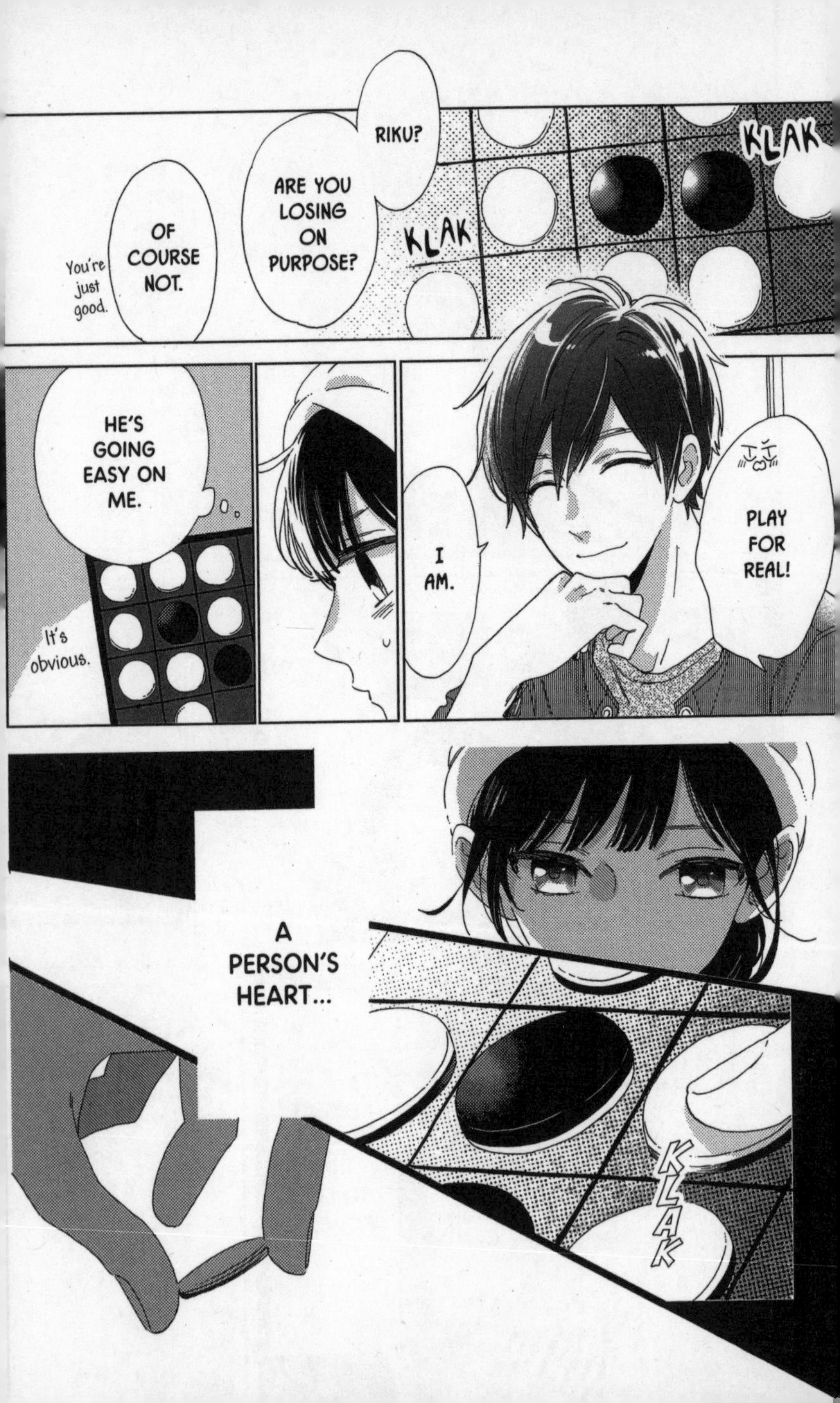
KLAK
RIKU?
ARE YOU LOSING ON PURPOSE?
KLAK
OF COURSE NOT.
You're just good.
PLAY FOR REAL!
I AM.
HE'S GOING EASY ON ME.
It's obvious.
A PERSON'S HEART...
KLAK

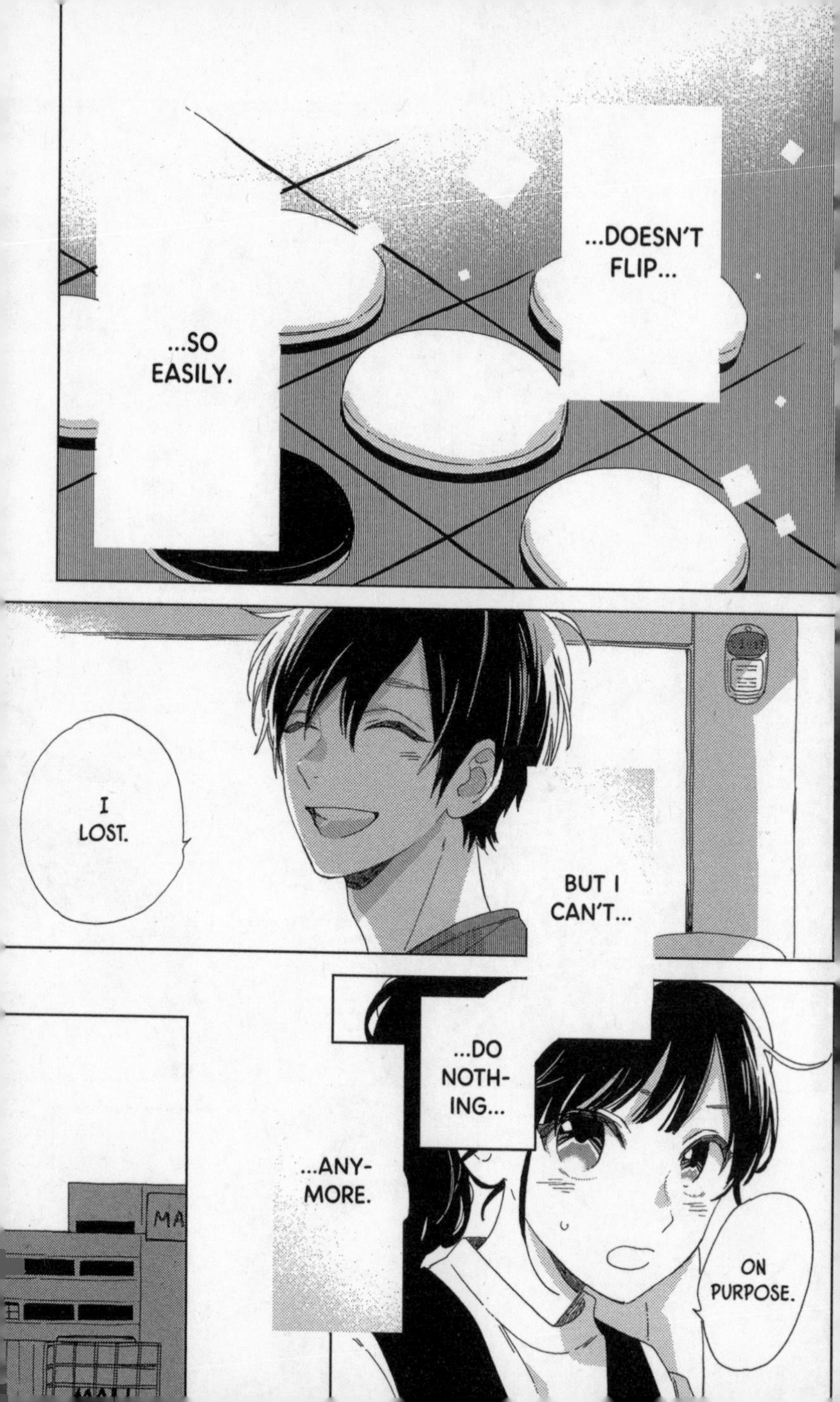
...DOESN'T FLIP...
...SO EASILY.
I LOST.
BUT I CAN'T...
...DO NOTHING...
...ANYMORE.
ON PURPOSE.
MA

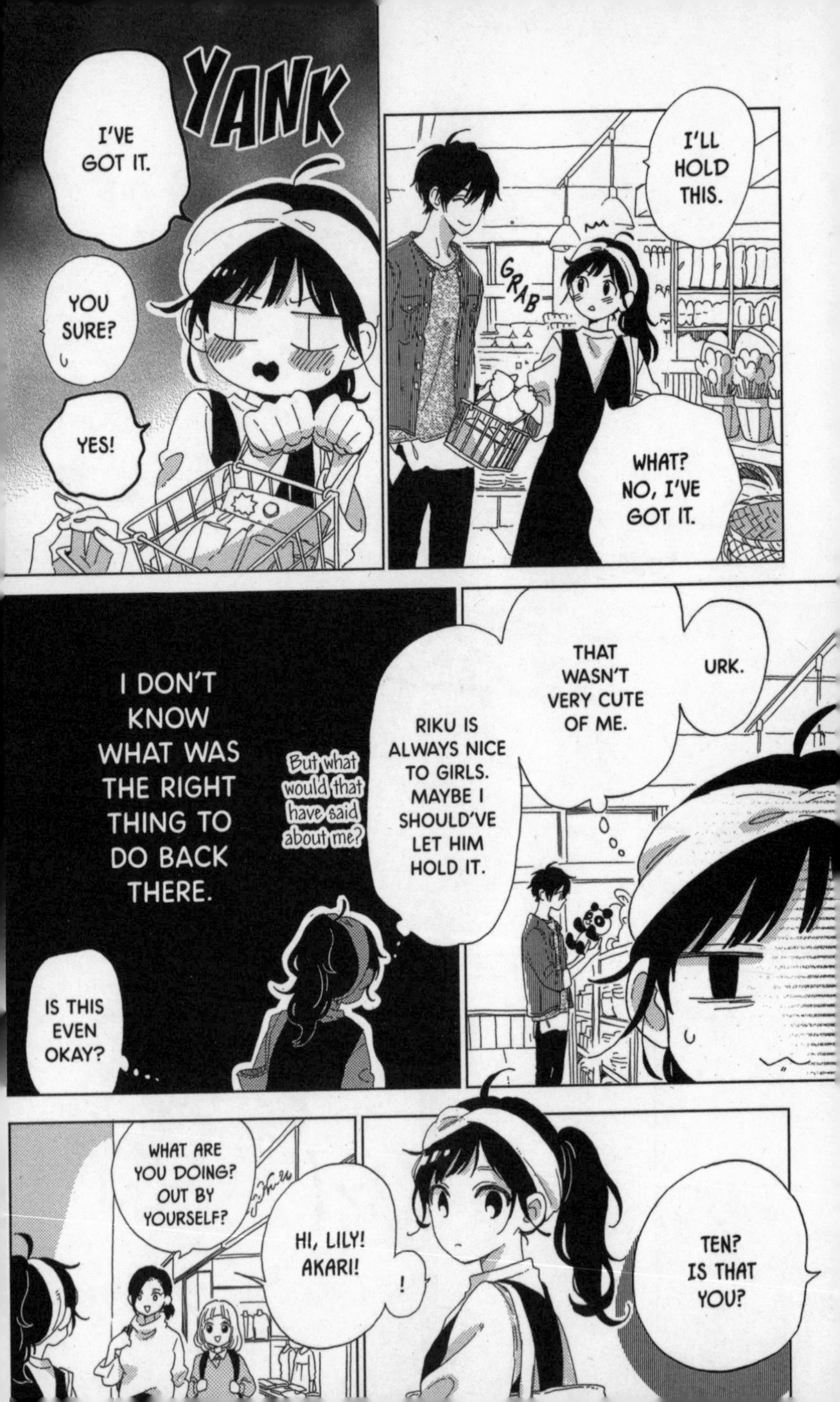
I'LL HOLD THIS.
GRAB
WHAT? NO, I'VE GOT IT.
YANK
I'VE GOT IT.
YOU SURE?
YES!
URK.
THAT WASN'T VERY CUTE OF ME.
RIKU IS ALWAYS NICE TO GIRLS. MAYBE I SHOULD'VE LET HIM HOLD IT.
I DON'T KNOW WHAT WAS THE RIGHT THING TO DO BACK THERE.
But what would that have said about me?
IS THIS EVEN OKAY?
TEN? IS THAT YOU?
!
HI, LILY! AKARI!
WHAT ARE YOU DOING? OUT BY YOURSELF?

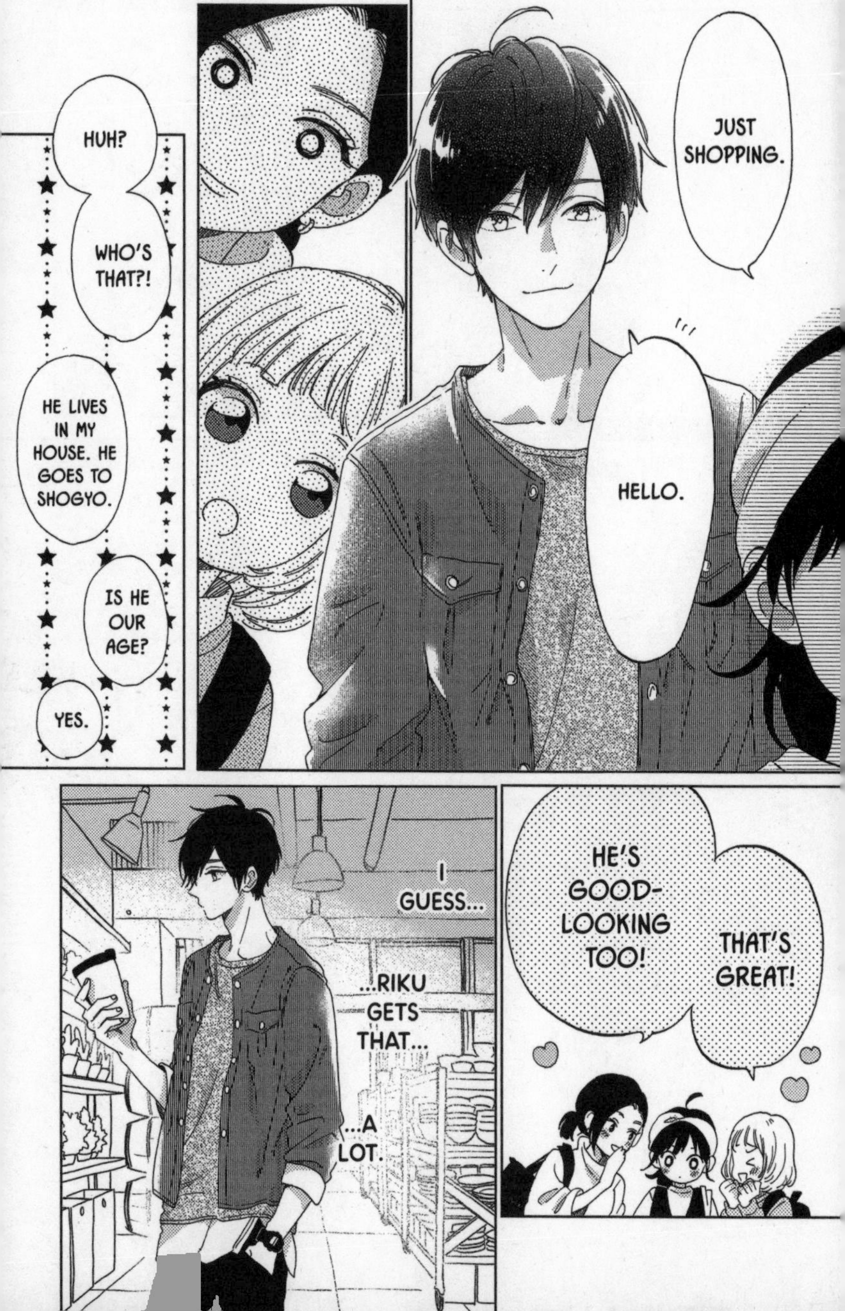
JUST SHOPPING.
HELLO.
HUH?
WHO'S THAT?!
HE LIVES IN MY HOUSE. HE GOES TO SHOGYO.
IS HE OUR AGE?
YES.
THAT'S GREAT!
HE'S GOOD-LOOKING TOO!
I GUESS...
...RIKU GETS THAT...
...A LOT.

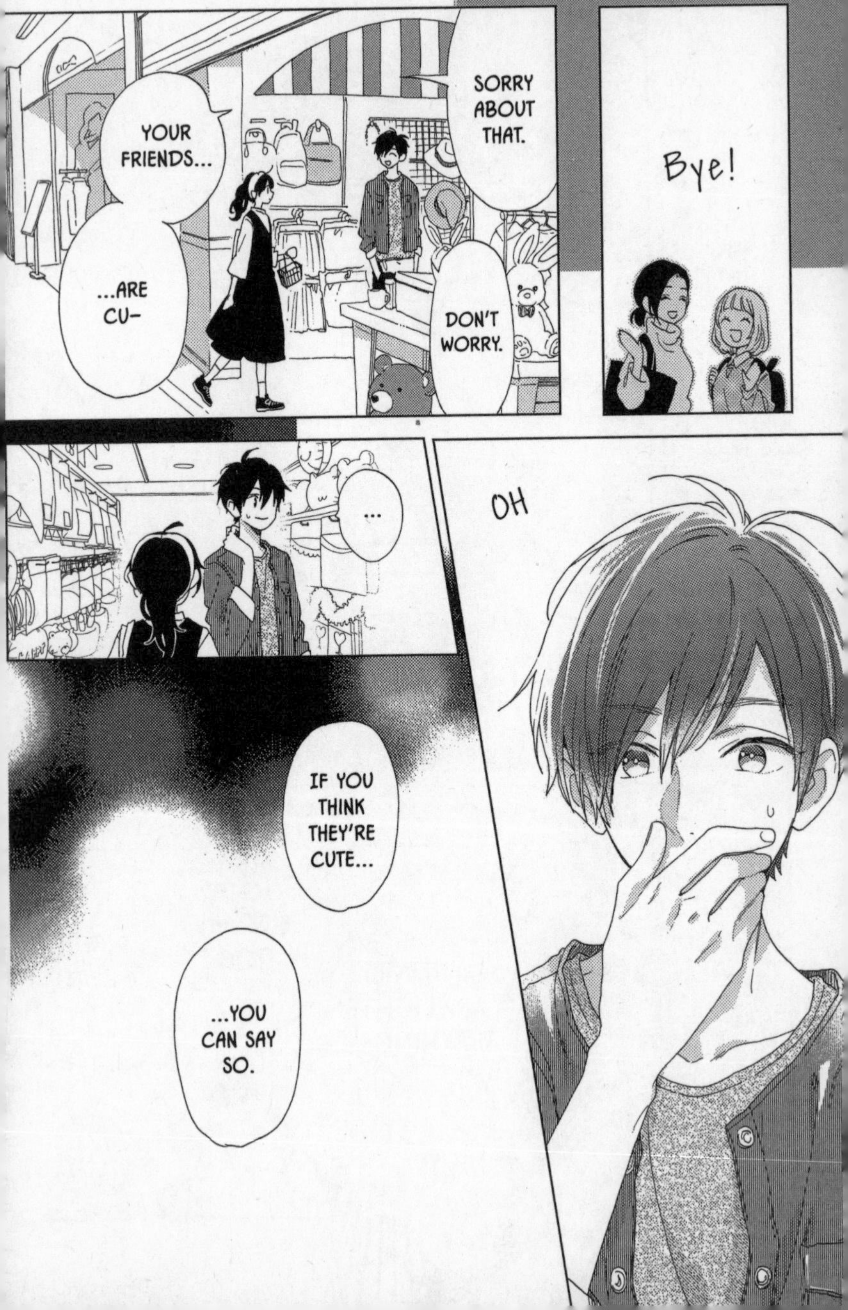
Bye!
SORRY ABOUT THAT.
YOUR FRIENDS...
...ARE CU-
DON'T WORRY.
OH
...
IF YOU THINK THEY'RE CUTE...
...YOU CAN SAY SO.

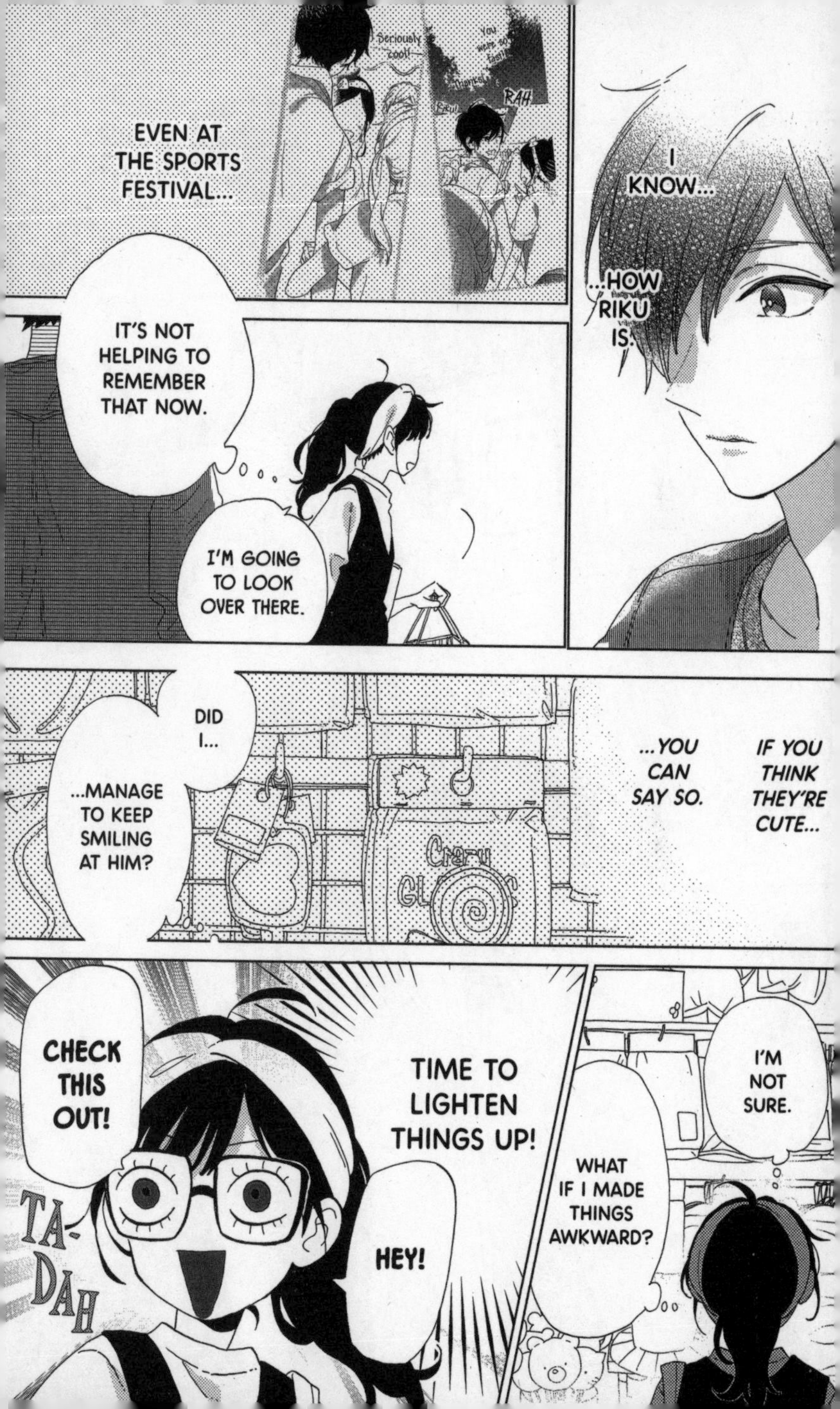
I KNOW...
...HOW RIKU IS.
You were so fast!
RAH
Thanks!
Riku!
Seriously cool!
EVEN AT THE SPORTS FESTIVAL...
IT'S NOT HELPING TO REMEMBER THAT NOW.
I'M GOING TO LOOK OVER THERE.
IF YOU THINK THEY'RE CUTE...
...YOU CAN SAY SO.
DID I...
...MANAGE TO KEEP SMILING AT HIM?
I'M NOT SURE.
WHAT IF I MADE THINGS AWKWARD?
TIME TO LIGHTEN THINGS UP!
HEY!
CHECK THIS OUT!
TA-DAH

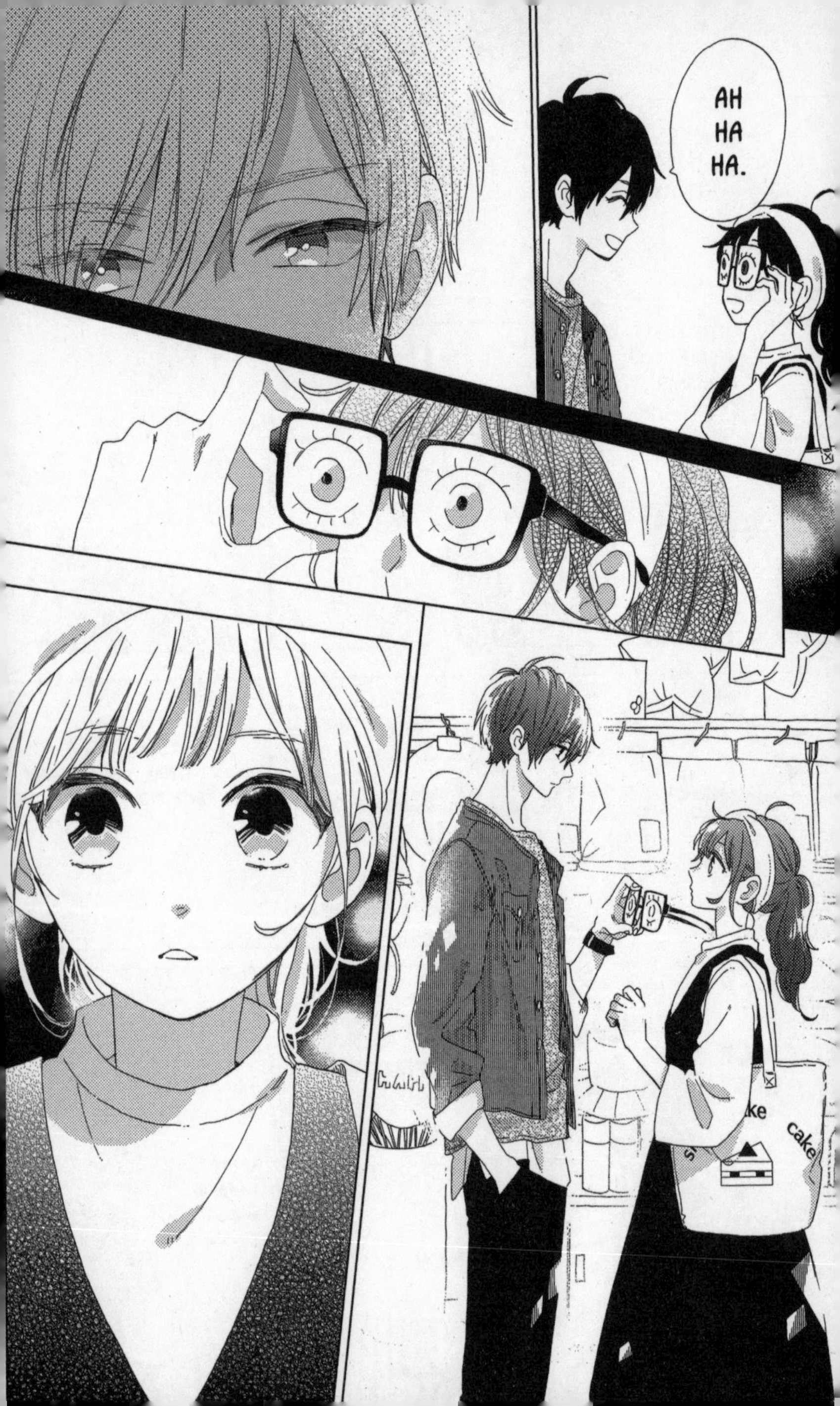
AH HA HA.
cake

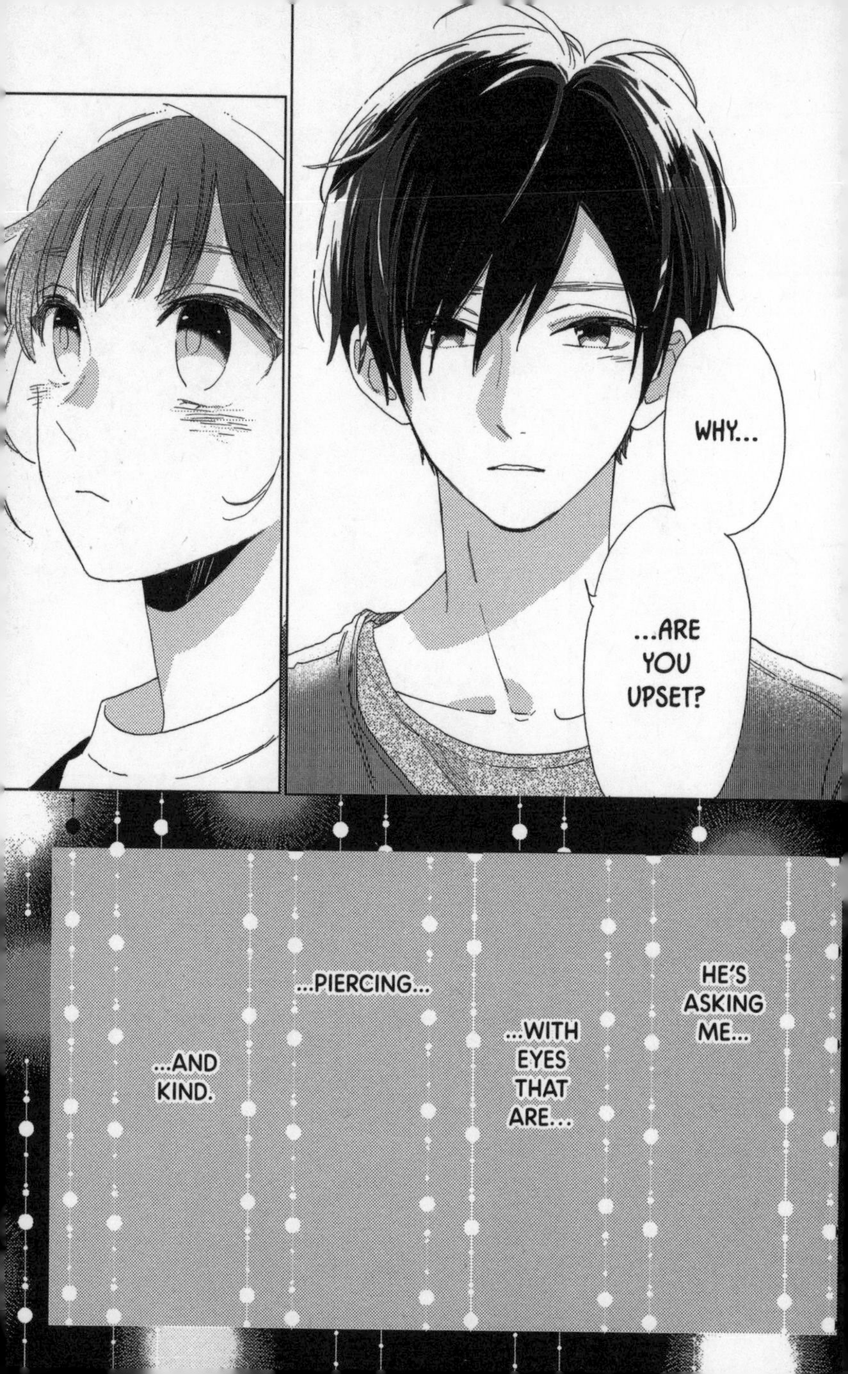
WHY...
...ARE YOU UPSET?
HE'S ASKING ME...
...WITH EYES THAT ARE...
...PIERCING...
...AND KIND.

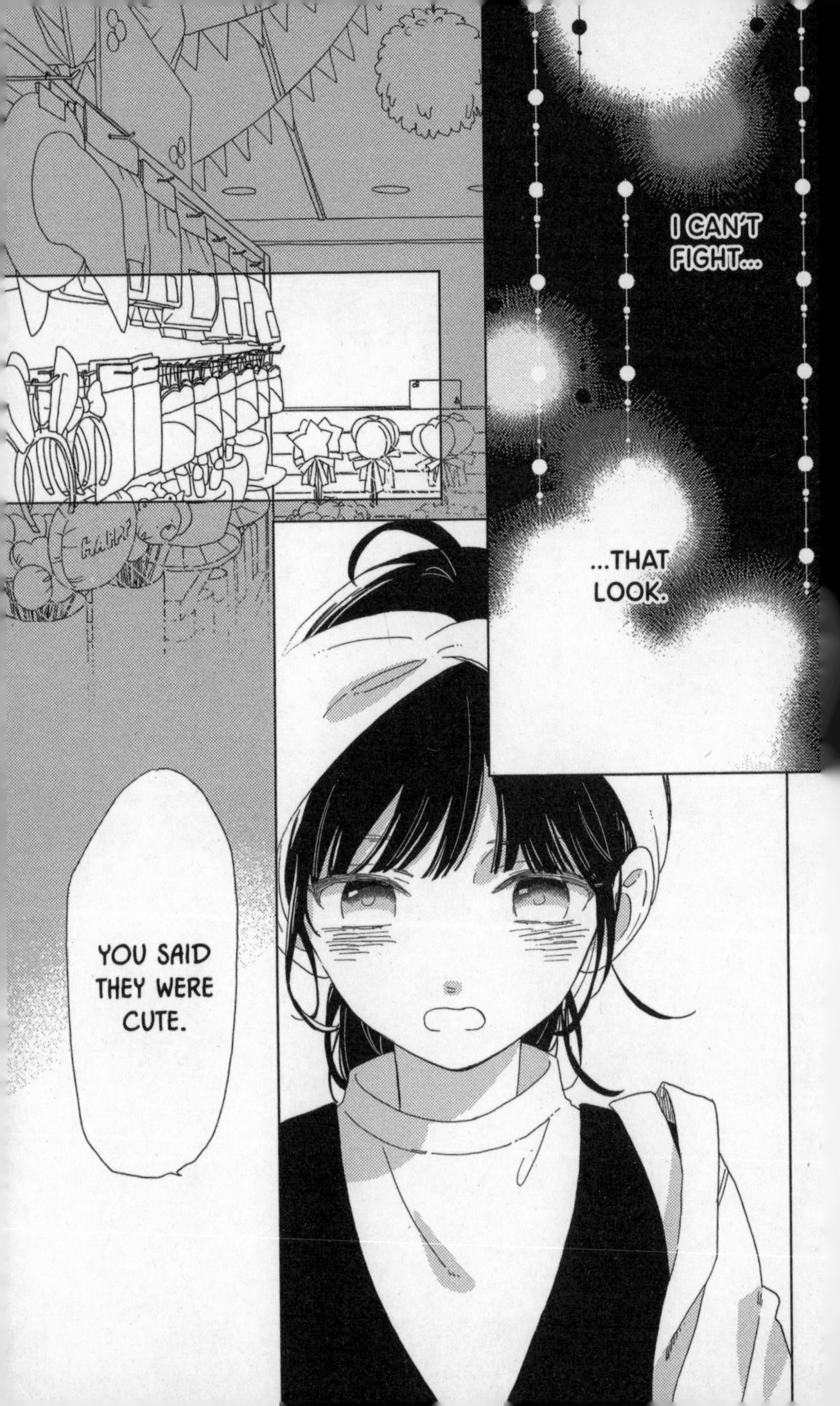
I CAN'T FIGHT...
...THAT LOOK.
YOU SAID THEY WERE CUTE.

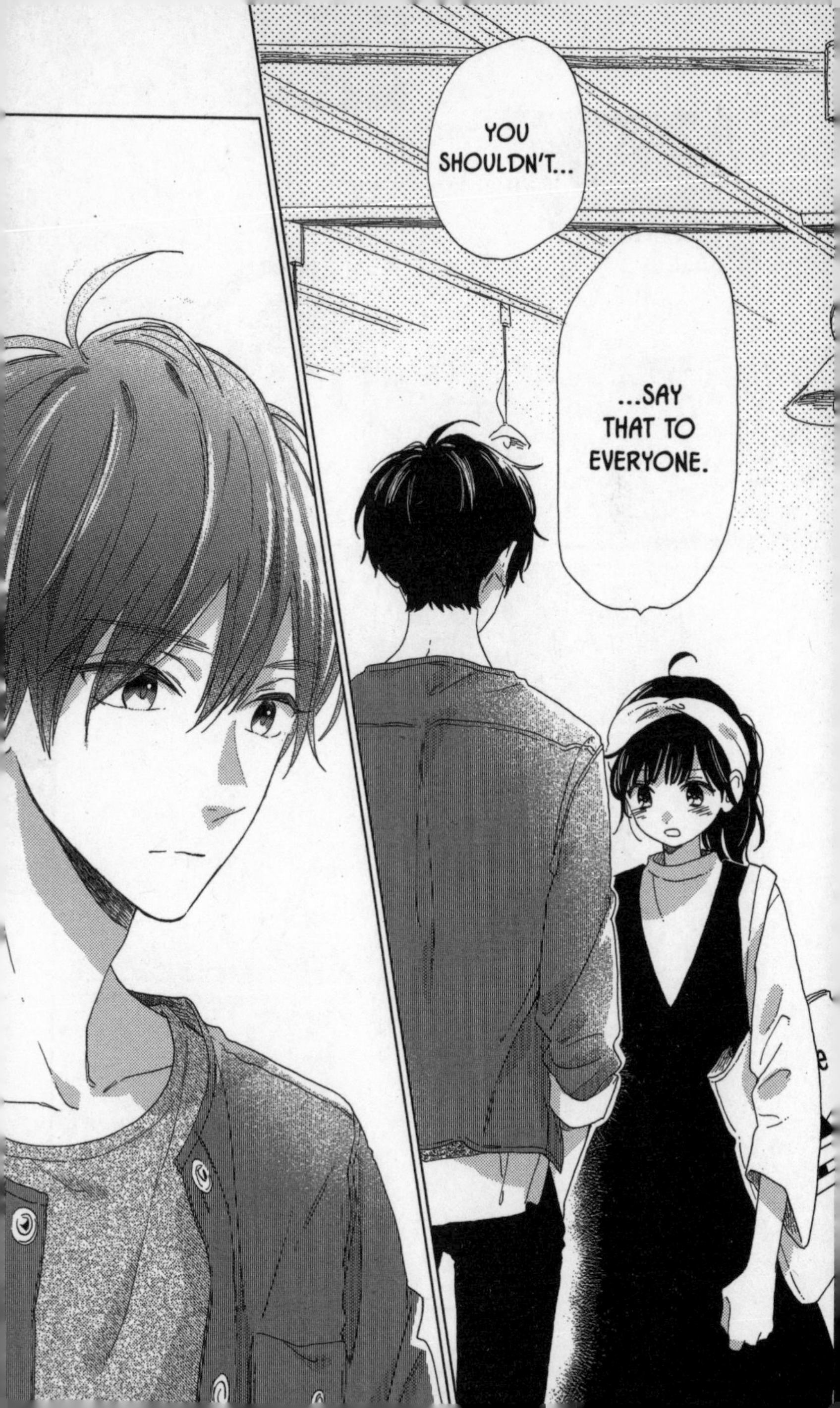
YOU SHOULDN'T...
...SAY THAT TO EVERYONE.

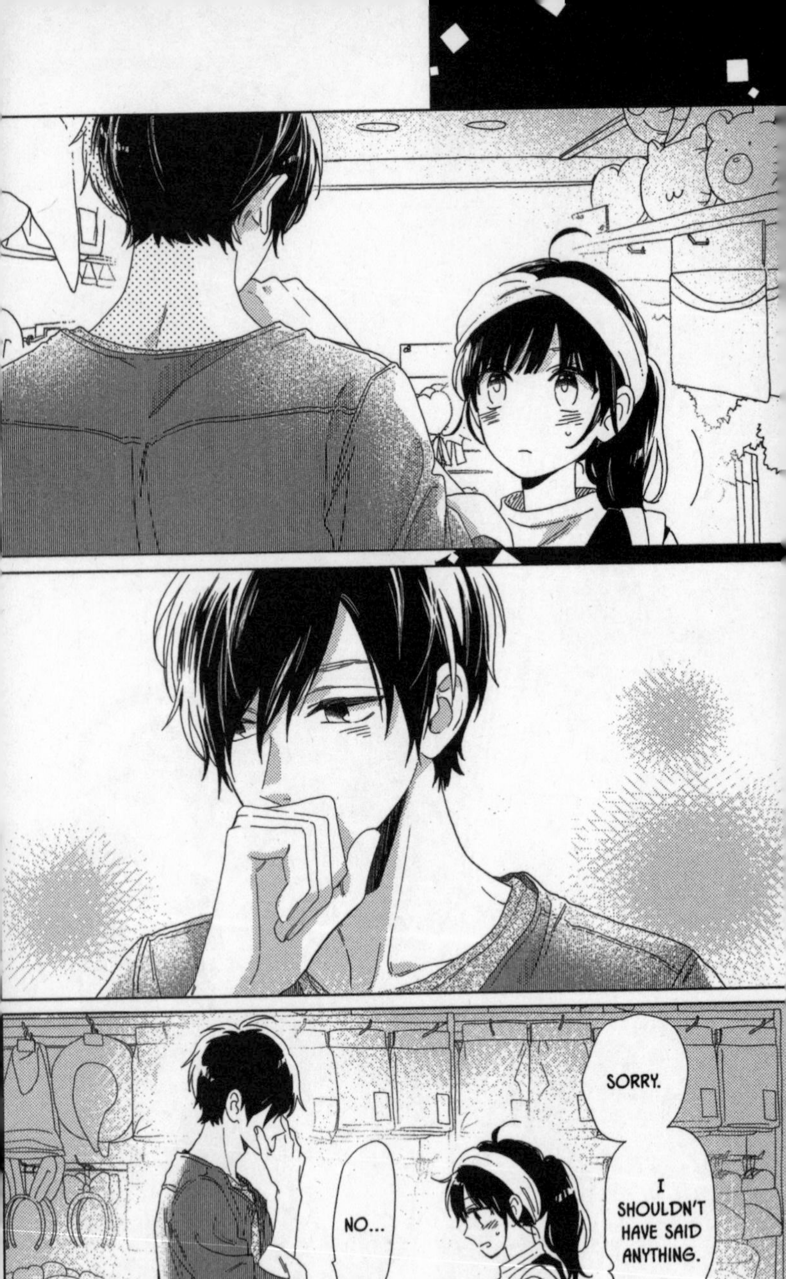
SORRY.
I SHOULDN'T HAVE SAID ANYTHING.
NO...

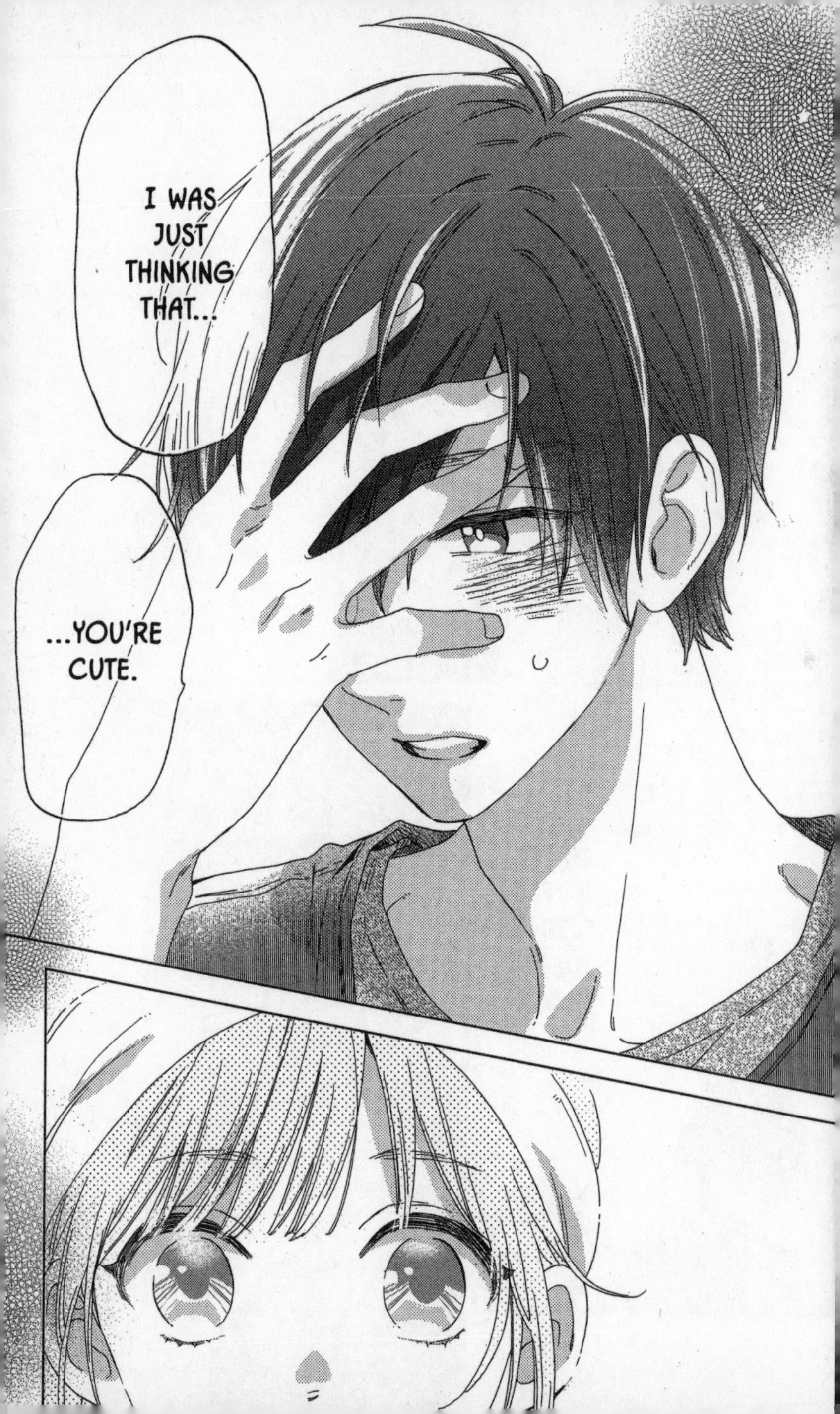
I WAS JUST THINKING THAT...
...YOU'RE CUTE.

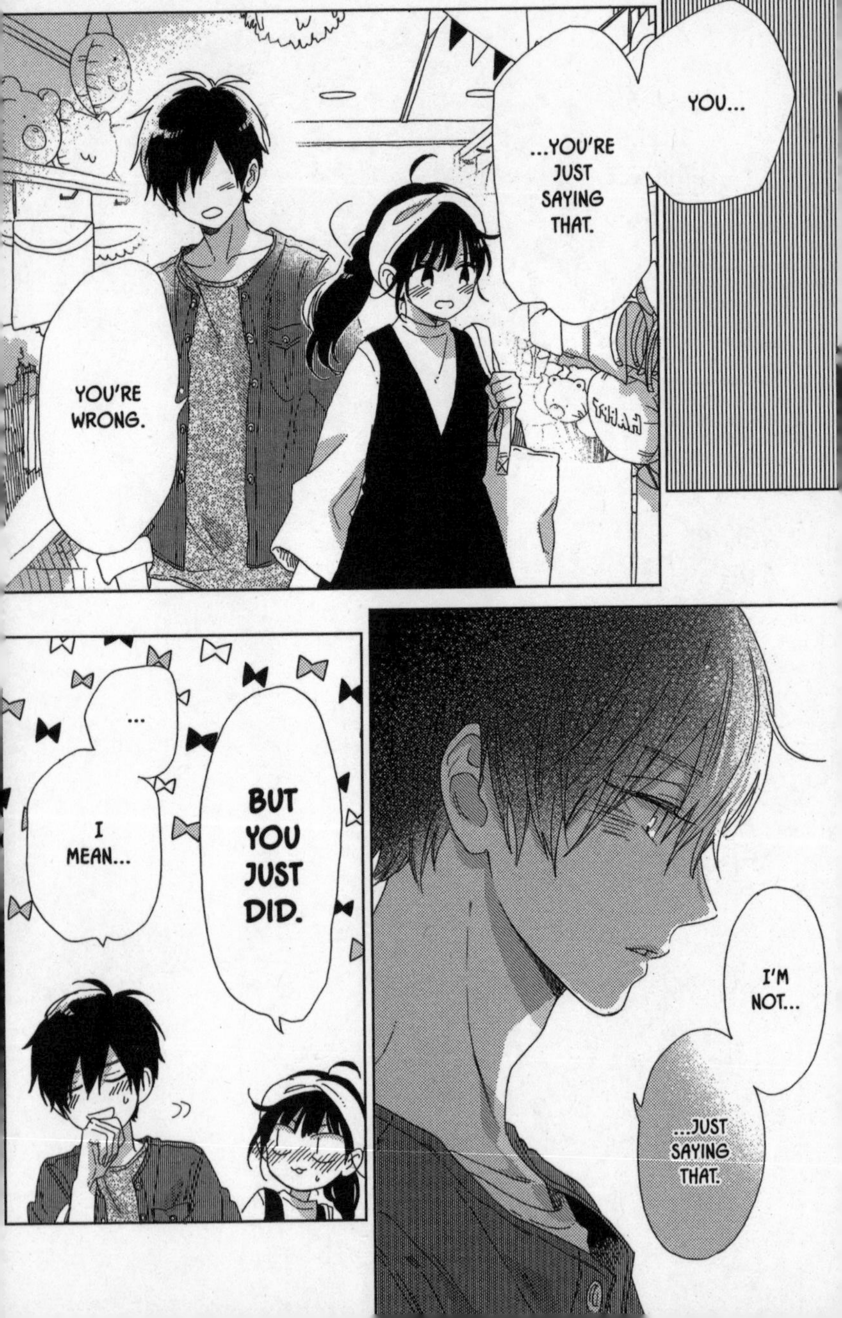
YOU...
...YOU'RE JUST SAYING THAT.
YOU'RE WRONG.
I'M NOT...
...JUST SAYING THAT.
BUT YOU JUST DID.
...
I MEAN...

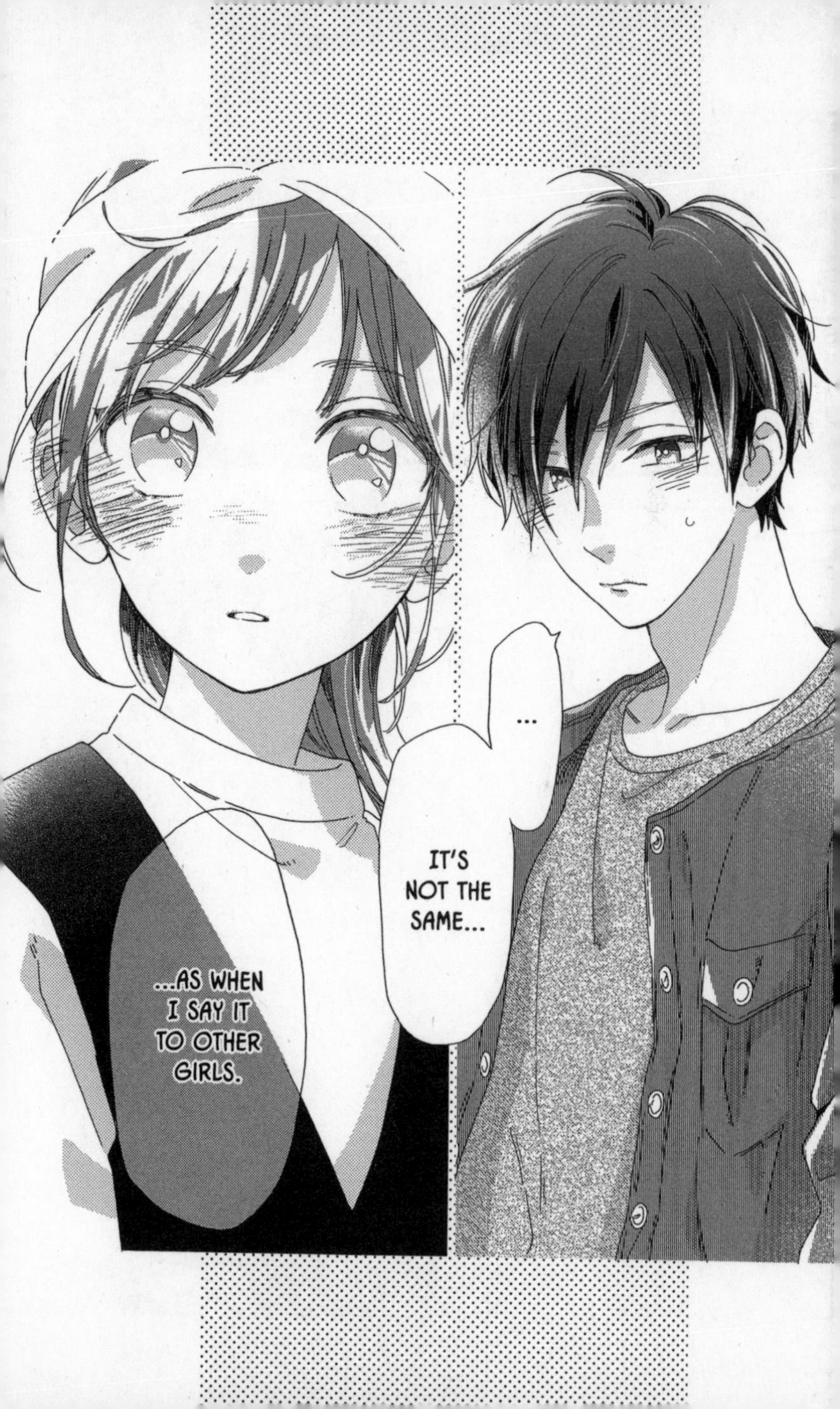
...
IT'S NOT THE SAME...
...AS WHEN I SAY IT TO OTHER GIRLS.

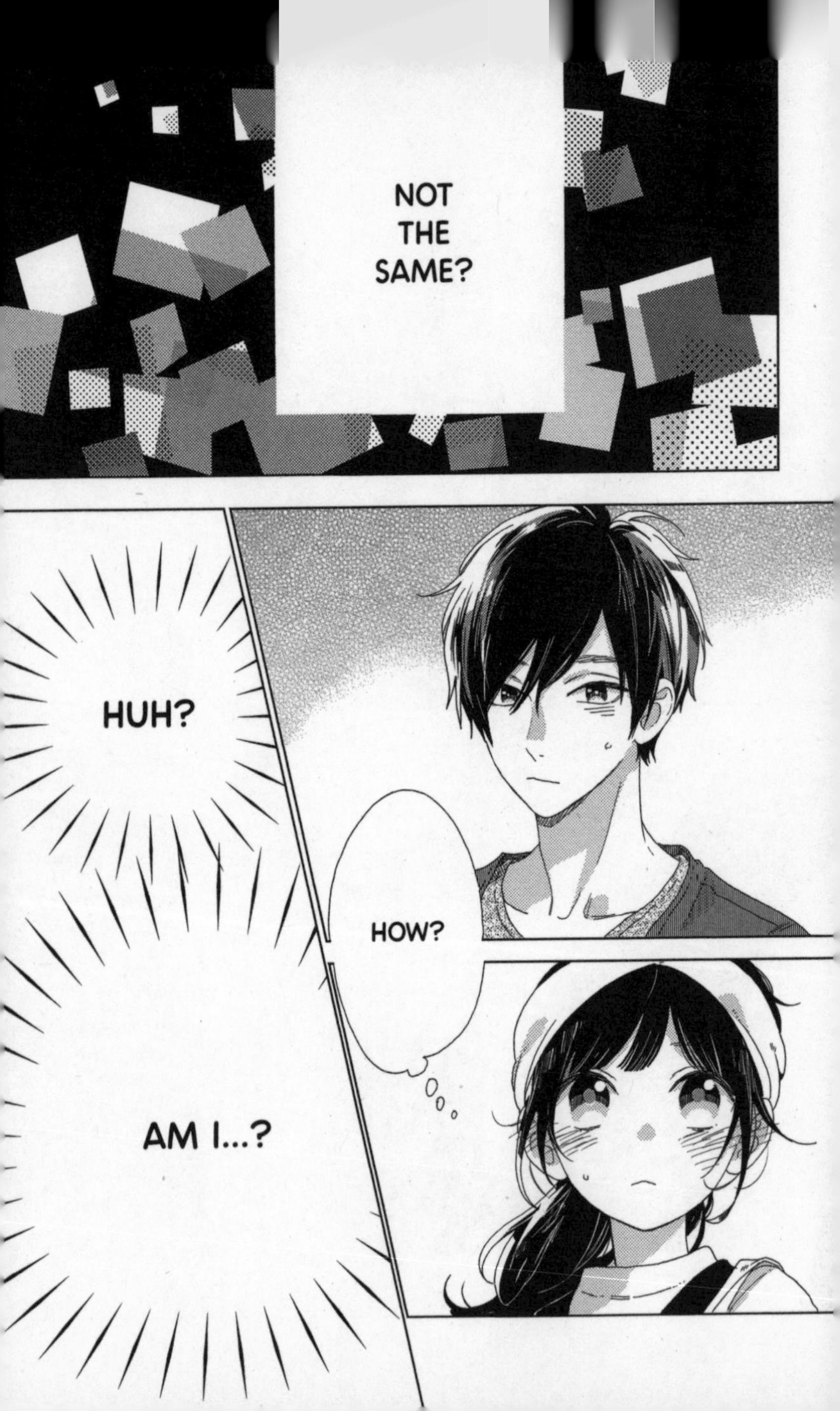
NOT THE SAME?
HOW?
HUH?
AM I...?

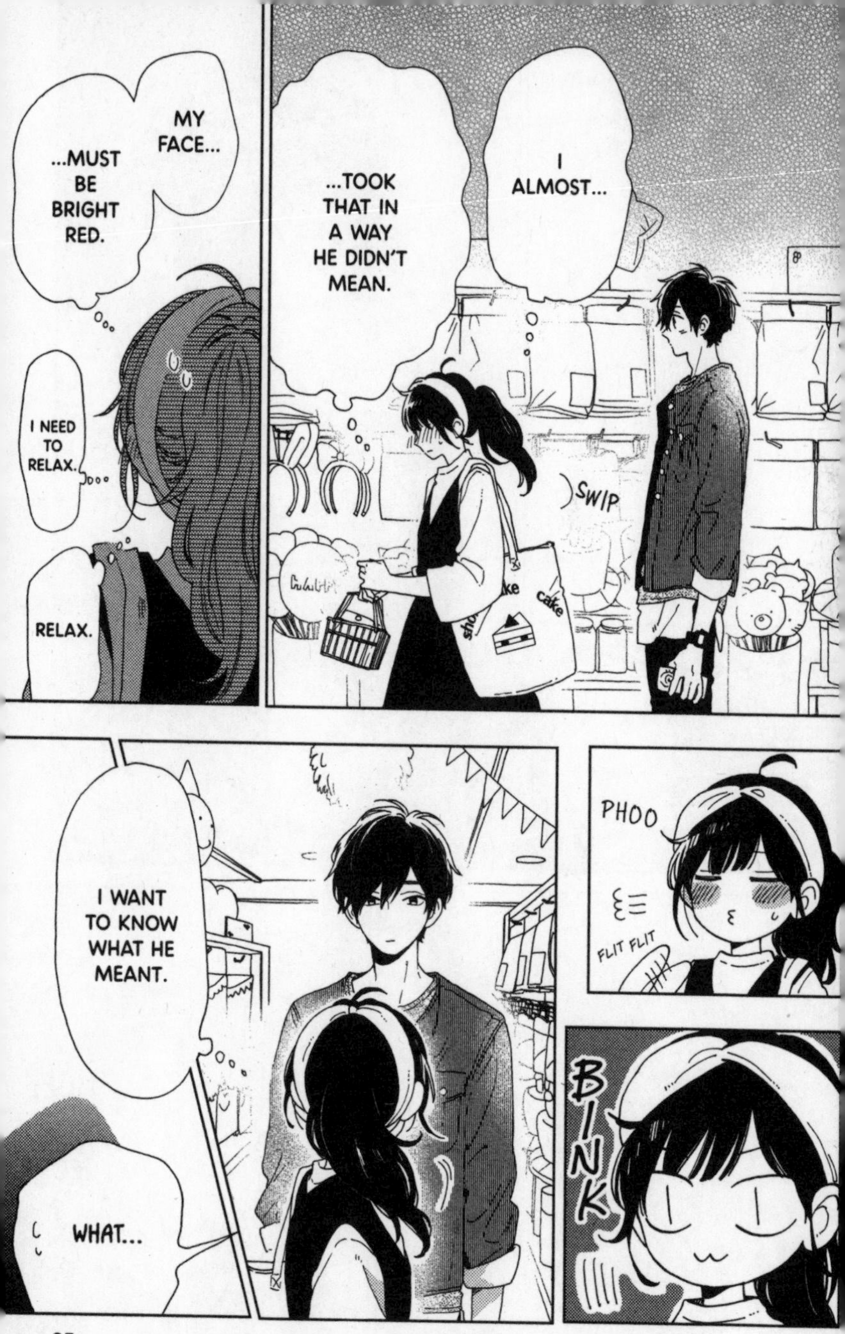
I ALMOST...
...TOOK THAT IN A WAY HE DIDN'T MEAN.
SWIP
MY FACE...
...MUST BE BRIGHT RED.
I NEED TO RELAX.
RELAX.
PHOO
FLIT FLIT
BINK
I WANT TO KNOW WHAT HE MEANT.
WHAT...

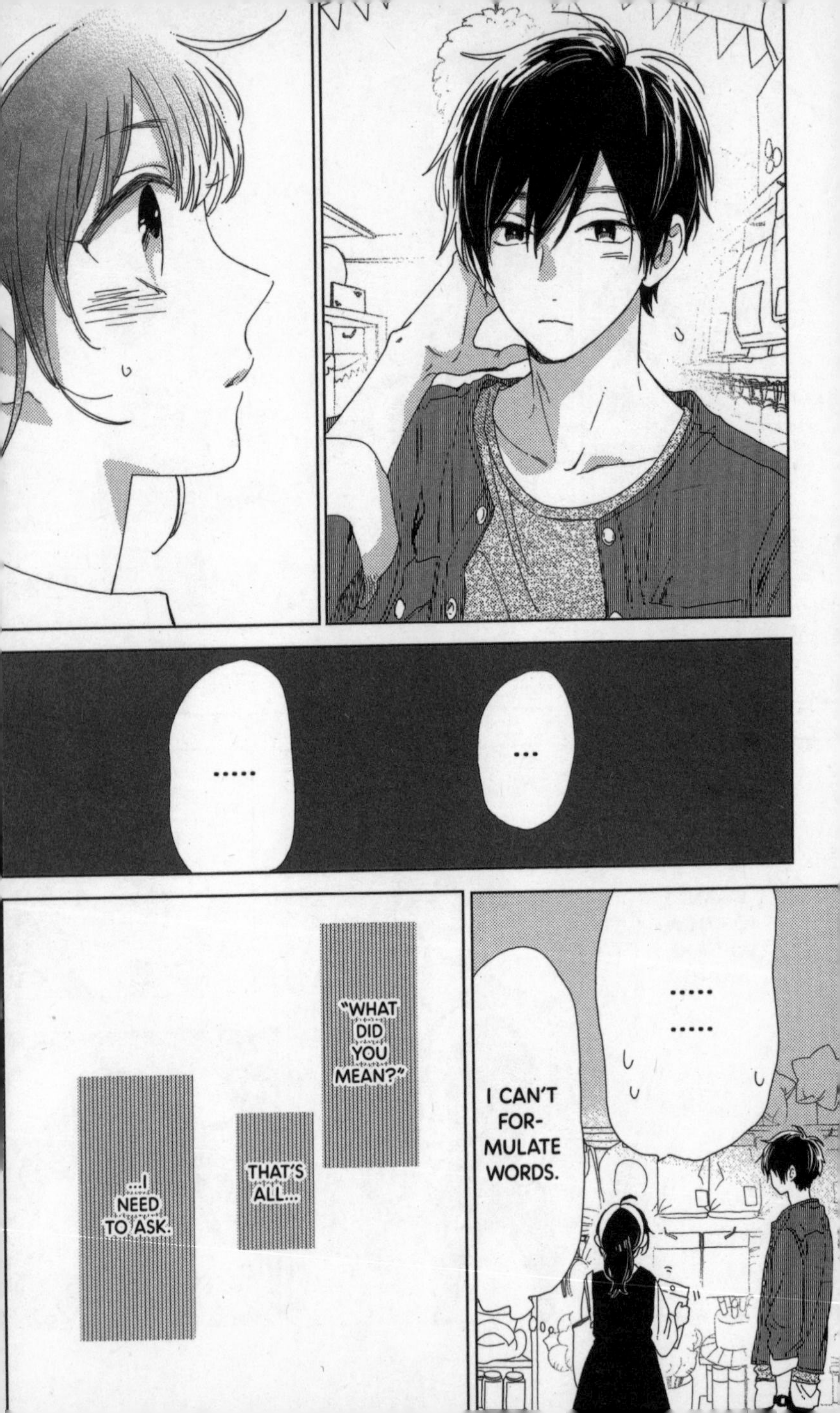
...
.....
.....
.....
I CAN'T FOR-MULATE WORDS.
"WHAT DID YOU MEAN?"
THAT'S ALL...
...I NEED TO ASK.

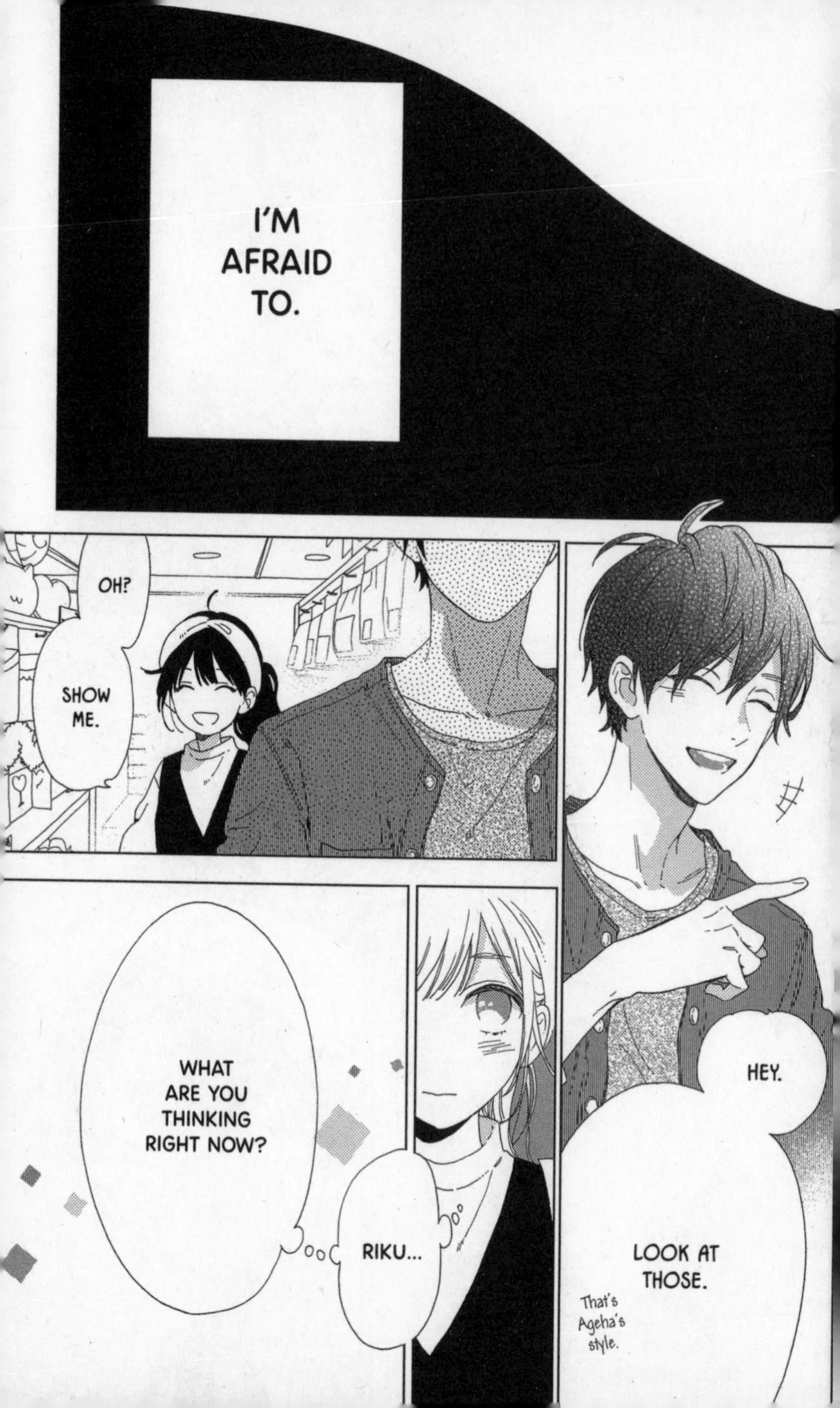
I'M AFRAID TO.
OH?
SHOW ME.
HEY.
LOOK AT THOSE.
That's Ageha's style.
WHAT ARE YOU THINKING RIGHT NOW?
RIKU...

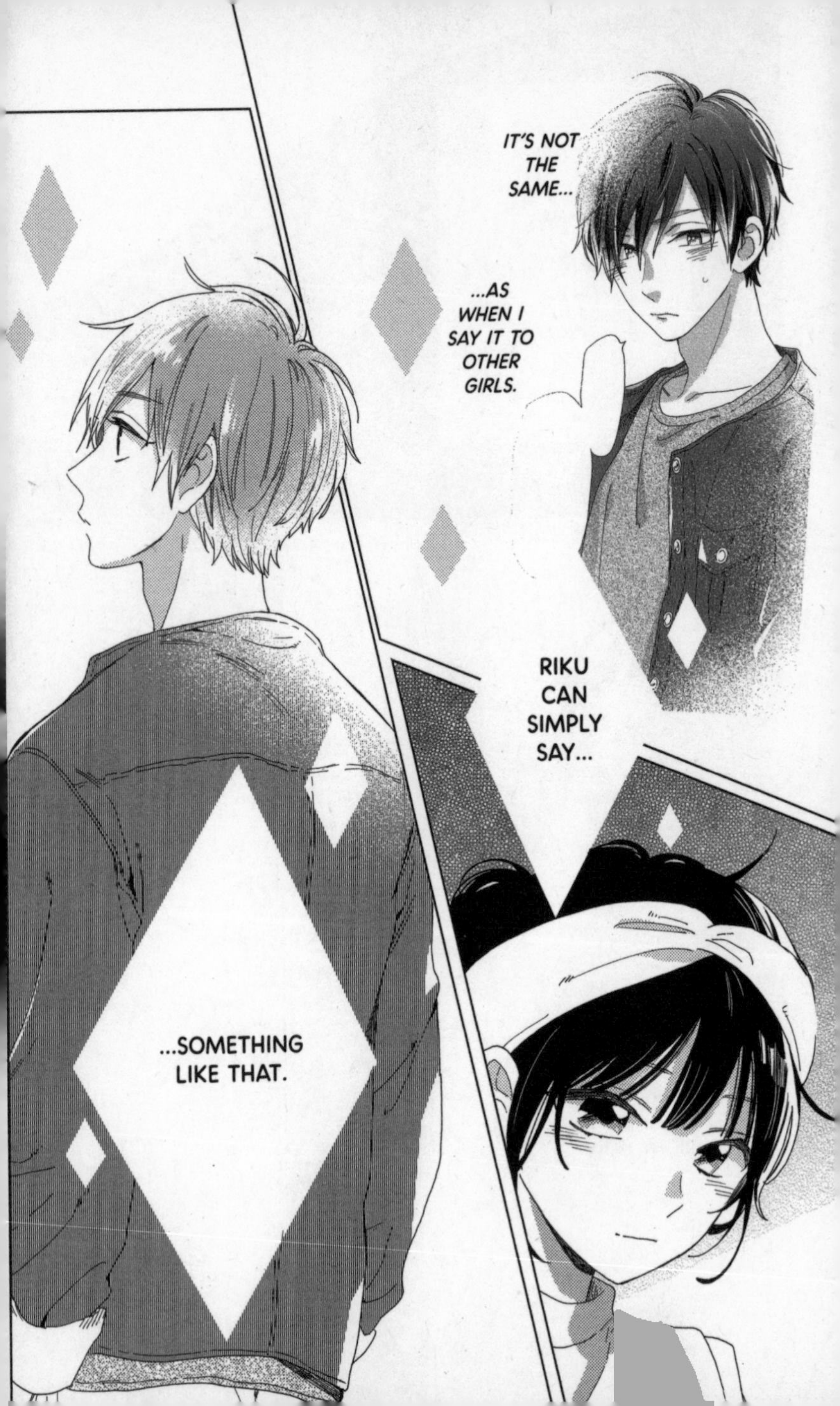
IT'S NOT THE SAME...
...AS WHEN I SAY IT TO OTHER GIRLS.
RIKU CAN SIMPLY SAY...
...SOMETHING LIKE THAT.

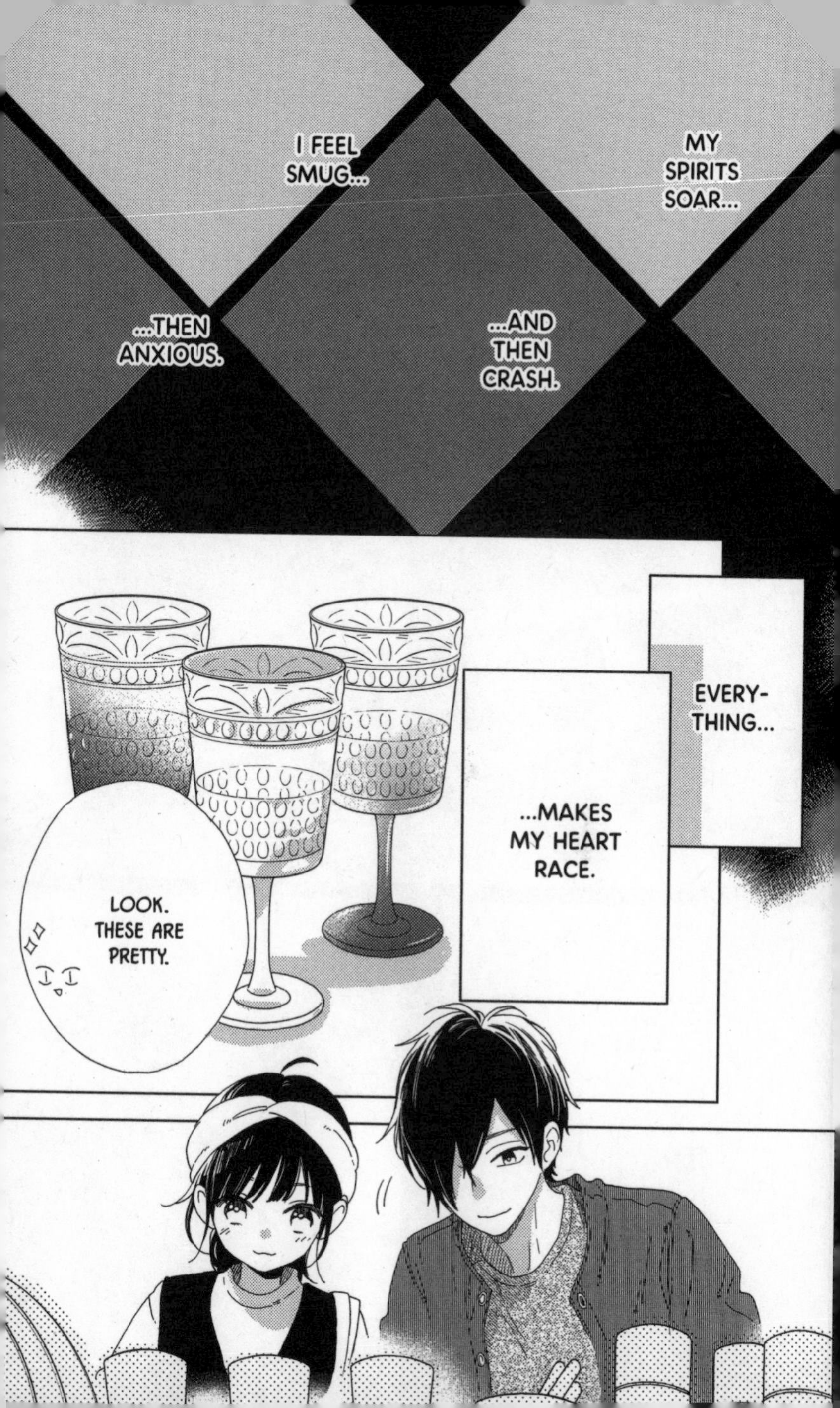
MY SPIRITS SOAR...
...AND THEN CRASH.
I FEEL SMUG...
...THEN ANXIOUS.
EVERY-THING...
...MAKES MY HEART RACE.
LOOK. THESE ARE PRETTY.

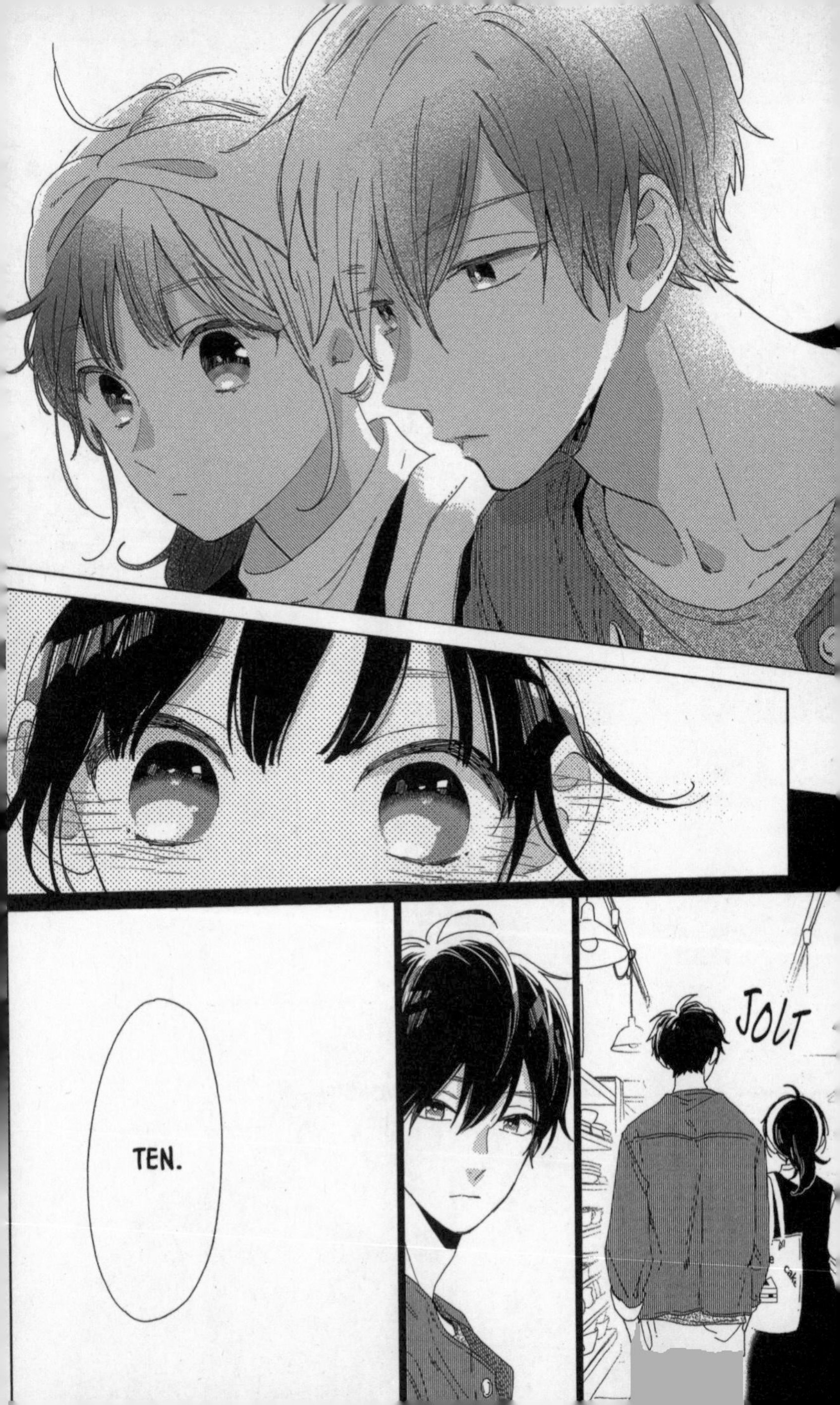
JOLT
TEN.

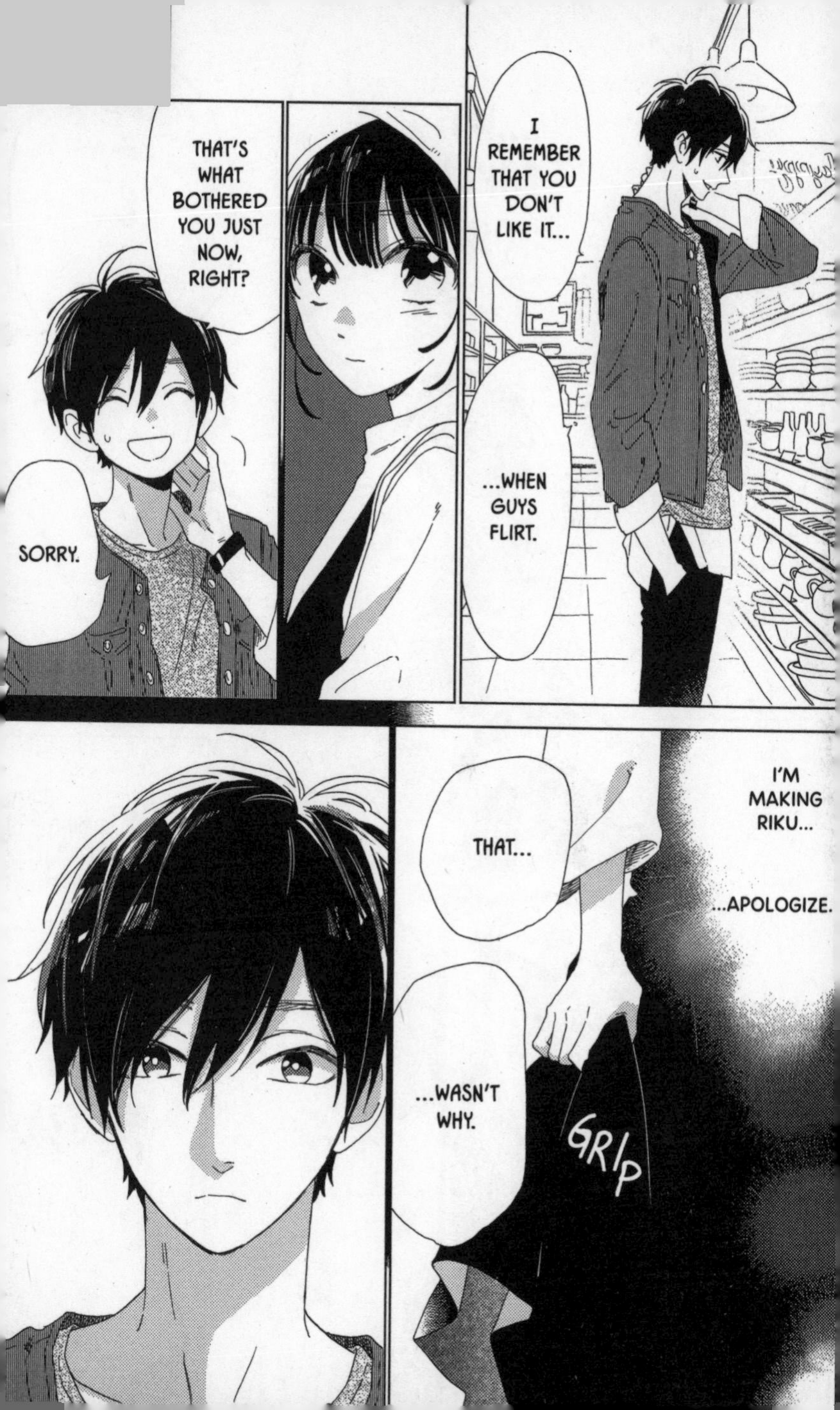
I REMEMBER THAT YOU DON'T LIKE IT...
...WHEN GUYS FLIRT.
THAT'S WHAT BOTHERED YOU JUST NOW, RIGHT?
SORRY.
I'M MAKING RIKU...
...APOLOGIZE.
THAT...
...WASN'T WHY.
GRIP

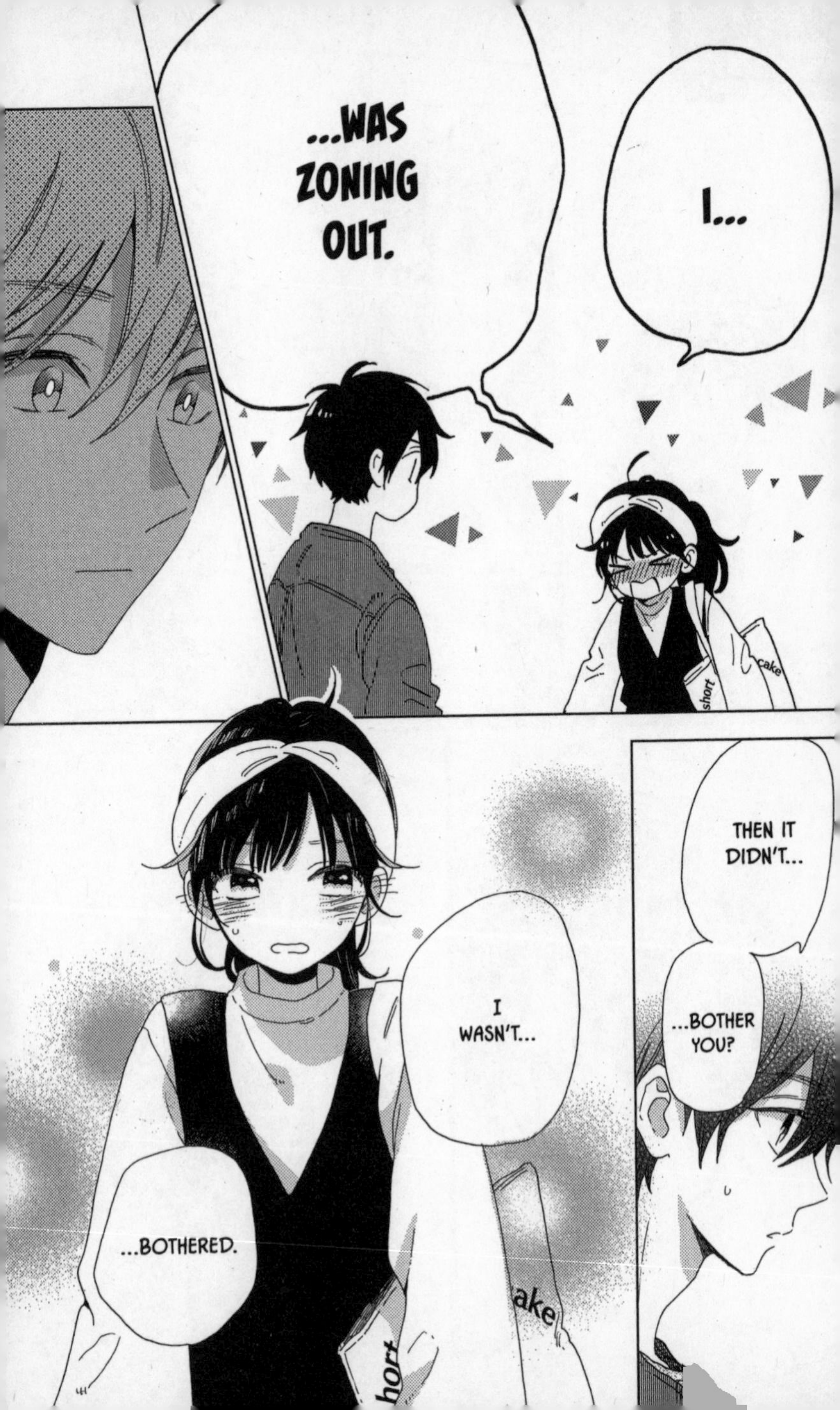
I...
...WAS ZONING OUT.
short
cake
THEN IT DIDN'T...
...BOTHER YOU?
I WASN'T...
...BOTHERED.

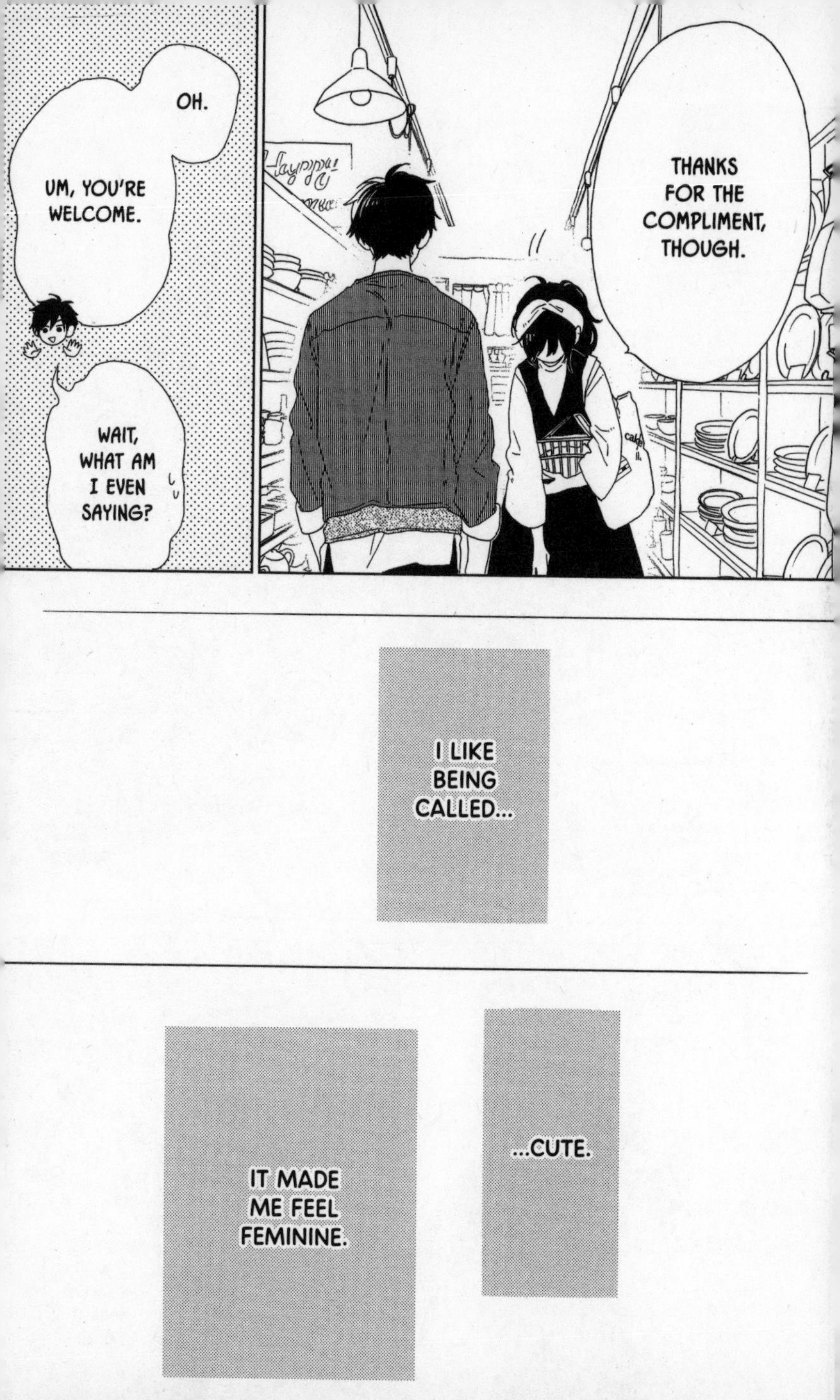
THANKS FOR THE COMPLIMENT, THOUGH.
OH.
UM, YOU'RE WELCOME.
WAIT, WHAT AM I EVEN SAYING?
I LIKE BEING CALLED...
...CUTE.
IT MADE ME FEEL FEMININE.

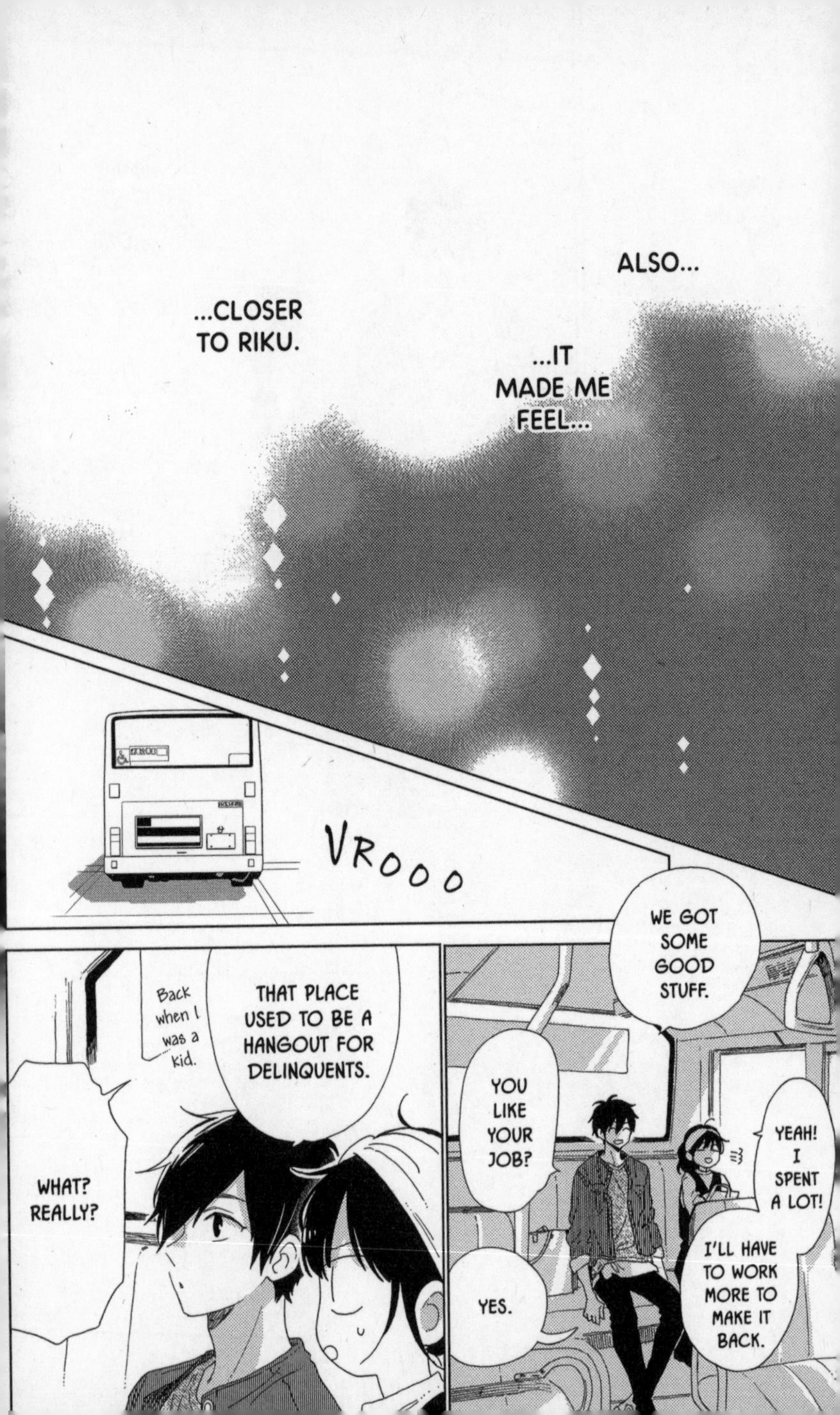
ALSO...
...IT MADE ME FEEL...
...CLOSER TO RIKU.
VROOOO
WE GOT SOME GOOD STUFF.
YEAH! I SPENT A LOT!
I'LL HAVE TO WORK MORE TO MAKE IT BACK.
YOU LIKE YOUR JOB?
YES.
THAT PLACE USED TO BE A HANGOUT FOR DELINQUENTS.
Back when I was a kid.
WHAT? REALLY?

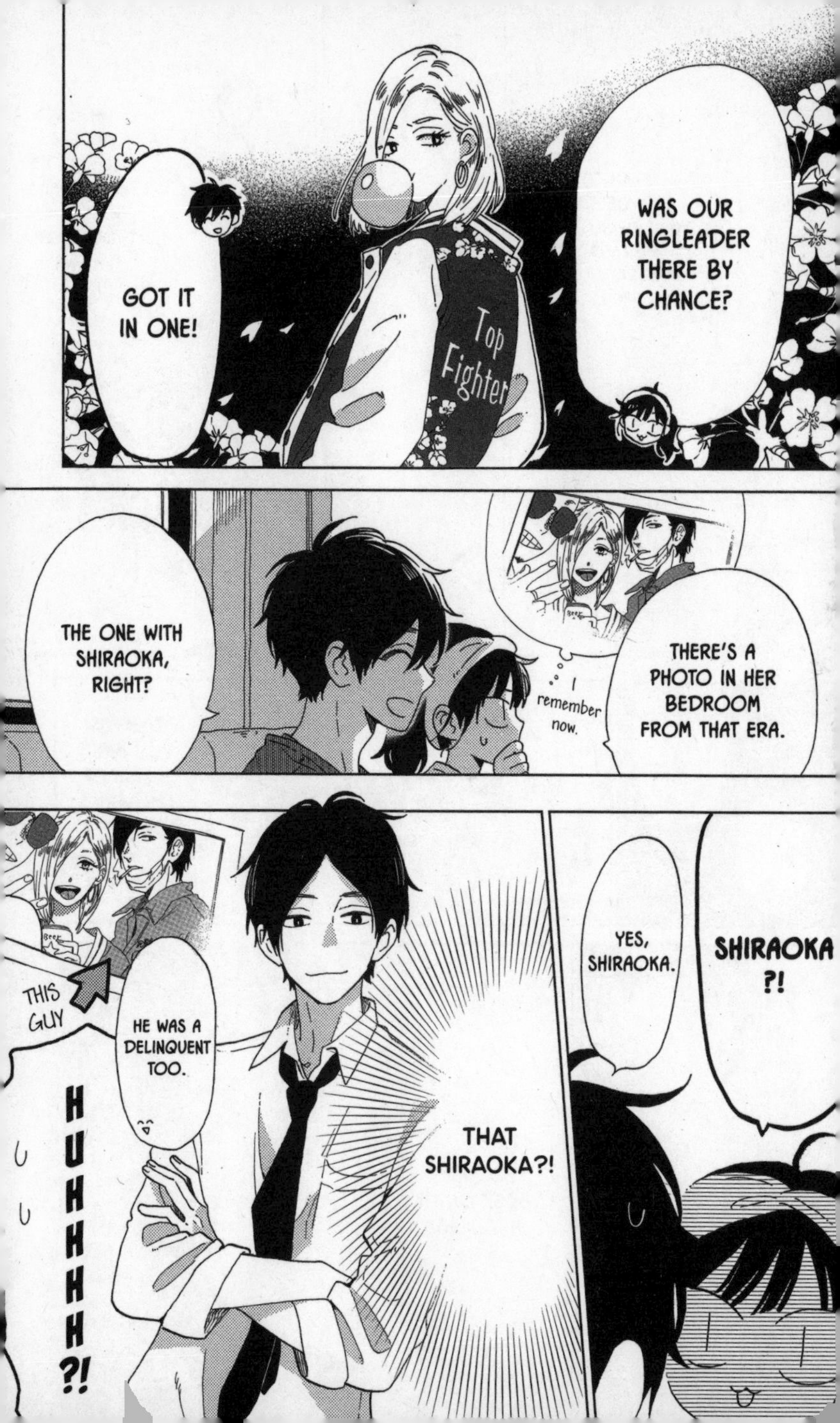
WAS OUR RINGLEADER THERE BY CHANCE?
Top Fighter
GOT IT IN ONE!
THERE'S A PHOTO IN HER BEDROOM FROM THAT ERA.
I remember now.
THE ONE WITH SHIRAOKA, RIGHT?
SHIRAOKA ?!
YES, SHIRAOKA.
THAT SHIRAOKA?!
HE WAS A DELINQUENT TOO.
THIS GUY
HUHHHHH?!

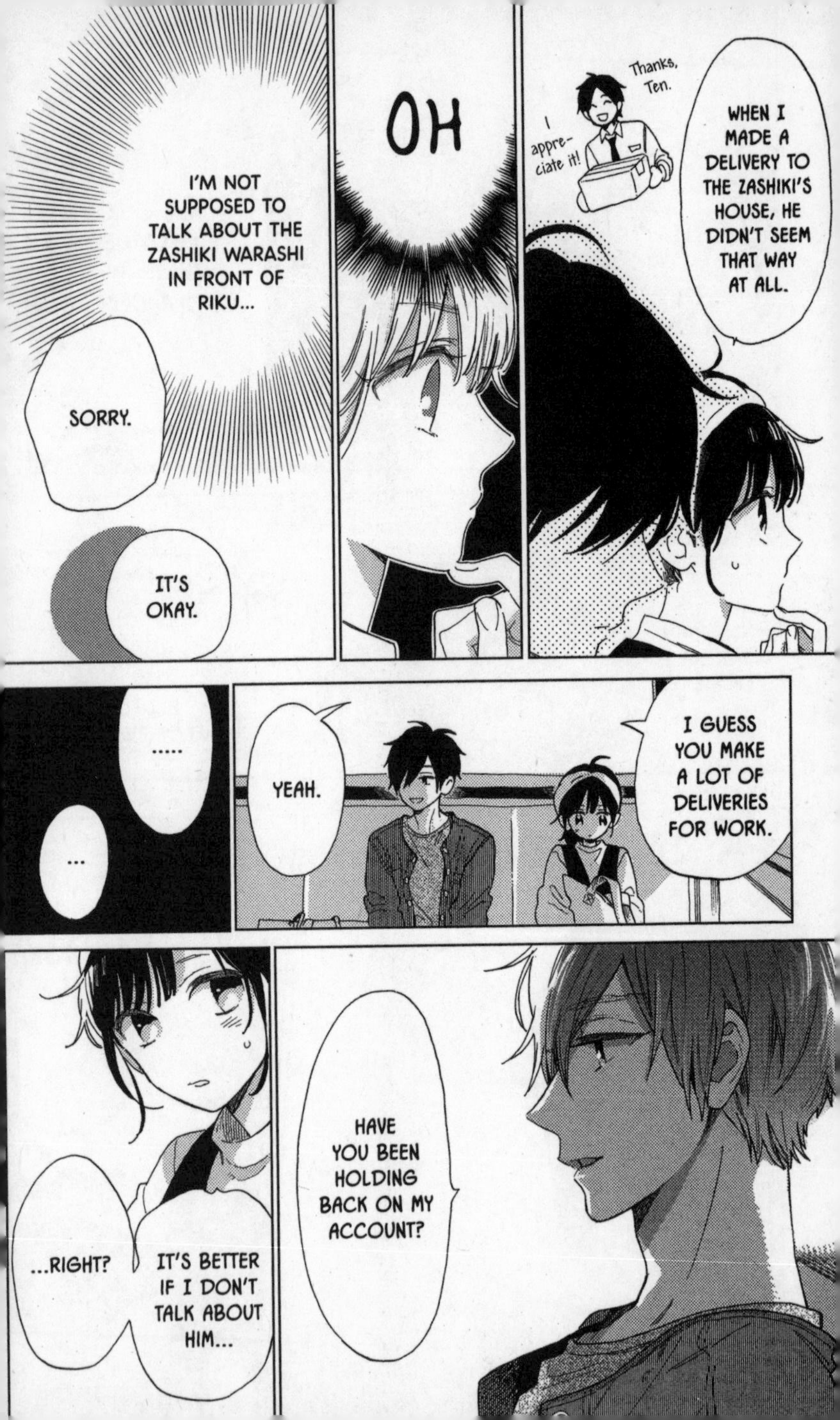
WHEN I MADE A DELIVERY TO THE ZASHIKI'S HOUSE, HE DIDN'T SEEM THAT WAY AT ALL.
Thanks, Ten.
I appreciate it!
OH
I'M NOT SUPPOSED TO TALK ABOUT THE ZASHIKI WARASHI IN FRONT OF RIKU...
SORRY.
IT'S OKAY.
I GUESS YOU MAKE A LOT OF DELIVERIES FOR WORK.
YEAH.
.....
...
HAVE YOU BEEN HOLDING BACK ON MY ACCOUNT?
IT'S BETTER IF I DON'T TALK ABOUT HIM...
...RIGHT?

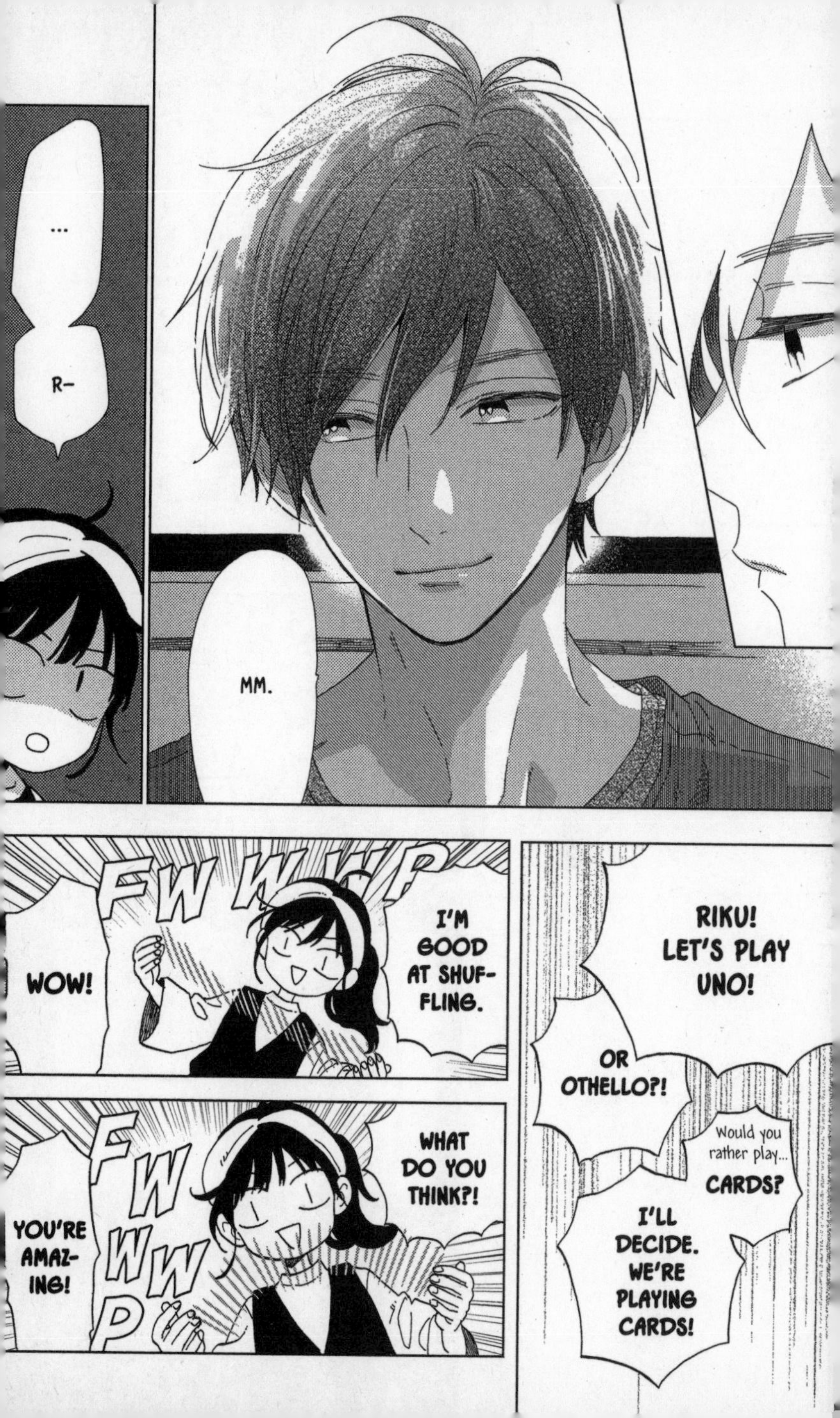
MM.
...
R-
RIKU! LET'S PLAY UNO!
OR OTHELLO?!
Would you rather play... CARDS?
I'LL DECIDE. WE'RE PLAYING CARDS!
FWWWP
I'M GOOD AT SHUF-FLING.
WOW!
FWWWP
WHAT DO YOU THINK?!
YOU'RE AMAZ-ING!

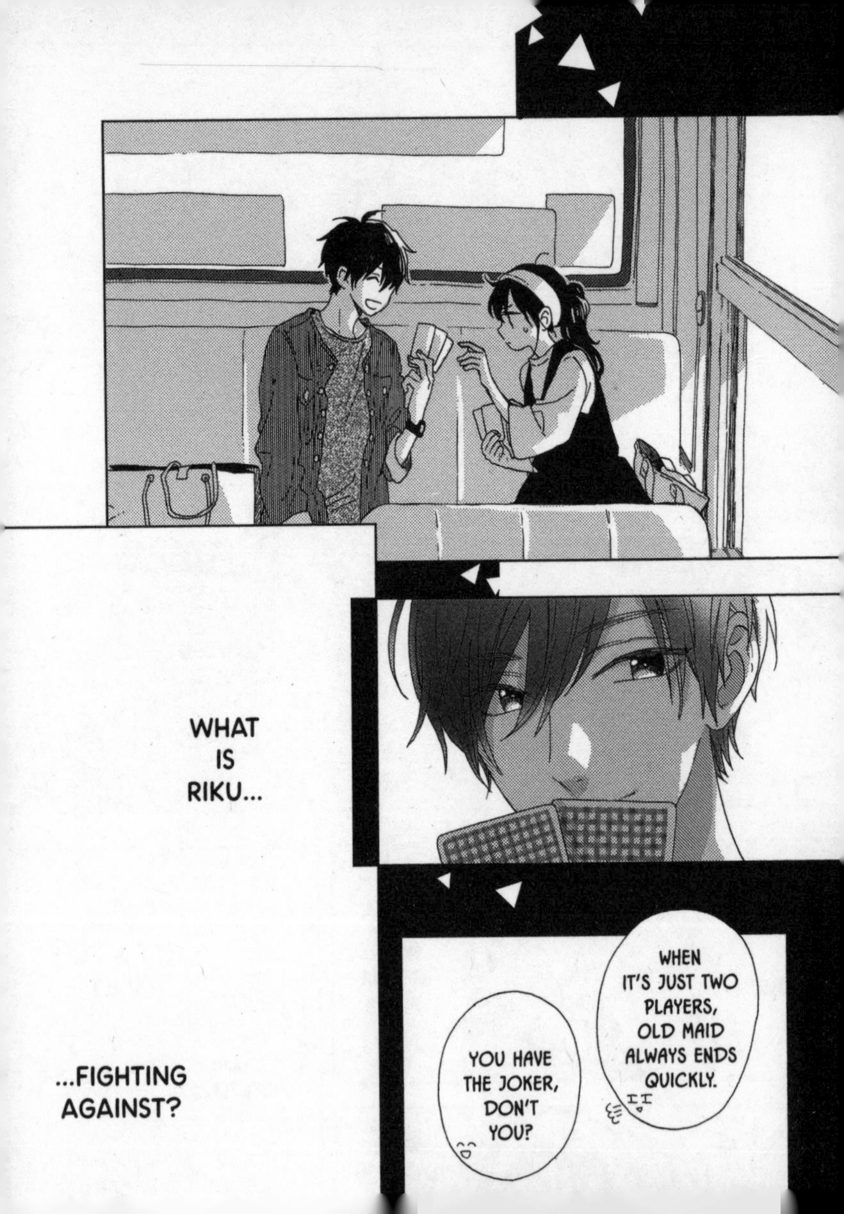
WHEN IT'S JUST TWO PLAYERS, OLD MAID ALWAYS ENDS QUICKLY.
YOU HAVE THE JOKER, DON'T YOU?
WHAT IS RIKU...
...FIGHTING AGAINST?

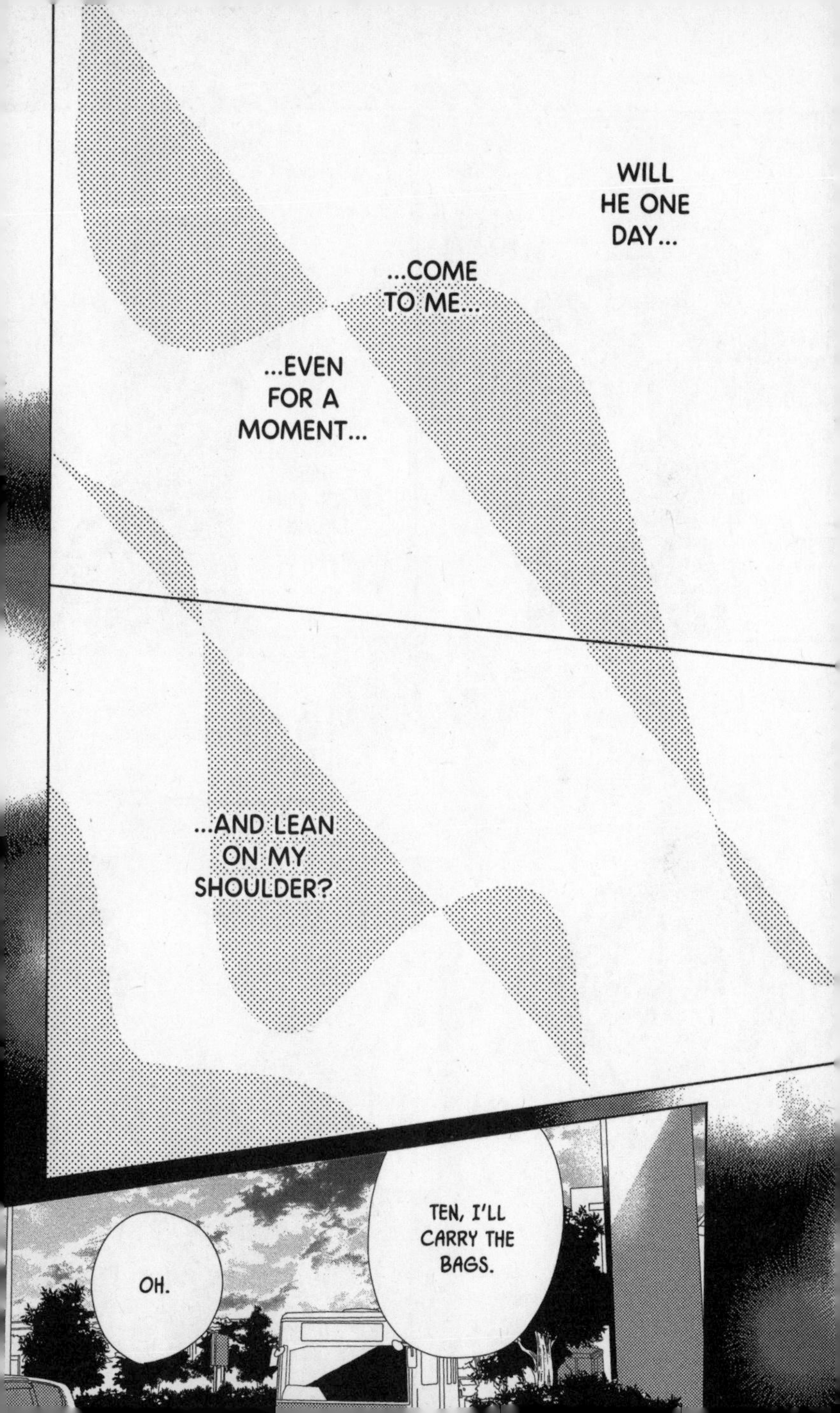
WILL HE ONE DAY...
...COME TO ME...
...EVEN FOR A MOMENT...
...AND LEAN ON MY SHOULDER?
TEN, I'LL CARRY THE BAGS.
OH.

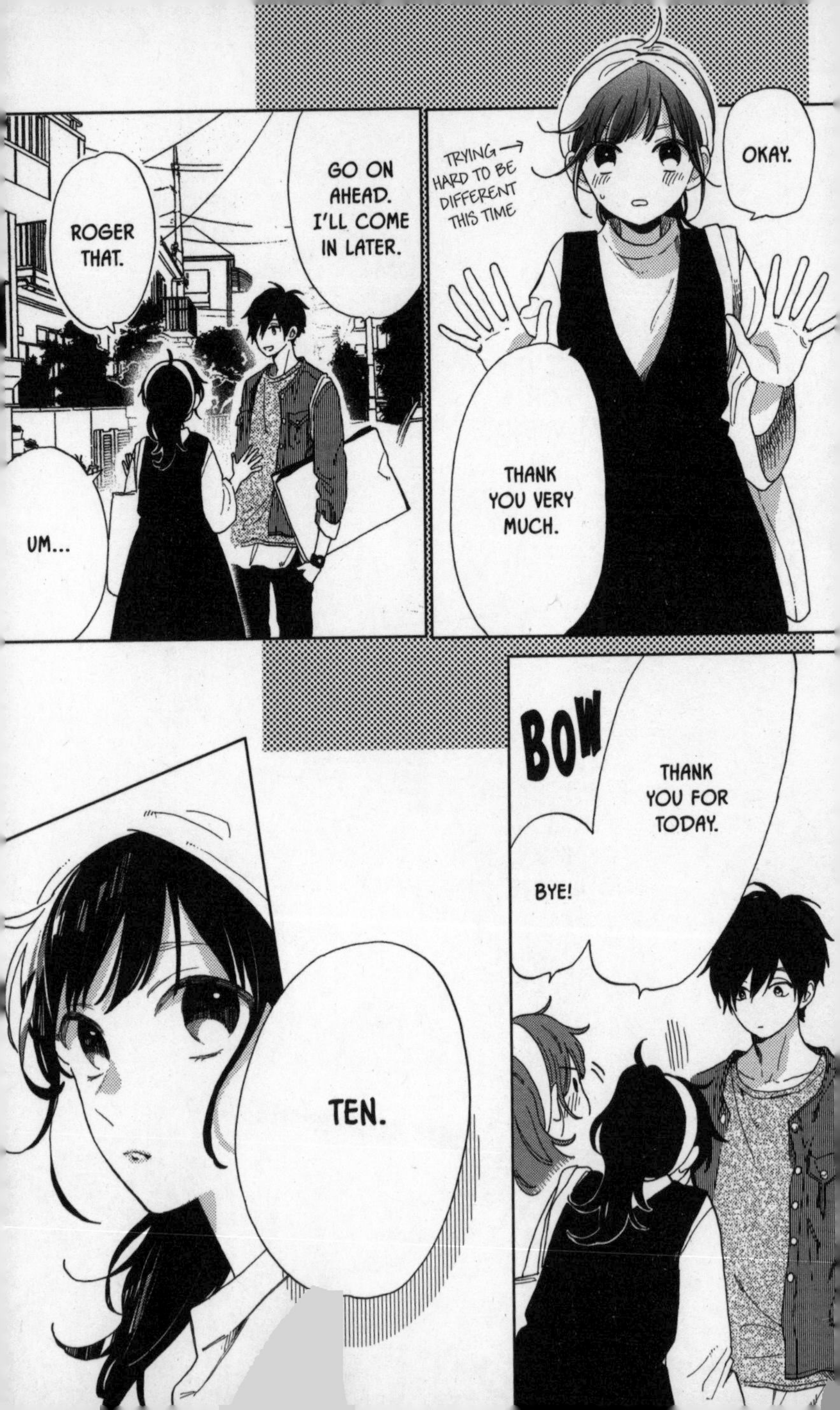
OKAY.
TRYING HARD TO BE DIFFERENT THIS TIME
THANK YOU VERY MUCH.
GO ON AHEAD. I'LL COME IN LATER.
ROGER THAT.
UM...
THANK YOU FOR TODAY.
BOW
BYE!
TEN.

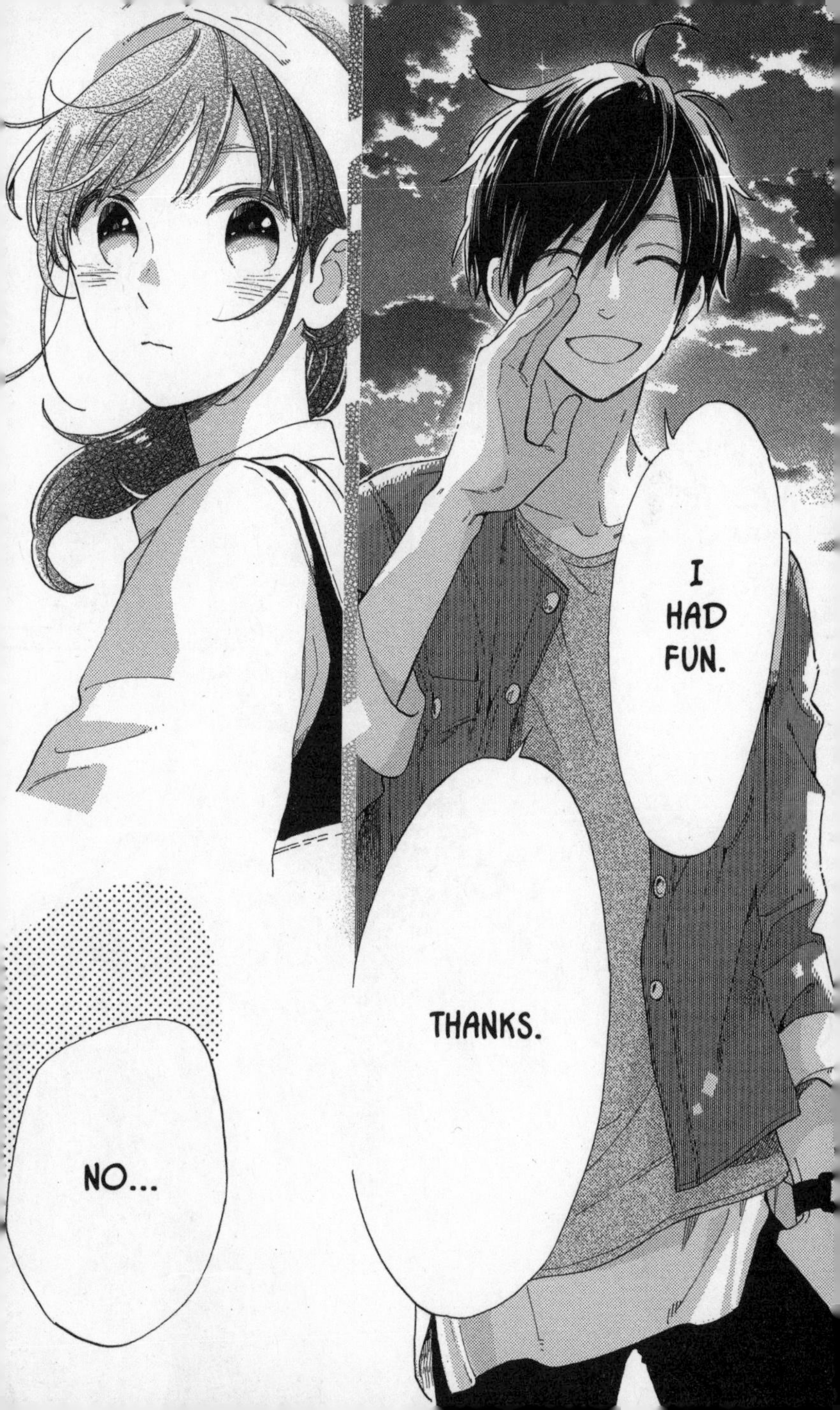
I HAD FUN.
THANKS.
NO...

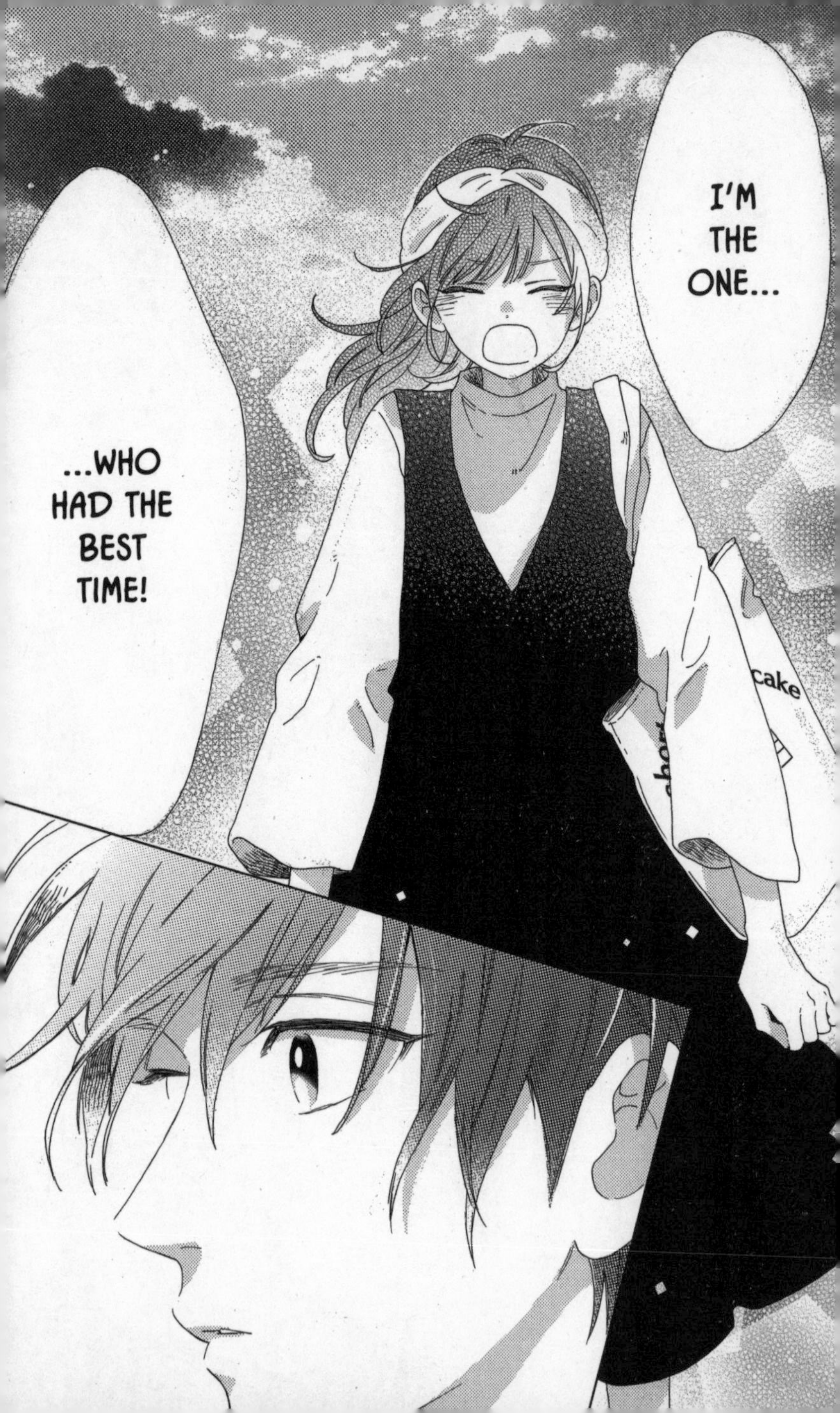
I'M THE ONE...
...WHO HAD THE BEST TIME!
cake

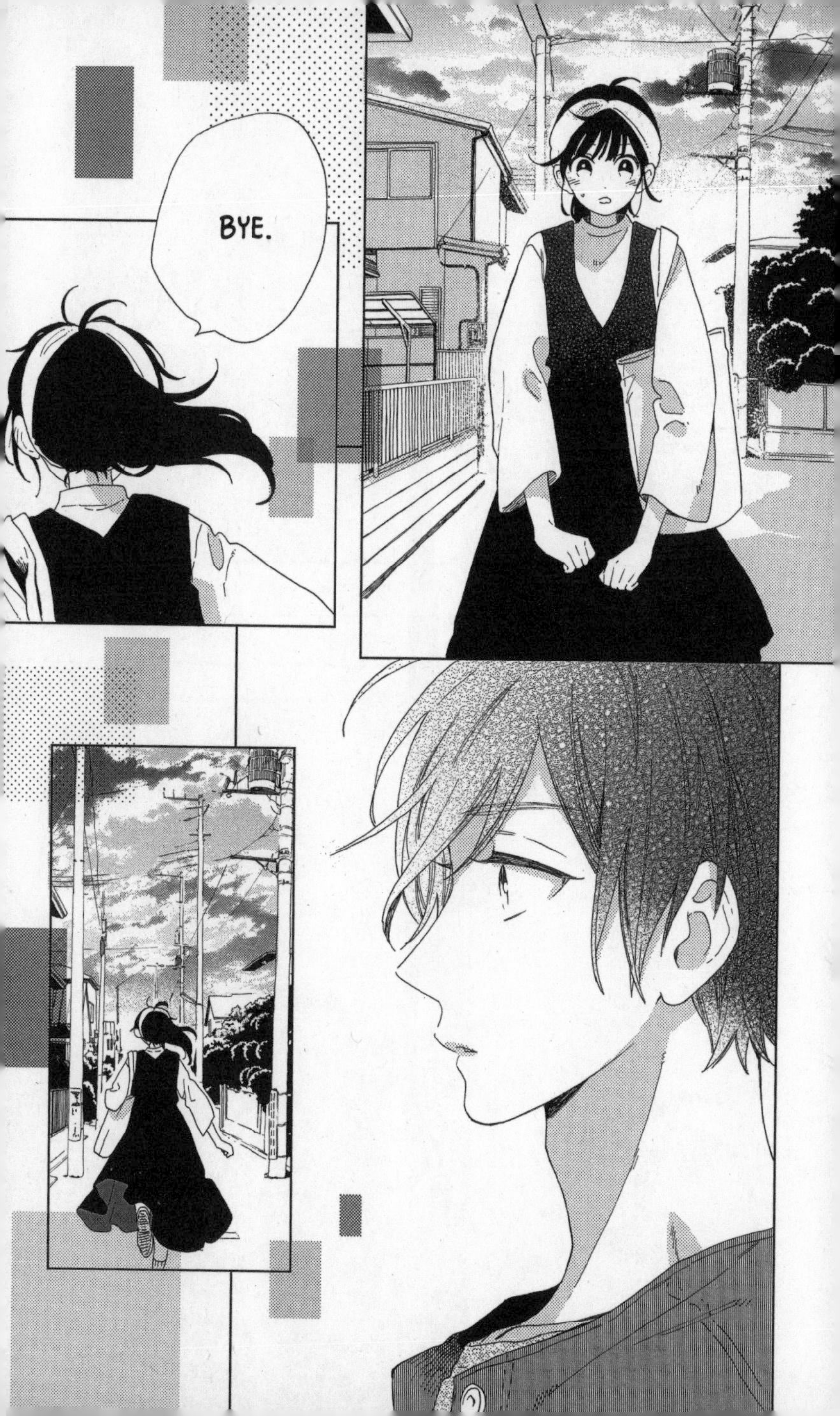
BYE.

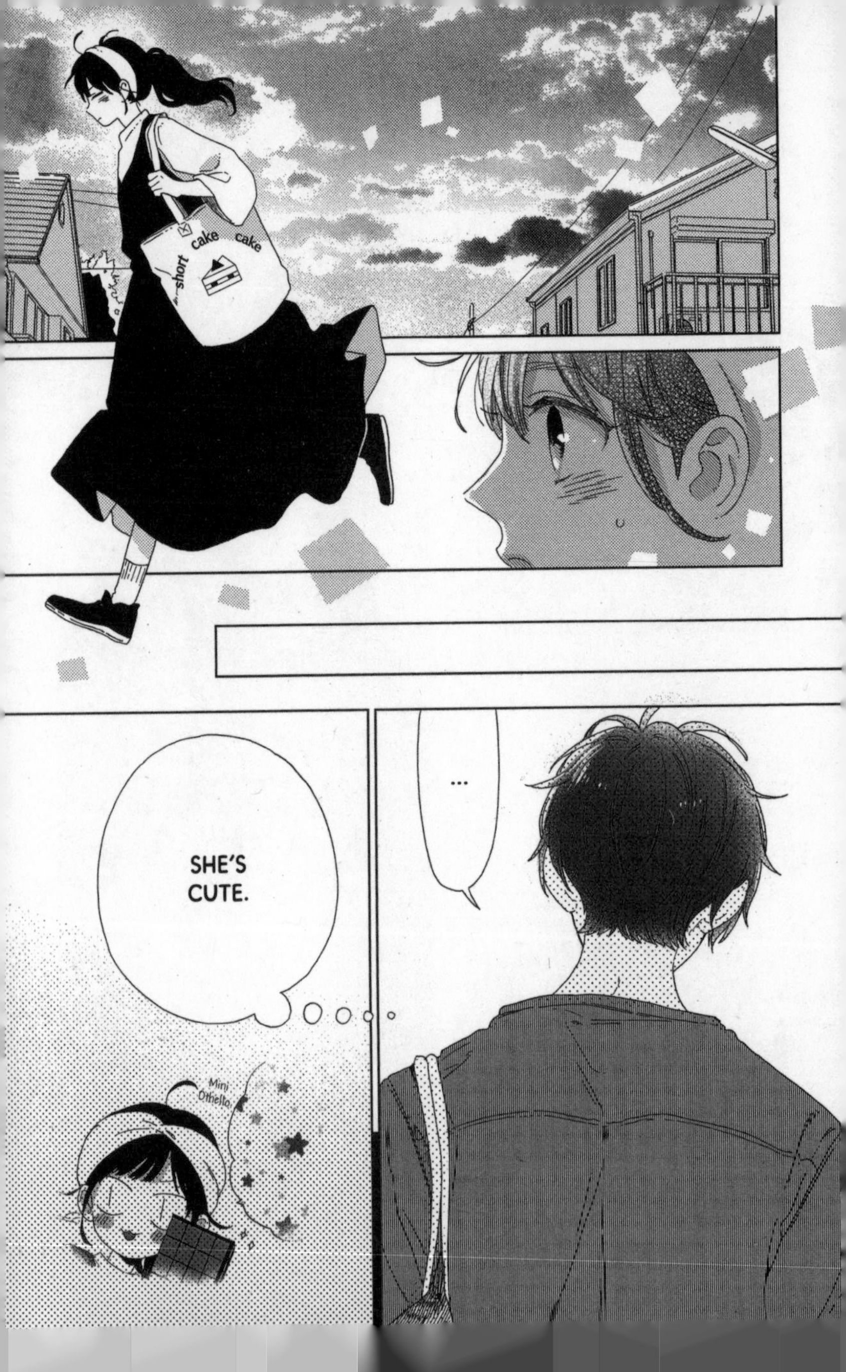
short cake cake
...
SHE'S CUTE.
Mini Othello

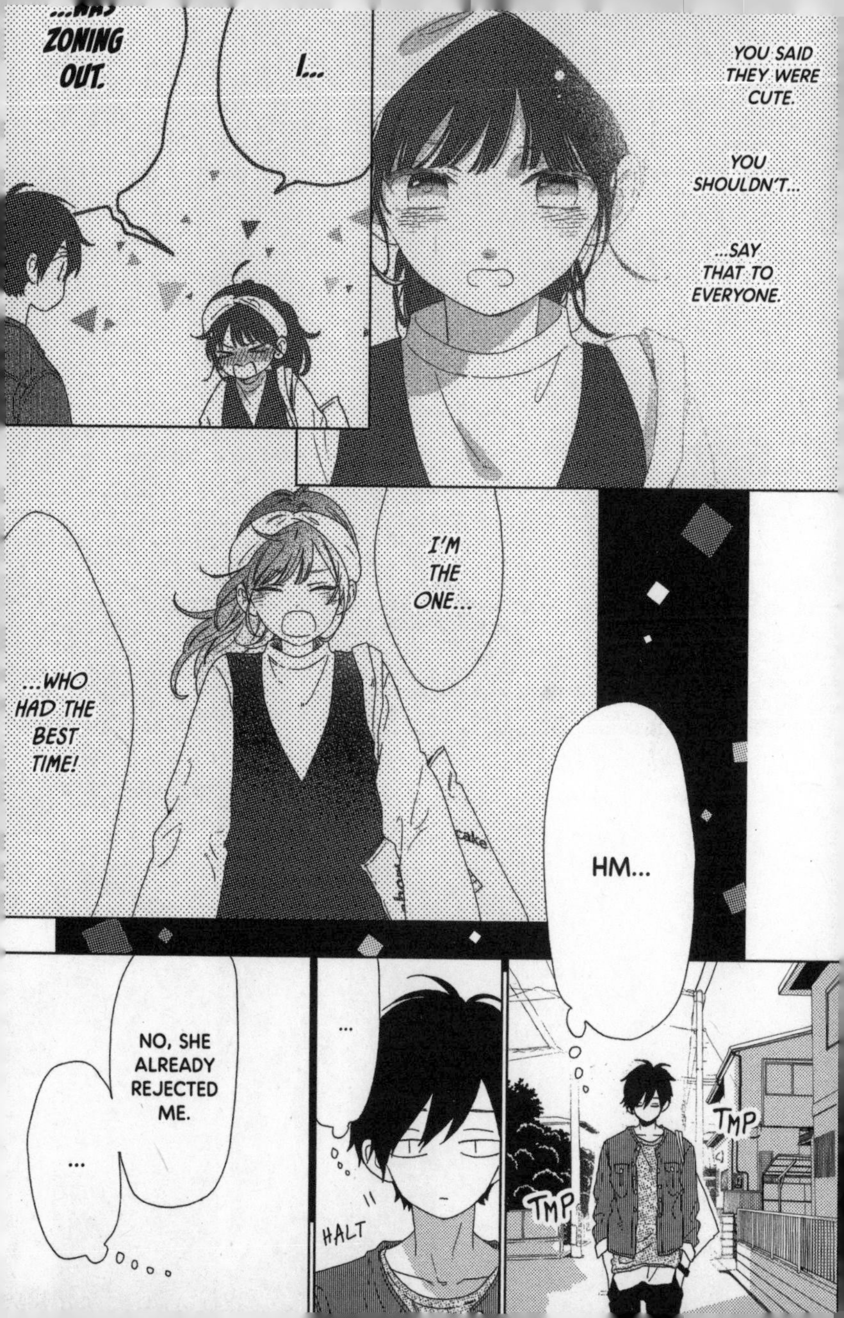
YOU SAID THEY WERE CUTE.
YOU SHOULDN'T...
...SAY THAT TO EVERYONE.
I...
...WAS ZONING OUT.
I'M THE ONE...
...WHO HAD THE BEST TIME!
HM...
TMP
TMP
...
HALT
NO, SHE ALREADY REJECTED ME.
...

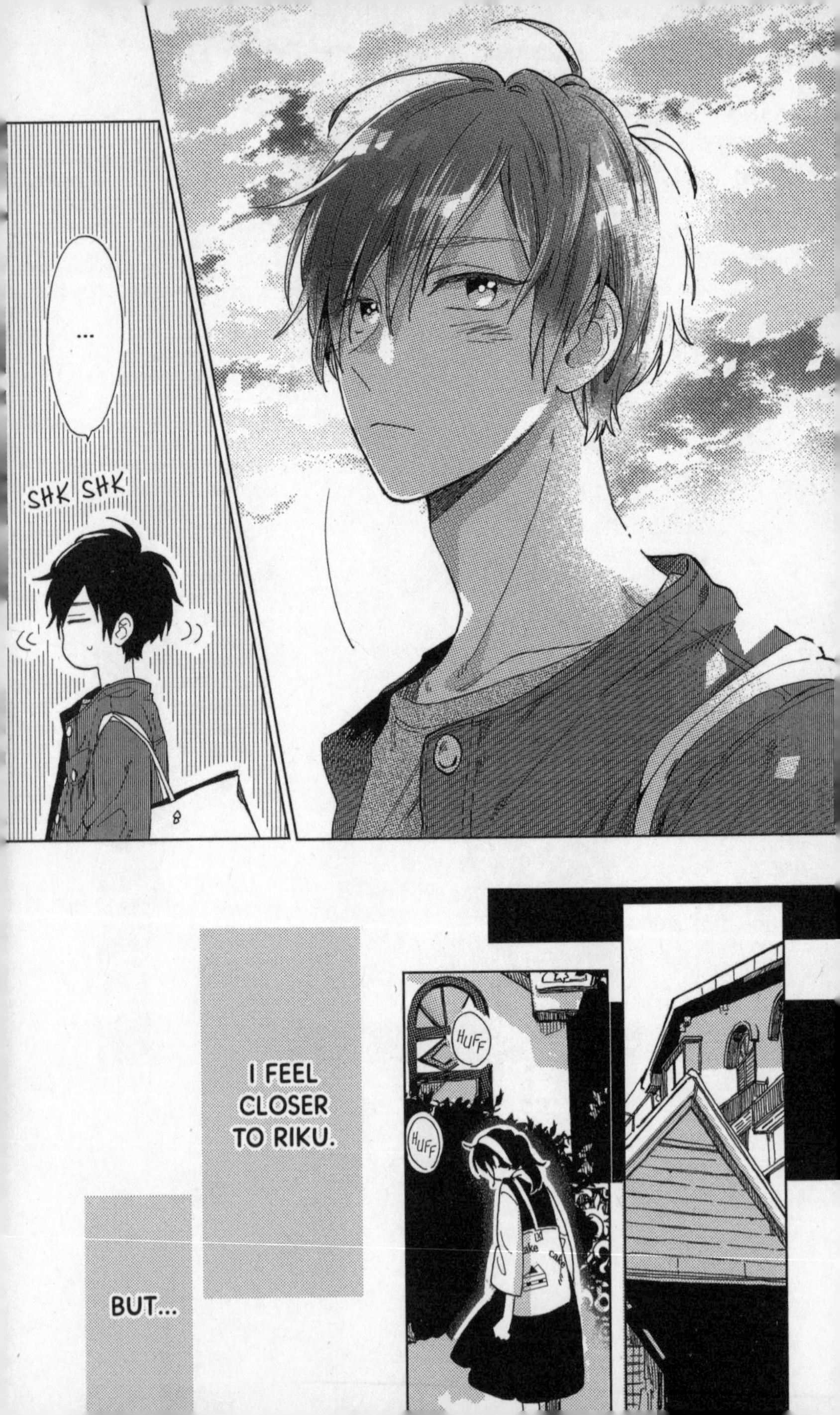
...
SHK SHK
HUFF
HUFF
I FEEL CLOSER TO RIKU.
BUT...

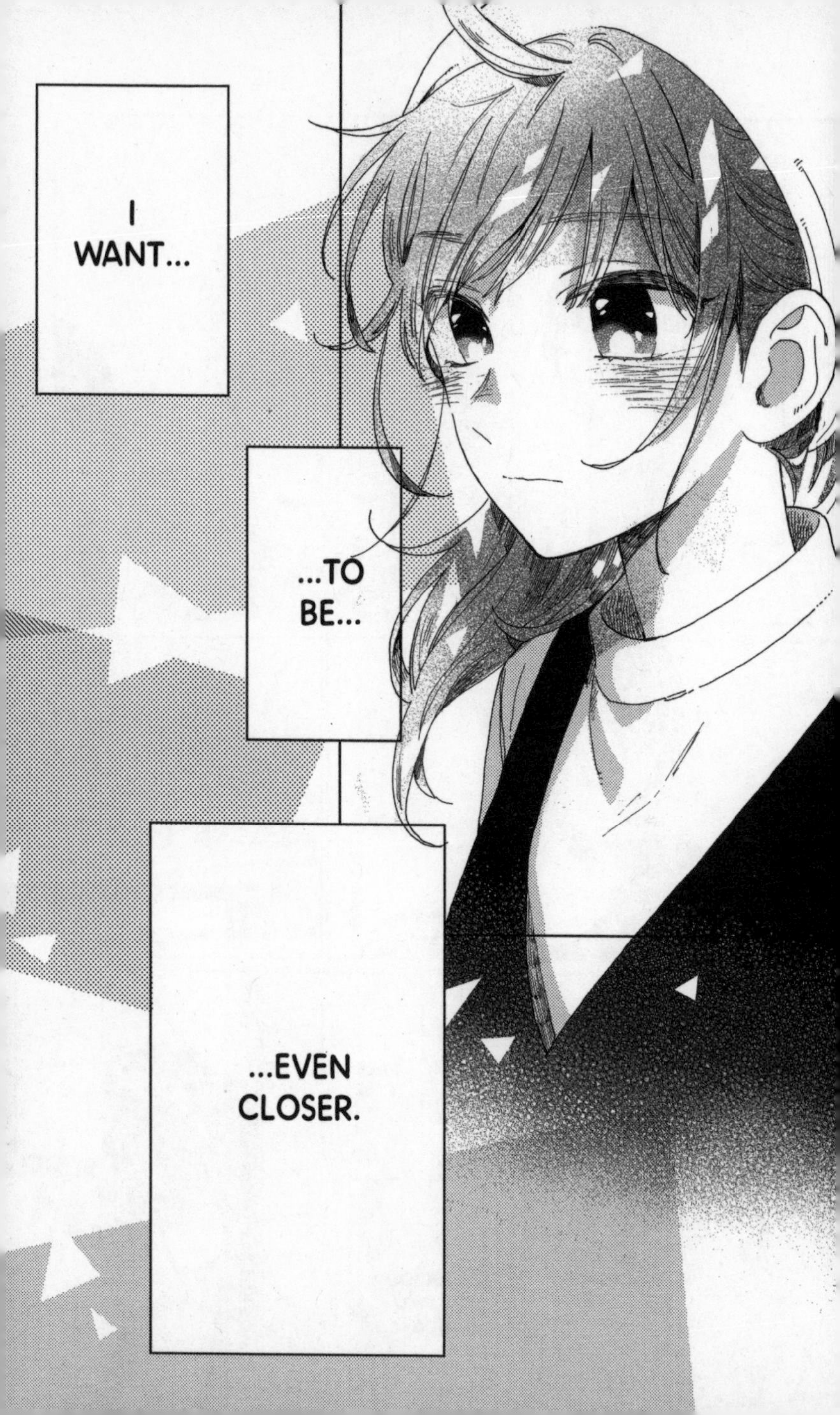
I WANT...
...TO BE...
...EVEN CLOSER.

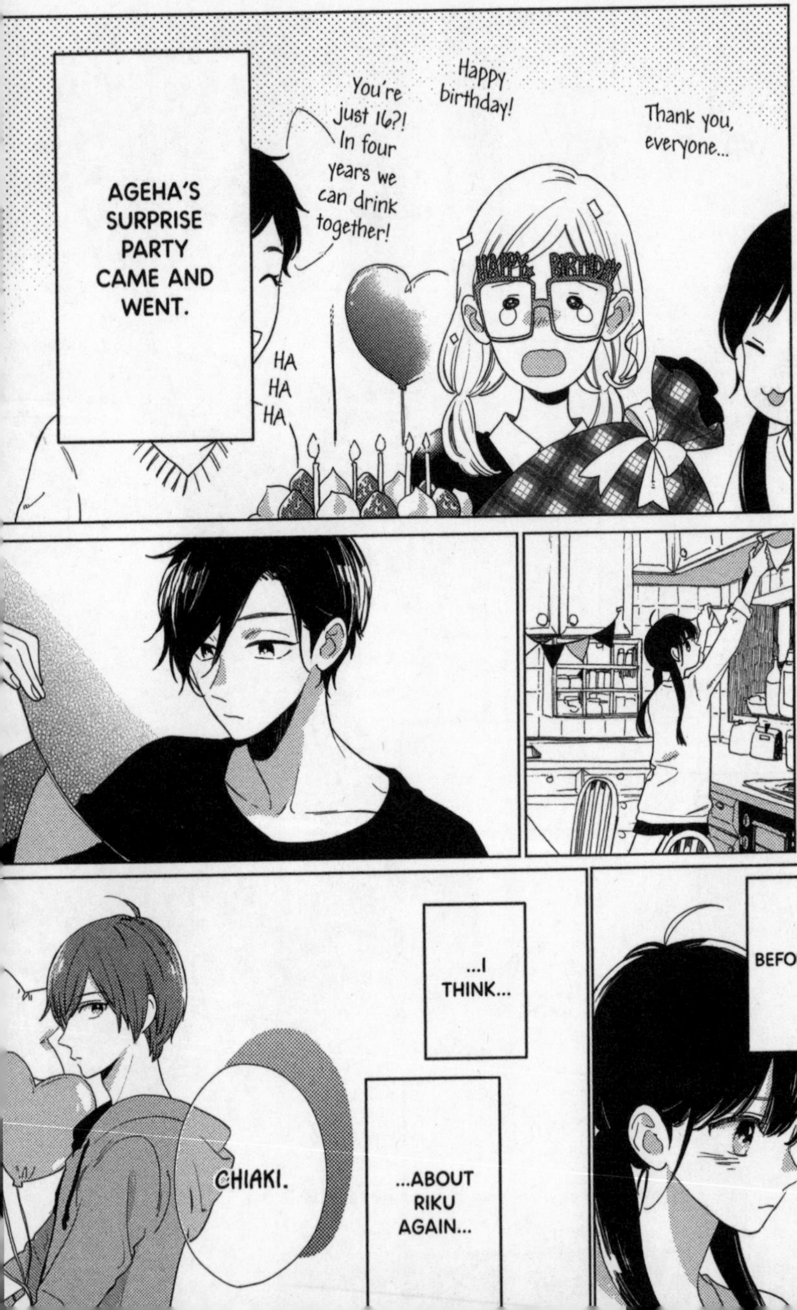
Thank you, everyone...
Happy birthday!
You're just 16?! In four years we can drink together!
AGEHA'S SURPRISE PARTY CAME AND WENT.
HA HA HA
BEFORE...
...I THINK...
...ABOUT RIKU AGAIN...
CHIAKI.

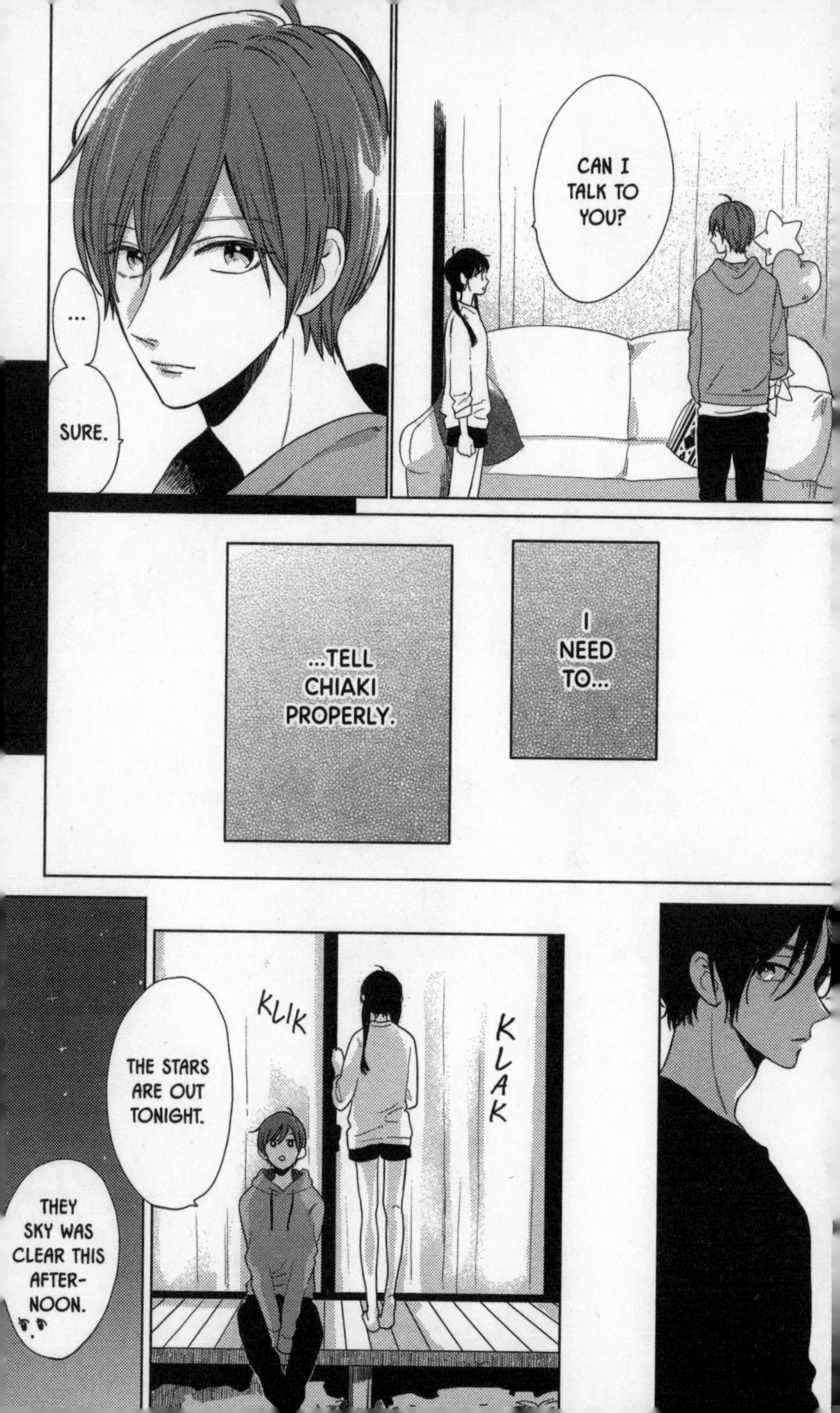
CAN I TALK TO YOU?
...
SURE.
I NEED TO...
...TELL CHIAKI PROPERLY.
KLAK
KLIK
THE STARS ARE OUT TONIGHT.
THEY SKY WAS CLEAR THIS AFTER-NOON.

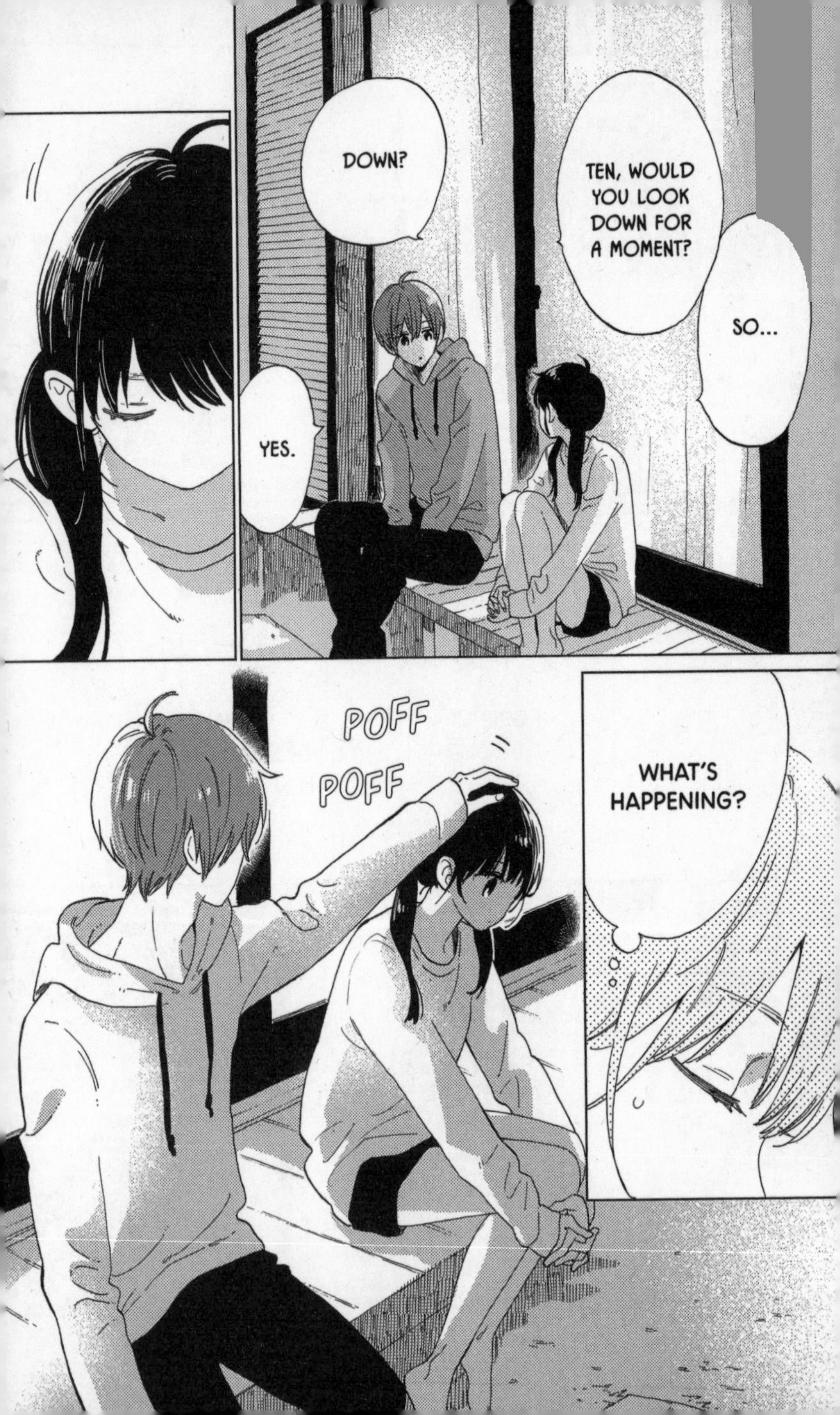
SO...
TEN, WOULD YOU LOOK DOWN FOR A MOMENT?
DOWN?
YES.
WHAT'S HAPPENING?
POFF
POFF

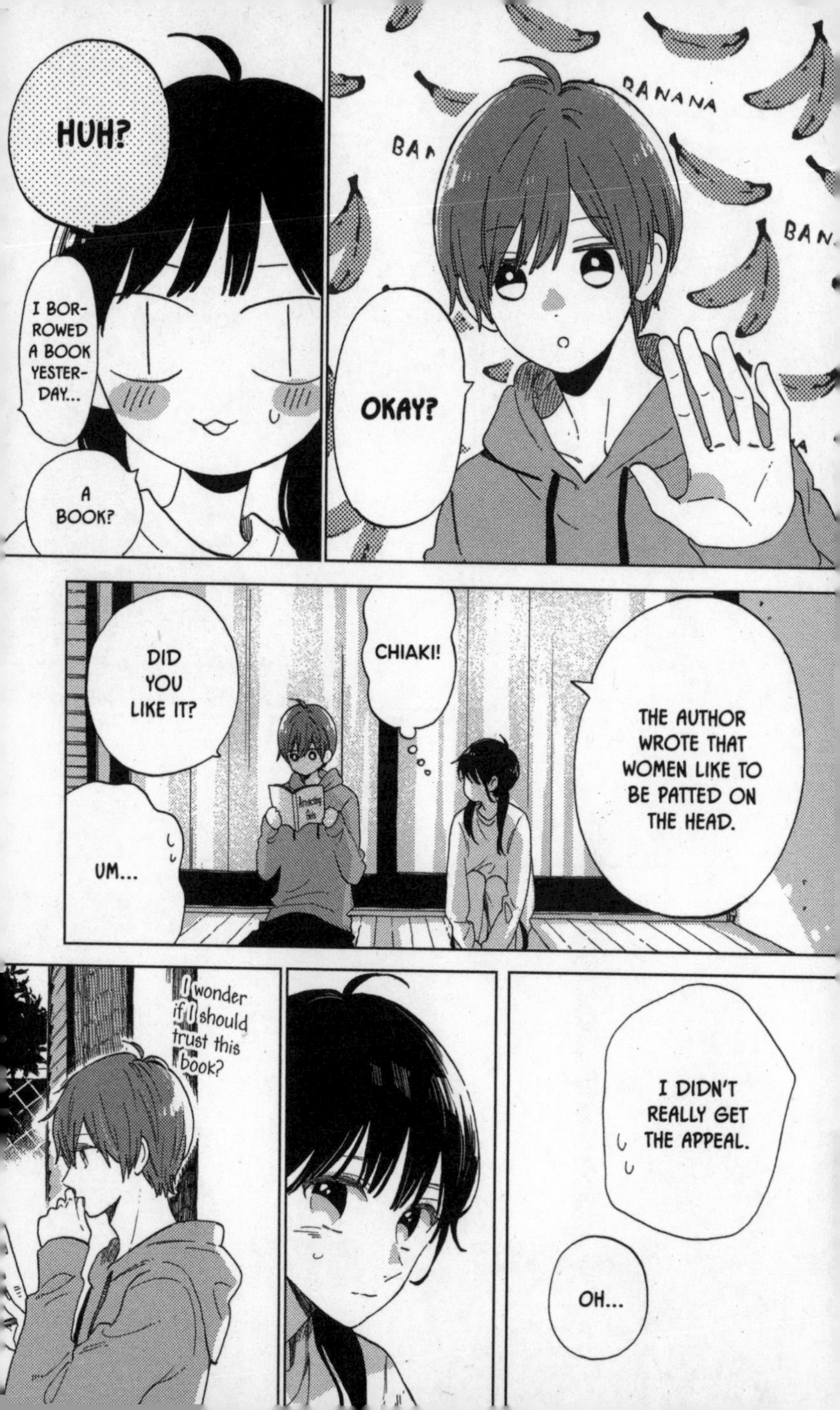
BANANA
BAN
BAN
OKAY?
HUH?
I BORROWED A BOOK YESTERDAY...
A BOOK?
THE AUTHOR WROTE THAT WOMEN LIKE TO BE PATTED ON THE HEAD.
CHIAKI!
DID YOU LIKE IT?
UM...
I DIDN'T REALLY GET THE APPEAL.
OH...
I wonder if I should trust this book?

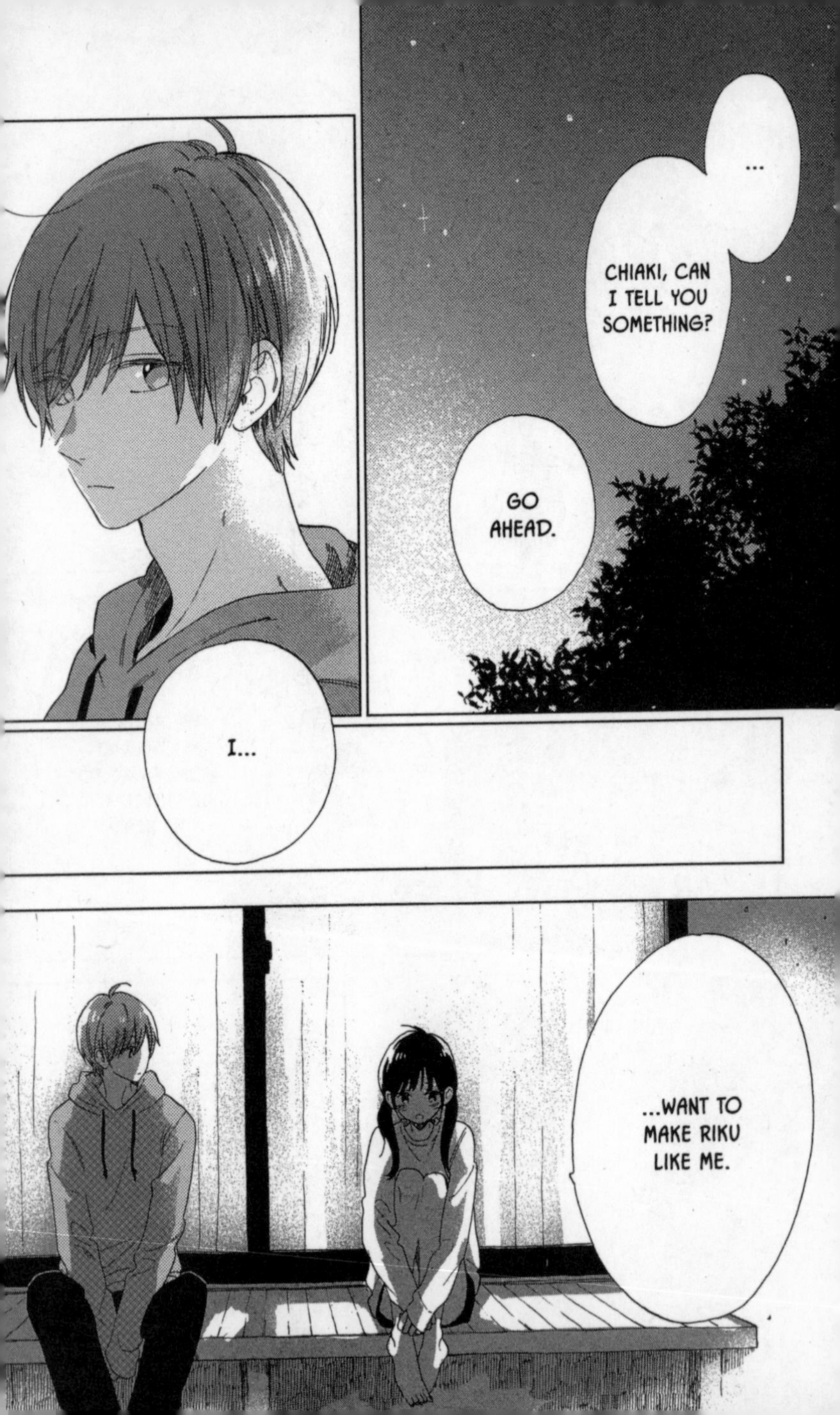
...
CHIAKI, CAN I TELL YOU SOMETHING?
GO AHEAD.
I...
...WANT TO MAKE RIKU LIKE ME.

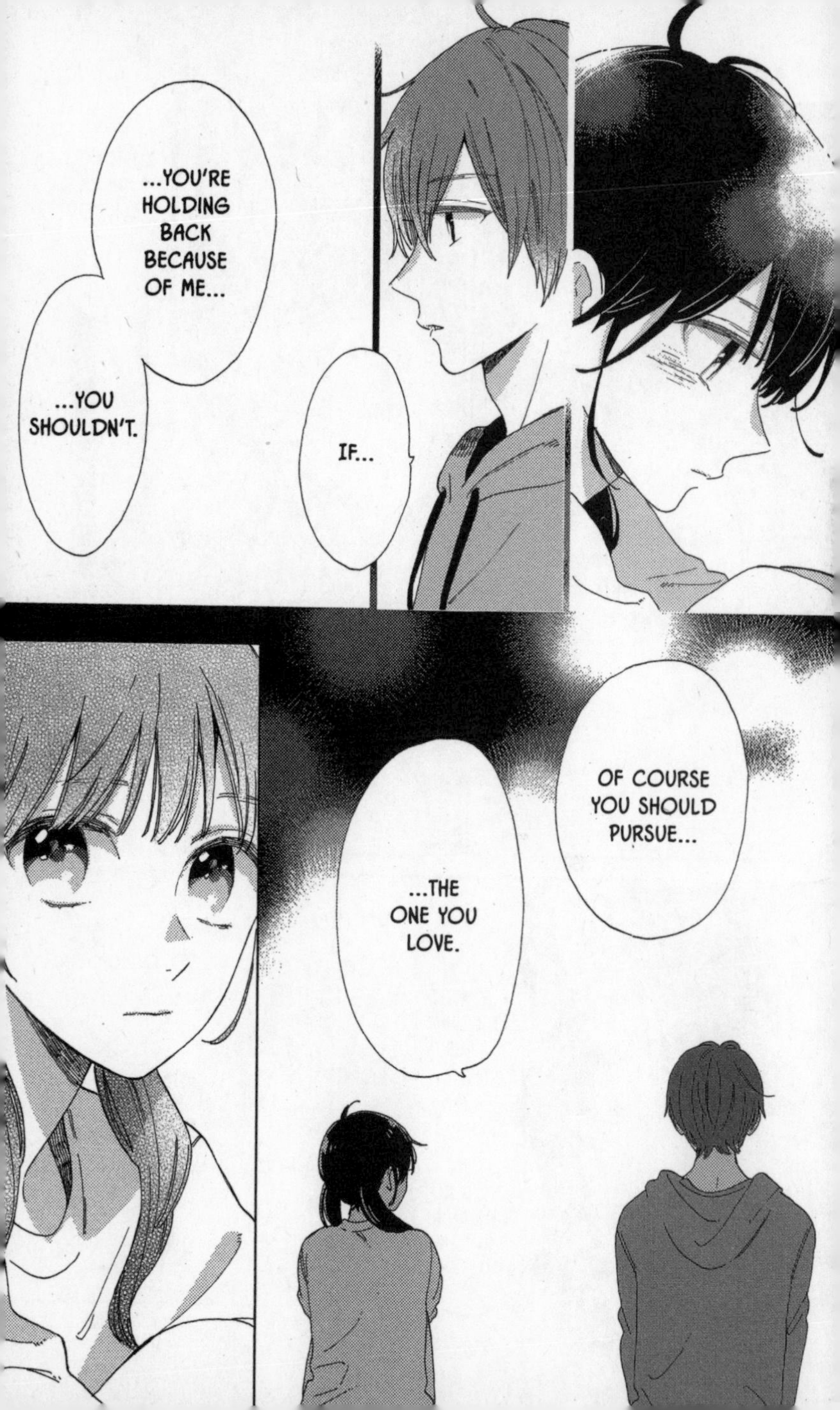
IF...
...YOU'RE HOLDING BACK BECAUSE OF ME...
...YOU SHOULDN'T.
OF COURSE YOU SHOULD PURSUE...
...THE ONE YOU LOVE.

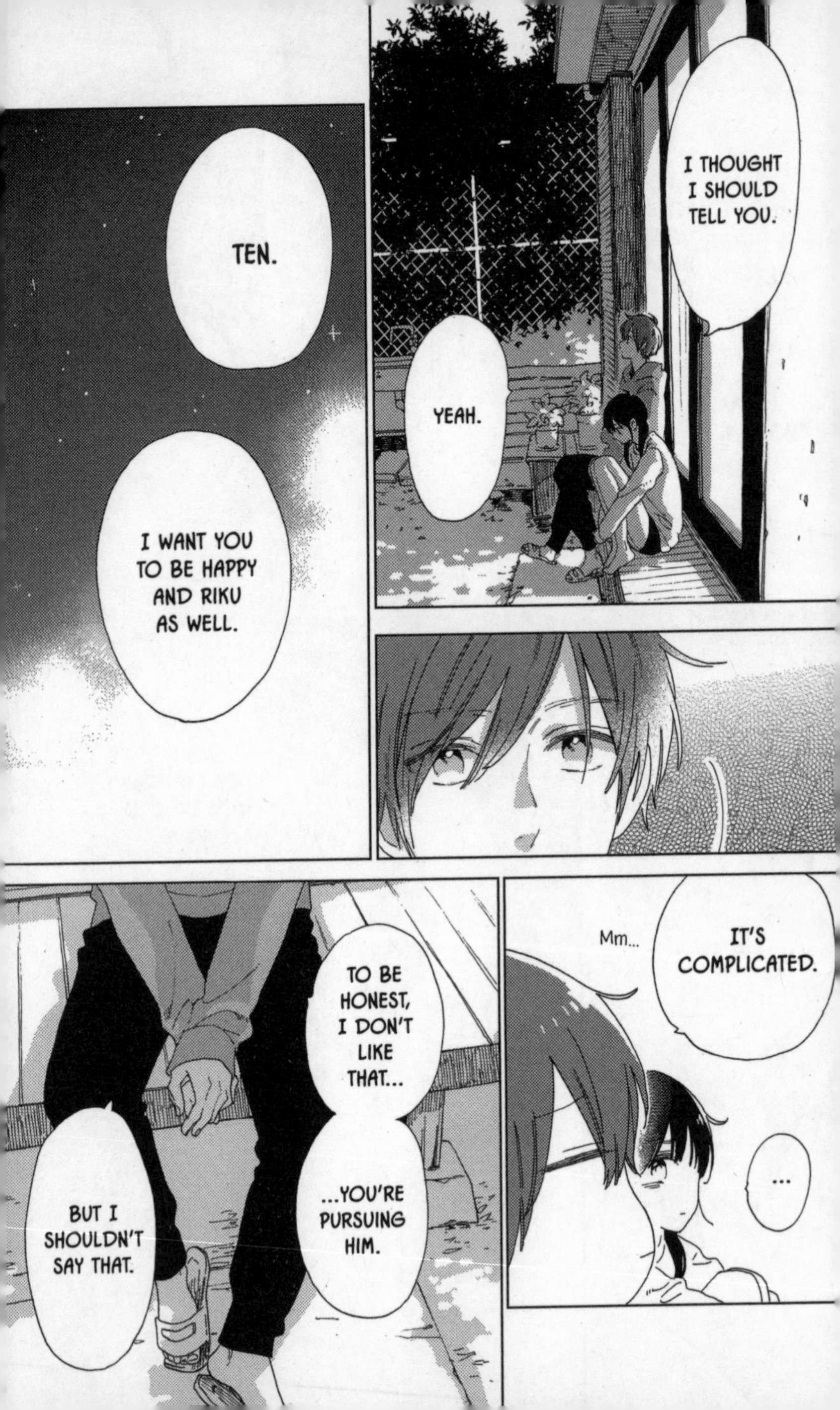
I THOUGHT I SHOULD TELL YOU.
YEAH.
TEN.
I WANT YOU TO BE HAPPY AND RIKU AS WELL.
IT'S COMPLICATED.
Mm...
...
TO BE HONEST, I DON'T LIKE THAT...
...YOU'RE PURSUING HIM.
BUT I SHOULDN'T SAY THAT.

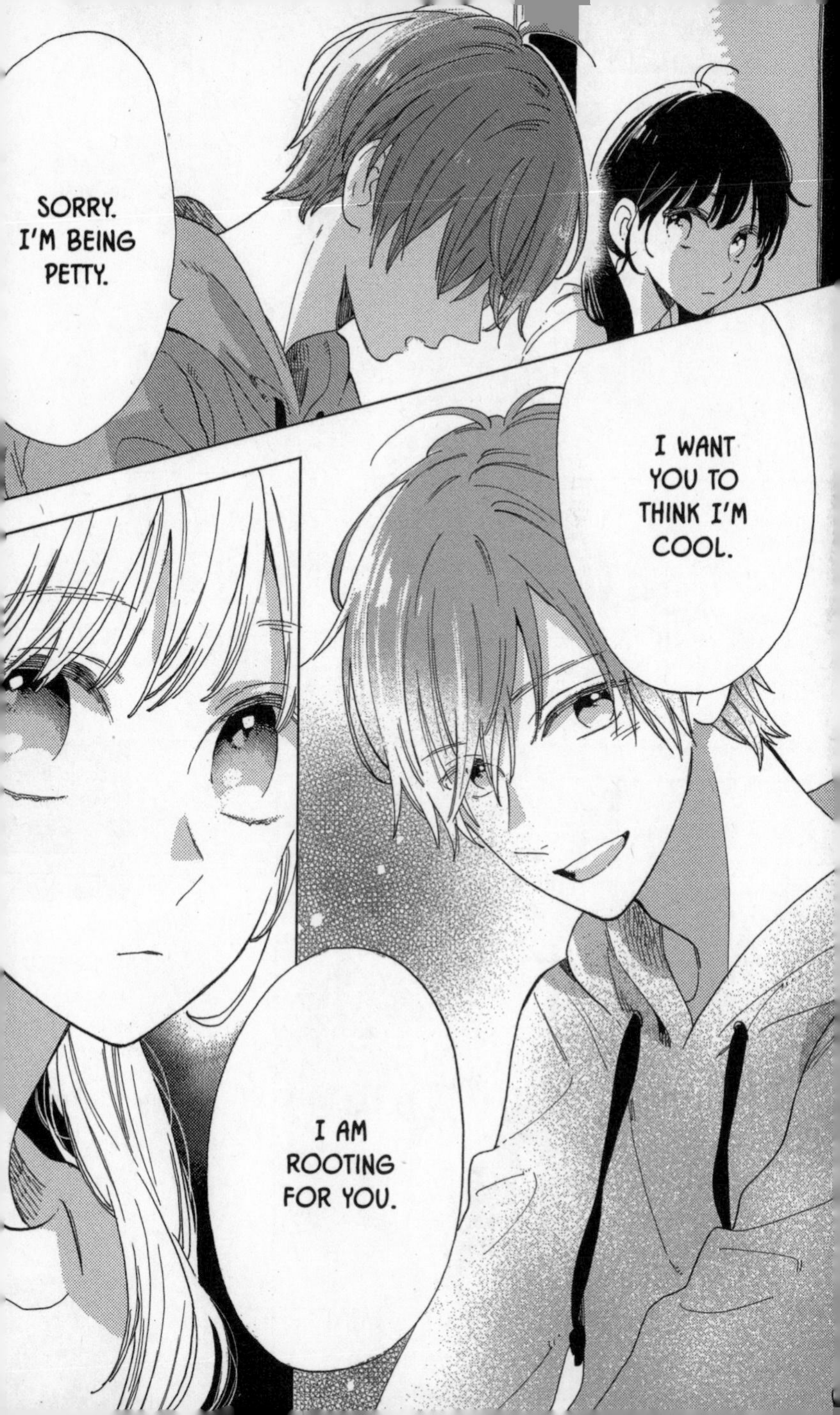
SORRY. I'M BEING PETTY.
I WANT YOU TO THINK I'M COOL.
I AM ROOTING FOR YOU.

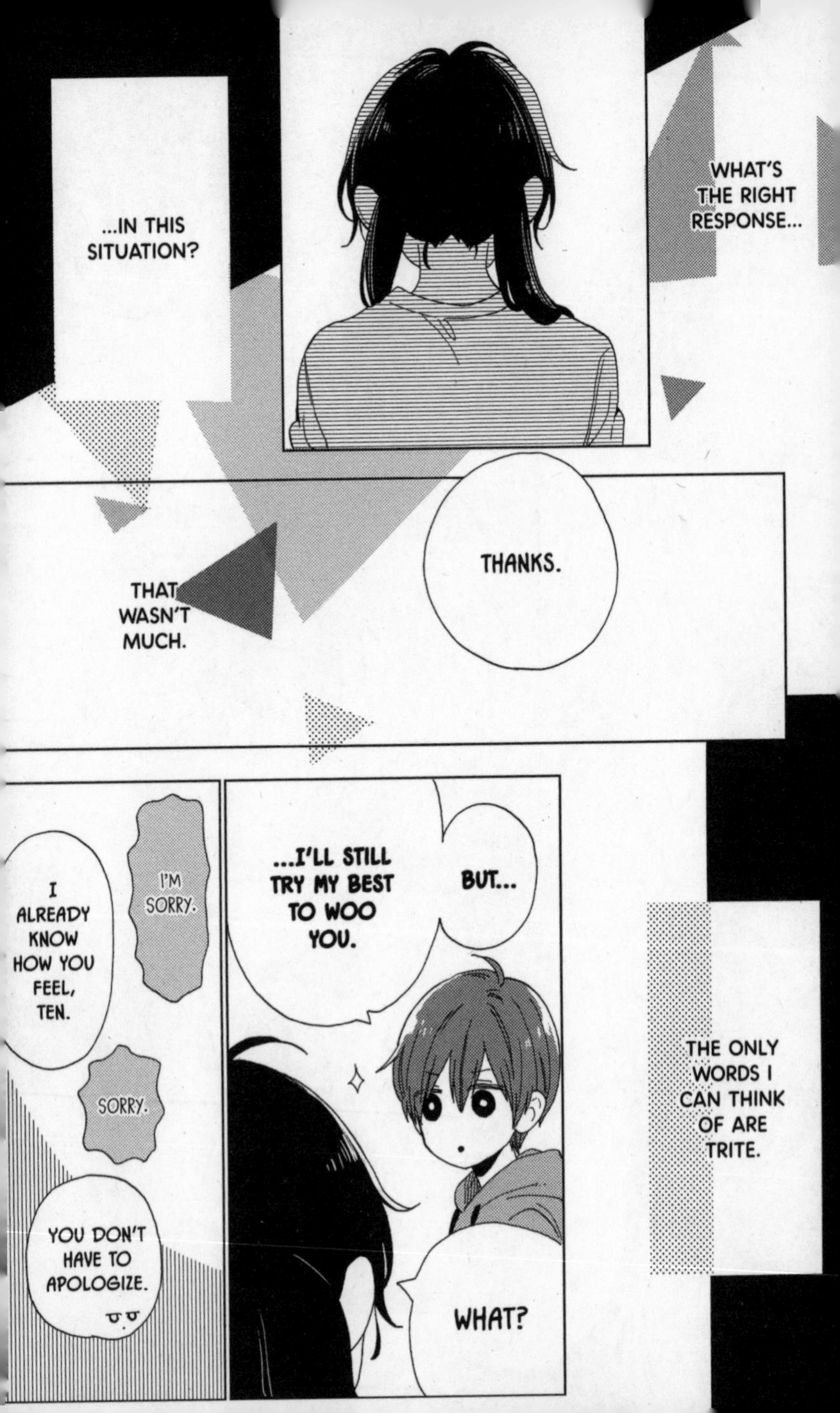
WHAT'S THE RIGHT RESPONSE...
...IN THIS SITUATION?
THANKS.
THAT WASN'T MUCH.
THE ONLY WORDS I CAN THINK OF ARE TRITE.
BUT...
...I'LL STILL TRY MY BEST TO WOO YOU.
WHAT?
I'M SORRY.
I ALREADY KNOW HOW YOU FEEL, TEN.
SORRY.
YOU DON'T HAVE TO APOLOGIZE.

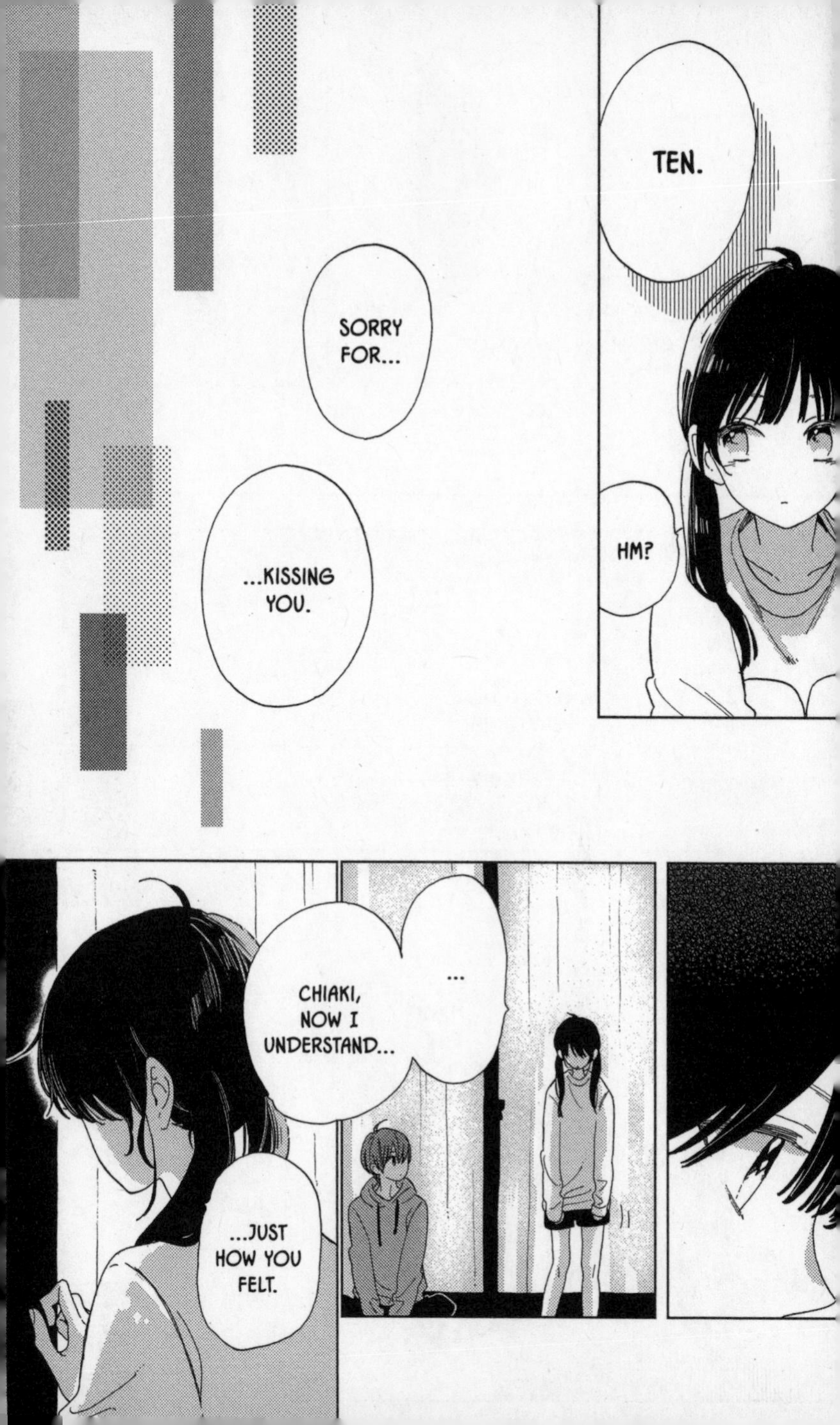
TEN.
HM?
SORRY FOR...
...KISSING YOU.
...
CHIAKI, NOW I UNDERSTAND...
...JUST HOW YOU FELT.

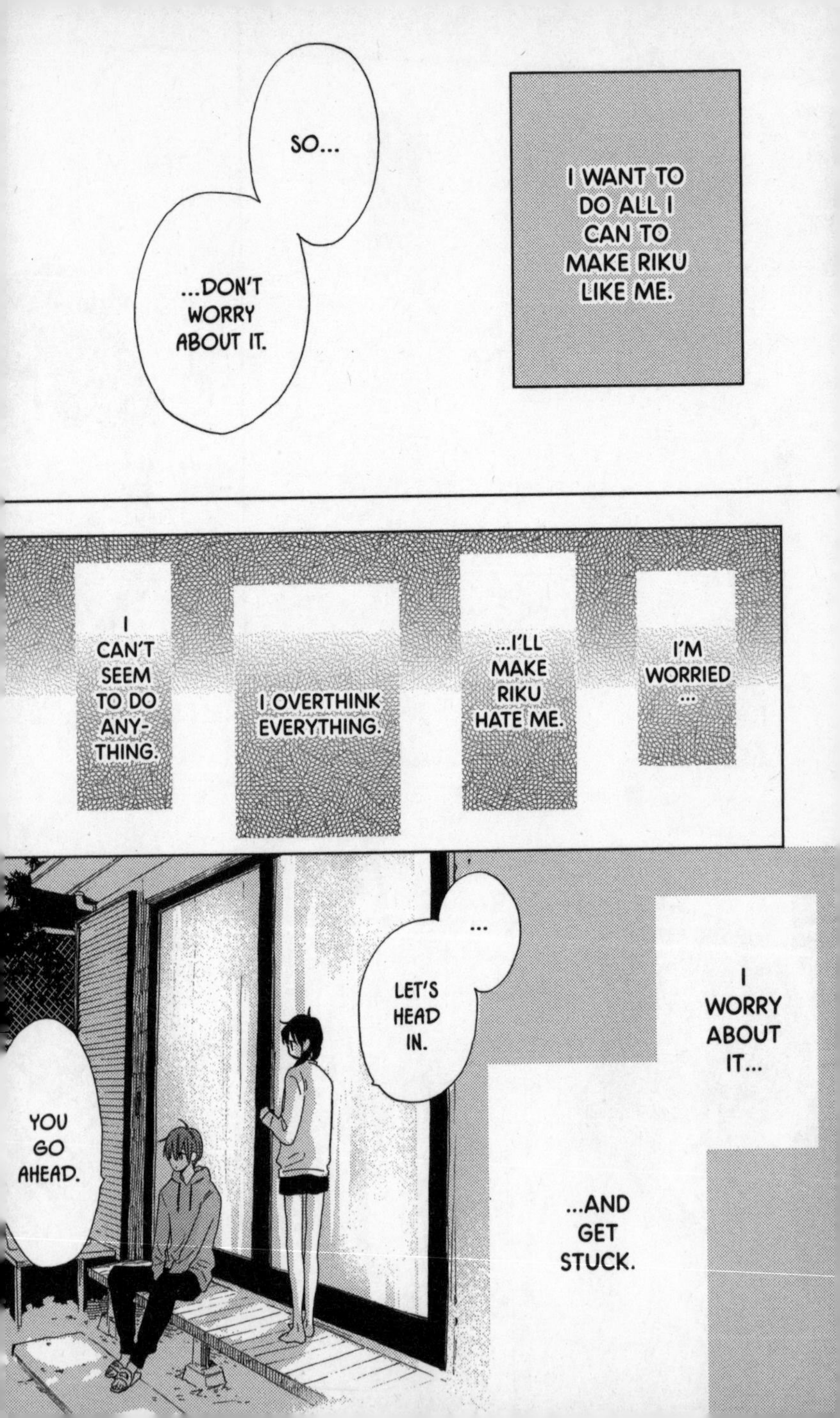
I WANT TO DO ALL I CAN TO MAKE RIKU LIKE ME.
SO...
...DON'T WORRY ABOUT IT.
I'M WORRIED...
...I'LL MAKE RIKU HATE ME.
I OVERTHINK EVERYTHING.
I CAN'T SEEM TO DO ANY-THING.
I WORRY ABOUT IT...
...AND GET STUCK.
...
LET'S HEAD IN.
YOU GO AHEAD.

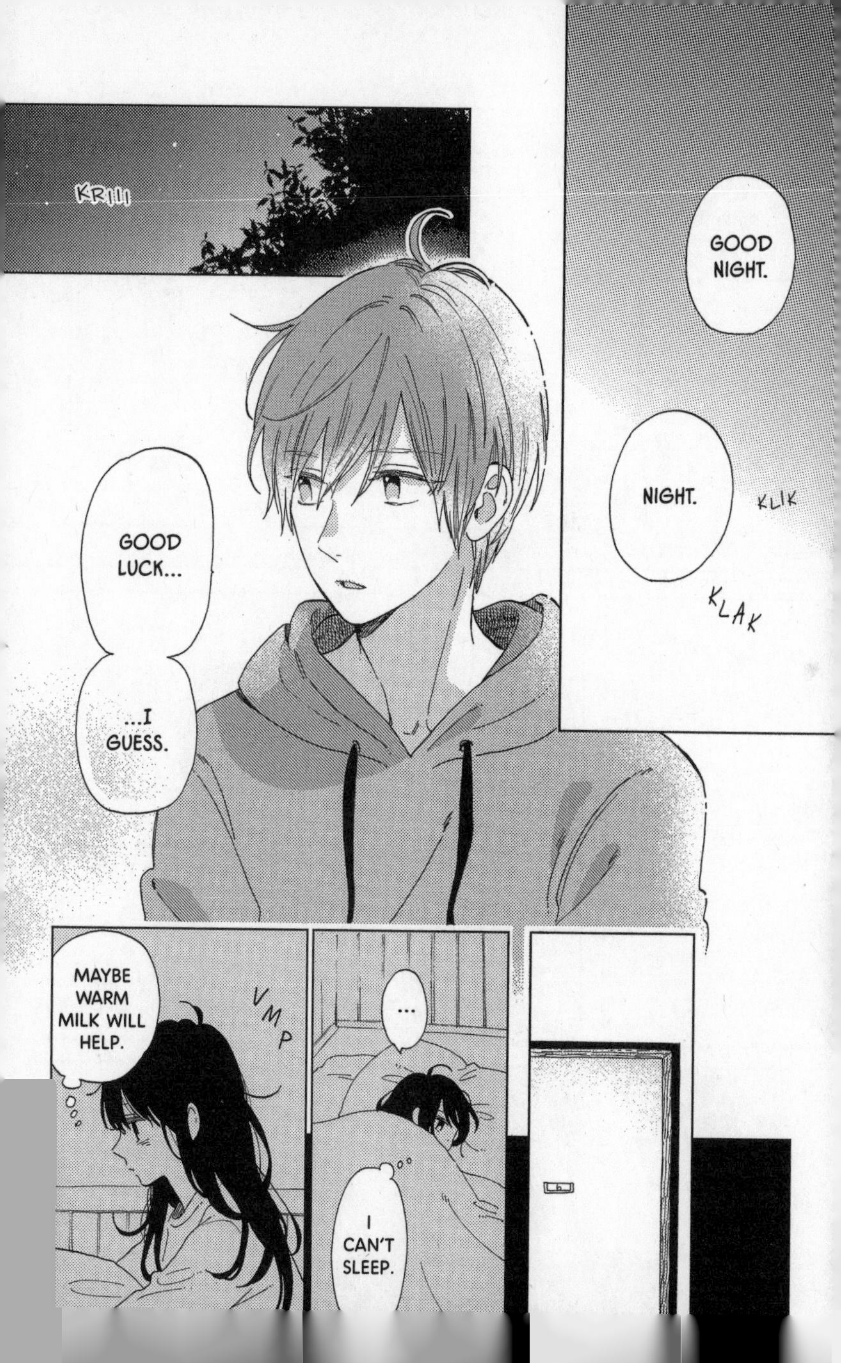
GOOD NIGHT.
NIGHT.
KLIK
KLAK
KRIII
GOOD LUCK...
...I GUESS.
...
I CAN'T SLEEP.
MAYBE WARM MILK WILL HELP.
VMP

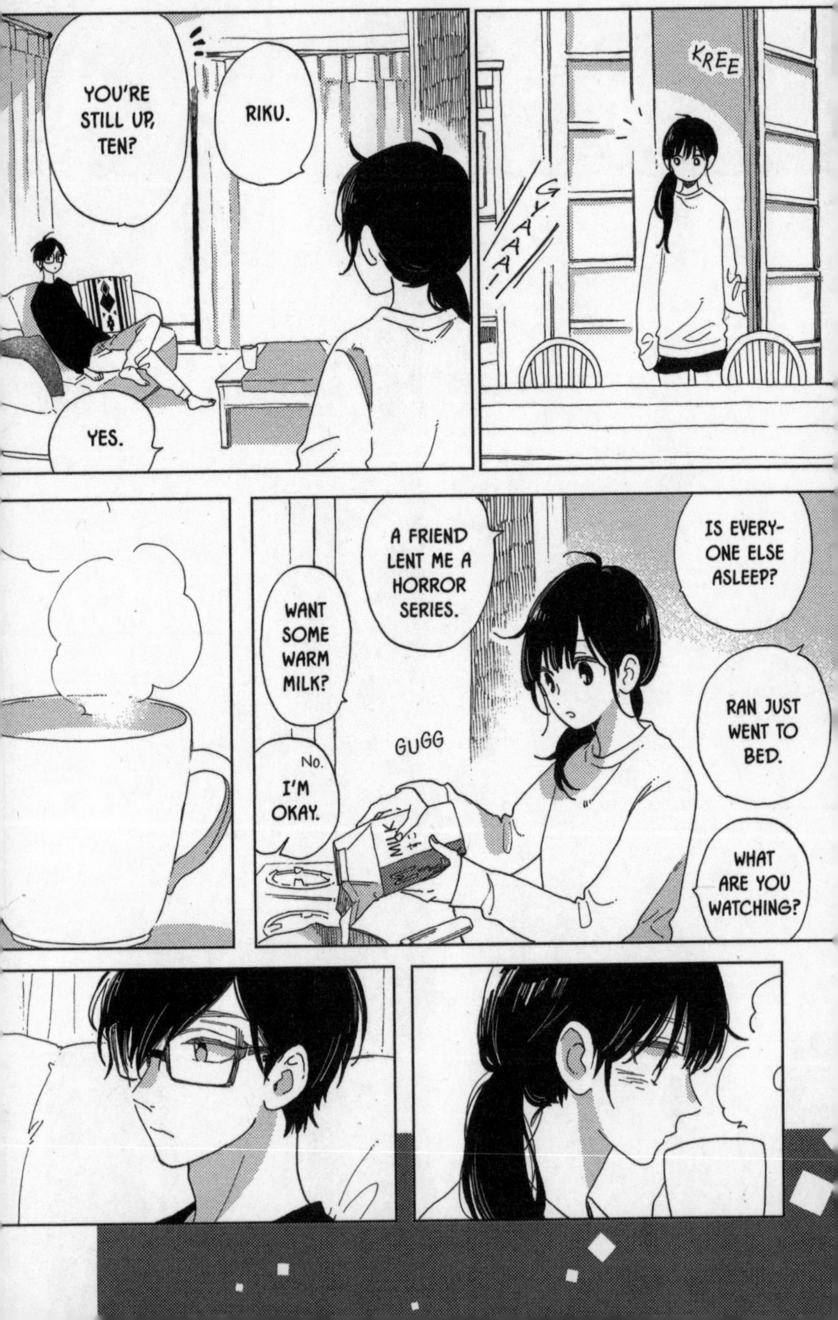
KREE
GYAAA!
RIKU.
YOU'RE STILL UP, TEN?
YES.
IS EVERY-ONE ELSE ASLEEP?
RAN JUST WENT TO BED.
WHAT ARE YOU WATCHING?
A FRIEND LENT ME A HORROR SERIES.
WANT SOME WARM MILK?
GUGG
No. I'M OKAY.
MILK

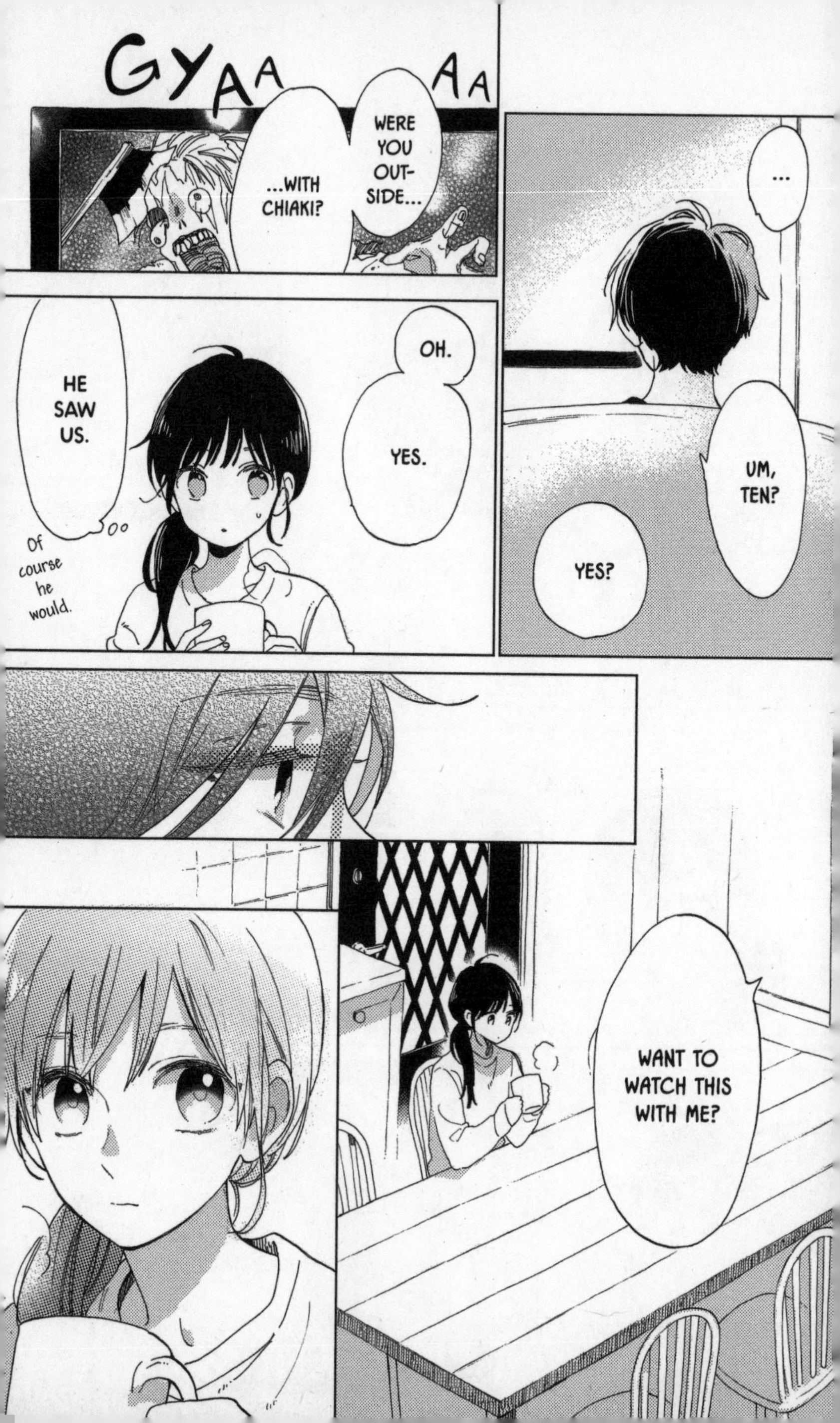
...
UM, TEN?
YES?
GYAAAA
WERE YOU OUTSIDE...
...WITH CHIAKI?
OH.
YES.
HE SAW US.
Of course he would.
WANT TO WATCH THIS WITH ME?

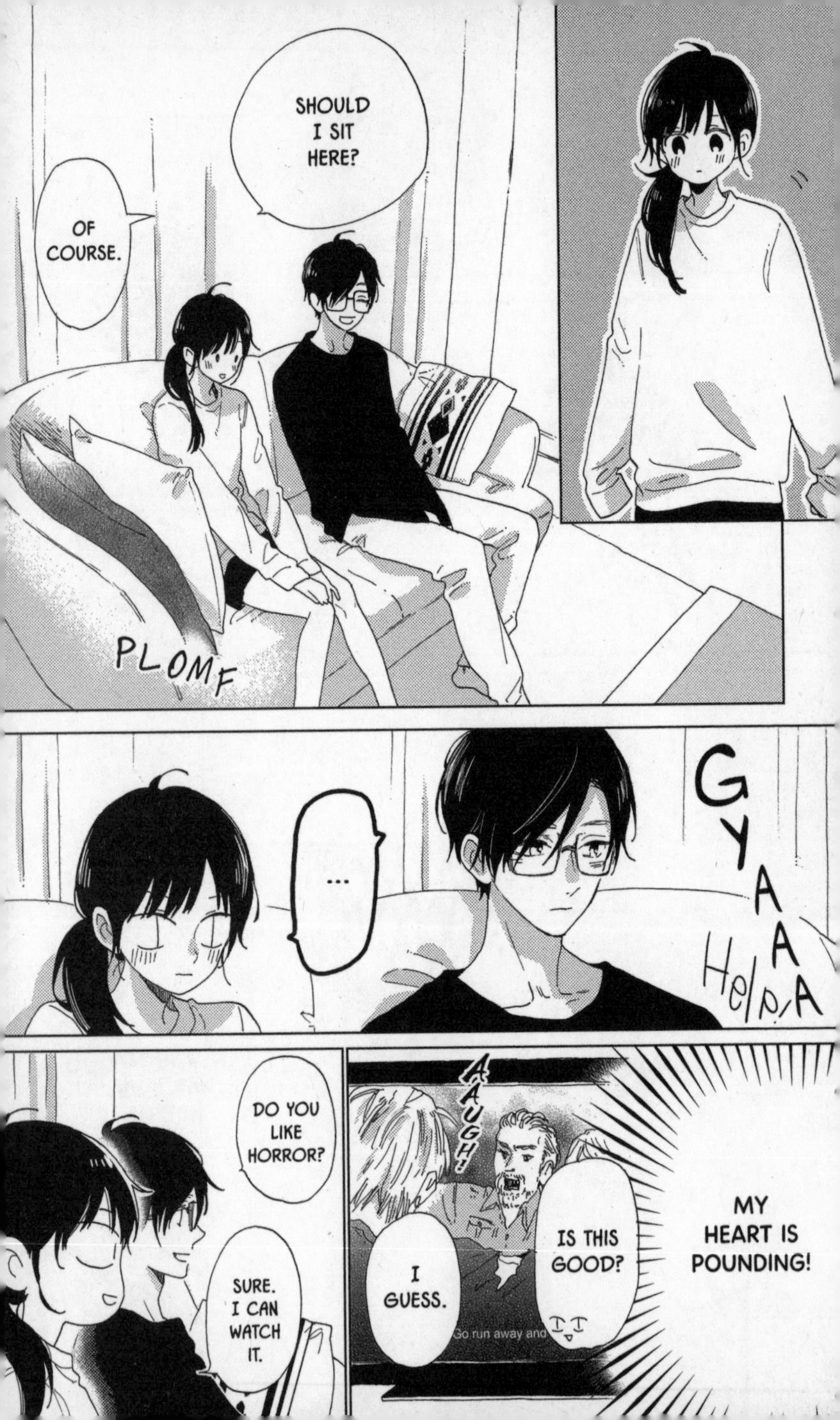
SHOULD I SIT HERE?
OF COURSE.
PLOMF
GYAAA
Help
...
MY HEART IS POUNDING!
AAUGH!
IS THIS GOOD?
I GUESS.
Go run away and
DO YOU LIKE HORROR?
SURE. I CAN WATCH IT.

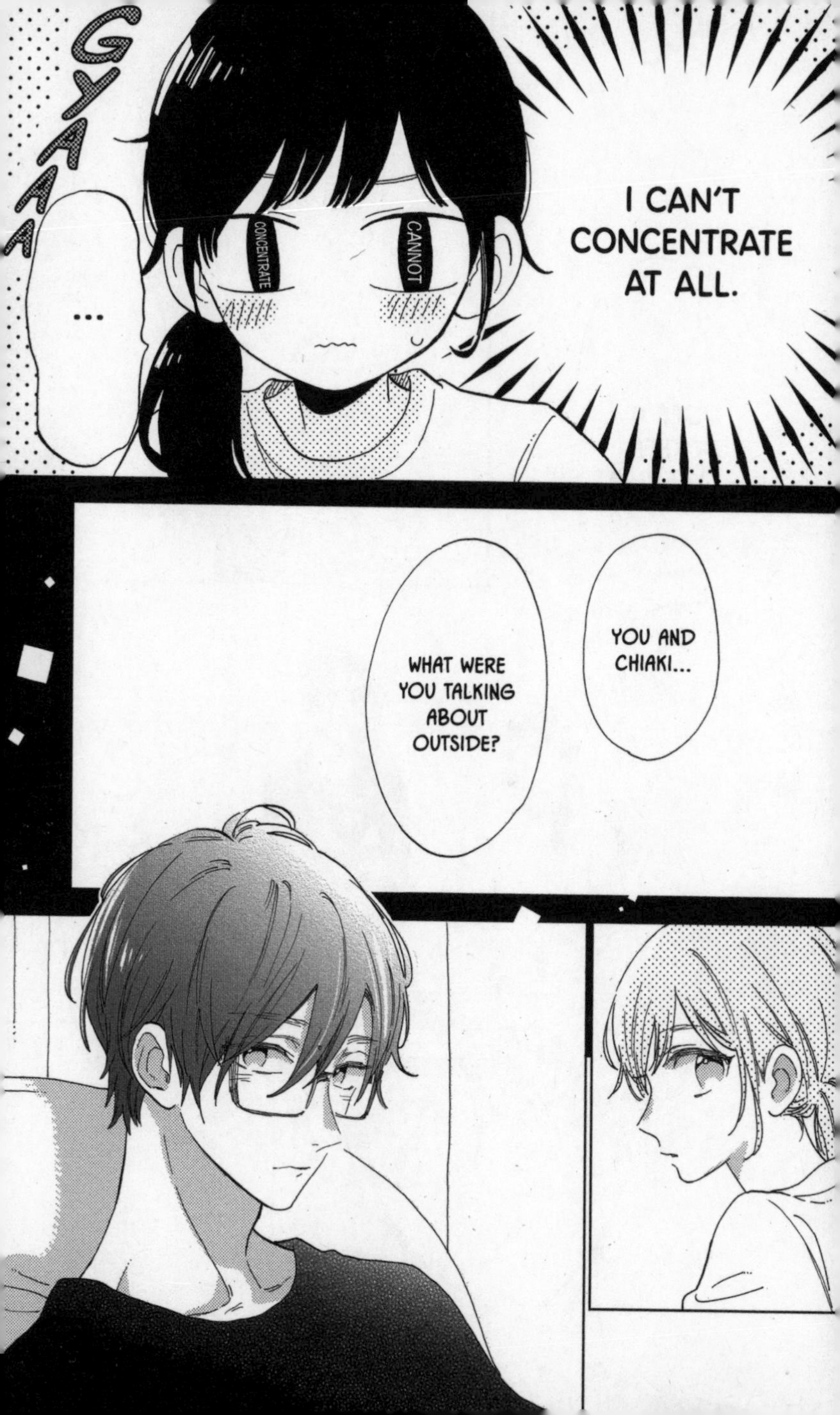
I CAN'T CONCENTRATE AT ALL.
CANNOT
CONCENTRATE
GYAAAA
...
YOU AND CHIAKI...
WHAT WERE YOU TALKING ABOUT OUTSIDE?

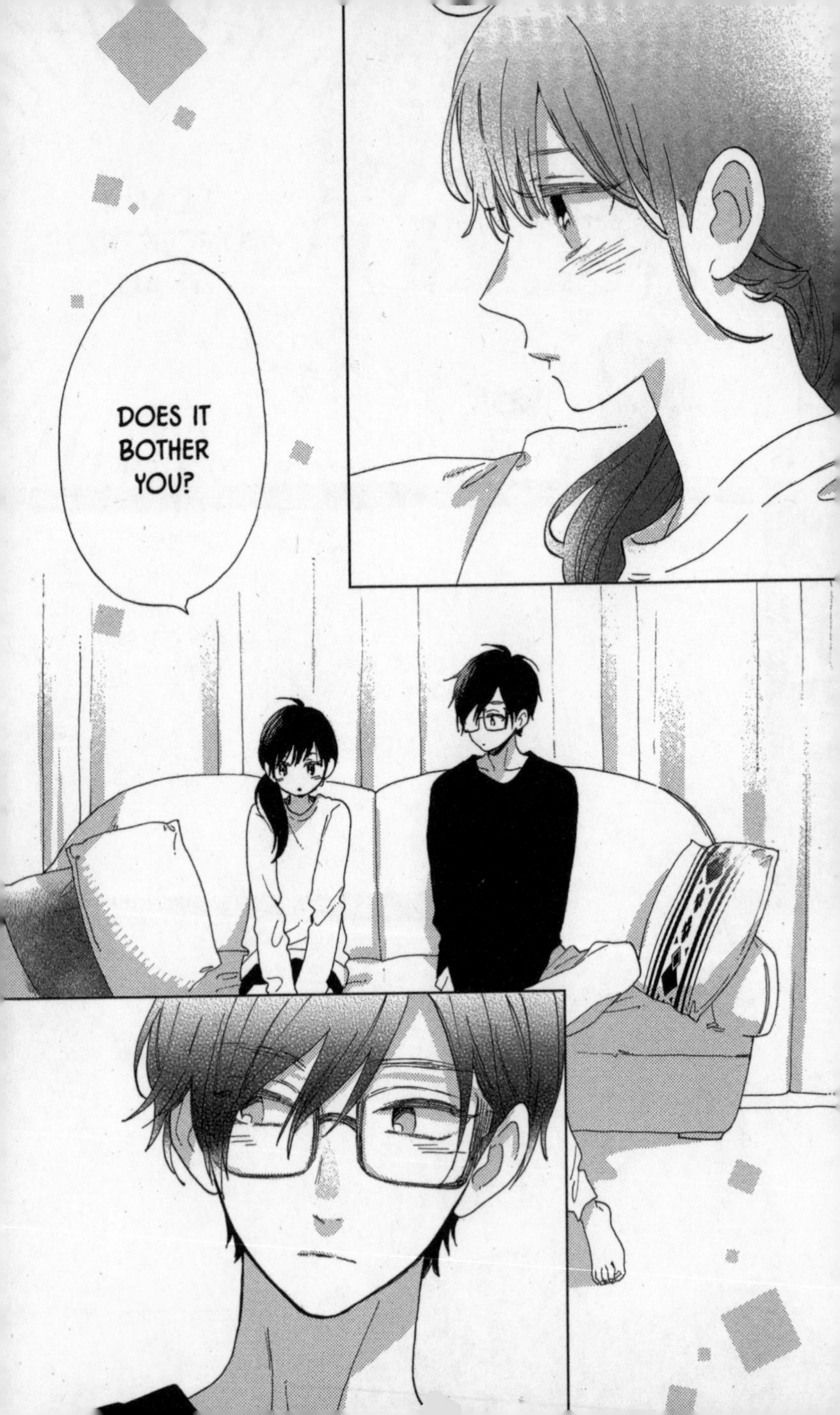
DOES IT BOTHER YOU?

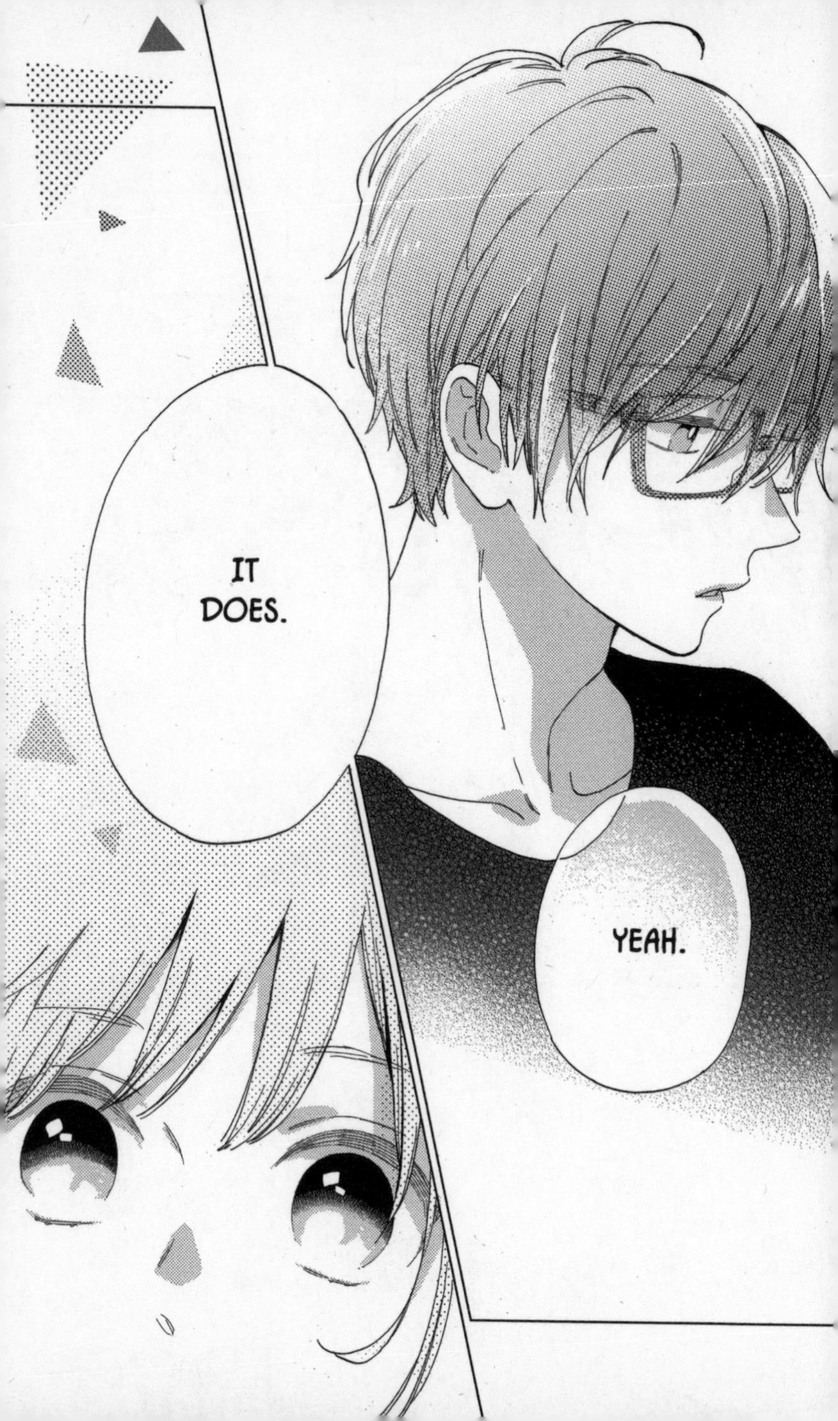
IT DOES.
YEAH.

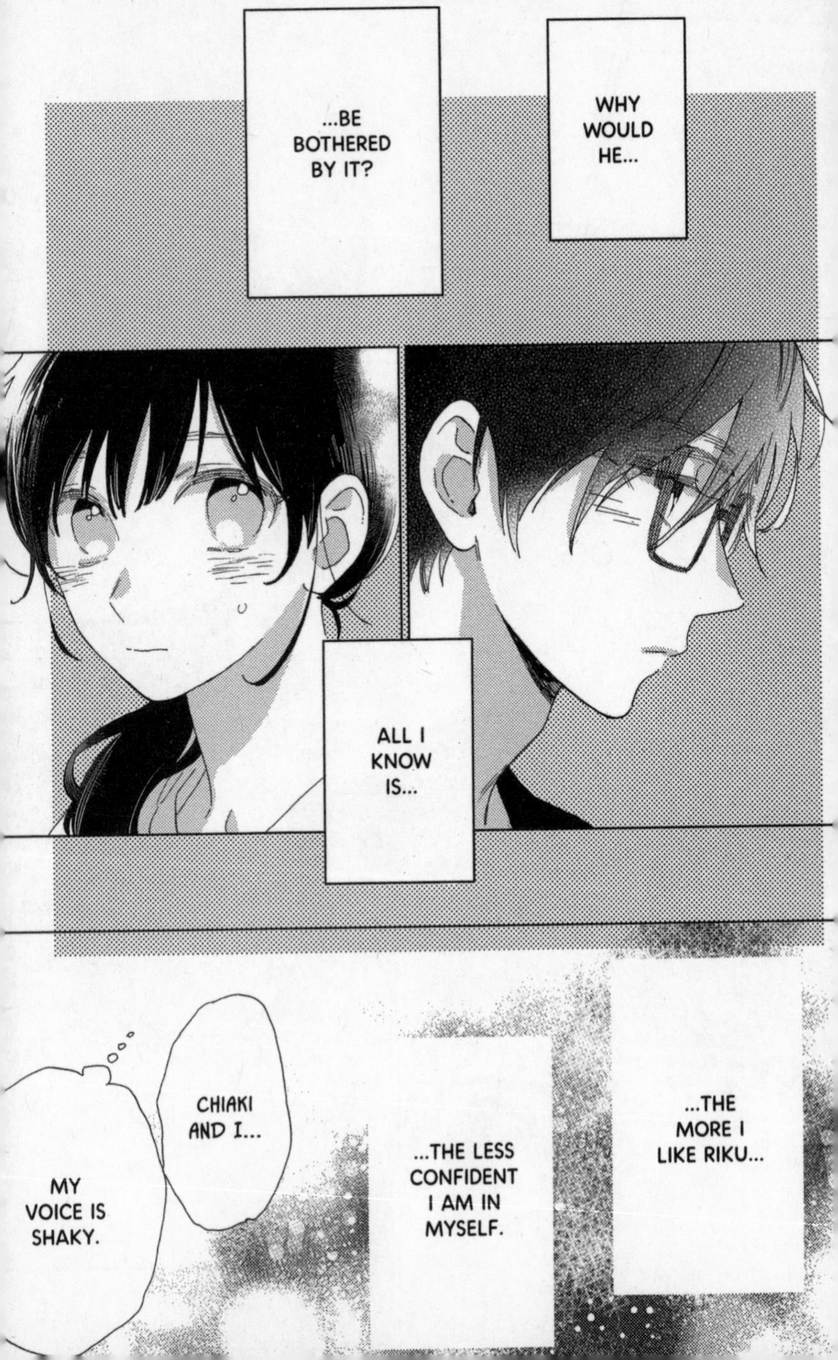
WHY WOULD HE...
...BE BOTHERED BY IT?
ALL I KNOW IS...
...THE MORE I LIKE RIKU...
...THE LESS CONFIDENT I AM IN MYSELF.
CHIAKI AND I...
MY VOICE IS SHAKY.

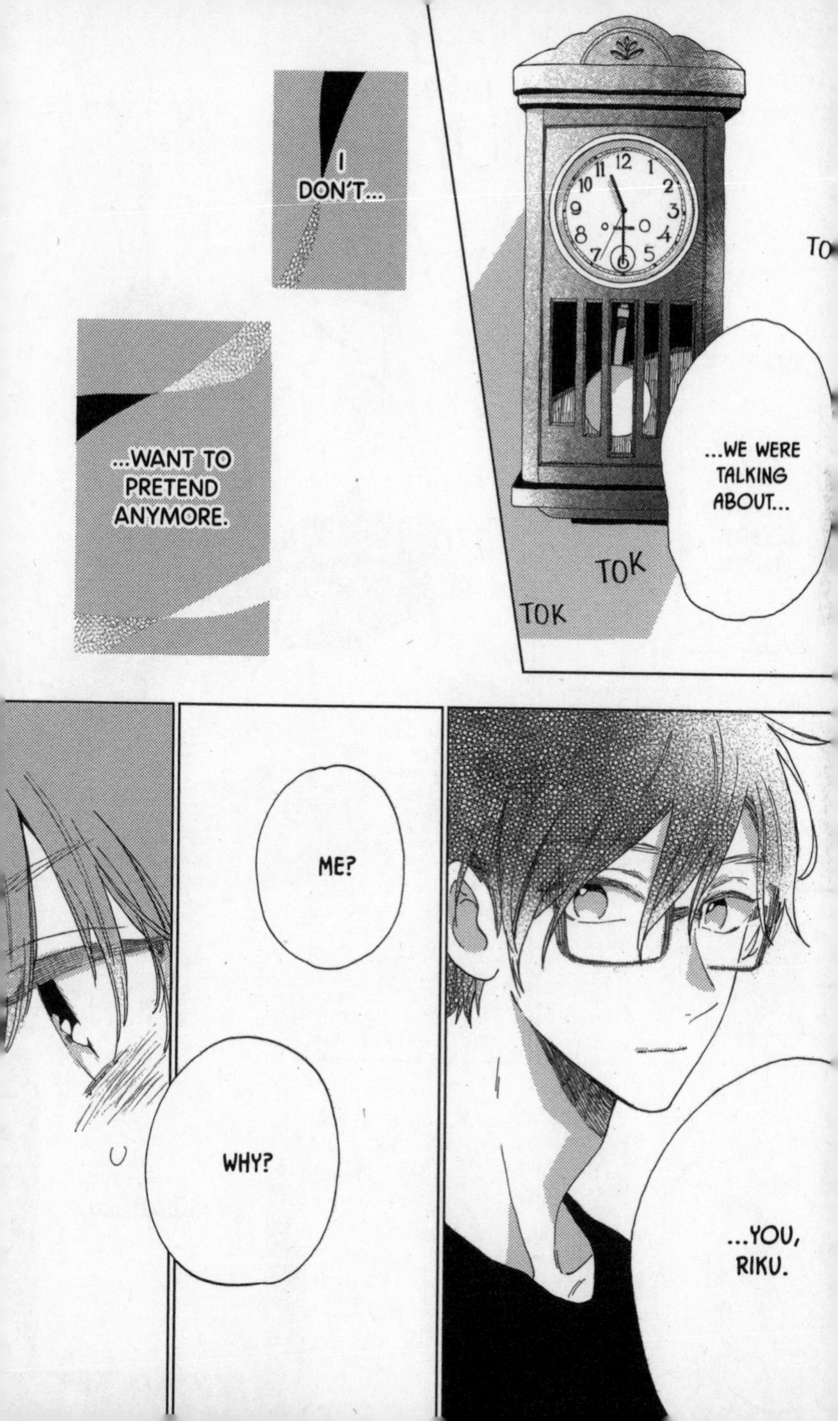
TO
...WE WERE TALKING ABOUT...
TOK
TOK
I DON'T...
...WANT TO PRETEND ANYMORE.
...YOU, RIKU.
ME?
WHY?

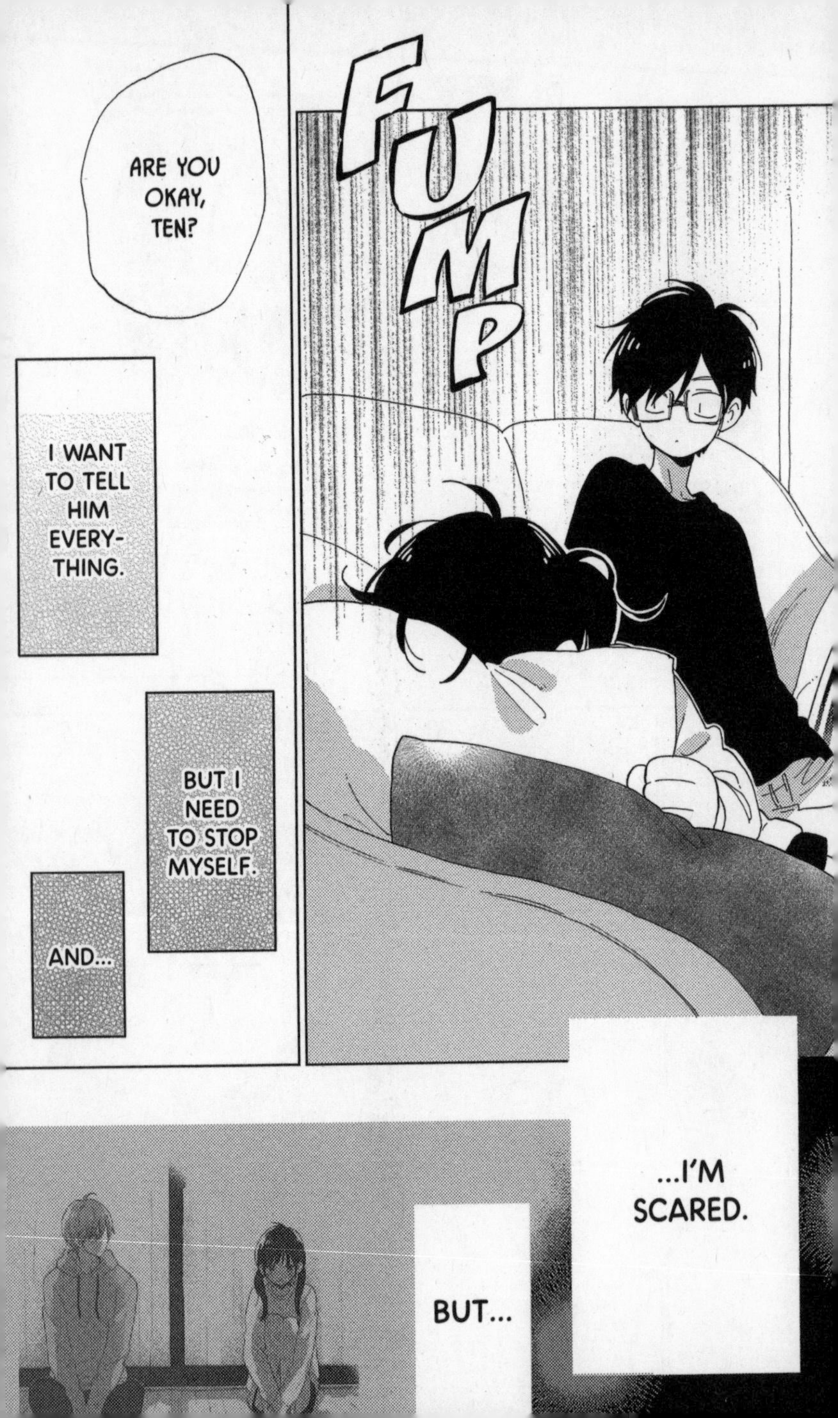
FUMP
ARE YOU OKAY, TEN?
I WANT TO TELL HIM EVERY-THING.
BUT I NEED TO STOP MYSELF.
AND...
...I'M SCARED.
BUT...

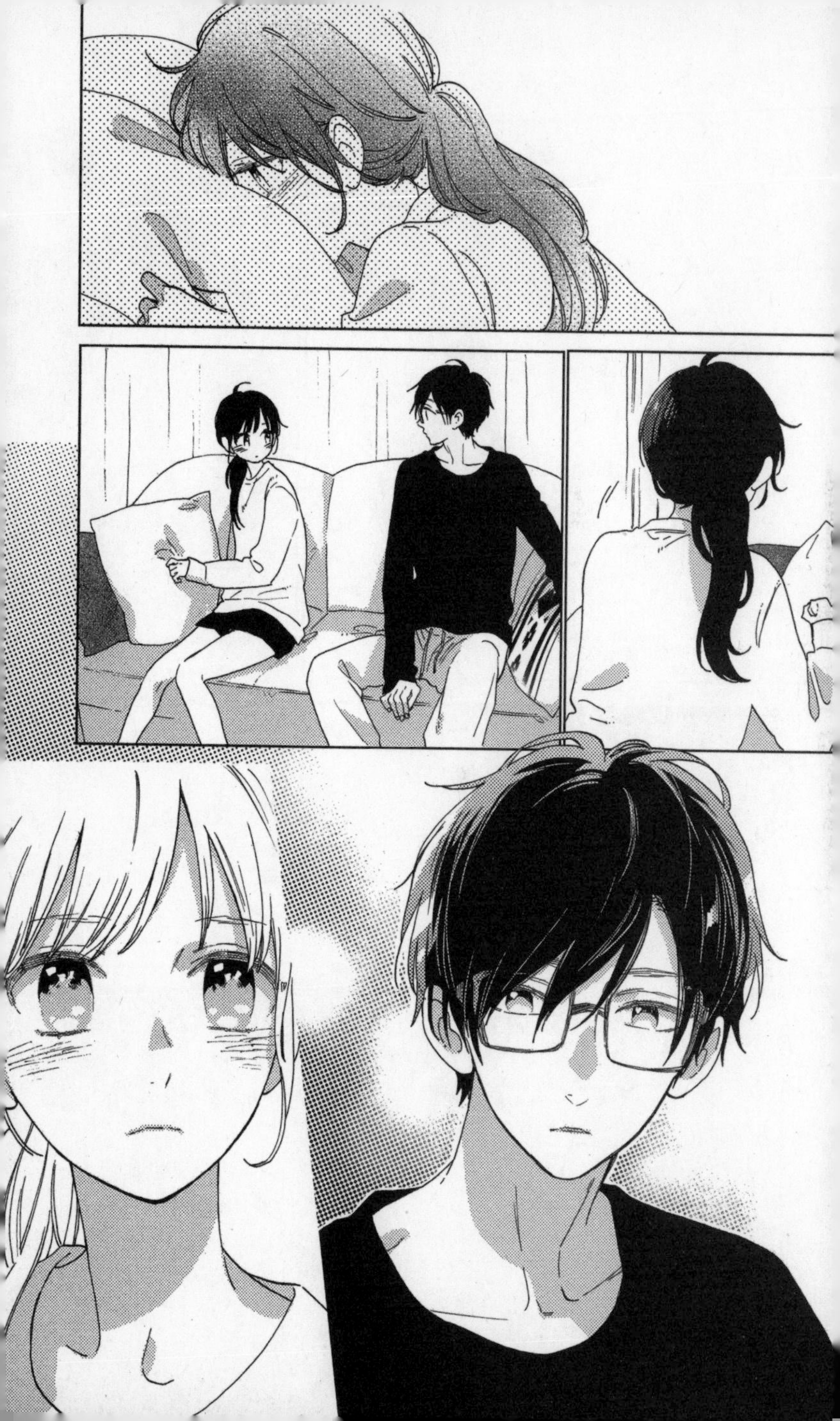

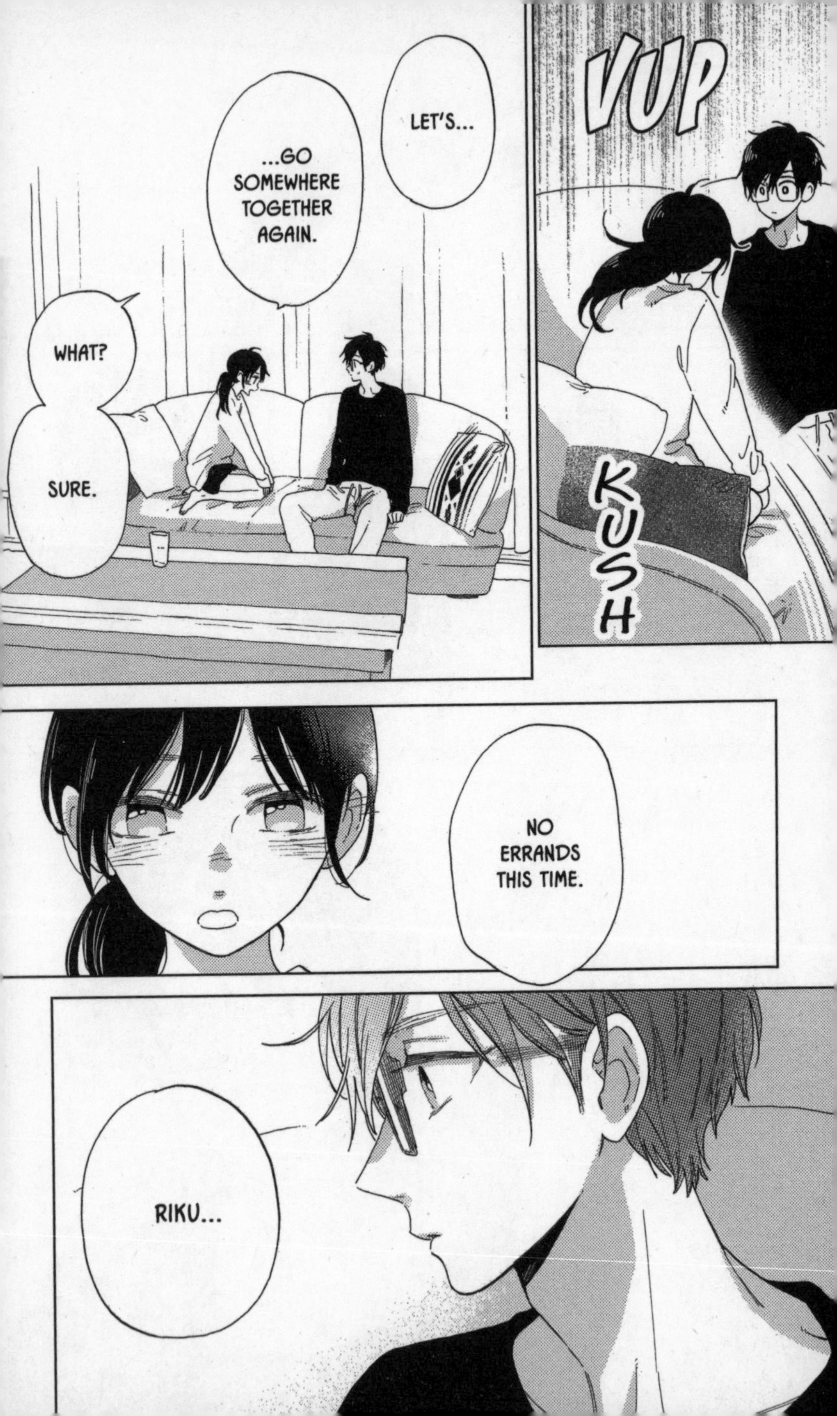
VUP
KUSH
LET'S...
...GO SOMEWHERE TOGETHER AGAIN.
WHAT?
SURE.
NO ERRANDS THIS TIME.
RIKU...

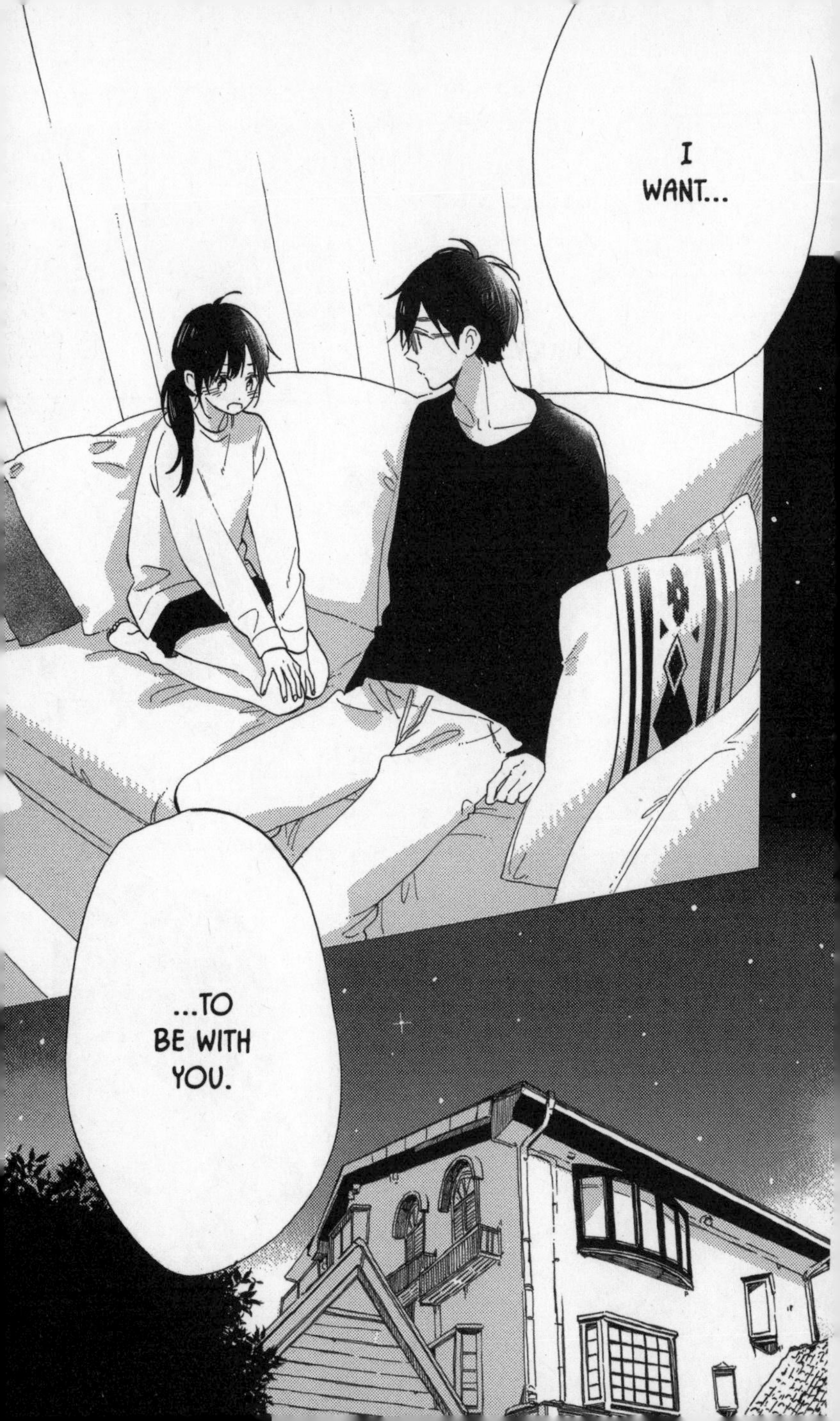
I WANT...
...TO BE WITH YOU.

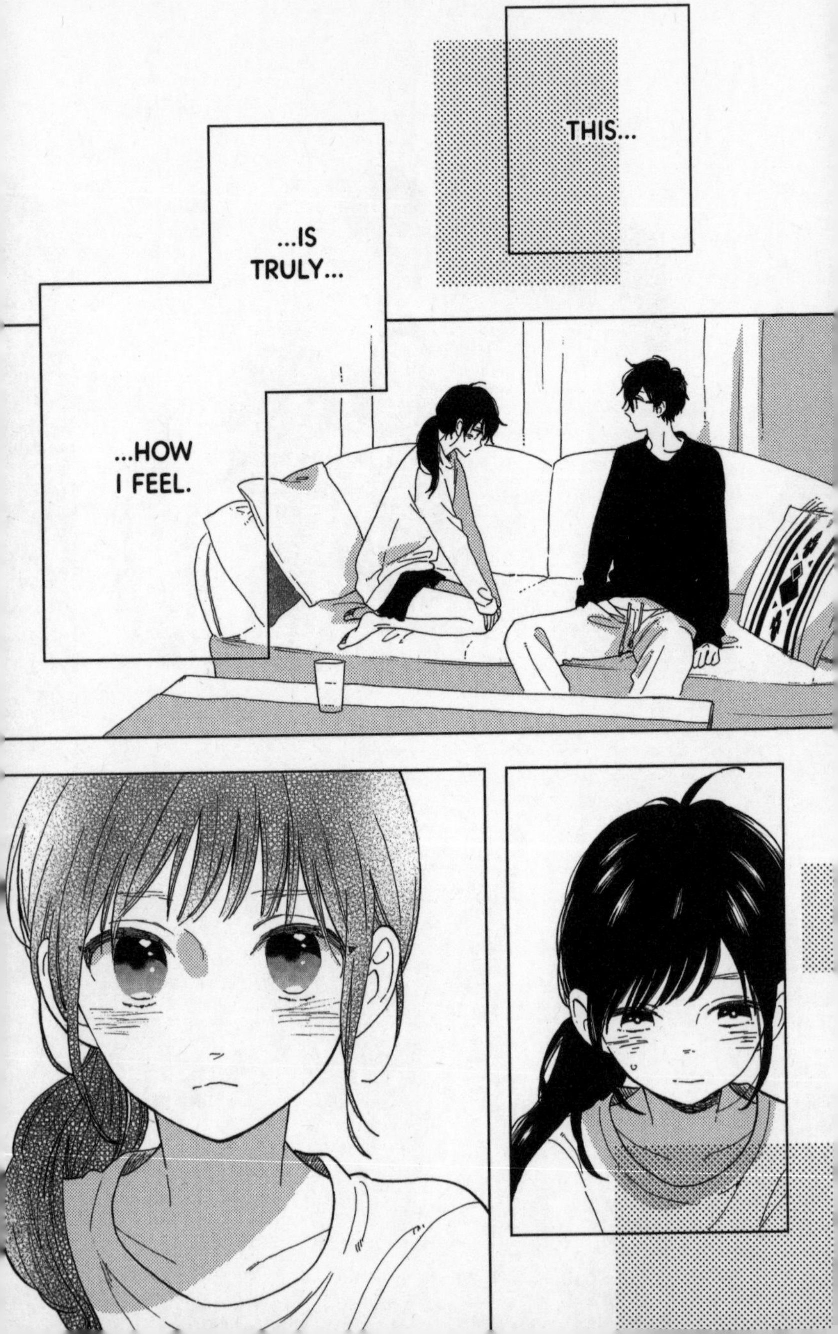
THIS...
...IS TRULY...
...HOW I FEEL.

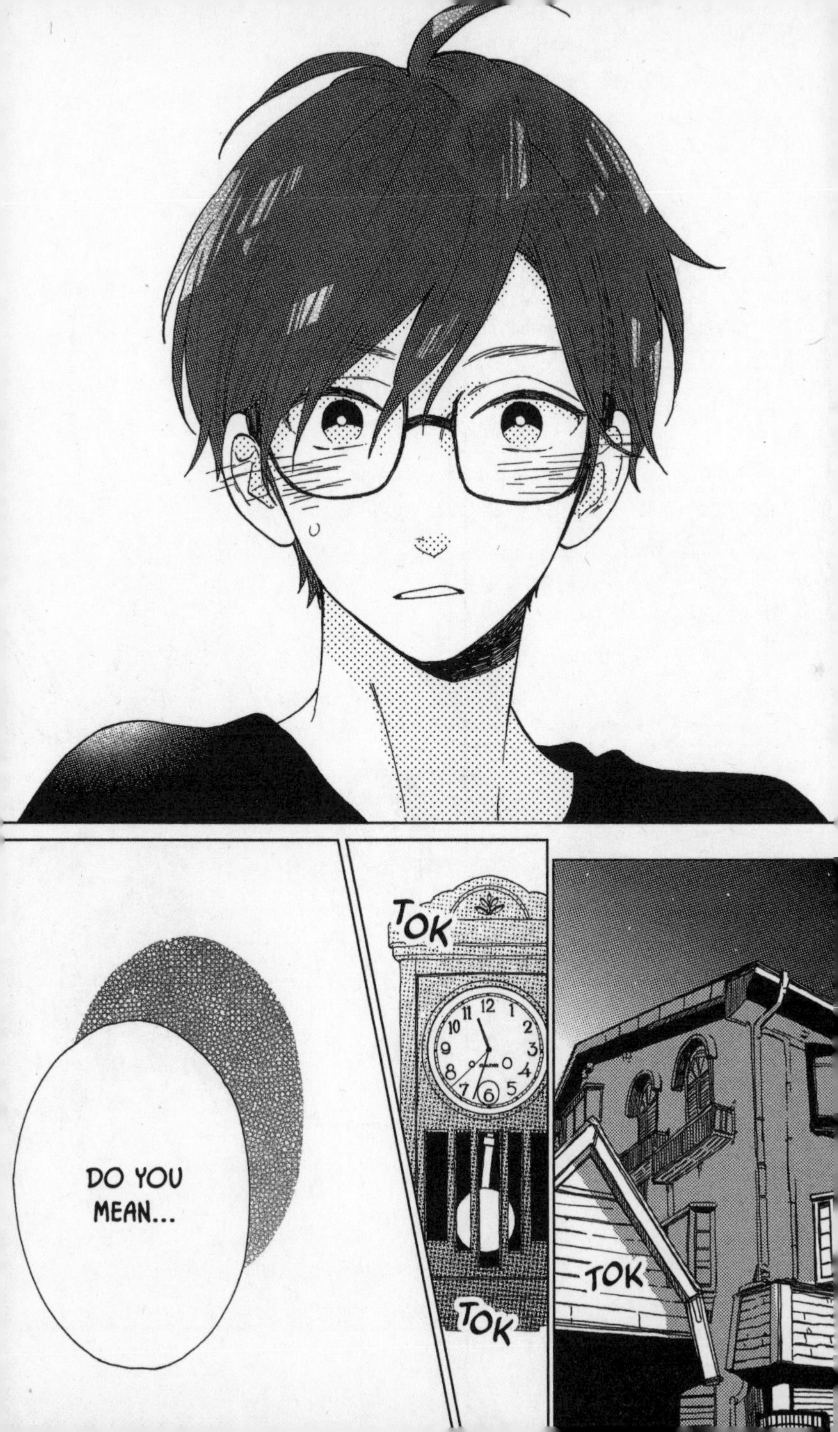
TOK
TOK
TOK
DO YOU MEAN...

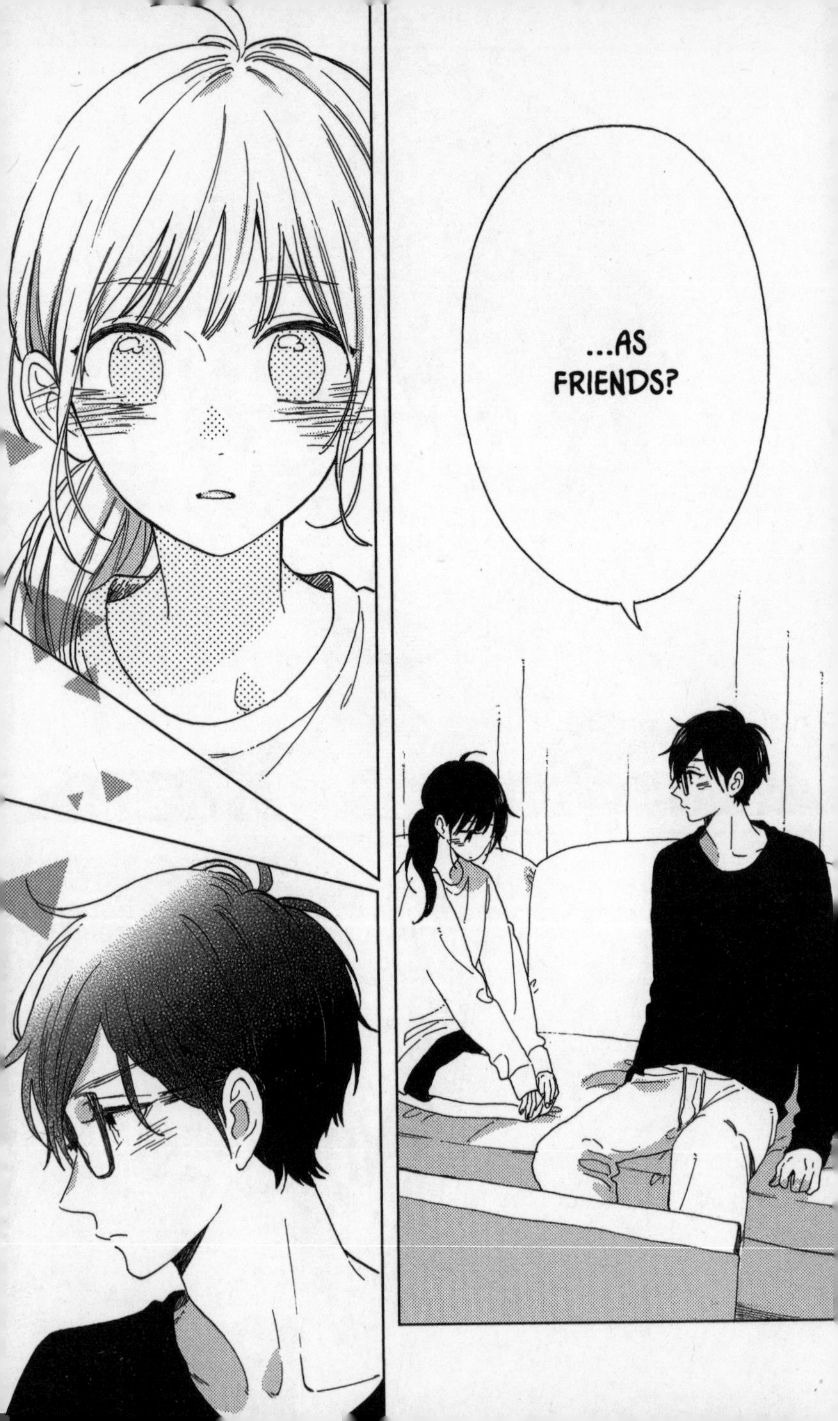
...AS FRIENDS?

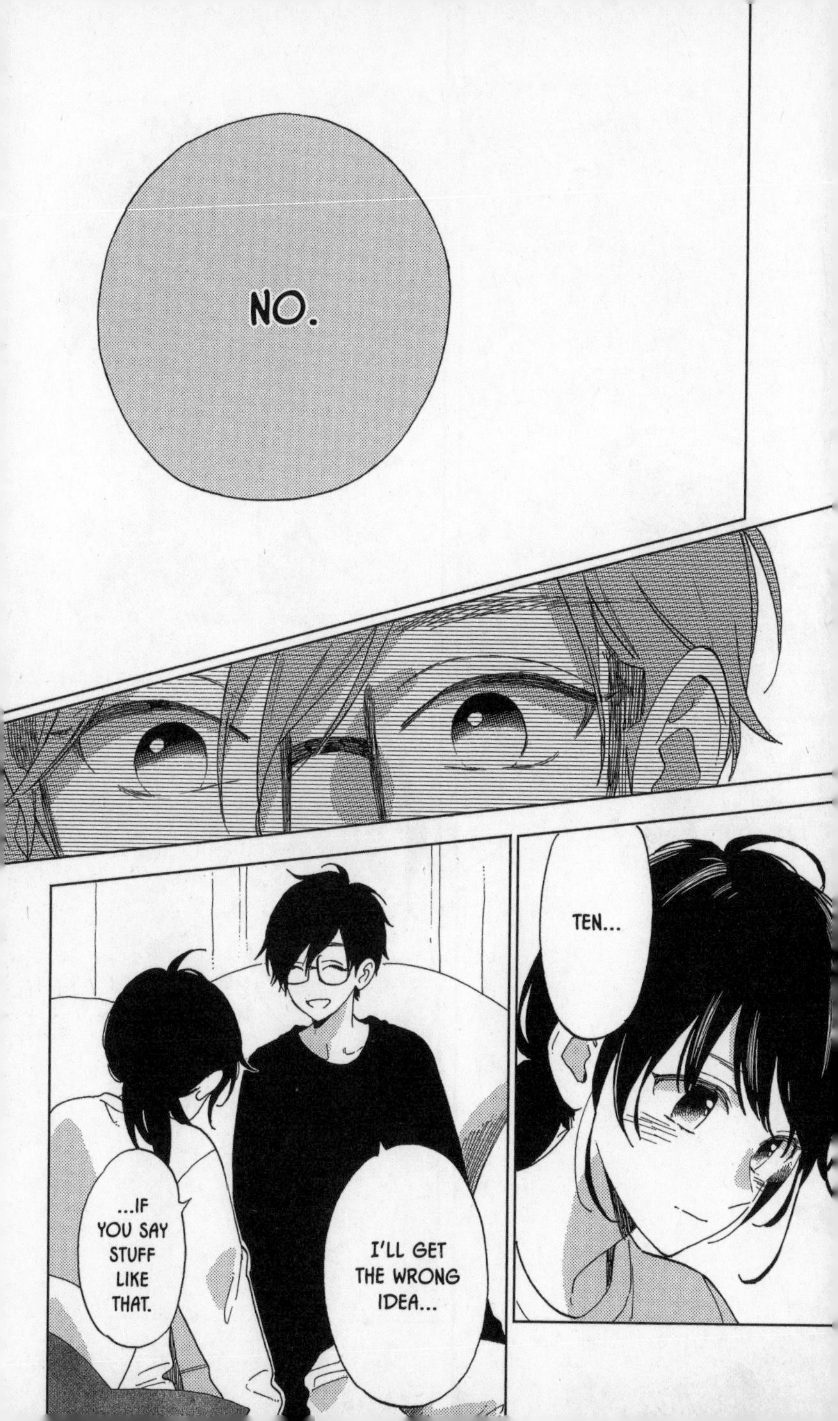
NO.
TEN...
I'LL GET THE WRONG IDEA...
...IF YOU SAY STUFF LIKE THAT.

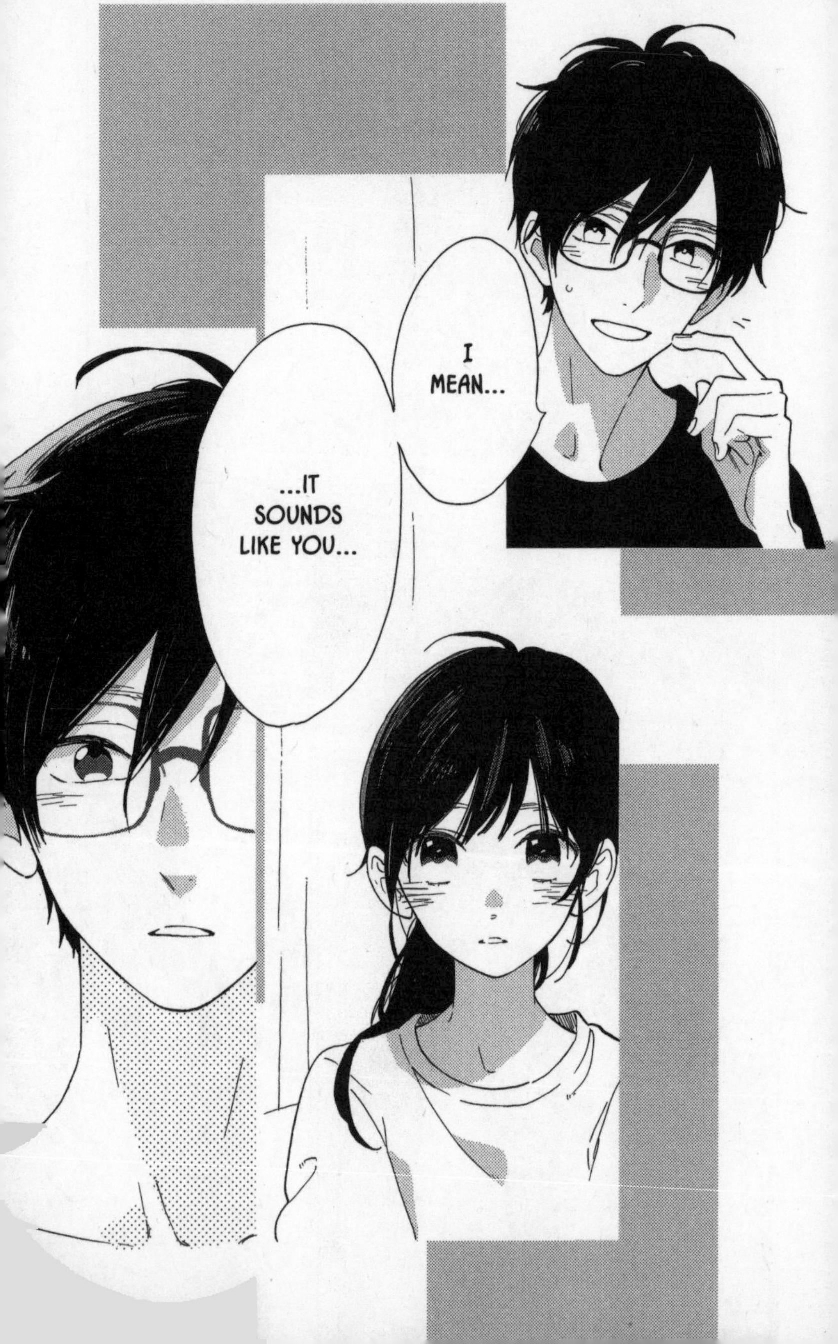
I MEAN...
...IT SOUNDS LIKE YOU...

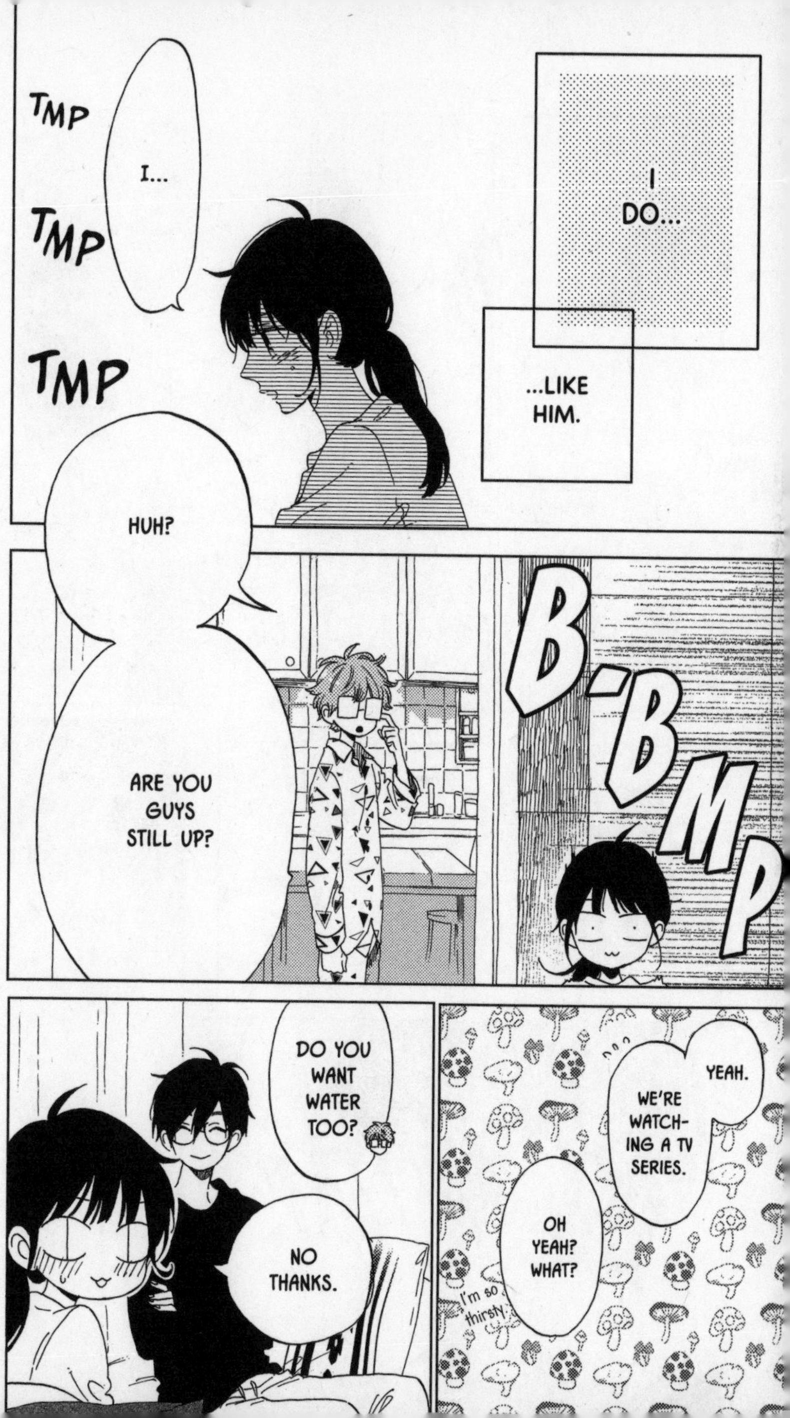
I DO...
...LIKE HIM.
TMP
TMP
TMP
I...
HUH?
ARE YOU GUYS STILL UP?
B-BMP
YEAH.
WE'RE WATCHING A TV SERIES.
OH YEAH? WHAT?
I'm so thirsty.
DO YOU WANT WATER TOO?
NO THANKS.

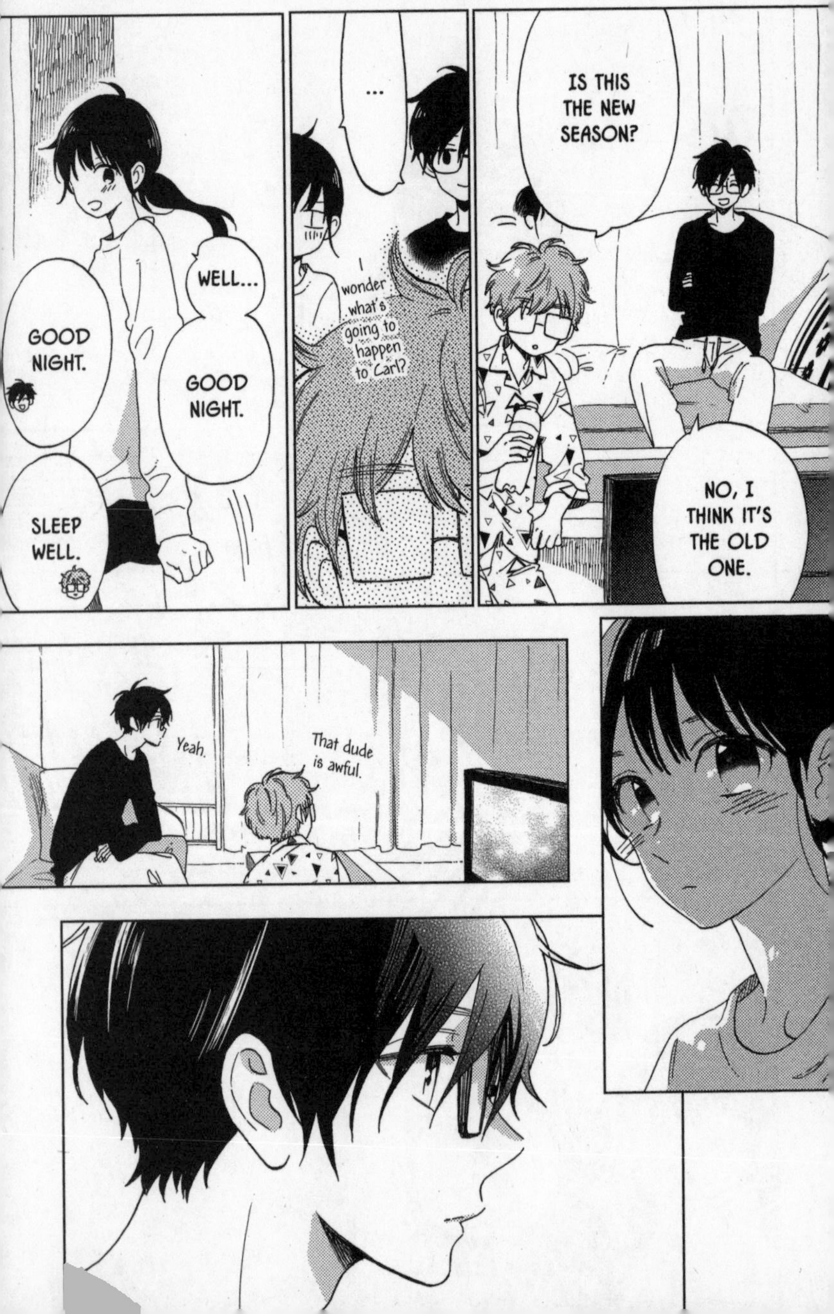
IS THIS THE NEW SEASON?
NO, I THINK IT'S THE OLD ONE.
...
I wonder what's going to happen to Carl?
WELL...
GOOD NIGHT.
GOOD NIGHT.
SLEEP WELL.
That dude is awful.
Yeah.

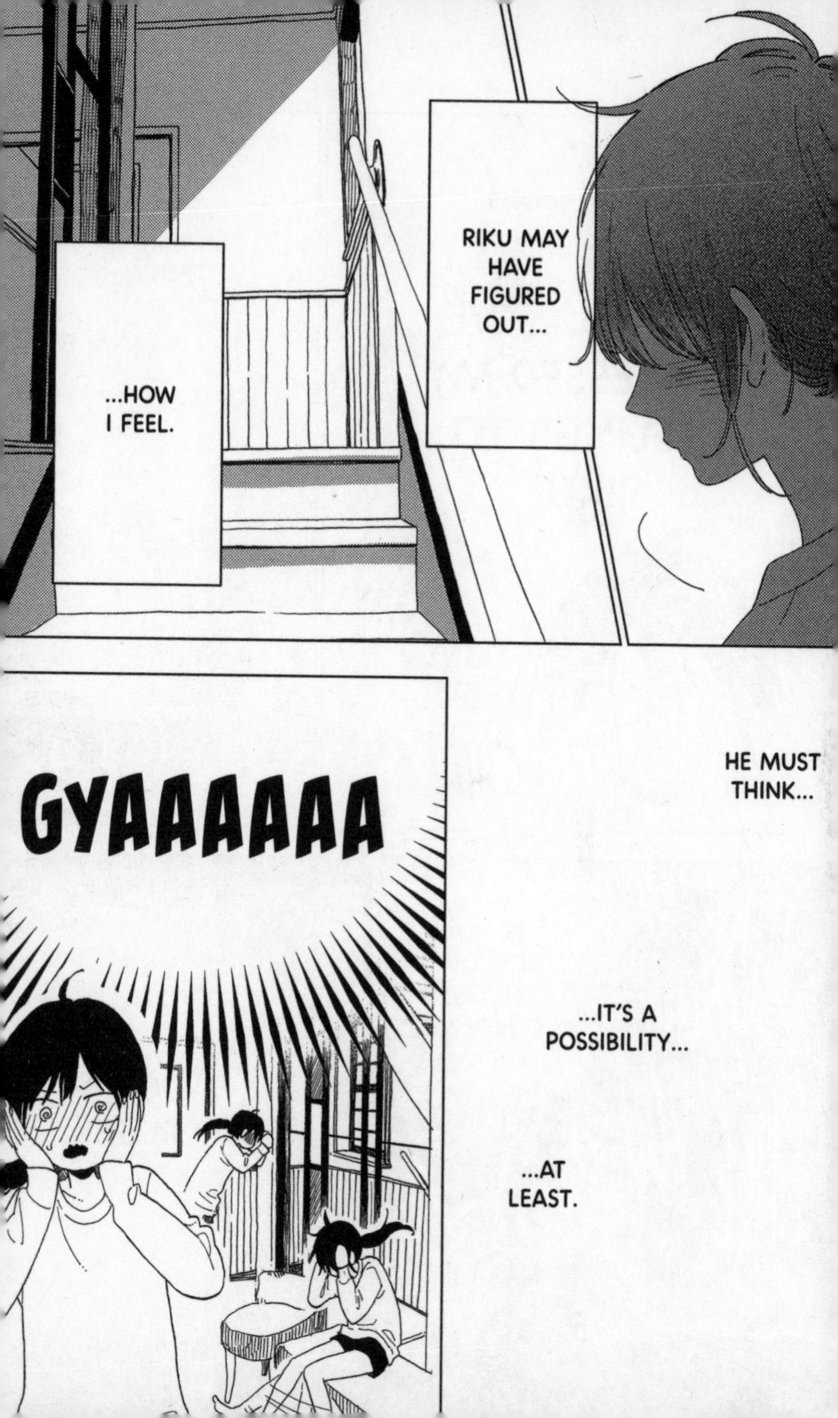
RIKU MAY HAVE FIGURED OUT...
...HOW I FEEL.
HE MUST THINK...
...IT'S A POSSIBILITY...
...AT LEAST.
GYAAAAAAA

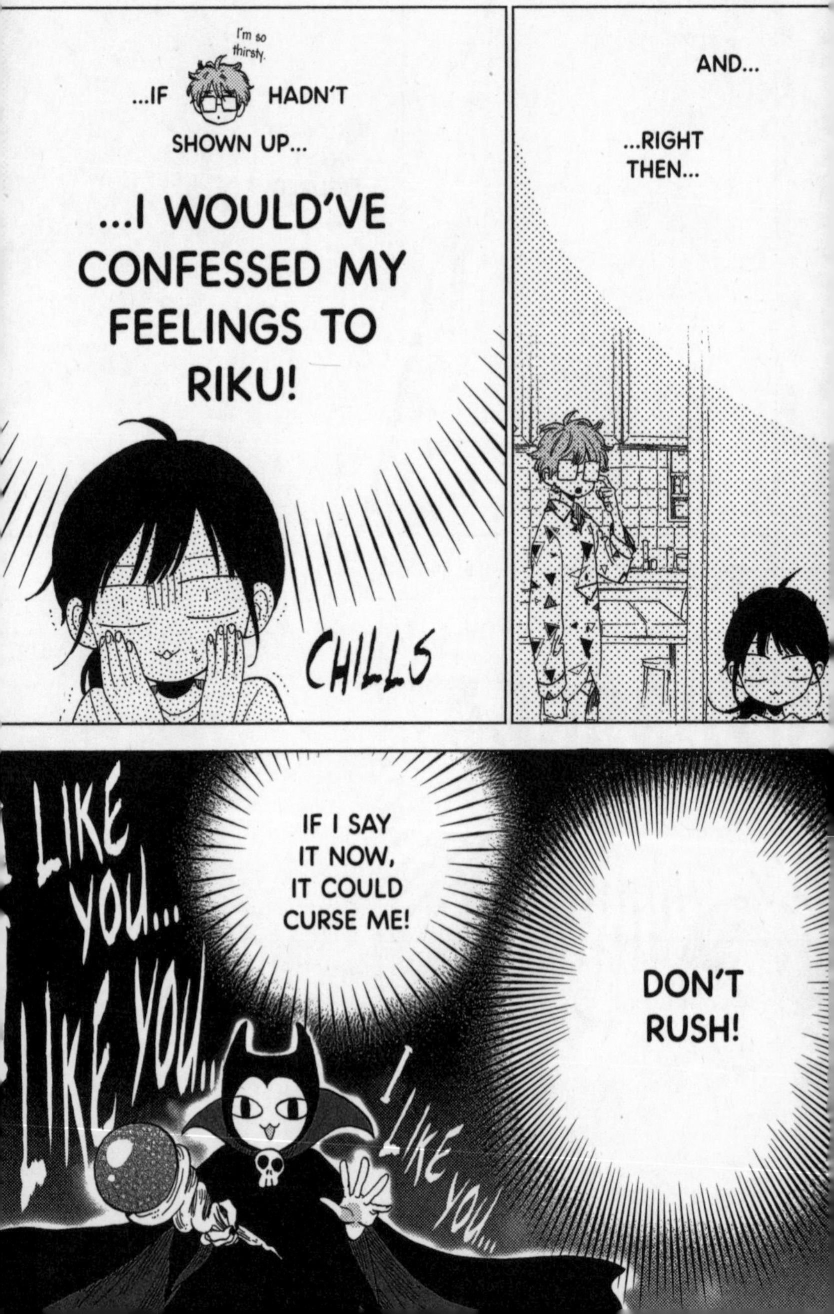
AND...
...RIGHT THEN...
I'm so thirsty.
...IF HADN'T SHOWN UP...
...I WOULD'VE CONFESSED MY FEELINGS TO RIKU!
CHILLS
DON'T RUSH!
IF I SAY IT NOW, IT COULD CURSE ME!
I LIKE YOU...
LIKE YOU...
LIKE YOU...
LIKE YOU...

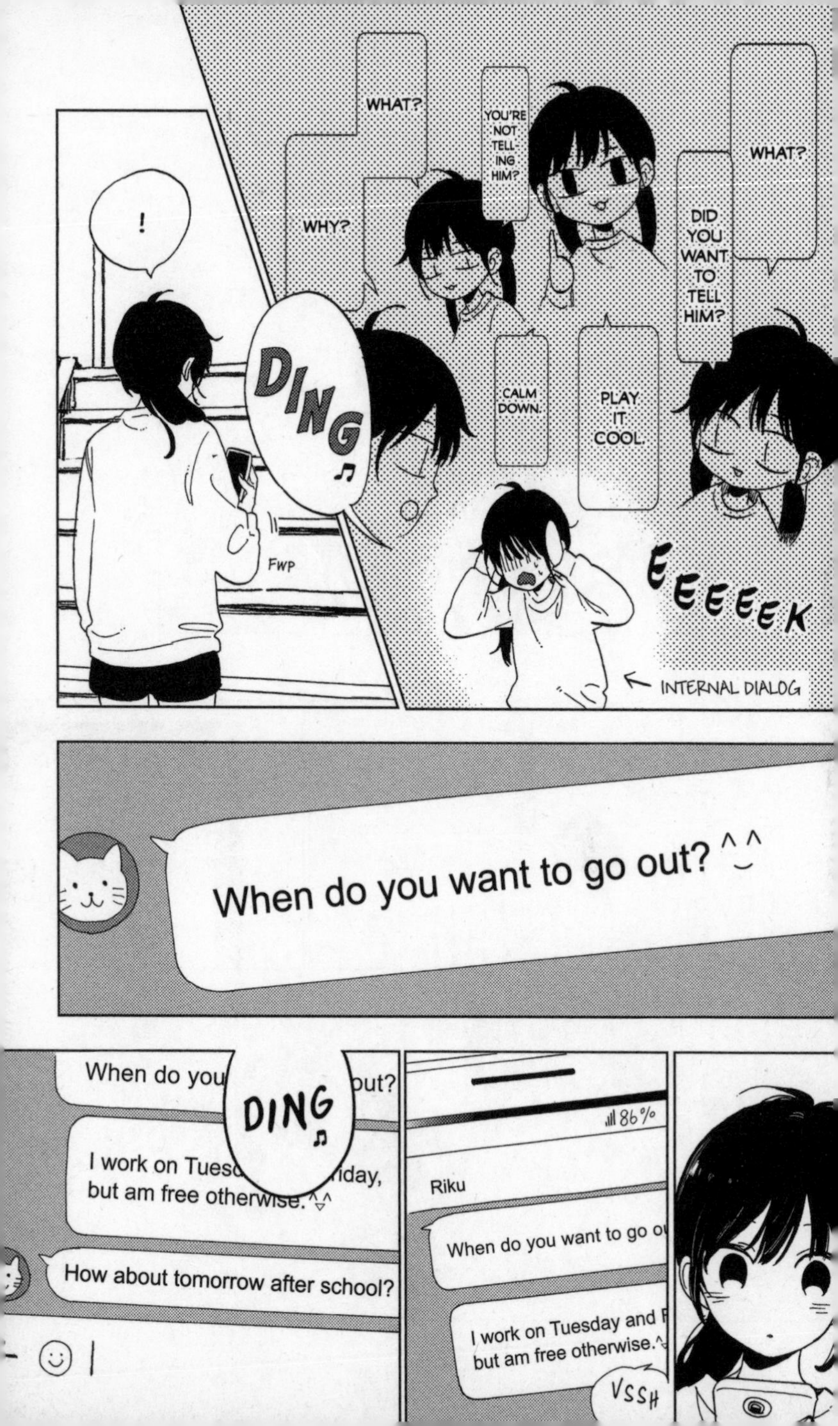
WHAT?
DID YOU WANT TO TELL HIM?
YOU'RE NOT TELL-ING HIM?
WHAT?
WHY?
PLAY IT COOL.
CALM DOWN.
EEEEEEK
INTERNAL DIALOG
!
DING ♫
FWP
When do you want to go out? ^‿^
86%
Riku
When do you want to go o
I work on Tuesday and F
but am free otherwise.^
VSSH
When do you
out?
DING ♫
I work on Tues
riday,
but am free otherwise. ^▽^
How about tomorrow after school?

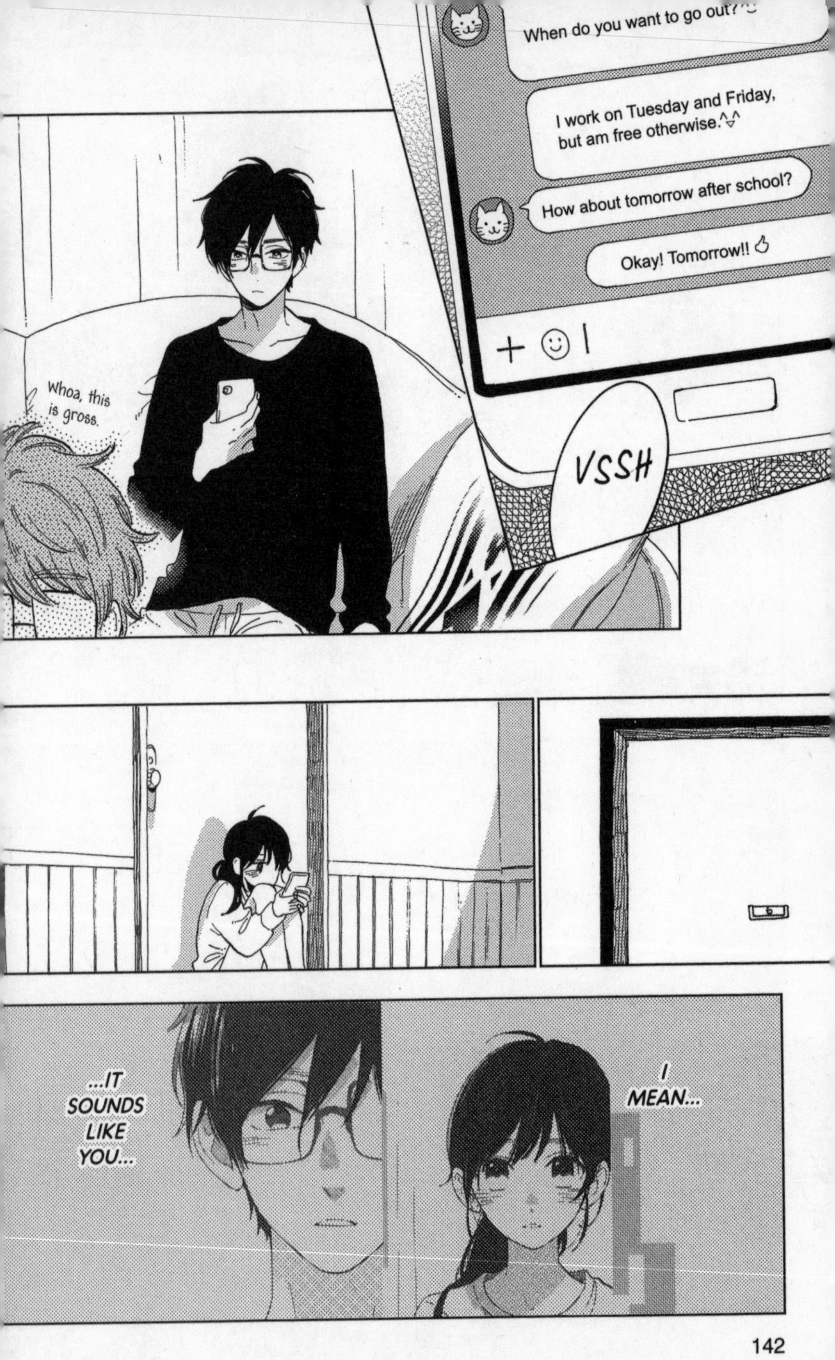
When do you want to go out?
I work on Tuesday and Friday, but am free otherwise.^▽^
How about tomorrow after school?
Okay! Tomorrow!!
VSSH
Whoa, this is gross.
I MEAN...
...IT SOUNDS LIKE YOU...

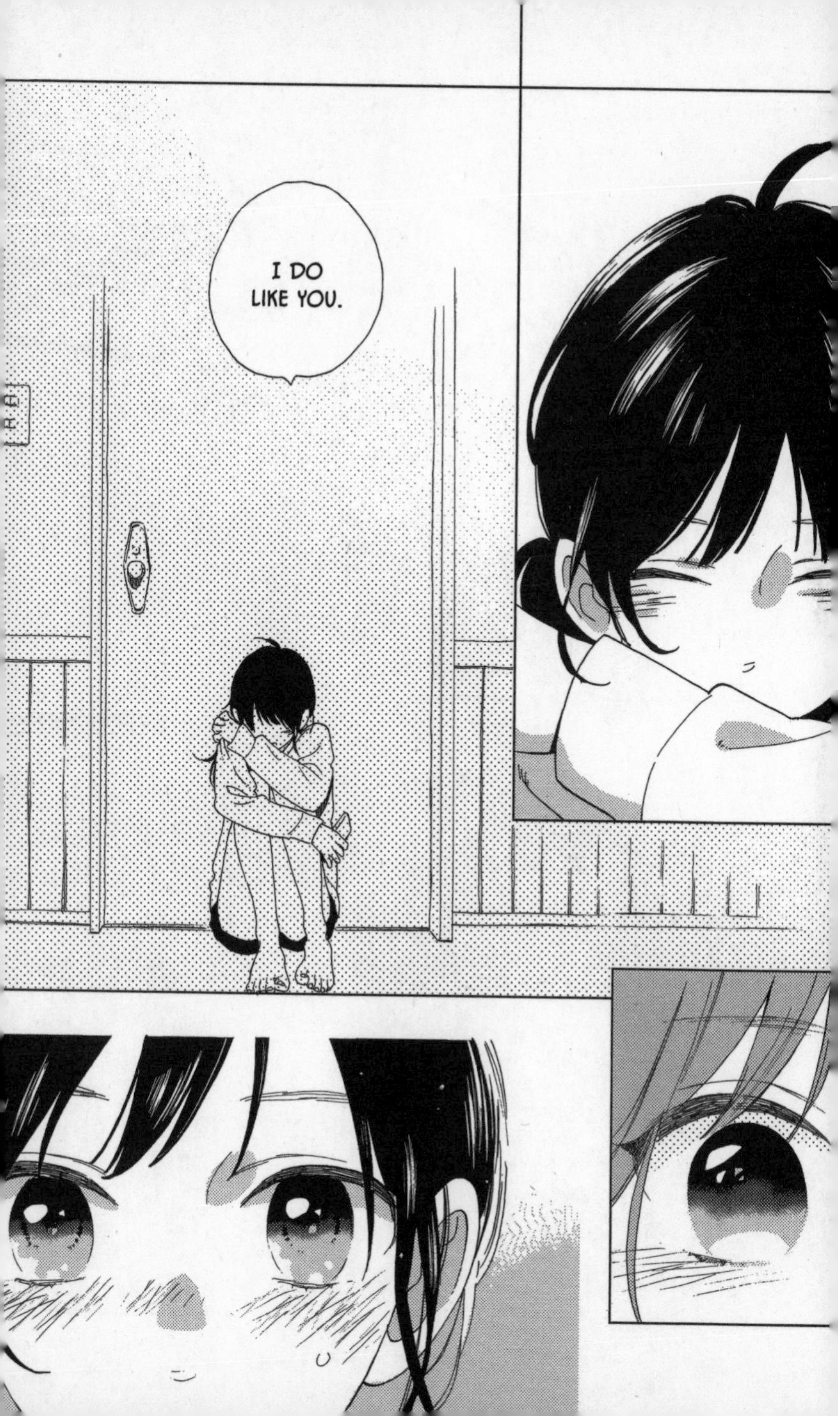
I DO LIKE YOU.

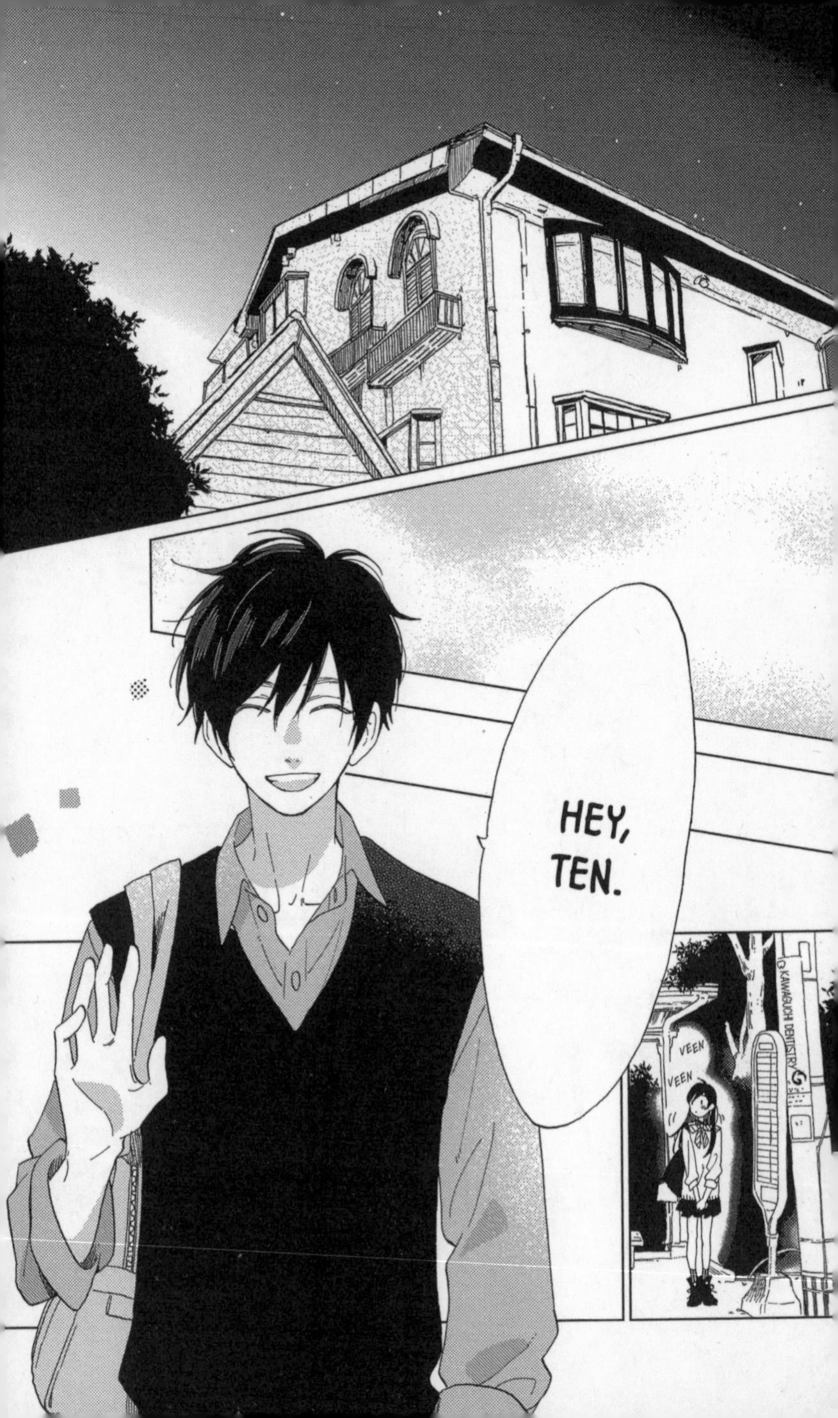
HEY, TEN.
KAWAGUCHI DENTISTRY
VEEN
VEEN

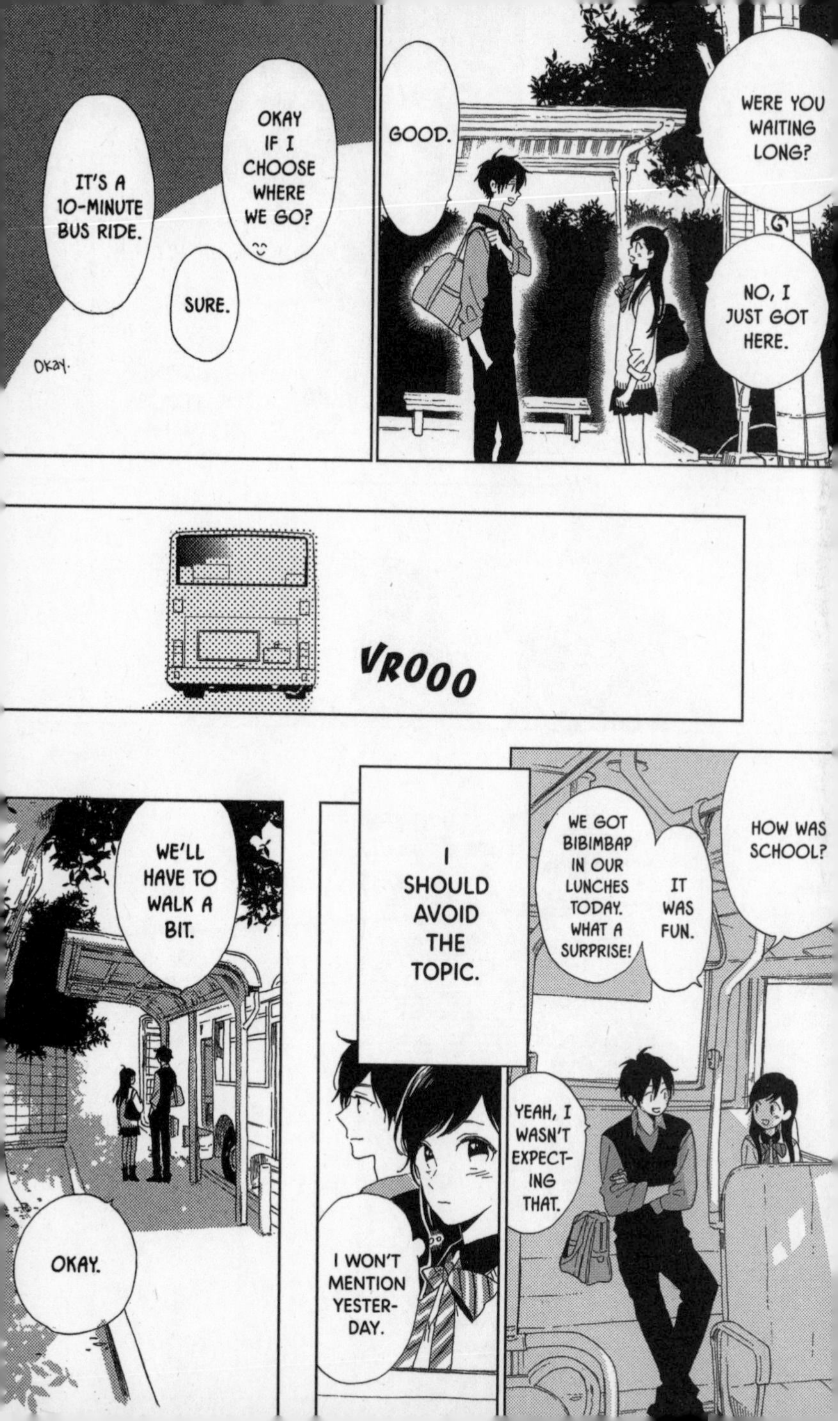
WERE YOU WAITING LONG?
NO, I JUST GOT HERE.
GOOD.
OKAY IF I CHOOSE WHERE WE GO?
IT'S A 10-MINUTE BUS RIDE.
SURE.
Okay.
VROOO
HOW WAS SCHOOL?
IT WAS FUN.
WE GOT BIBIMBAP IN OUR LUNCHES TODAY. WHAT A SURPRISE!
YEAH, I WASN'T EXPECT-ING THAT.
I SHOULD AVOID THE TOPIC.
I WON'T MENTION YESTER-DAY.
WE'LL HAVE TO WALK A BIT.
OKAY.

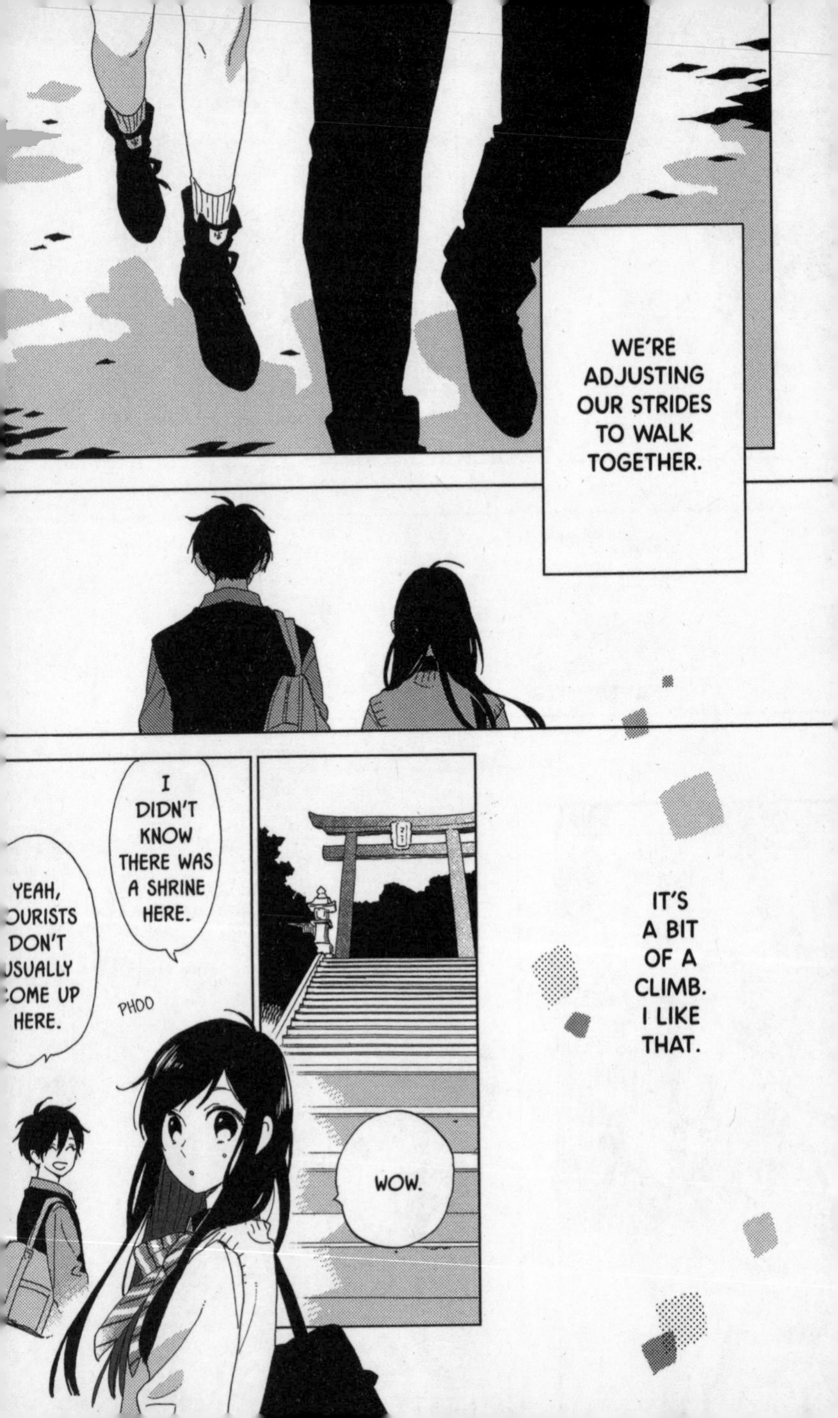
WE'RE ADJUSTING OUR STRIDES TO WALK TOGETHER.
IT'S A BIT OF A CLIMB. I LIKE THAT.
WOW.
I DIDN'T KNOW THERE WAS A SHRINE HERE.
PHOO
YEAH, OURISTS DON'T USUALLY OME UP HERE.

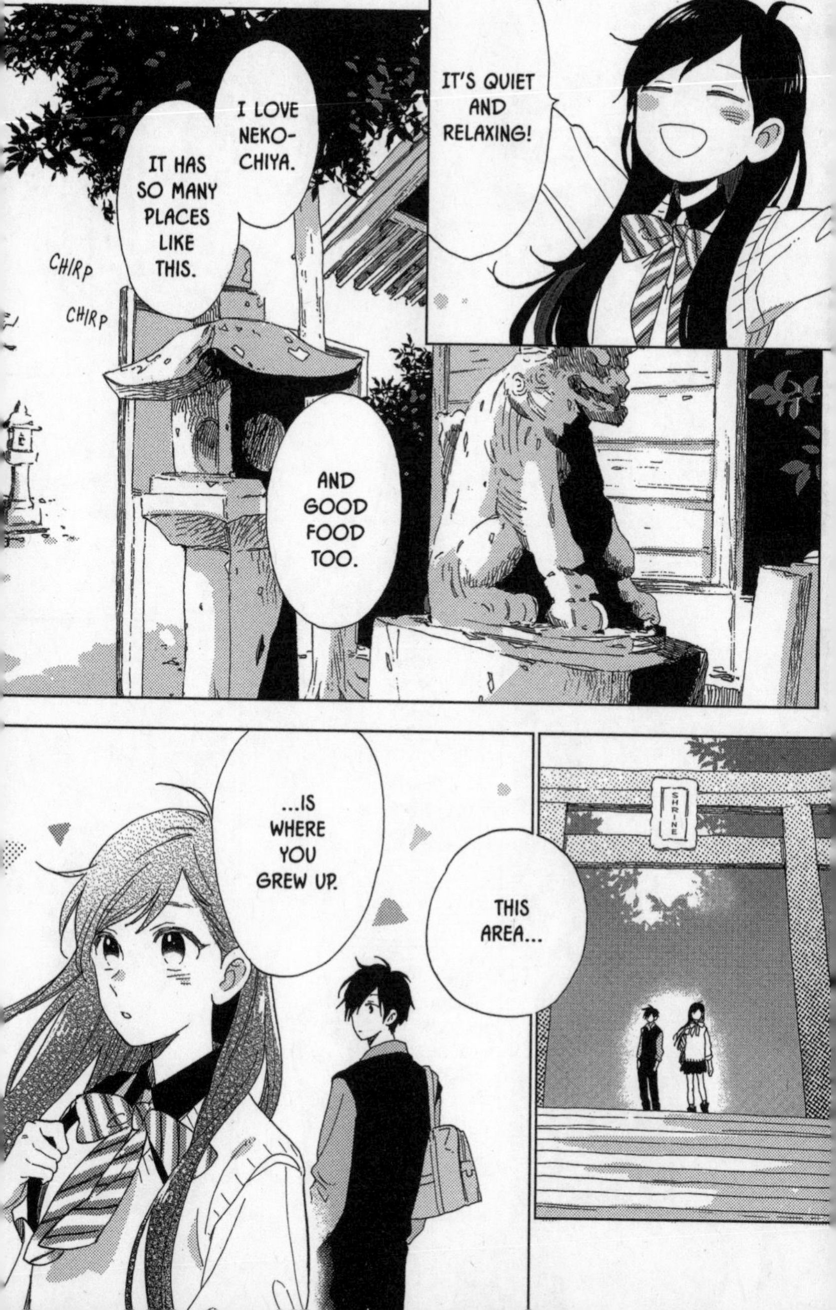
IT'S QUIET AND RELAXING!
I LOVE NEKO-CHIYA.
IT HAS SO MANY PLACES LIKE THIS.
CHIRP
CHIRP
AND GOOD FOOD TOO.
SHRINE
THIS AREA...
...IS WHERE YOU GREW UP.

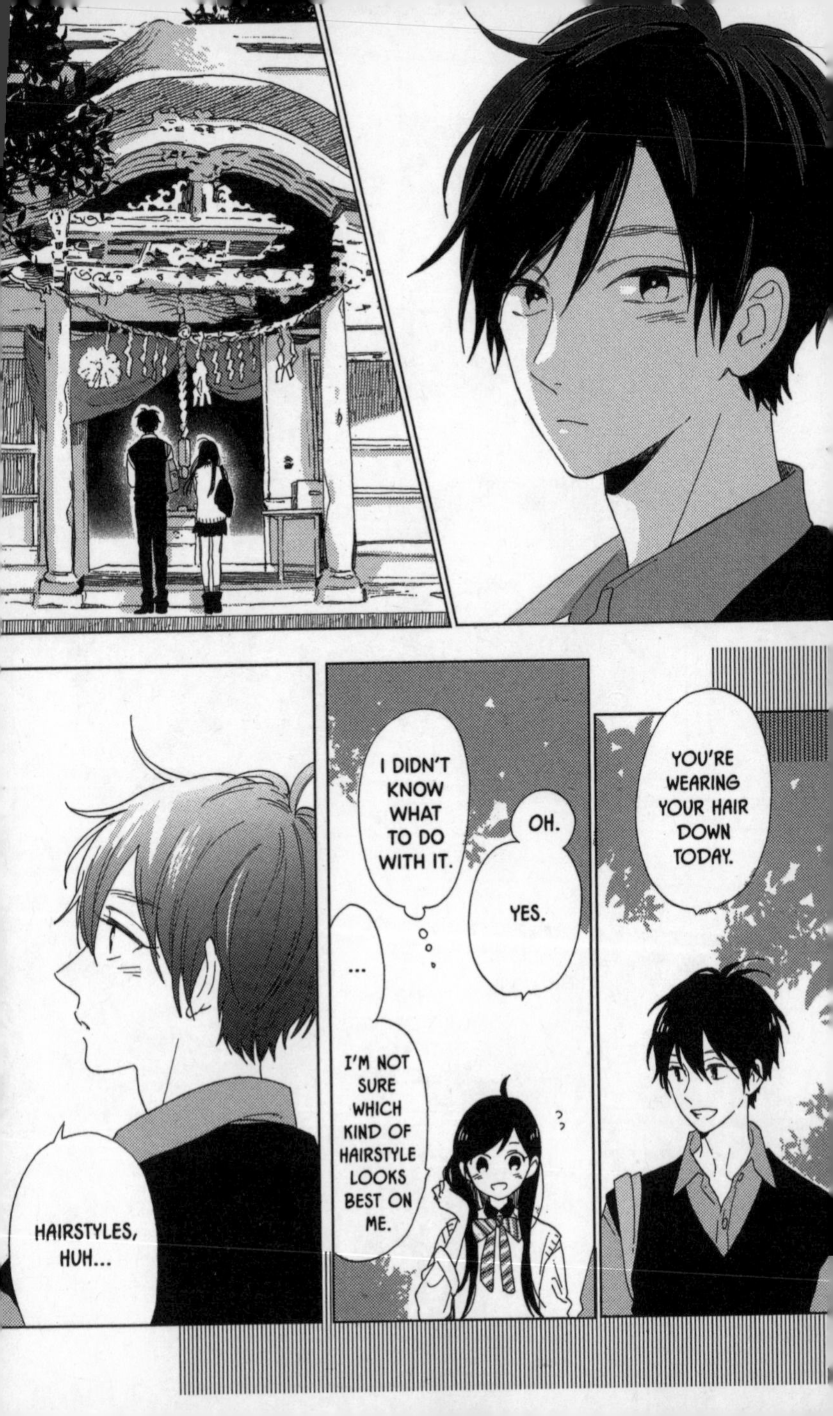
YOU'RE WEARING YOUR HAIR DOWN TODAY.
OH.
YES.
I DIDN'T KNOW WHAT TO DO WITH IT.
...
I'M NOT SURE WHICH KIND OF HAIRSTYLE LOOKS BEST ON ME.
HAIRSTYLES, HUH...

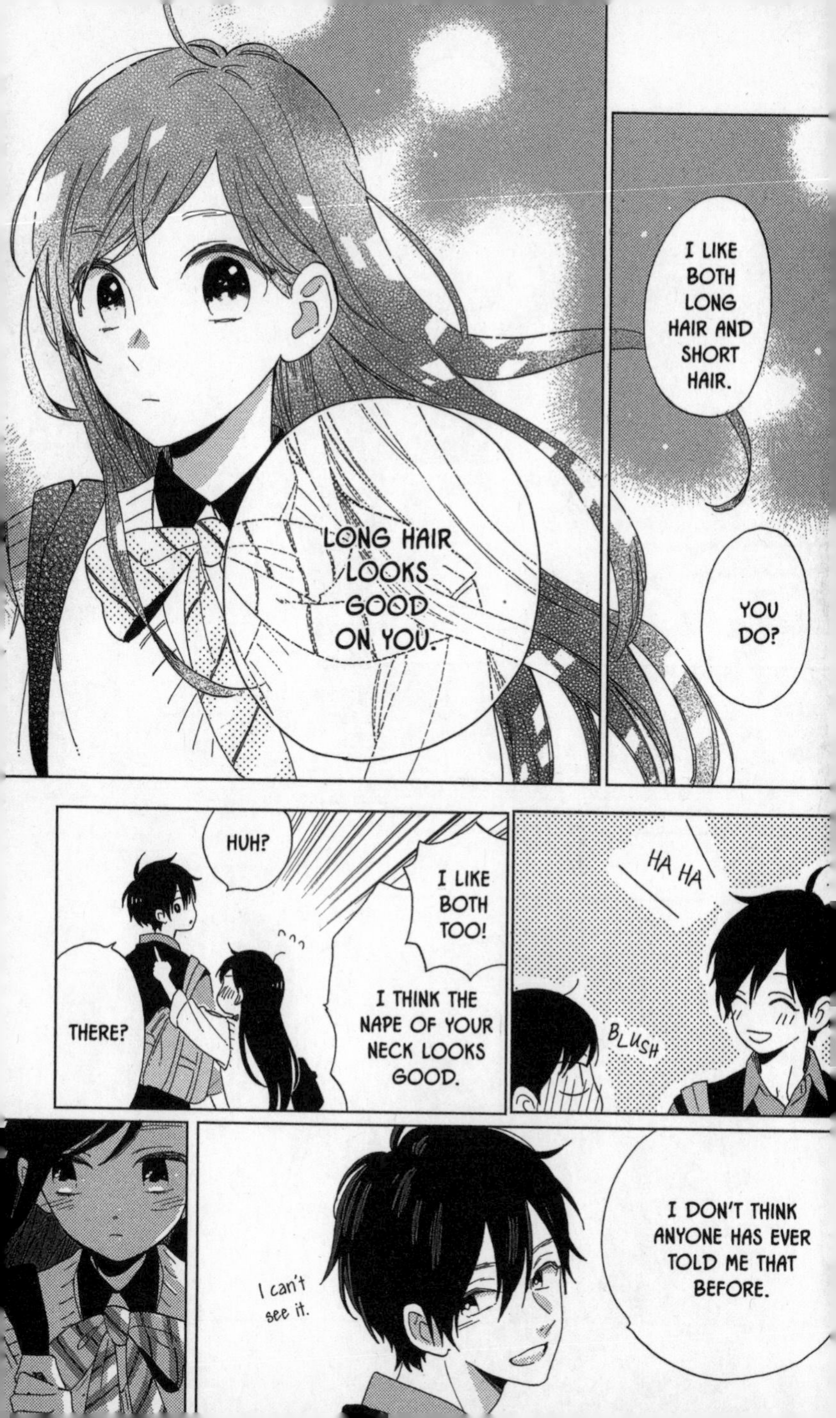
I LIKE BOTH LONG HAIR AND SHORT HAIR.
YOU DO?
LONG HAIR LOOKS GOOD ON YOU.
HA HA
BLUSH
I LIKE BOTH TOO!
HUH?
I THINK THE NAPE OF YOUR NECK LOOKS GOOD.
THERE?
I DON'T THINK ANYONE HAS EVER TOLD ME THAT BEFORE.
I can't see it.

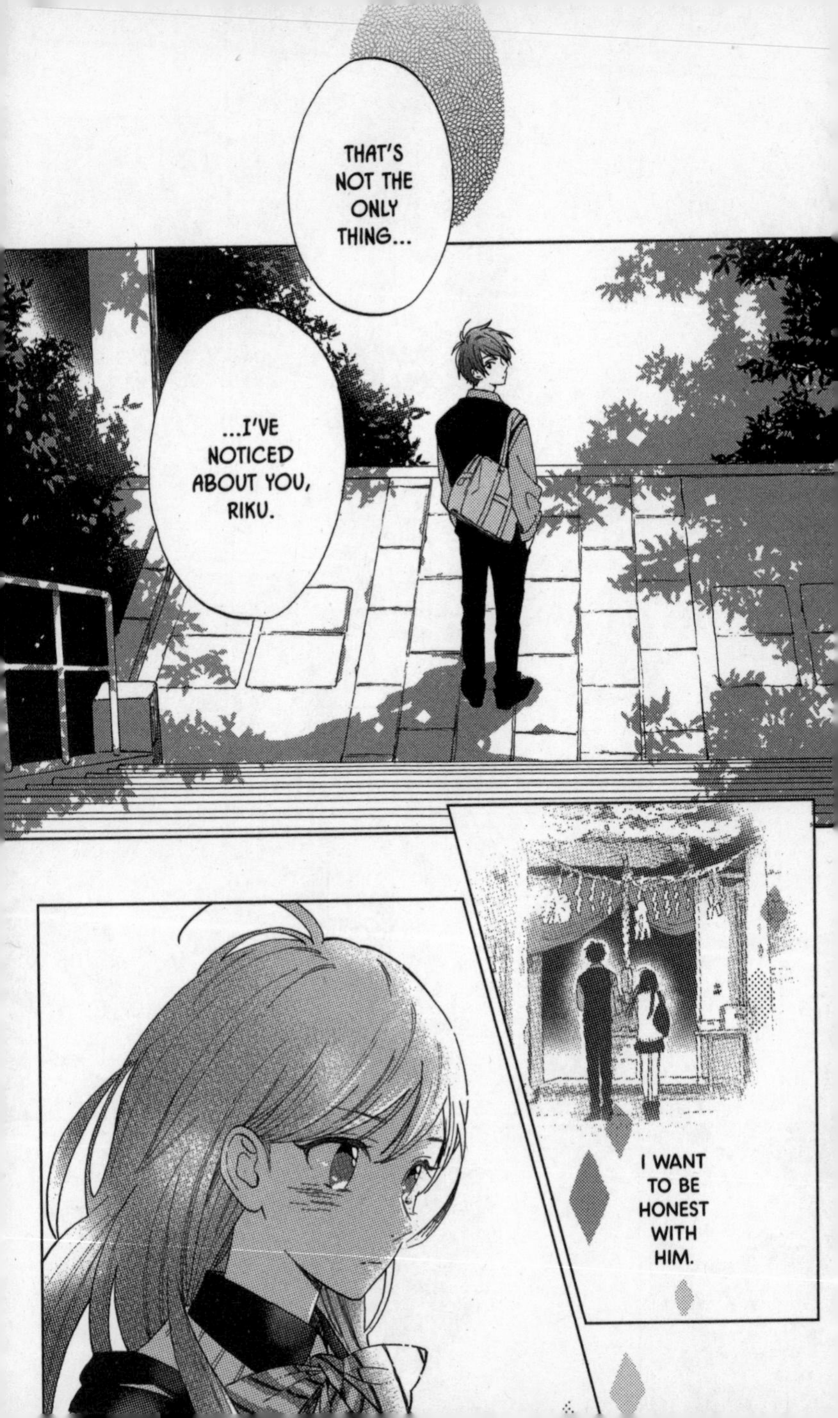
THAT'S NOT THE ONLY THING...
...I'VE NOTICED ABOUT YOU, RIKU.
I WANT TO BE HONEST WITH HIM.

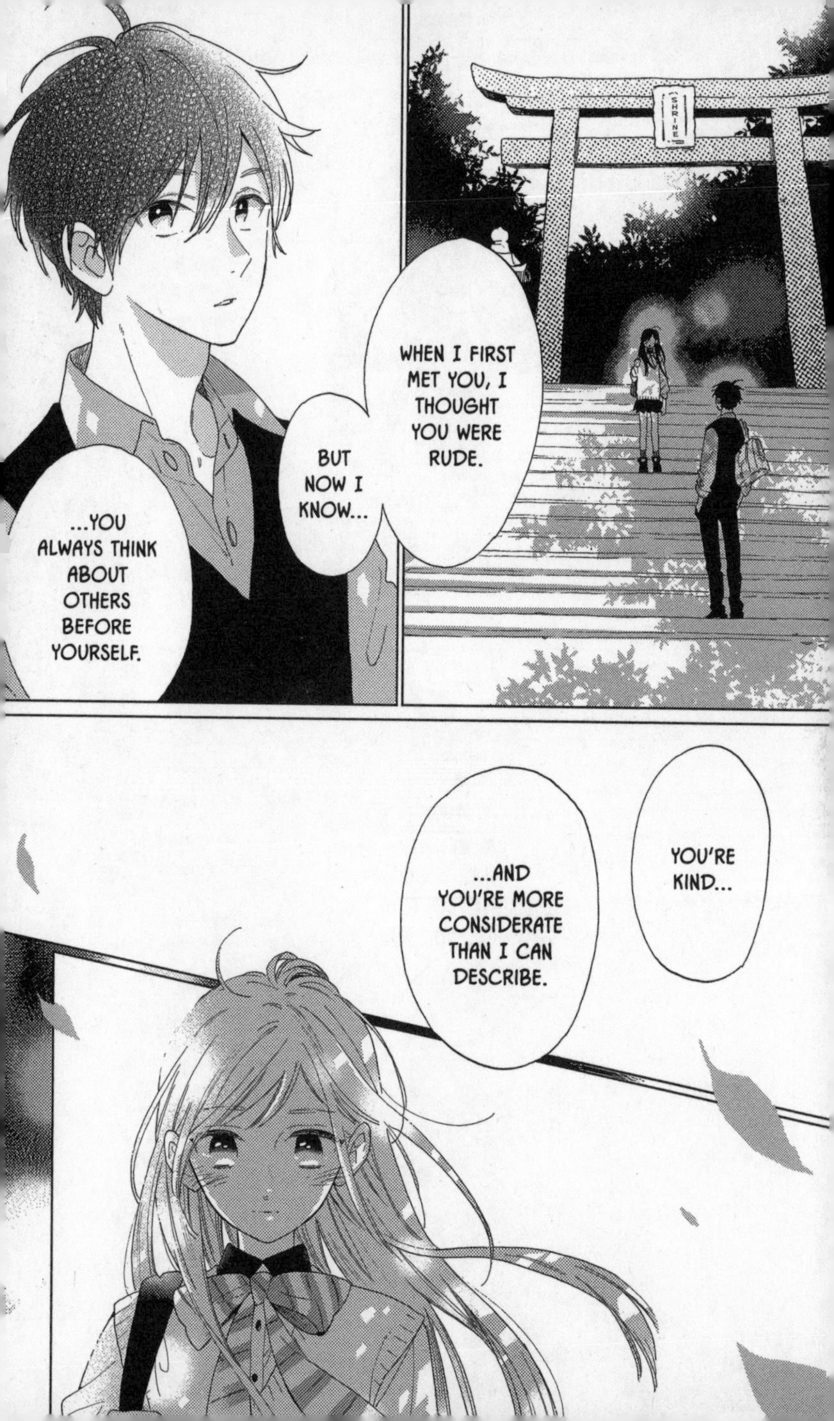
SHRINE
WHEN I FIRST MET YOU, I THOUGHT YOU WERE RUDE.
BUT NOW I KNOW...
...YOU ALWAYS THINK ABOUT OTHERS BEFORE YOURSELF.
YOU'RE KIND...
...AND YOU'RE MORE CONSIDERATE THAN I CAN DESCRIBE.

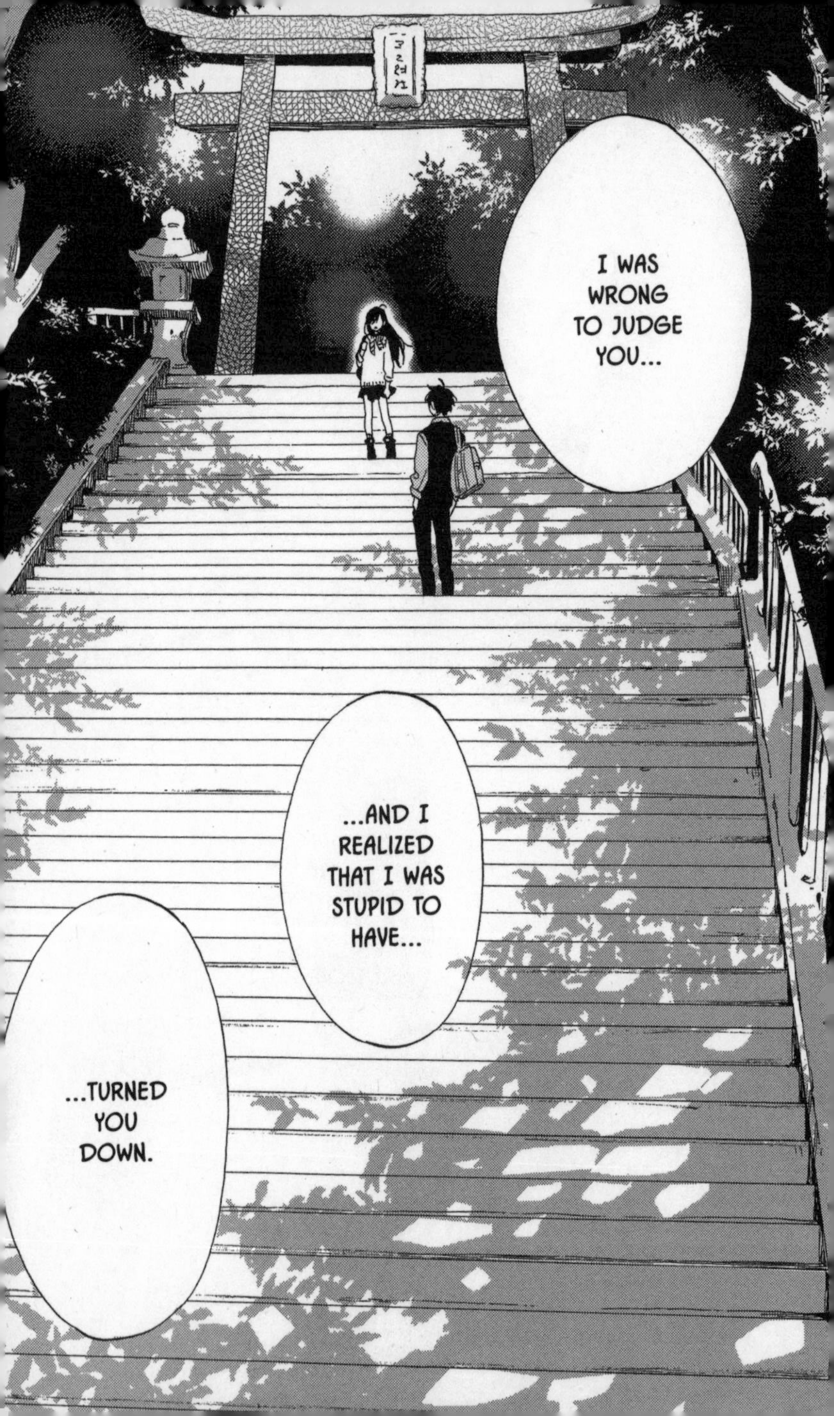
I WAS WRONG TO JUDGE YOU...
...AND I REALIZED THAT I WAS STUPID TO HAVE...
...TURNED YOU DOWN.

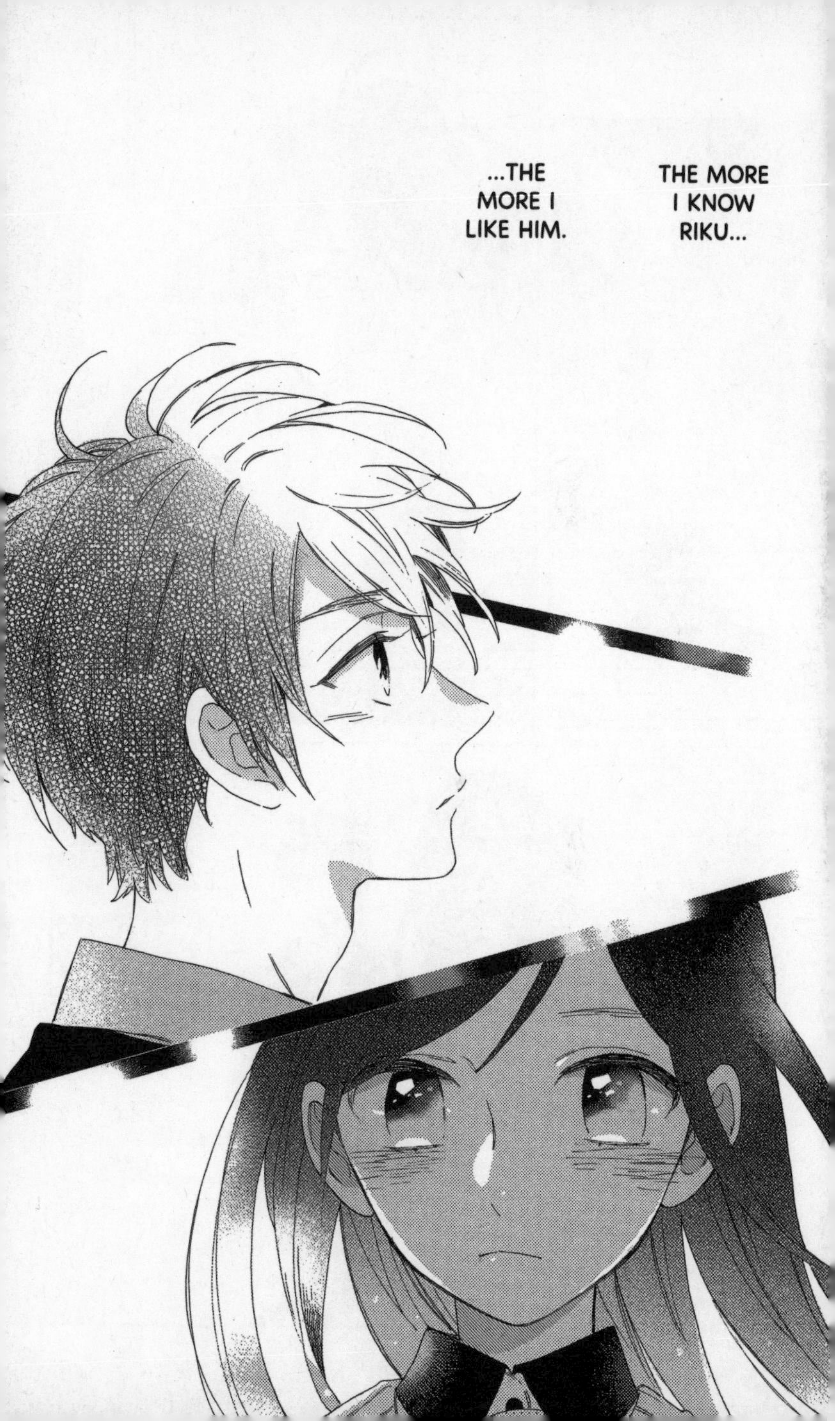
THE MORE I KNOW RIKU...
...THE MORE I LIKE HIM.

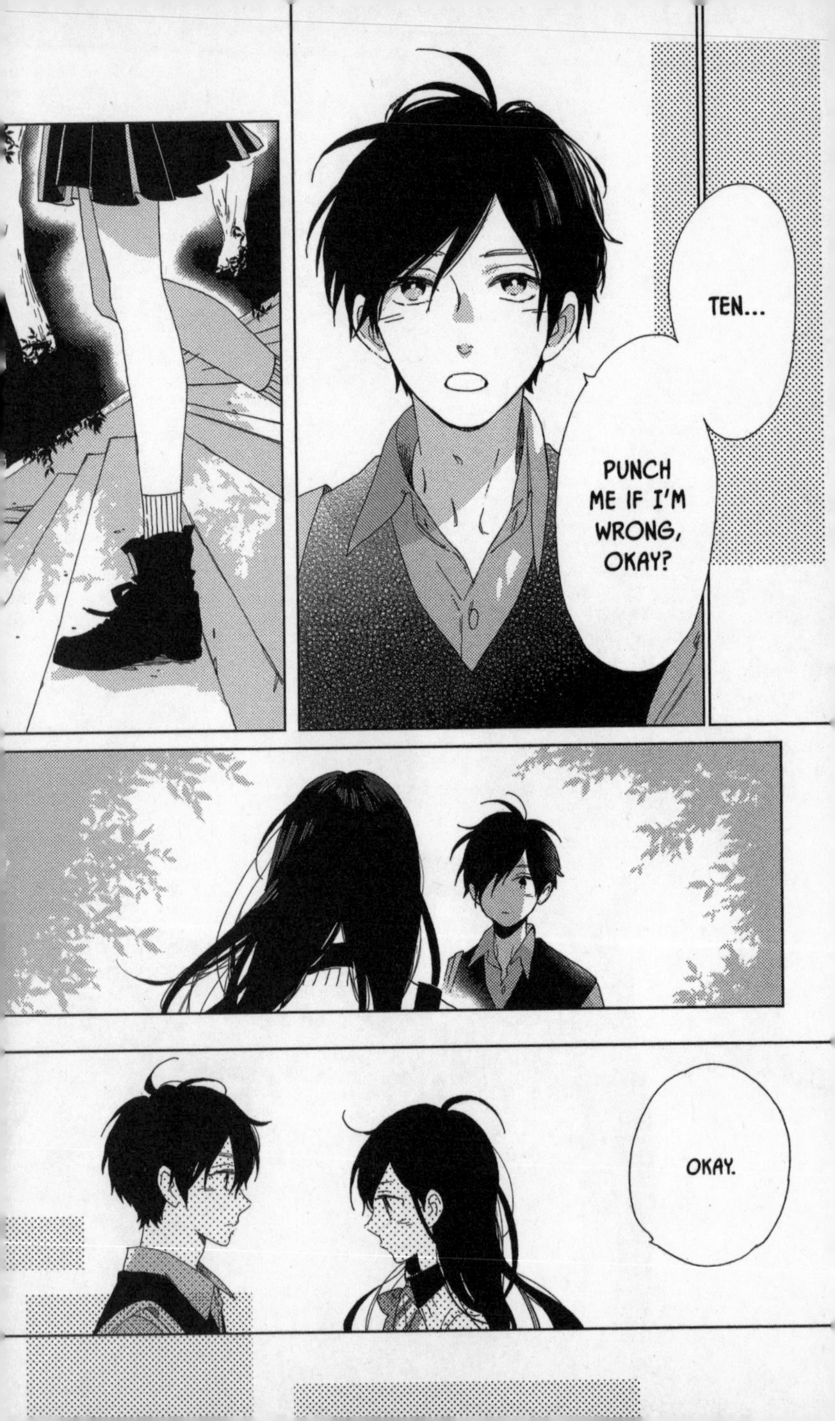
TEN...
PUNCH ME IF I'M WRONG, OKAY?
OKAY.

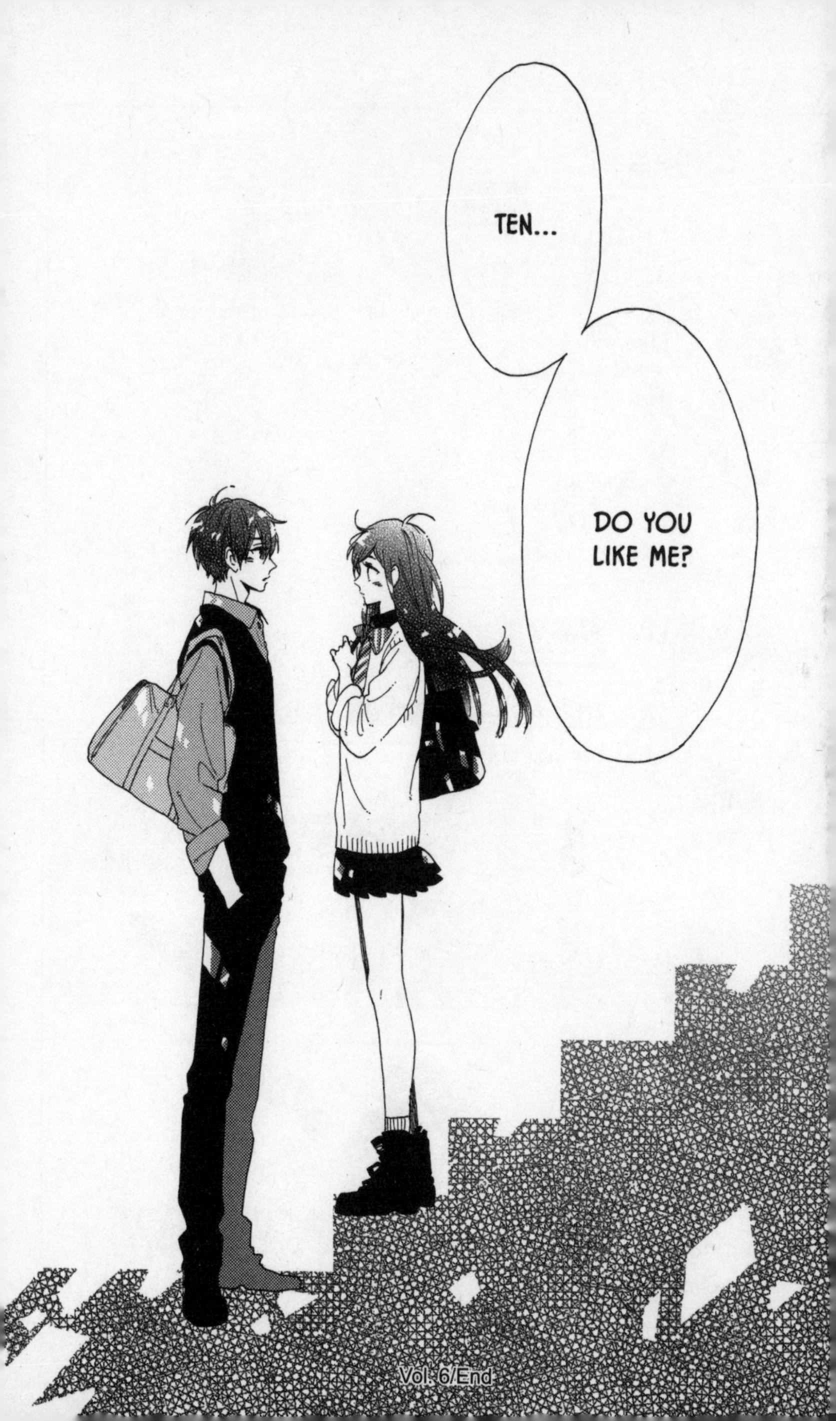
TEN...
DO YOU LIKE ME?
Vol. 6/End

## ▽▲△ Series Details ▽▲▽

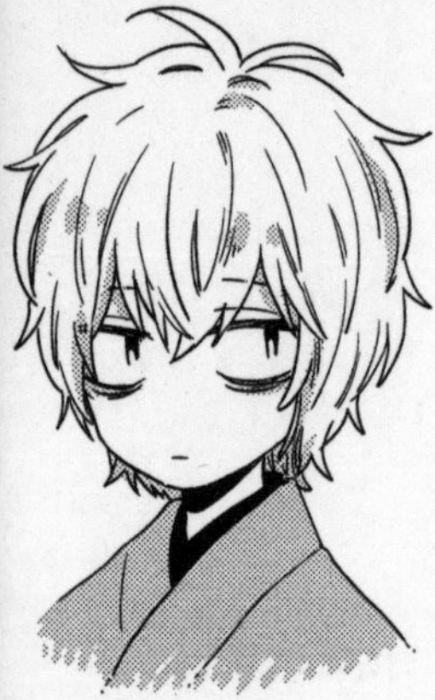

### REI

I imagine his hair to be shades of brown, rather like a milk-tea color. It's a bright brown.

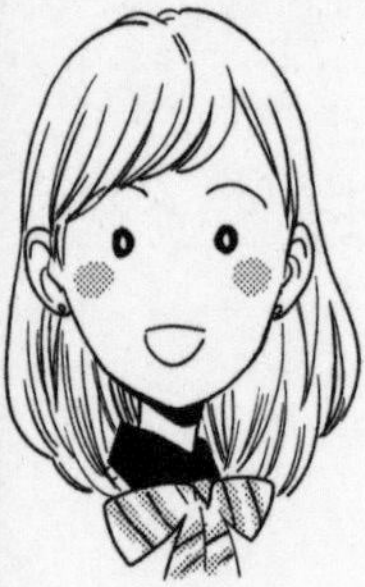

### AGEHA

She's a brunette, and she dyes her hair a little.

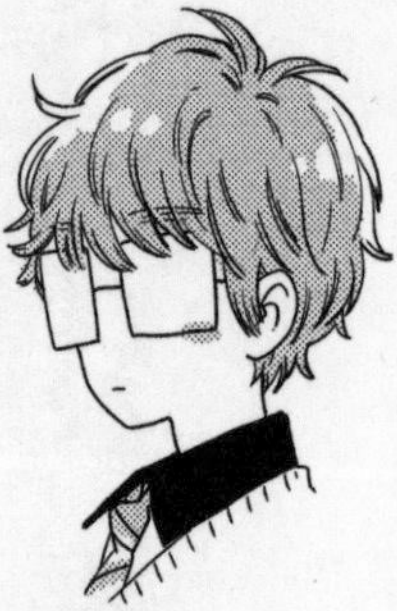

### YUTO

His hair is chestnut and naturally wavy.

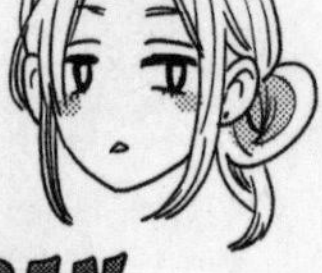

### RAN

She dyes her hair blonde, but it's usually a bit brown on top like flan.

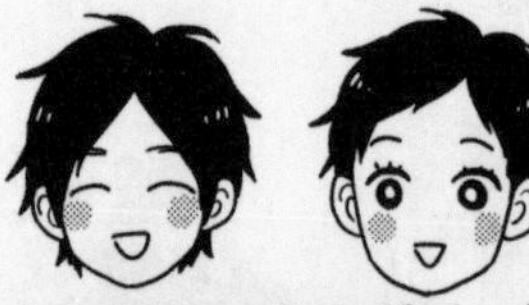

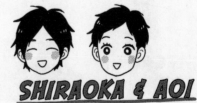

### SHIRAOKA & AOI

Both have plain black hair.

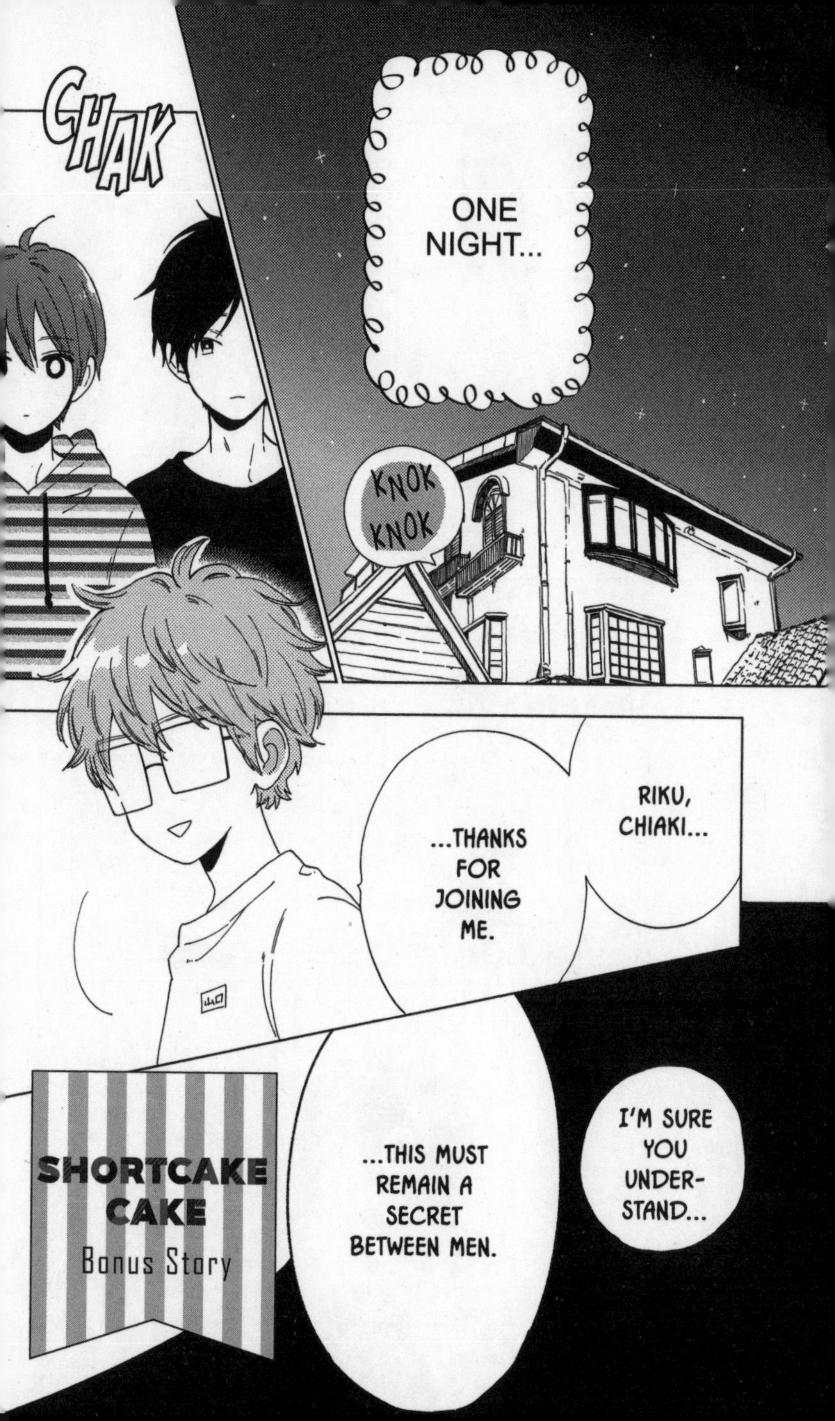
ONE NIGHT...
KNOK KNOK
CHAK
RIKU, CHIAKI...
...THANKS FOR JOINING ME.
I'M SURE YOU UNDER-STAND...
...THIS MUST REMAIN A SECRET BETWEEN MEN.
SHORTCAKE CAKE
Bonus Story

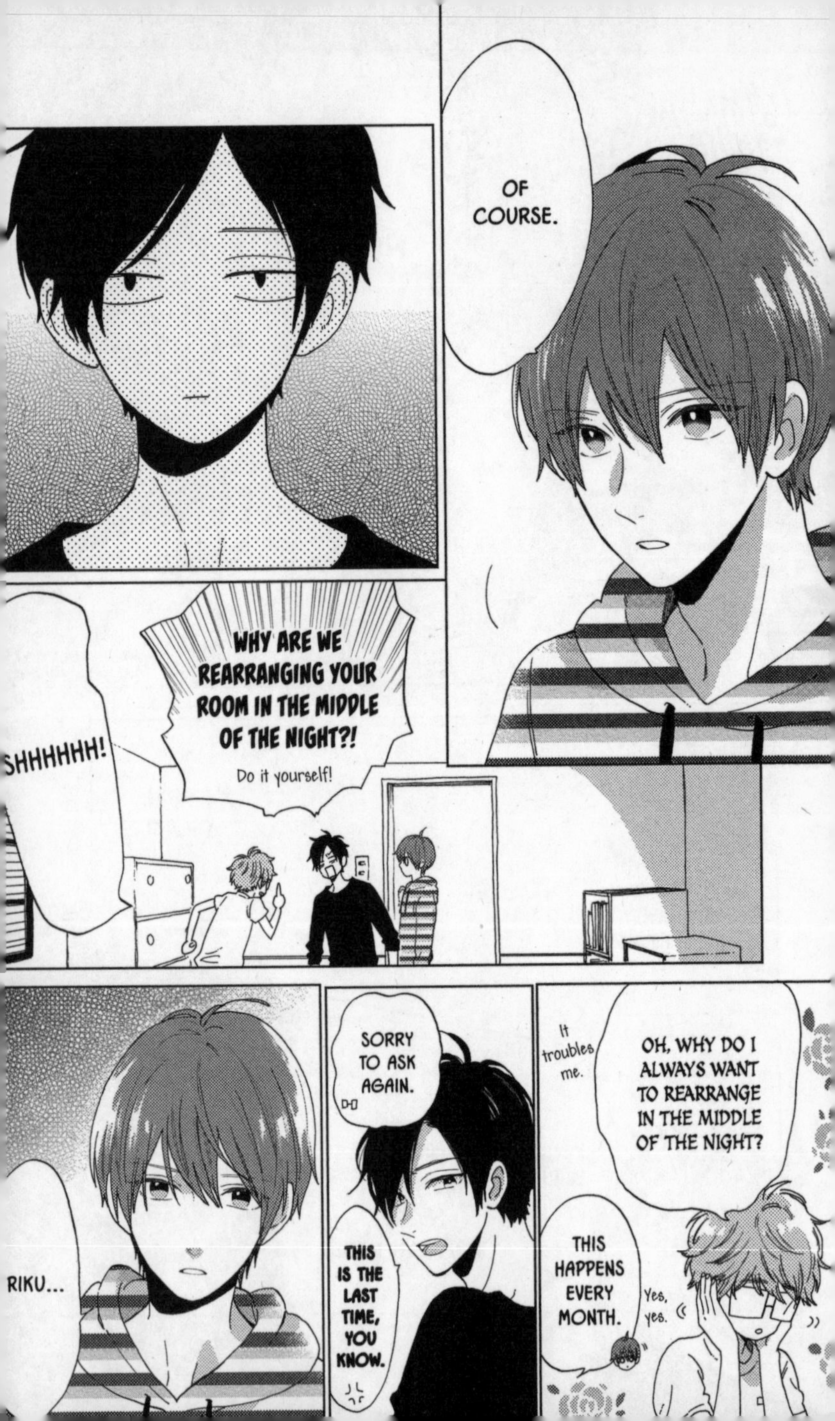
OF COURSE.
WHY ARE WE REARRANGING YOUR ROOM IN THE MIDDLE OF THE NIGHT?!
Do it yourself!
SHHHHHH!
OH, WHY DO I ALWAYS WANT TO REARRANGE IN THE MIDDLE OF THE NIGHT?
It troubles me.
Yes, yes.
THIS HAPPENS EVERY MONTH.
SORRY TO ASK AGAIN.
THIS IS THE LAST TIME, YOU KNOW.
RIKU...

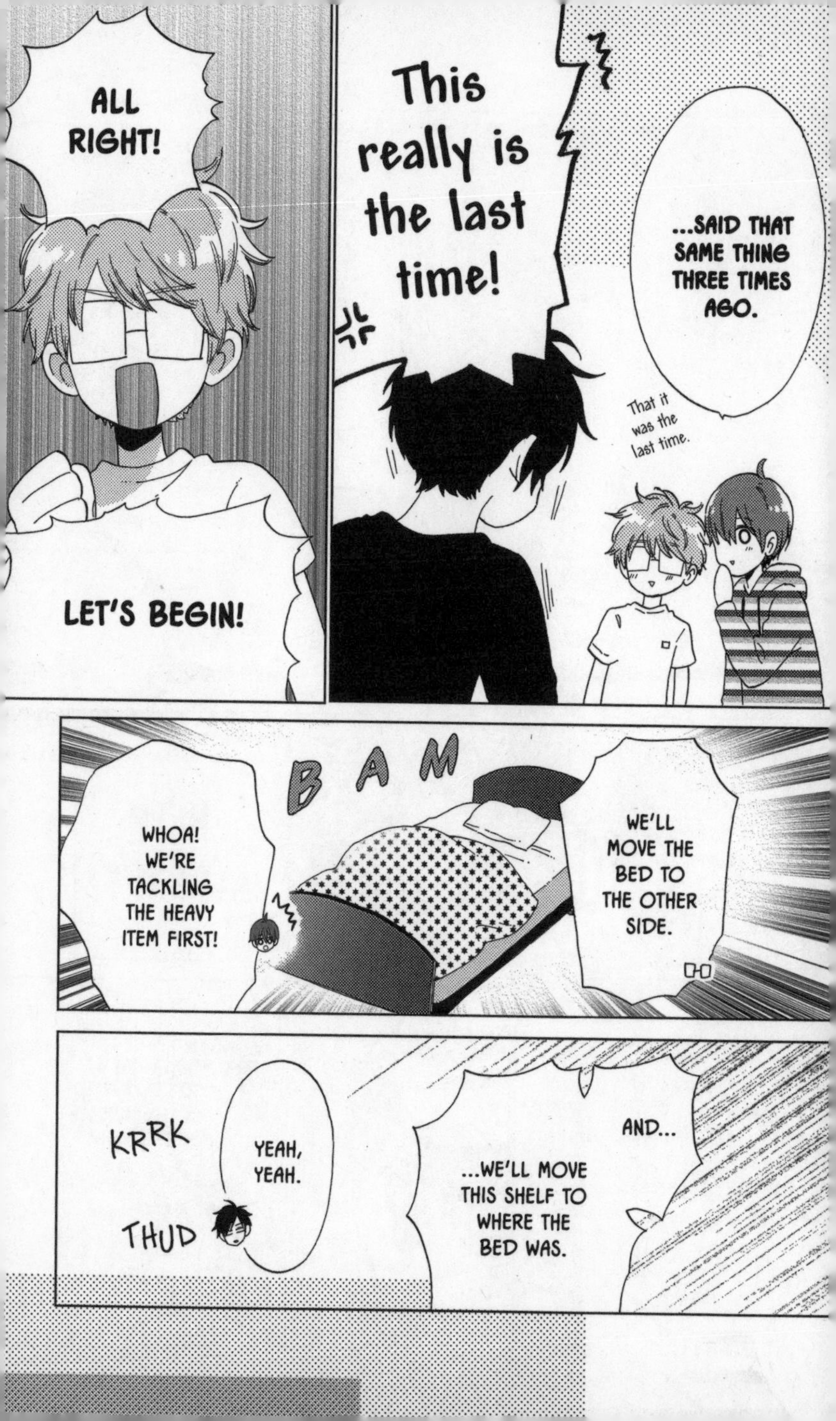
This really is the last time!
...SAID THAT SAME THING THREE TIMES AGO.
That it was the last time.
ALL RIGHT!
LET'S BEGIN!
WE'LL MOVE THE BED TO THE OTHER SIDE.
BAM
WHOA! WE'RE TACKLING THE HEAVY ITEM FIRST!
AND...
...WE'LL MOVE THIS SHELF TO WHERE THE BED WAS.
YEAH, YEAH.
KRRK
THUD

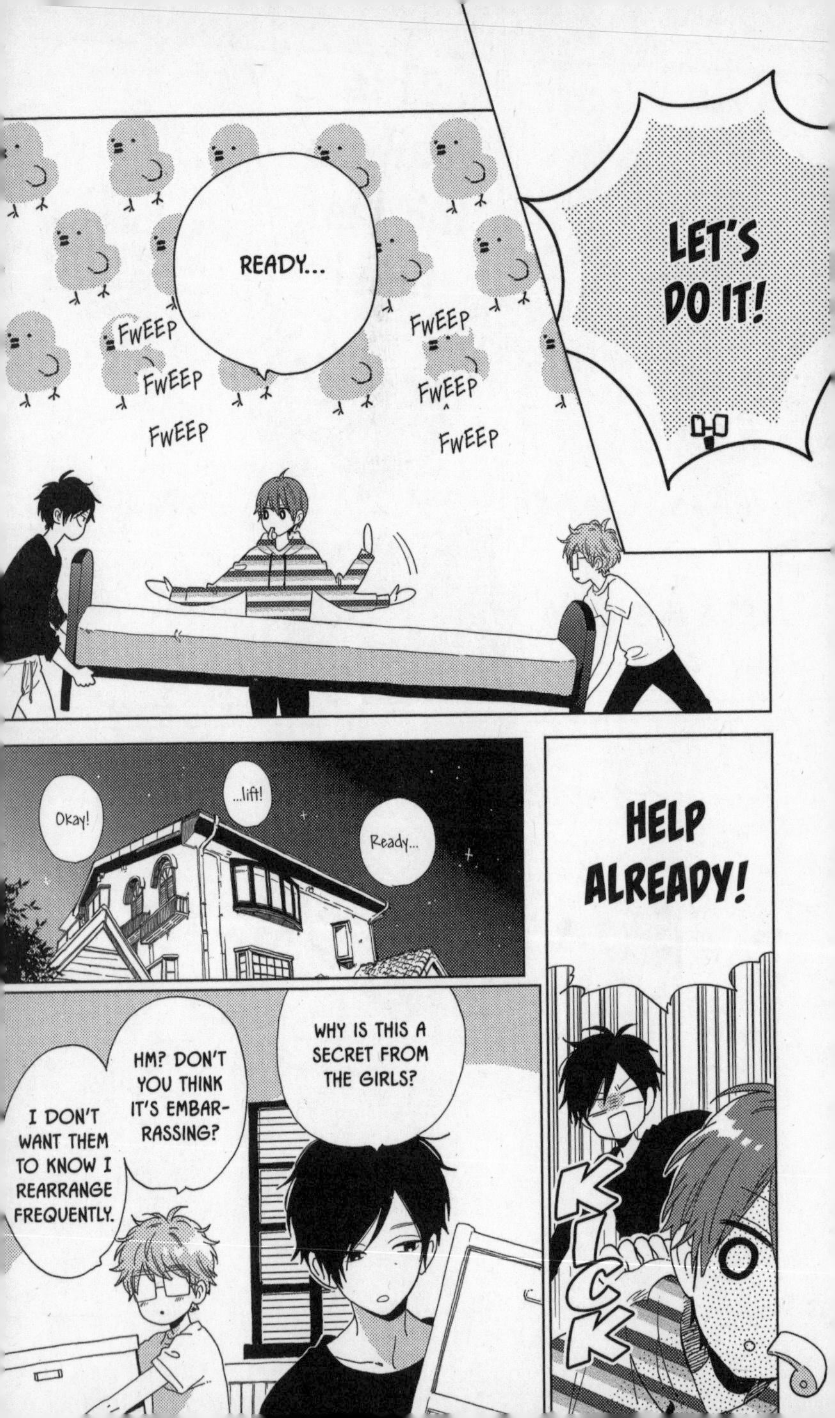
LET'S DO IT!
READY...
FWEEP
FWEEP
FWEEP
FWEEP
FWEEP
FWEEP
HELP ALREADY!
KICK
Ready...
...lift!
Okay!
WHY IS THIS A SECRET FROM THE GIRLS?
HM? DON'T YOU THINK IT'S EMBAR-RASSING?
I DON'T WANT THEM TO KNOW I REARRANGE FREQUENTLY.

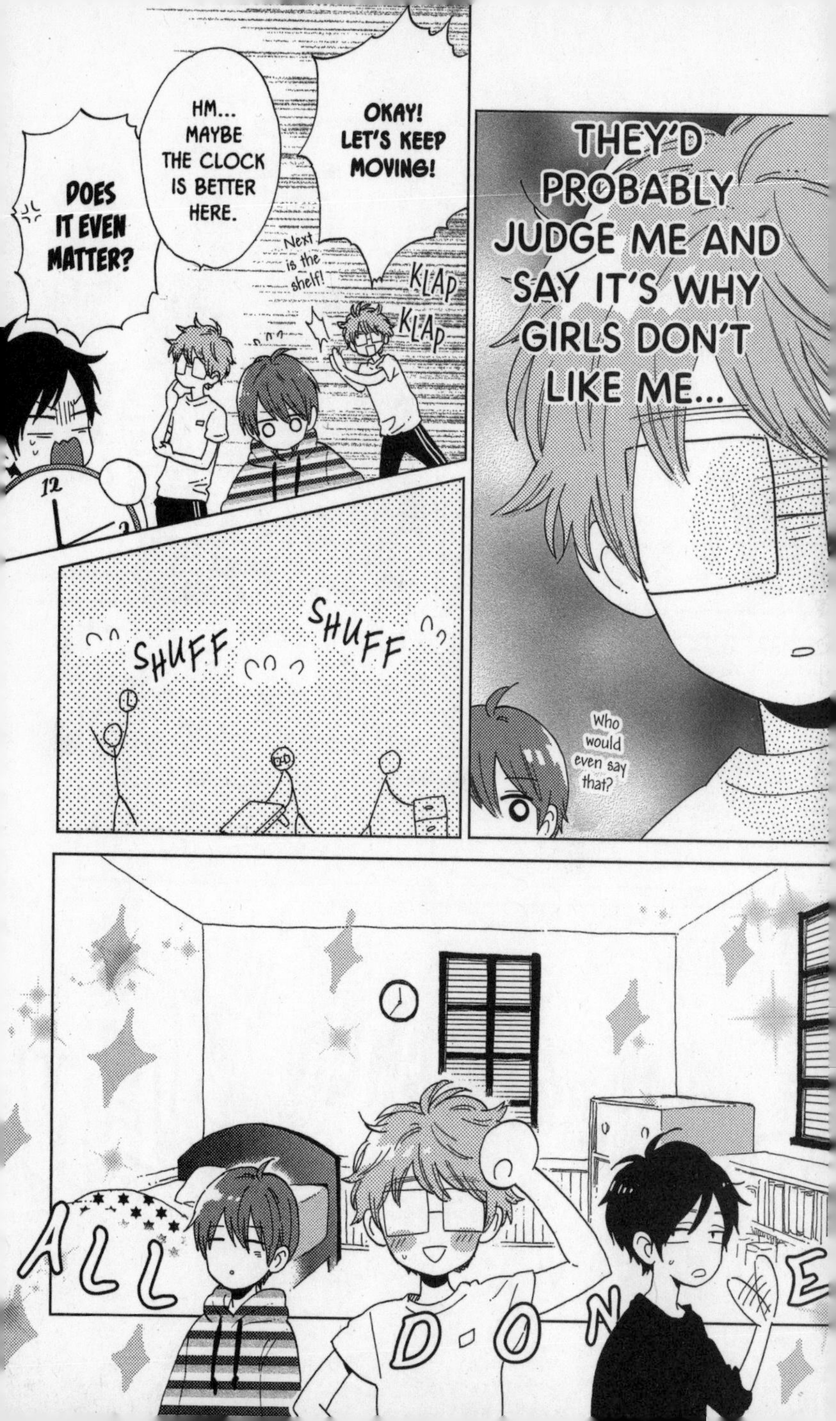
OKAY! LET'S KEEP MOVING!
HM... MAYBE THE CLOCK IS BETTER HERE.
DOES IT EVEN MATTER?
Next is the shelf!
KLAP KLAP
12
SHUFF SHUFF
THEY'D PROBABLY JUDGE ME AND SAY IT'S WHY GIRLS DON'T LIKE ME...
Who would even say that?
ALL DONE

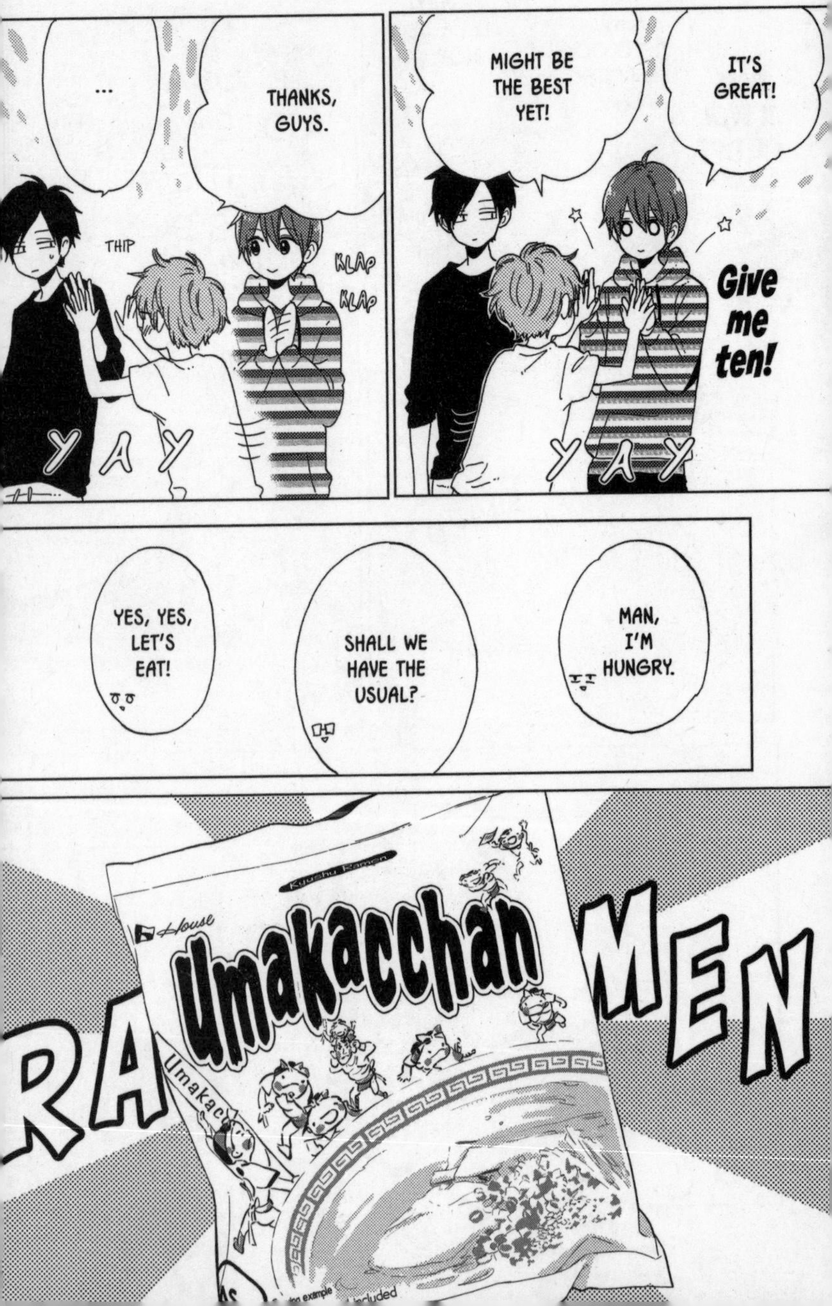
IT'S GREAT!
MIGHT BE THE BEST YET!
Give me ten!
YAY
THANKS, GUYS.
...
KLAP
KLAP
THIP
YAY
MAN, I'M HUNGRY.
SHALL WE HAVE THE USUAL?
YES, YES, LET'S EAT!
RAMEN
Kyushu Ramen
House
Umakacchan

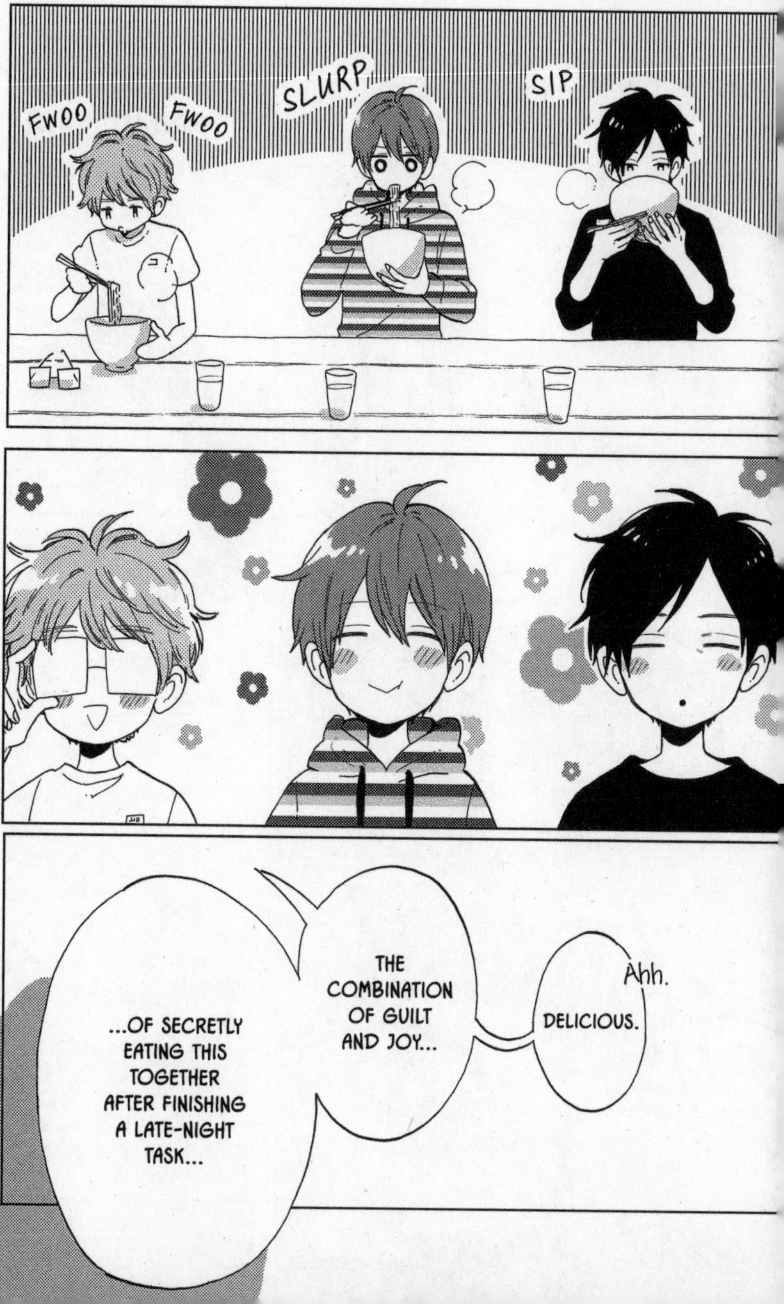
SIP
SLURP
FWOO
FWOO
Ahh.
DELICIOUS.
THE COMBINATION OF GUILT AND JOY...
...OF SECRETLY EATING THIS TOGETHER AFTER FINISHING A LATE-NIGHT TASK...

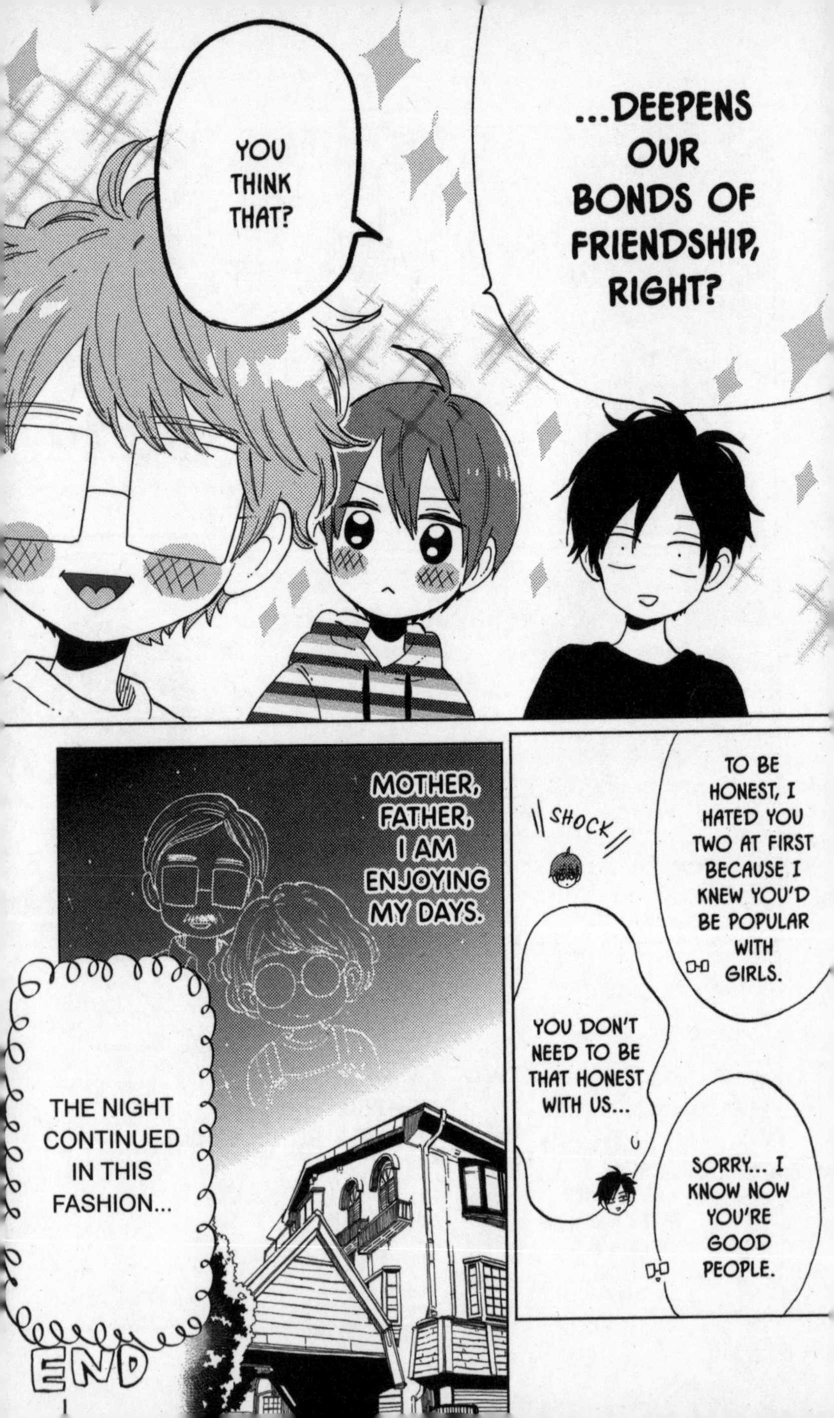
...DEEPENS OUR BONDS OF FRIENDSHIP, RIGHT?
YOU THINK THAT?
TO BE HONEST, I HATED YOU TWO AT FIRST BECAUSE I KNEW YOU'D BE POPULAR WITH GIRLS.
SHOCK
YOU DON'T NEED TO BE THAT HONEST WITH US...
SORRY... I KNOW NOW YOU'RE GOOD PEOPLE.
MOTHER, FATHER, I AM ENJOYING MY DAYS.
THE NIGHT CONTINUED IN THIS FASHION...
END

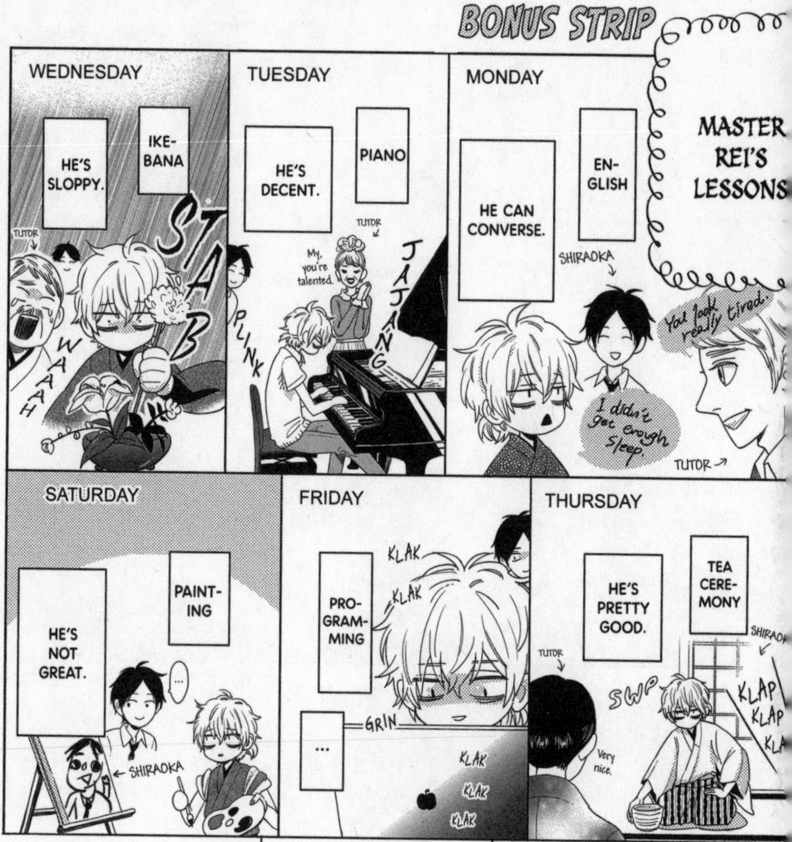
BONUS STRIP
MASTER REI'S LESSONS
You look really tired.
TUTOR
I didn't get enough sleep.
MONDAY
SHIRAOKA
ENGLISH
HE CAN CONVERSE.
TUESDAY
PIANO
TUTOR
HE'S DECENT.
My, you're talented.
JAJANG
PLINK
WEDNESDAY
IKEBANA
HE'S SLOPPY.
STAB
TUTOR
WAAAH
THURSDAY
TEA CEREMONY
SHIRAOKA
HE'S PRETTY GOOD.
KLAP KLAP KLAP
SWP
TUTOR
Very nice.
FRIDAY
PROGRAMMING
KLAK
KLAK
GRIN
...
KLAK KLAK KLAK
SATURDAY
PAINTING
HE'S NOT GREAT.
...
SHIRAOKA
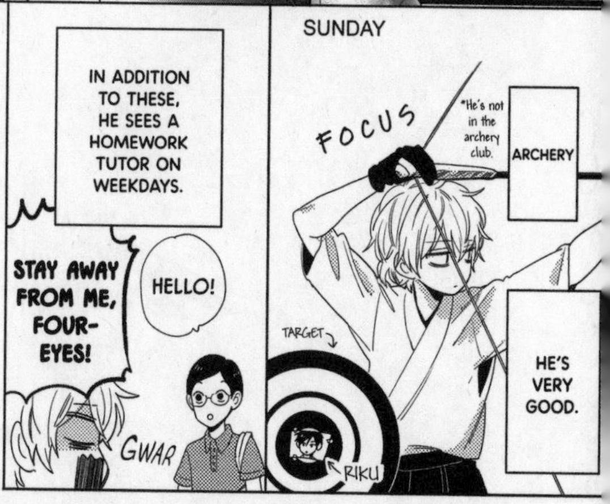
SUNDAY
ARCHERY
*He's not in the archery club.
FOCUS
HE'S VERY GOOD.
TARGET
RIKU
IN ADDITION TO THESE, HE SEES A HOMEWORK TUTOR ON WEEKDAYS.
HELLO!
STAY AWAY FROM ME, FOUR-EYES!
GWAR

Thanks for reading volume 6!

Hope to see you again in volume 7!

**Special Thanks**

- Tanyaka
- The Margaret editorial team
- Our designer, Yasuhisa Kawatani
- Our assistant, Nao Hamaguchi
- Our assistant's helper, Kame-chimu

And all our readers

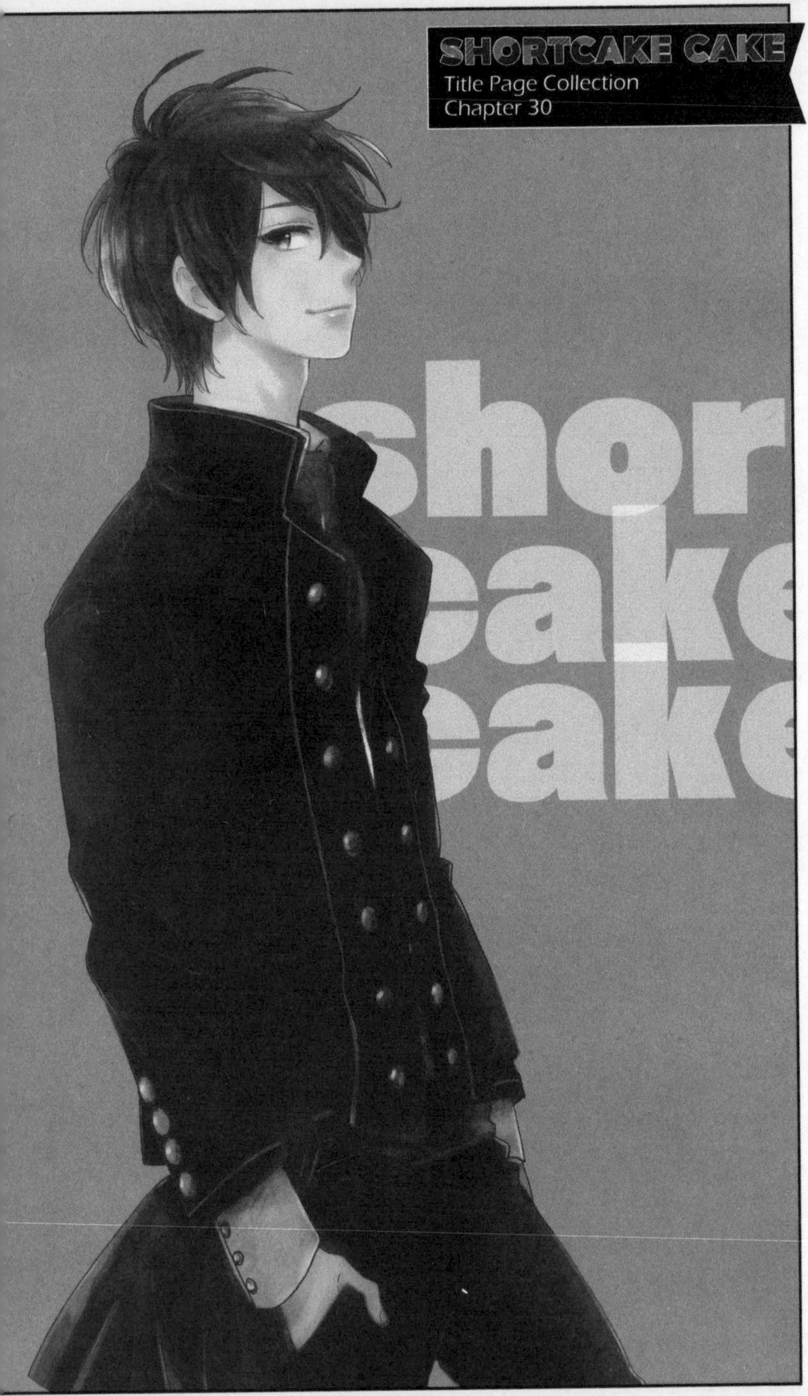
SHORTCAKE CAKE
Title Page Collection
Chapter 30

**SHORTCAKE CAKE**
Title Page Collection
Issue 9 Magazine Cover

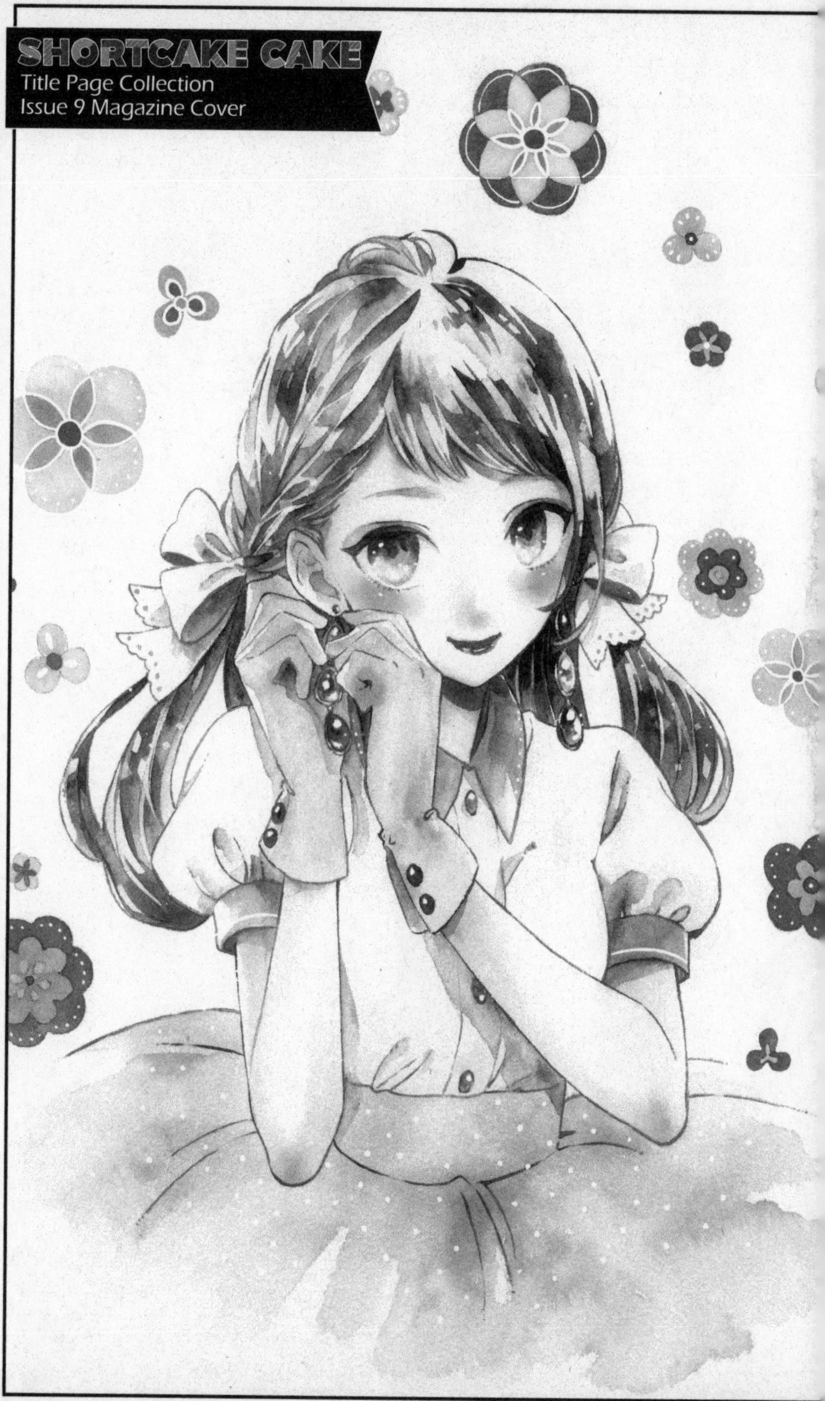

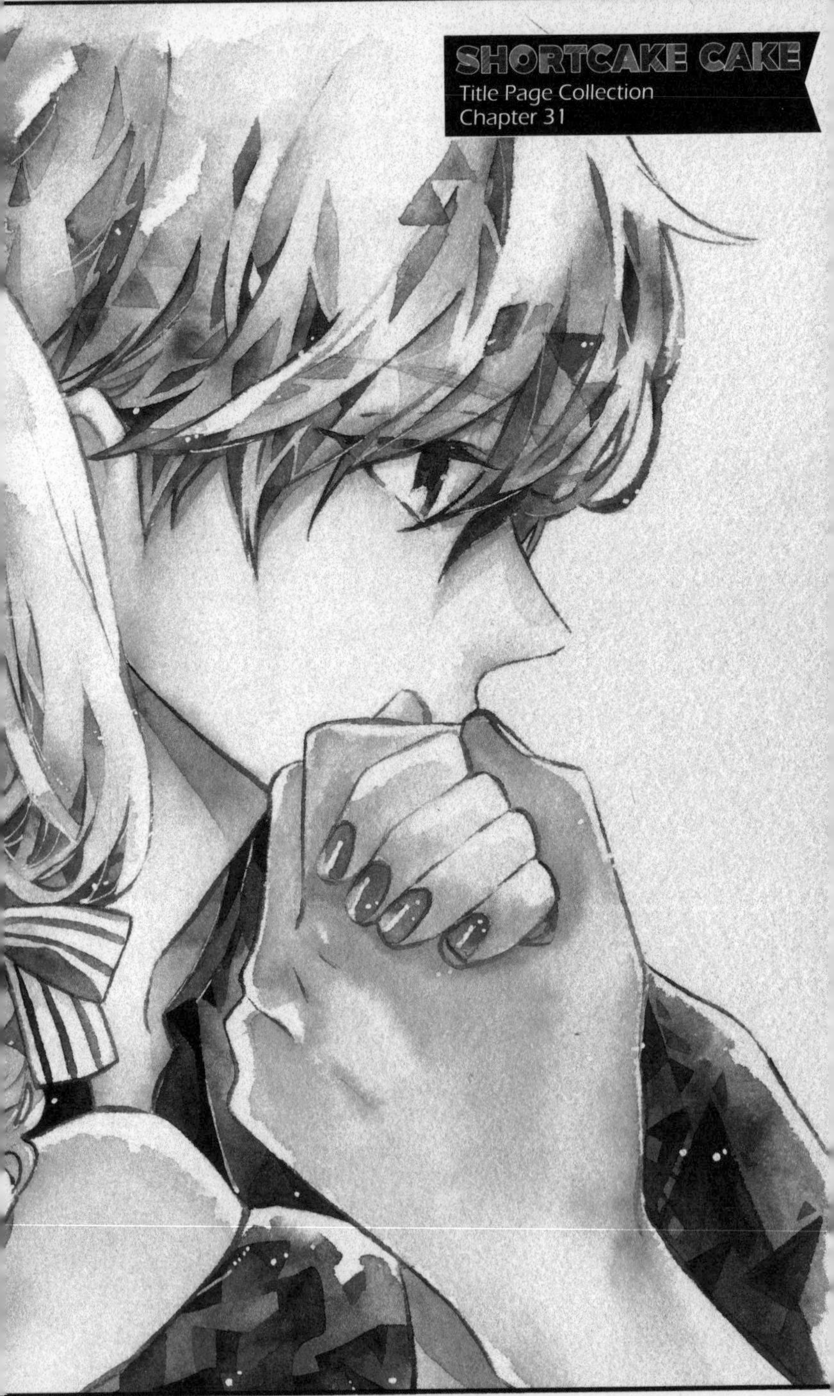
SHORTCAKE CAKE
Title Page Collection
Chapter 31

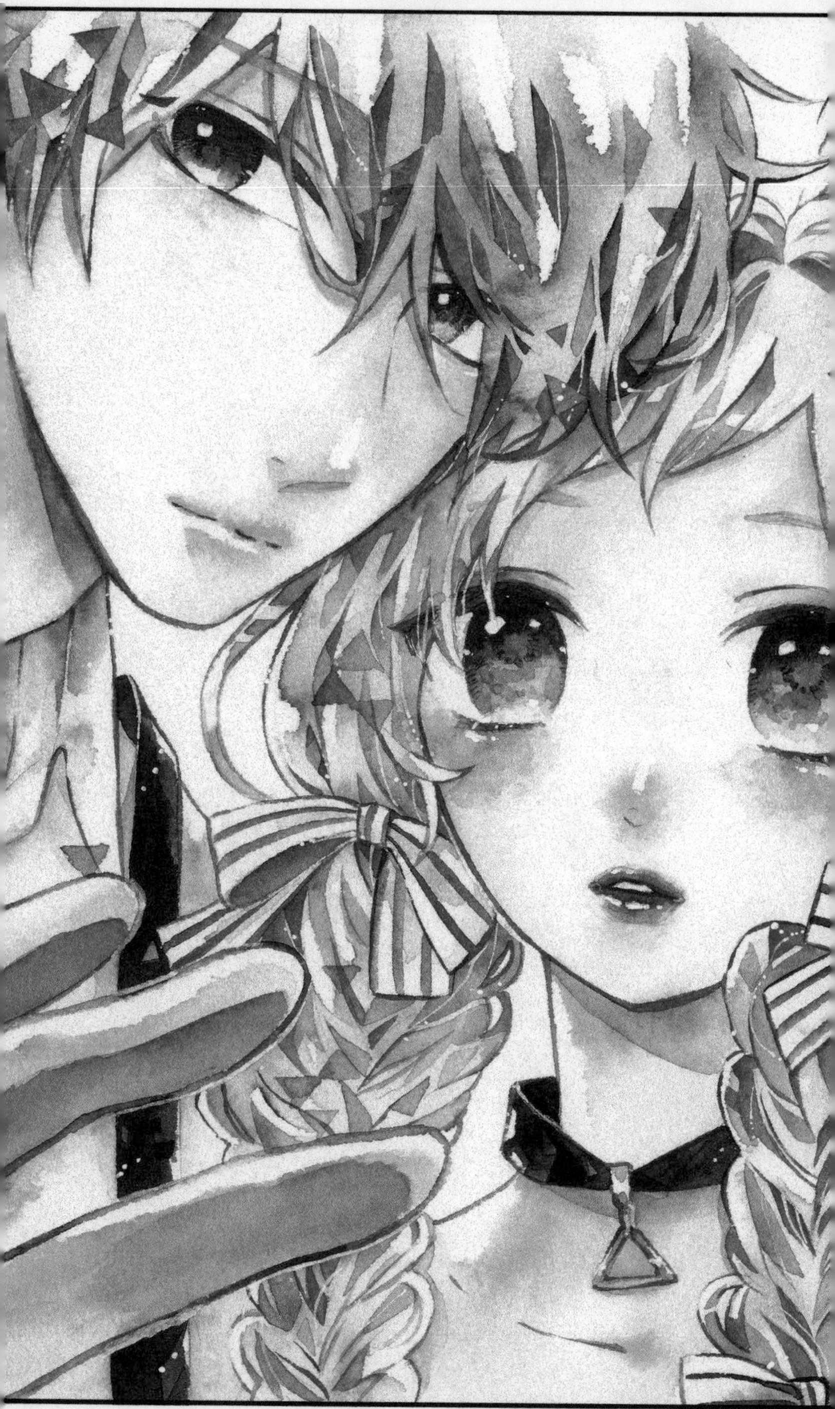

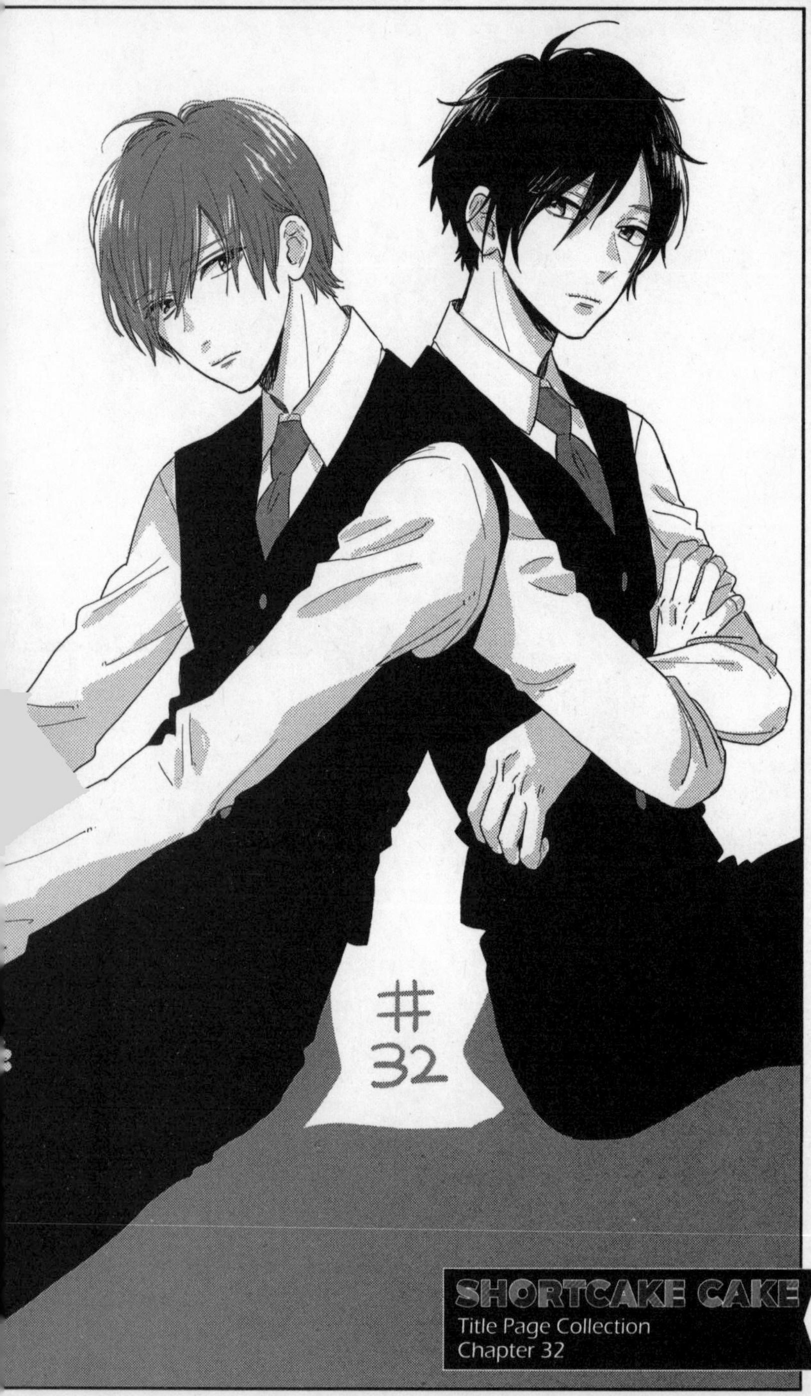
#
32
SHORTCAKE CAKE
Title Page Collection
Chapter 32

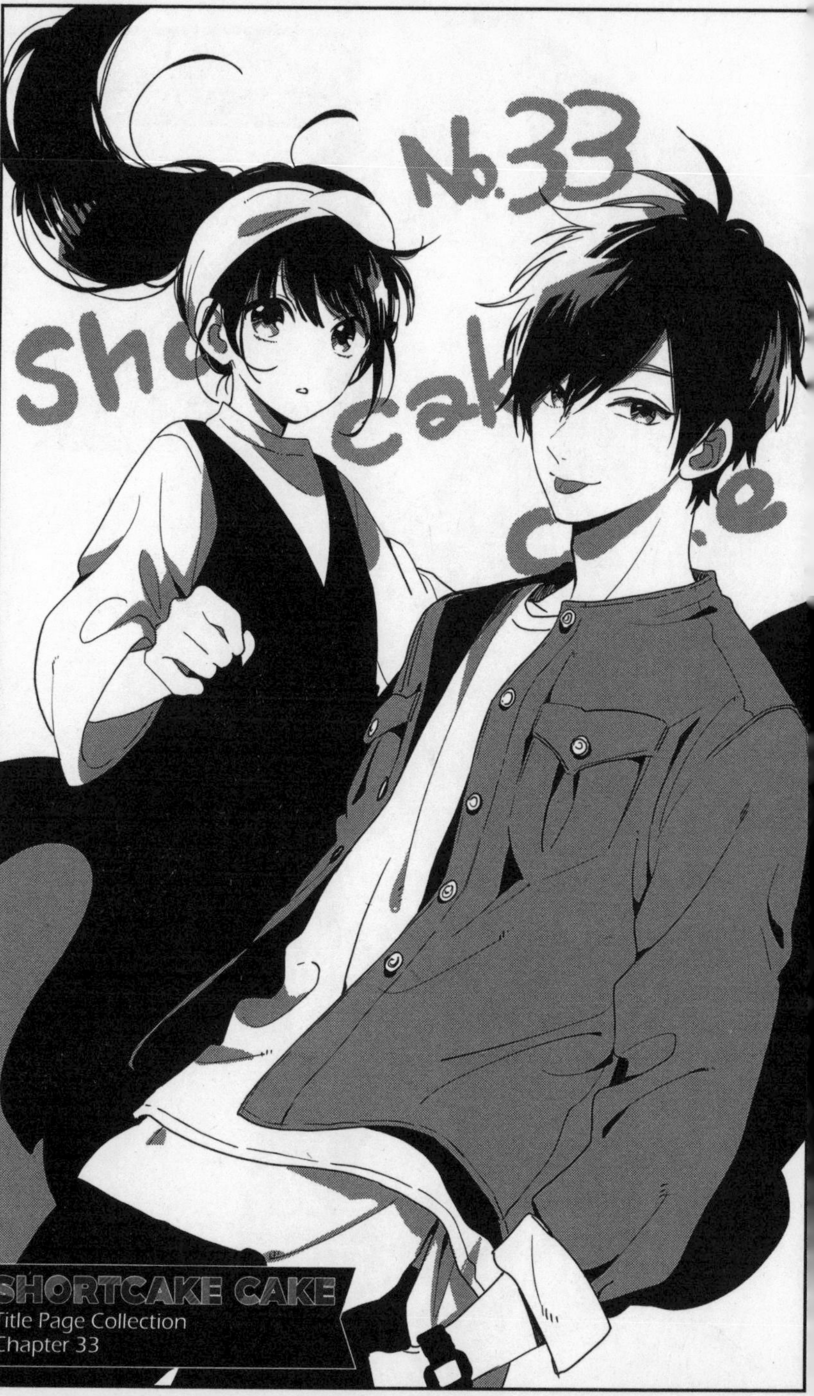
No.33

SHORTCAKE CAKE
Title Page Collection
Chapter 33

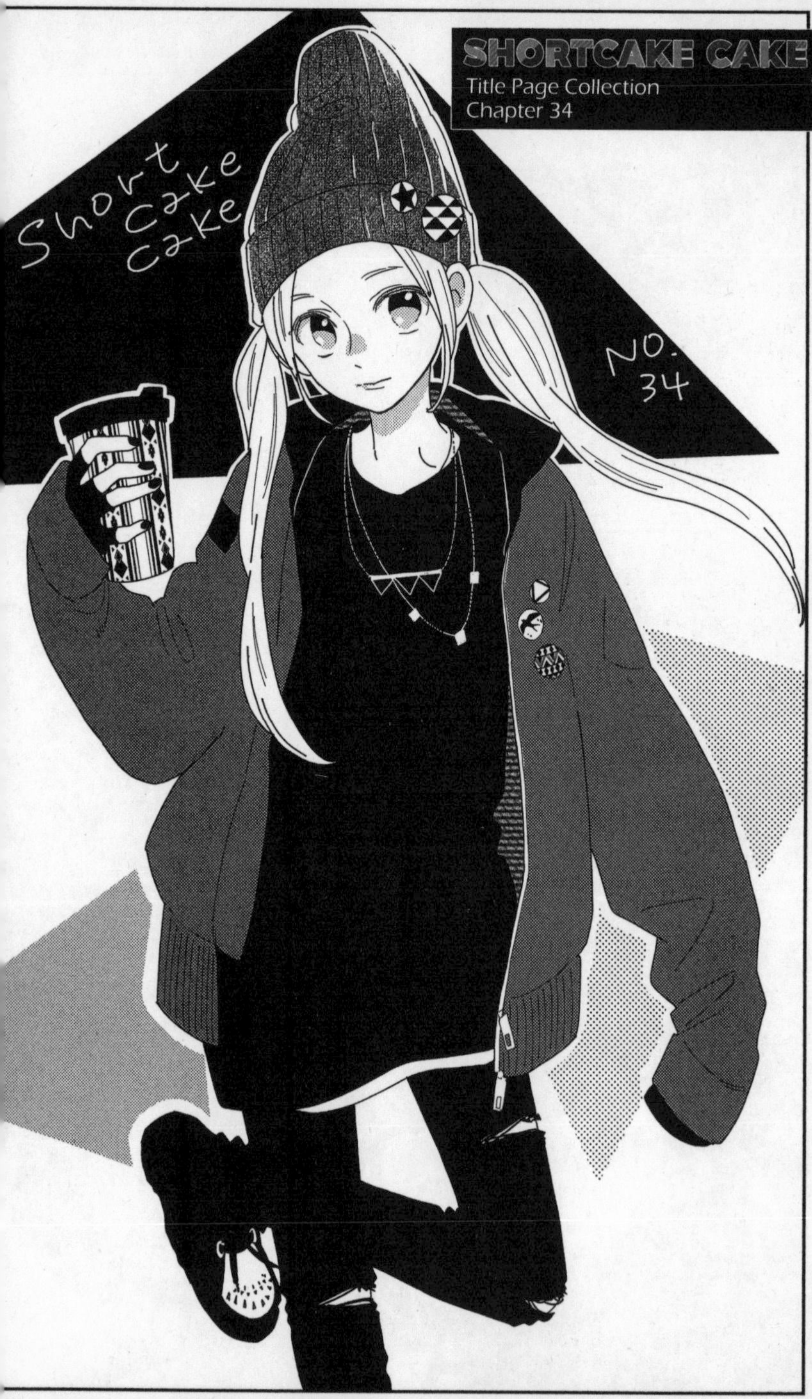
SHORTCAKE CAKE
Title Page Collection
Chapter 34
Short cake cake
NO. 34

**SHORTCAKE CAKE**
Title Page Collection
Chapter 35

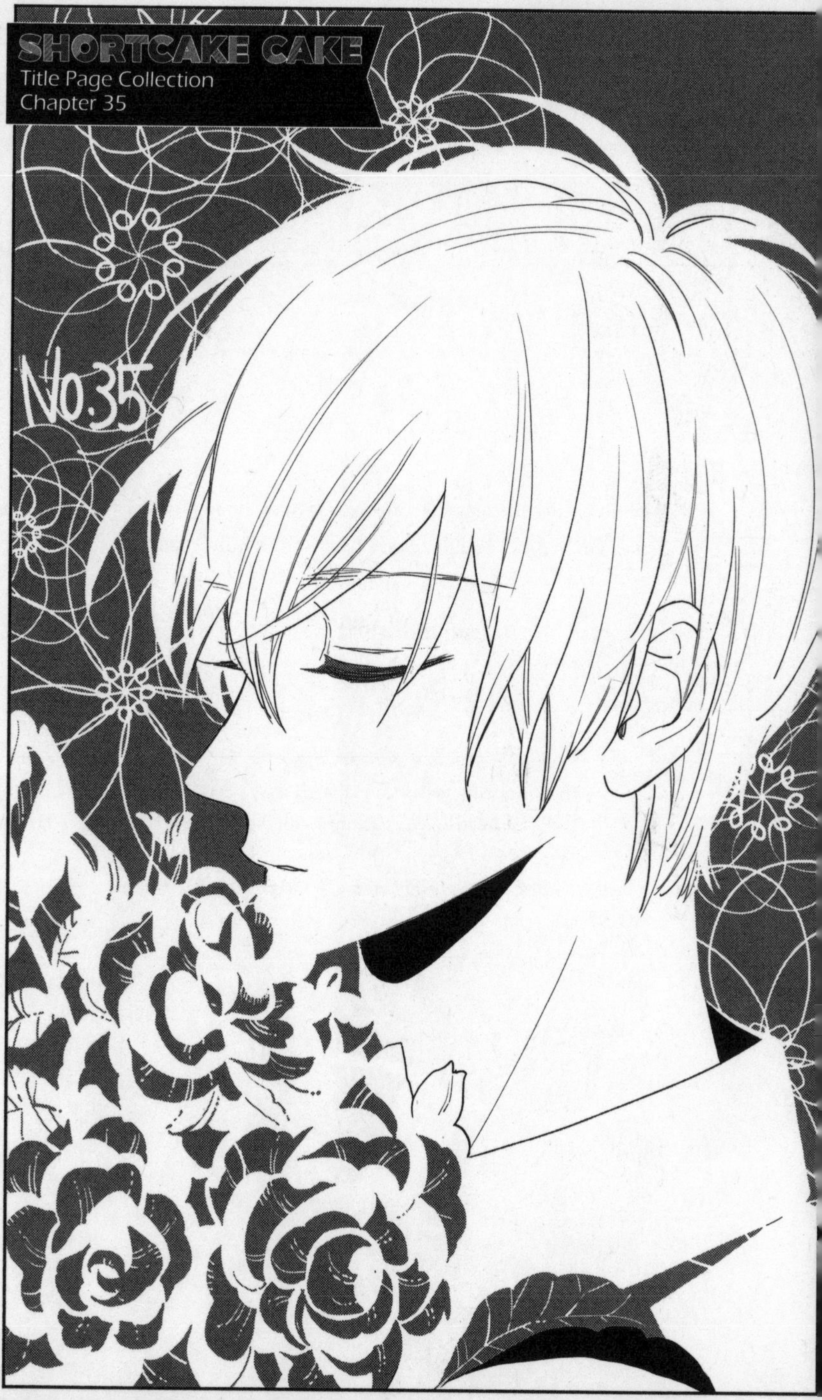
No.35

I've been eating Umakacchan instant noodles since I was
a kid, and I'm happy I could include them in the bonus story.
They're so yummy!

**—suu Morishita**

suu Morishita is a creator duo.
The story is by Makiro, and the art is by
Nachiyan. In 2010 they debuted with the
one-shot "Anote Konote." Their works include
*Hibi Chouchou* and *Shortcake Cake*.